Bargaining

Emin Karagözoğlu · Kyle B. Hyndman
Editors

Bargaining

Current Research and Future Directions

palgrave
macmillan

Editors
Emin Karagözoğlu
Department of Economics
Bilkent University
Ankara, Turkey

Kyle B. Hyndman
The University of Texas at Dallas
Richardson, TX, USA

ISBN 978-3-030-76665-8 ISBN 978-3-030-76666-5 (eBook)
https://doi.org/10.1007/978-3-030-76666-5

This Palgrave Macmillan imprint is published by the registered company Springer Nature Switzerland AG
The registered company address is: Gewerbestrasse 11, 6330 Cham, Switzerland

Acknowledgements

This book would not have been possible without the contributions of the authors, as well as the reviewers who generously provided feedback to the authors. We would also like to thank Arlindo Skenderaj for his work in bringing this book into shape. We also thank Ashwini Elango for her work.

Contents

1	**Introduction** *Emin Karagözoğlu and Kyle B. Hyndman*	1
Part I	**Theoretical and Behavioral Foundations**	
2	**Commitment Tactics in Bargaining Under Complete Information** *Topi Miettinen*	11
3	**Reputational Bargaining** *Jack Fanning and Alexander Wolitzky*	35
4	**Dynamic Bargaining with Private Information** *William Fuchs and Andrzej Skrzypacz*	61
5	**Reference Dependence in Bargaining Models** *Kerim Keskin*	87
6	**Focal Points in Experimental Bargaining Games** *Andrea Isoni, Robert Sugden, and Jiwei Zheng*	109

7 **Between Utilitarianism and Egalitarianism: Some Ethical Aspects of the Nash Bargaining Solution** 131
Shiran Rachmilevitch

8 **Dynamic Legislative Bargaining** 151
Hülya Eraslan, Kirill S. Evdokimov, and Jan Zápal

Part II Applications

9 **Legislative Bargaining Experiments** 179
Marina Agranov

10 **Market Institutions, Prices and Distribution of Surplus: A Theoretical and Experimental Investigation** 203
Nick Feltovich and Nejat Anbarcı

11 **Empirical Models of Bargaining with Externalities in IO and Trade** 227
Ali Yürükoğlu

12 **Bargaining in Healthcare Markets: Applications of Nash-in-Nash and Extensions** 249
Matthew Grennan and Ashley Swanson

13 **Bargaining and Climate Change Negotiations** 271
Alejandro Caparrós

14 **Bargaining and War** 293
Bahar Leventoğlu

15 **Bargaining in Operations Management Research** 317
Andrew M. Davis

Part III Advances in Bargaining Research: New Platforms, Challenges and Techniques

16 **Field Experiments in Bargaining** 343
Burak Dindaroğlu and Seda Ertac

17 **Bargaining in Online Markets** 365
Matthew Backus, Thomas Blake, and Steven Tadelis

18 **Self-sufficient, Self-directed, and Interdependent Negotiation Systems: A Roadmap Toward Autonomous Negotiation Agents** 387
Tim Baarslag, Michael Kaisers, Enrico H. Gerding, Catholijn M. Jonker, and Jonathan Gratch

19 **Using Machine Learning to Understand Bargaining Experiments** 407
Colin F. Camerer, Hung-Ni Chen, Po-Hsuan Lin, Gideon Nave, Alec Smith, and Joseph Tao-yi Wang

20 **Emotions in Bargaining** 433
Gert-Jan Lelieveld and Eric van Dijk

21 **Gender Differences in Negotiation and Policy for Equalizing Outcomes** 455
María P. Recalde and Lise Vesterlund

Index 477

Contributors

Marina Agranov California Institute of Technology, Pasadena, CA, USA

Nejat Anbarcı Durham University, Durham, UK

Tim Baarslag Centrum Wiskunde & Informatica, Amsterdam, The Netherlands

Matthew Backus Columbia University, New York, NY, USA

Thomas Blake Amazon, San Jose, CA, USA

Colin F. Camerer California Institute of Technology, Pasadena, CA, USA

Alejandro Caparrós Department of Economics and Finance, Business School, University of Durham, Durham, UK

Hung-Ni Chen Ludwig Maximilians University of Munich, Munich, Germany

Andrew M. Davis SC Johnson College of Business, Cornell University, Ithaca, NY, USA

Eric van Dijk Leiden University, Leiden, The Netherlands

Burak Dindaroğlu İzmir Institute of Technology, Urla, Turkey

Hülya Eraslan Rice University, Houston, TX, USA

Seda Ertac Koç University, Istanbul, Turkey

Kirill S. Evdokimov Rice University, Houston, TX, USA

Jack Fanning Brown University, Providence, RI, USA

Nick Feltovich Monash University, Melbourne, VIC, Australia

William Fuchs University of Texas at Austin and Universidad Carlos III Madrid, Austin, TX, USA

Enrico H. Gerding University of Southampton, Southampton, UK

Jonathan Gratch University of Southern California, Los Angeles, CA, USA

Matthew Grennan University of California-Berkeley, Berkeley, CA, USA

Kyle B. Hyndman University of Texas at Dallas, Richardson, TX, USA

Andrea Isoni University of Warwick, Coventry, UK

Catholijn M. Jonker Delft University of Technology, Delft, The Netherlands

Michael Kaisers Centrum Wiskunde & Informatica, Amsterdam, The Netherlands

Emin Karagözoğlu Department of Economics, Bilkent University, Ankara, Turkey

Kerim Keskin ADA University, Baku, Azerbaijan

Gert-Jan Lelieveld Leiden University, Leiden, The Netherlands

Bahar Leventoğlu Duke University, Durham, NC, USA

Po-Hsuan Lin California Institute of Technology, Pasadena, CA, USA

Topi Miettinen Hanken School of Economics, Helsinki, Finland

Gideon Nave University of Pennsylvania, Philadelphia, PA, USA

Shiran Rachmilevitch Department of Economics, University of Haifa, Haifa, Israel

María P. Recalde University of Melbourne, Melbourne, Australia

Andrzej Skrzypacz Stanford University, Stanford, CA, USA

Alec Smith Virginia Tech, Blacksburg, VA, USA

Robert Sugden University of East Anglia, Norwich, UK

Ashley Swanson Columbia University, New York, NY, USA

Steven Tadelis University of California, Berkeley, Berkeley, CA, USA

Joseph Tao-yi Wang National Taiwan University, Taipei, Taiwan

Lise Vesterlund University of Pittsburgh, Pittsburgh, Pennsylvania, USA

Alexander Wolitzky Massachusetts Institute of Technology, Cambridge, MA, USA

Ali Yürükoğlu Stanford University, Stanford, CA, USA

Jiwei Zheng Lancaster University, Lancaster, UK

Jan Zápal CERGE-EI, a joint workplace of Charles University and the Economics Institute of the Czech Academy of Sciences, Prague, Czech Republic

List of Figures

Fig. 4.1	In the limit, if $P(v)$ were strictly above $c(v)$, the seller would want to lower the price infinitely fast to immediately capture all the profits. Therefore, in equilibrium $P(v)$ must be lower	66
Fig. 4.2	Graphical explanation of the equilibrium reservation prices	68
Fig. 4.3	Equilibrium path for Prices and Cutoffs and agreement atom at the deadline normalized to $T = 1$	76
Fig. 6.1	Two bargaining table games from Isoni et al. (2013)	121
Fig. 8.1	Equilibrium dynamics in the distributive model	158
Fig. 8.2	Indifference curves of the dynamic utility in the rotating dictator equilibrium	159
Fig. 8.3	A simple solution in the distributive model	161
Fig. 8.4	Asymmetric pure strategy equilibrium in the spatial model	163
Fig. 8.5	Symmetric mixed strategy equilibrium in the spatial model	166
Fig. 10.1	Sequence of decisions in the experiment (P = posting, H = haggling, F = flexible pricing)	205

Fig. 10.2 Bargaining set (hatched area) and bargaining solution, haggling and flexible-pricing treatments 207

Fig. 10.3 Normal form of the 2 × 2 market with flexible pricing (v_i = max $\{20 - p_i^p, 10\}$, with posted prices p_1^p, p_2^p) 208

Fig. 10.4 Bargaining results in Hagg treatment—cumulative distribution functions 215

Fig. 10.5 Bargaining results in Flex treatment—scatterplots of posted and transaction price 217

Fig. 10.6 Auction results in Flex treatment—scatterplots of posted and transaction price 220

Fig. 14.1 Bargaining range in the conflict 294

Fig. 15.1 Baseline bargaining experiment setting in OM 319

Fig. 17.1 Best offer on eBay (*Notes* This figure depicts a listing with the Best Offer feature enabled, which is why the "Make Offer" button appears underneath the "Buy It Now" and "Add to Cart" buttons. When a user clicks the Make Offer button, a panel appears, prompting an offer and, if desired, an accompanying message) 369

Fig. 17.2 Bargaining sequence patterns (*Notes* This figure summarizes the offer-level data in terms of the "game tree" of bargaining, and is borrowed from Backus et al. [2]) 371

Fig. 17.3 Best offer on eBay (*Notes* This scatterplot presents average first offers, normalized by the BIN price to be between zero and one, grouped by unit intervals of the BIN price, defined by $(z - 1, z]$. When the BIN price is on an interval rounded to a number ending in "00" or "50," it is represented by a red circle. The figure is borrowed from Backus et al. [4]) 374

Fig. 17.4 Seller acceptance rates (*Notes* This figure depicts the polynomial fit of the probability of acceptance for a given offer (normalized by the BIN) on items with listing prices between \$85 and \$115, plotted separately for \$100 "Round" listings and the remaining "Precise" listings. This figure is borrowed from Backus et al. [4]) 377

Fig. 18.1 By and large, negotiation research can be clustered around one of the three main orthogonal dimensions of autonomy: *self-sufficiency*, *self-directedness*, and *interdependence*. The efforts of the three need to be integrated to arrive at such truly autonomous negotiators that can progress along the *autonomy diagonal* 391
Fig. 19.1 (A) Initial offer screen: in the first two seconds of bargaining, both players can set their initial positions without revealing to the opponent. The pie size is on the top left corner and it only appears on informed player's screen. (B) Players communicate their offers using mouse click on the interface. (C) When two players' positions match, the green vertical stripe appears and this would be the deal if there is no change in the following 1.5 seconds. (D) After the bargaining round, both players would be notified about their payoffs and the pie size 417
Fig. 19.2 The deal rates under different pie sizes and treatments. The green bars stand for the average deal rates of baseline sessions at different pie sizes. The blue and red bars are for female-informed sessions and male-informed sessions, respectively. The standard errors (overlaid on the bars) are calculated at the session level 421
Fig. 19.3 The deal rates under different pie sizes and treatments. The green bars stand for the average deal rates of baseline sessions at different pie sizes. The blue and red bars are for the experienced sessions and high-stake sessions, respectively. The standard errors (overlaid on the bars) are calculated at the session level. Since there is only one session for experienced and high-stake treatment, the standard errors are not computable for these two treatments 422

Fig. 19.4 Receiver operating characteristic (ROC) for predicting disagreements, two, five, and seven seconds into the bargaining game. The dashed lines represent the false and true positive rates of a random classifier. (A1-C1) show the data from Camerer et al. [8] (Experiment 1) and (A2-C2) plot the result from Experiment 2 423
Fig. 19.5 Area under the curve (AUC) of disagreements classifiers using process data, pie size, and the two combined. Note that the classifier's input included only trials that were still in progress (when a deal has not yet been achieved), and excluded trials in which the offers and demand were equal at the relevant time stamp. The left figure is the original result from Camerer et al. [8] (Experiment 1) and the right one is the result from Experiment 2 424
Fig. 19.6 Bargaining Process Features Selected by the Classifier for Outcome Prediction (Deal= 1) and Their Estimated Marginal Effects. The left panel is the result from Camerer et al. [8] (Experiment 1) and the right panel is the result from Experiment 2. The pie sizes are excluded 425

List of Tables

Table 10.1	Theoretical predictions	209
Table 10.2	Aggregate observed behaviour (all sessions and rounds)	212
Table 10.3	Tobit results (average marginal effects, with standard errors in parentheses)	214
Table 10.4	Factors affecting bargaining proposals (average MEs unless noted)	218
Table 10.5	Auction results, Hagg and Flex treatments	219
Table 15.1	Behavioral OM papers related to bargaining	336
Table 18.1	Overview of major challenges in autonomous negotiation and the main dimensions of autonomy to which they relate. Each challenge is subdivided in building blocks along with example opportunities and a solution roadmap	390
Table 19.1	Summary statistics for different treatments	420

1

Introduction

Emin Karagözoğlu and Kyle B. Hyndman

It goes almost without saying that bargaining is ubiquitous and has been a part of the human experience for thousands of years. It is arguably one of the most natural forms of social interaction. As Schelling [6] famously put it, "most conflict situations are bargaining situations." Hence, it is not surprising to see that a great deal of attention has been paid to it in terms of academic research in multiple disciplines. Among many other notable works, some of these appear in the survey by Roth [5], an excellent handbook edited by Bolton and Croson [1], and a book by McMillan [3]. We, the editors of this book, are thrilled to see that even

E. Karagözoğlu (✉)
Department of Economics, Bilkent University, Ankara, Turkey
e-mail: karagozoglu@bilkent.edu.tr

K. B. Hyndman
University of Texas at Dallas, Richardson, TX, USA
e-mail: kyleb.hyndman@utdallas.edu

E. Karagözoğlu and K. B. Hyndman (eds.), *Bargaining*,
https://doi.org/10.1007/978-3-030-76666-5_1

after decades of research on bargaining, it is still a dynamic and evolving field, and we hope that the readers of this book will share our enthusiasm.

Our goal in this edited volume is to bring together a collection of essays that highlight both classical and new theoretical foundations, as well as shedding new light on traditional applications to bargaining research and, finally, to introduce the reader to some of the newest and most interesting avenues of current and future research in bargaining. In so doing, we hope that the book will be a source of inspiration for future research in this continuously evolving and inter-disciplinary domain, which touches almost every sphere of life. In line with our goal, most chapters in this volume start with an up-to-date survey of the existing literature to inform the reader about the *frontier* and continue with the challenges, open questions, and future directions. In this introduction, we will provide a brief overview of the chapters that readers of this volume will be exposed to.

As alluded to, this book is divided into three parts. The first, *Theoretical and Behavioral Foundations* provides a foundation of many classical—as well as some more recent—theoretical and behavioral underpinnings that serve as a foundation for more applied research. The seven chapters in Part I, explore commitment tactics, reputational bargaining, dynamic bargaining with private information, reference dependence, the role of focal points, ethical aspects of the Nash bargaining solution, and dynamic models of legislative bargaining.

In Chapter 2, **Topi Miettinen** surveys the literature on commitment tactics in bargaining under complete information. Inspired by seminal works of Nash [4], Schelling [6], and Crawford [2], many scholars studied the influence of strategic commitments and threats on bargaining behavior and outcomes. The author provides an overview of this line of work with a particular focus on pre-commitment, which he defines as an explicit choice to restrict one's future action space.

In Chapter 3, **Jack Fanning** and **Alexander Wolitzky** focus on commitment in bargaining games with incomplete information. In these models, whether a player is a rational type or a commitment type is his private information and the existence of commitment types introduces a strategic incentive for the rational players to mimic a commitment type player. The authors' survey spans a rich variety of models with single or multiple commitment types, endogenous commitment demands, non-stationary types and environments as well as possible applications in search markets and mediation.

William Fuchs and **Andrzej Skrzypacz** delve into the challenging environment of private information and bargaining in Chapter 4. Their survey mostly covers recent, cutting-edge theoretical models which are characterized by private information and dynamically evolving factors with a special emphasis on the influence of the outside environment. The arrival of new trading parties, the existence of a deadline, the arrival of relevant information or outside options are some examples. Their discussion of possible avenues for future research underlines the importance of endogenous outside options and continuous-time models for this line of work.

In Chapter 5, **Kerim Keskin** explains the various ways reference points and reference-dependent behavior are incorporated into bargaining models. His overview includes both axiomatic and strategic models of bargaining. Moreover, his analysis is not restricted only to models based on Prospect Theory, but also contains bargaining games or problems where the reference point does not enter agents' utility functions but just acts as a salient point coordinating their expectations.

In Chapter 6, **Andrea Isoni**, **Robert Sugden**, and **Jiwei Zheng** provide us with a thorough survey of the experimental literature on the role of focal points in bargaining, highlighting the differing effects of *payoff-based* and *label-based* focal points on bargaining behavior and outcomes. They discuss efficiency and equality as some possible sources of *payoff-based* focality, and player labels, strategy labels, and bargaining table design for the *label-based* focality.

Shiran Rachmilevitch, in Chapter 7, discusses the ethical aspects of the celebrated Nash bargaining solution. In particular, he presents results that reveal how the Nash bargaining solution offers a *perfect* compromise between two opposing notions of distributive justice, utilitarianism, and egalitarianism. He concludes with an engaging discussion on John Roemer's critique of the study of distributive justice using bargaining theory, and by explaining how the utilitarian-versus-egalitarian framework surveyed in the chapter can be useful in addressing ethical issues in distribution.

Legislative bargaining has been a very dynamic line of research in the last two decades. In Chapter 8, **Hülya Eraslan**, **Kirill Evdokimov**, and **Jan Zápal** survey the theoretical literature on legislative bargaining with a particular emphasis on models with endogenous status quo. The authors cover a wide set of issues including the existence and efficiency of equilibria, distributive and spatial policies, and policy convergence. Finally, they present concrete open questions and challenges, one of which is the incorporation of dynamic legislative bargaining models into macroeconomic models of dynamic taxation or evolving debt, where they have a great potential to offer new economic insights.

Part II, *Applications*, presents applications of bargaining theory in a rich variety of research fields ranging from political science to operations management. The seven chapters in this part explore legislative bargaining experiments, different market institutions and their impact on the distribution of surplus, empirical work on bargaining in IO and trade, applications of Nash-in-Nash bargaining in healthcare markets, climate change negotiations, applications of bargaining theory in the scientific study of war, and bargaining in operations management.

Following up on the earlier chapter, which focuses on theoretical aspects of legislative bargaining, in Chapter 9, **Marina Agranov** provides us with a thorough review of the still evolving experimental literature focusing on legislative bargaining. Her survey ends with a call for more research on standing committees and the dynamic interactions that take place in legislatures.

In Chapter 10, **Nicholas Feltovich** and **Nejat Anbarcı** revisit a well-studied problem on how the market institution underlying a trading mechanism affects prices and the allocation of surplus. They consider two extremes of posted price and negotiated price institutions, as well as a middle ground with flexible pricing. They show several interesting deviations from theory, including low efficiency and seller earnings when prices are negotiable.

Ali Yürükoğlu, in Chapter 11, surveys the relatively new and growing literature which leverages the workhorse Nash-in-Nash bargaining model to generate predictions, as well as the newly emerging data sets on bargaining outcomes in various industries. He provides examples from media content, healthcare, and grocery industries to highlight the many policy-relevant insights that are possible with this new approach.

In Chapter 12, **Matthew Grennan** and **Ashley Swanson**, dig deeper into the Nash-in-Nash empirical framework, focusing almost exclusively on the healthcare industry. They provide detailed examples of this framework being applied to real-world and policy-relevant problems for purchasing medical devices and pharmaceuticals, as well as hospital mergers and insurance networks. They end with a call to devote more attention to modeling asymmetric information and expanding models to include other important factors (e.g., leadership and incentives) that often wind up in the "residual."

In Chapter 13, **Alejandro Caparrós**, shows us that bargaining theory is also regularly applied to high stakes multilateral negotiations, with his discussion of bargaining and climate negotiations. He argues strongly that the change in approach to climate negotiations brought about by the Paris Climate Accord creates a need for new approaches to model this paradigm.

War is a way to resolve conflict, but a rather costly one. A natural alternative could be peaceful resolution through negotiated settlements. In Chapter 14, **Bahar Leventoǧlu** surveys the literature on bargaining and war that mostly grew in the realms of political science. Shifting bargaining power, information problems, and commitment problems are some issues that receive special attention in this chapter.

A great deal of research in operations management (OM) focuses on contracting between parties at various levels of the supply chain, meaning that bargaining research is fundamentally important in OM. **Andrew Davis**, in Chapter 15, sheds light on bargaining theory and, especially experiments in this field, and how they are similar to and different from those found in the economics literature more generally.

Part III, *Advances in Bargaining Research: New Platforms, Challenges and Techniques*, contains six chapters where the authors explore field experiments, bargaining in online platforms, autonomous negotiation agents, applications of machine learning in analyzing data from bargaining experiments, the role and effect of emotions in bargaining, and policies that aim to avoid the gender wage-gap in the presence of gender differences in bargaining.

In Chapter 16, **Burak Dindaroğlu** and **Seda Ertaç**, provide a broad overview of the growing literature which takes bargaining research into the field. Their main focus is on discrimination in the marketplace, as well as bargaining within the household, and gender-specific aspects of bargaining more broadly.

Another new and interesting application of bargaining in the field comes in Chapter 17, by **Matthew Backus**, **Thomas Blake**, and **Steven Tadelis**. They exploit data from eBay's roll-out of the Best Offer Platform and provide insights on both the role of communication and how agents learn to communicate when a new trading institution is brought to the market.

Self-sufficient, autonomous decision-making units are an extremely fertile and rapidly progressing field of research. Although it is mostly the human-like robots or self-driving cars that make it to the news, the research in the field is not restricted to these. Chapter 18, written by **Tim Baarslag**, **Michael Kaisers**, **Enrico Gerding**, **Catholijn Jonker** and **Jonathan Gratch** is proof. The authors present a summary of the progress made on autonomous negotiation agents, and explore various technological, societal, and ethical challenges that result from using autonomous negotiation systems.

The world is witnessing a data revolution. One that, naturally, triggers significant progress in statistical and econometric tools, and spreads their use in almost all research fields. In Chapter 19, **Colin Camerer**, **Hung-Ni Chen**, **Po-Hsuan Lin**, **Gideon Nave**, **Alec Smith**, and **Joseph Tao-yi Wang** present results from the first set of bargaining experiments, where the authors used machine learning methods to study the effect of process variables on bargaining outcomes.

Although not often explicitly noted in much of the bargaining literature found in economics, emotions can be expected to play a key role in bargaining behavior, especially when we observe deviations from the normative theoretical prediction. In Chapter 20, **Gert-Jan Lelieveld** and **Eric van Dijk** provide a broad overview of the research in social psychology that explicitly tries to link emotions to negotiation strategies and outcomes, as well as the underlying psychological theory.

The economics research in the last 20+ years report gender differences in negotiation as one of the potential factors contributing to the gender wage gap. That said, it is not totally clear what type of policies should be used to avoid this gap. Should one "fix the women" or "fix the institutions" or both? **María Recalde** and **Lise Vesterlund**, in Chapter 21, survey the experimental literature on gender differences and discuss challenging questions related to policies that can improve the wage equality across men and women.

References

1. Gary E. Bolton and Rachel T. A. Croson, editors. *The Oxford Handbook of Economic Conflict Resolution.* Oxford University Press, 2012.
2. Vincent P. Crawford. A Theory of Disagreement in Bargaining. *Econometrica,* 50(3):607–637, 1982.
3. John McMillan. *Reinventing the Bazaar: A Natural History of Markets.* W. W. Norton Company, 2003.
4. John F. Nash. Two-Person Cooperative Games. *Econometrica,* 21(1):128–140, 1953.
5. Alvin E. Roth. *The Handbook of Expeirmental Economics,* chapter Bargaining Experiments, pages 253–291. Princeton University Press, 1995.
6. Thomas C. Schelling. *The Strategy of Conflict.* Harvard University Press, Cambridge, MA, 1960.

Part I

Theoretical and Behavioral Foundations

2

Commitment Tactics in Bargaining Under Complete Information

Topi Miettinen

2.1 Introduction

For a long time economists deemed bargaining problems indeterminate (Edgeworth 1881; Hicks 1935). The received wisdom was that the solution must satisfy both individual and collective rationality, i.e., that the agreement should not be worse for either party than not agreeing, and that the outcome should be Pareto efficient. Yet, there was no theory to

This review article was prepared for the book "Current Research and Future Directions in Bargaining", Emin Karagözoğlu and Kyle Hyndman (eds.), Palgrave, Macmillan. I would like to thank the editors, an anonymous reviewer, Volker Britz, Vincent Crawford, Tore Ellingsen, Jack Fanning, Emin Karagözoğlu and Tomas Sjöström for comments. Financial support of the Fulbright Finland Foundation, the Norwegian Research Council (250506), the Yrjö Jahnsson Foundation is gratefully acknowledged.

T. Miettinen (✉)
Hanken School of Economics, Helsinki, Finland
e-mail: topi.miettinen@hanken.fi

E. Karagözoğlu and K. B. Hyndman (eds.), *Bargaining*,
https://doi.org/10.1007/978-3-030-76666-5_2

select which of the individually rational and Pareto efficient agreements would be chosen.

Zeuthen (1930, Chapter 4) proposes a formal structure and an intuition on how to reach a solution to the problem. He considers a protocol where parties may bind themselves to mutually incompatible commitment positions, and yet, potentially back down and concede if necessary. Zeuthen argues that the party which has less to lose in case of conflict and more to win in case of unilateral success will be more willing to insist. Zeuthen's solution of the problem anticipates a game-theoretic fixed-point notion that was later developed by Nash. It is Nash's (1950, 1953) exact formalizations which are perceived to discover the first rational prediction for the bargaining problem.[1]

Nash (1953) investigates a two-stage model where the players first commit to threats which would be carried out if negotiations stall. The parties then bargain under these threats. He shows how the commitments influence the bargaining outcomes. In line with his axiomatic model (Nash 1950) and the preceding received wisdom of the scholarship, the negotiators would come to an agreement in efficient and individually rational terms. Moreover, this sharing would depend on the chosen threats. Ever since, commitment tactics have been in the focus of game-theoretic bargaining scholarship.

Schelling (1956, 1960) adopts a different stance to commitment in bargaining, which in fact, in its vivid motivating rhetoric, closely mimics that of Zeuthen (1930).[2] He argues that parties might rather attempt to commit to reduce their strategic capacity (Schelling 1956, p. 286):

> ...it has not been uncommon for union officials to stir up excitement and determination on the part of the membership during or prior to a wage negotiation. If the union is going to insist on \$2 and expects the management to counter with \$1.60, an effort is made to persuade the membership not only that the management could pay \$2 but even perhaps that the negotiators themselves are incompetent if they fail to obtain close to \$2. The purpose ... is to make clear to the management

[1] Harsanyi (1956) illustrates that Zeuthen's solution can be considered largely equivalent to that of Nash.

[2] See also Ellsberg (1959) and Schelling (1966).

> that the negotiators could not accept less than $2 even if they wished to because they no longer control the members or because they would lose their own positions if they tried.

He also remarks that the commitment must be credible and successfully communicated to the other side of the bargaining table prior to the start of bargaining for the commitment to be effective. Arriving at the bargaining table with limited capacity to agree on unfavorable deals would force other parties to make concessions in order not to delay agreement. He argues that this type of commitment tactic could lead to mutually incompatible bargaining positions if pre-commitments are made simultaneously or unbeknownst of each other's moves. Superficially, Schelling seems to build directly on Nash merely changing the timing of commitments and what the commitments concern. Underneath, however, there is a more fundamental difference in approaches: whereas Nash aspires to offer a unique generally applicable rationality prescription, Schelling takes a more descriptive perspective admitting that unique efficient predictions are not consistent with what we observe in labor disputes, international conflicts, and experimental data. In his view, outcomes and strategies depend considerably on the context and human psychology.

Schelling supports his view with insightful experiments and encyclopedic anecdotal evidence. He expresses his ideas in approachable and clear English without any mathematical formulae. His ideas on pre-commitment are first put under rigorous game-theoretic scrutiny by Crawford (1982). Crawford sketches a two-stage model of bilateral bargaining where parties in the first round make attempts to tie their hands. In second stage, each chooses whether to back down from her commitment or not. In his model, the power to commit stems from the costs of revoking one's commitment. These costs are stochastic in the model and occasionally excessively high so as to rule out the capacity to back down and agree on any conceivable deal. Crawford shows that if excessively high commitment costs are not very likely, then the unique Perfect Bayesian Equilibrium involves aggressive commitments which, if successful, are mutually incompatible. Compelled by Schelling's more descriptive approach, Crawford also presents a boundedly rational version of the model where parties expect revoking probabilities to be independent of the commitment positions adopted in the first stage.

Contemporary to Crawford's work was both the celebrated perfect information alternating-offer bargaining model of Rubinstein (1982) and the incomplete information protocol-free inefficiency results of Myerson and Satterthwaite (1983). Rubinstein derives a unique outcome consistent with the Nash (1950) axioms based on the cost of delay and subgame perfection; the model has thereafter served as a primary motivation for the widespread use of the Nash bargaining solution in applied work. Myerson and Satterthwaite (1983) show that when parties are negotiating a transaction and valuations are privately known, there is no bargaining or other mechanism which would allow the parties to efficiently allocate the good. Much of the applied work that followed adopted the view that Nash bargaining solution is the right prediction for complete information bargaining and asymmetric information is the main, if not the only, source of delay and inefficiency in bargaining.

In the meanwhile, the commitment literature evolved to interesting new directions. Muthoo (1992, 1996) proposes an alternative justification for the Nash bargaining solution based on the cost of revoking commitments. The reputational bargaining literature with stubborn types (see the chapter by Fanning and Wolitzky), where Schelling's influence is clearly visible, leaped forward by the seminal contributions of Myerson (1991) and Abreu and Gul (2000). Relatedly, Fershtman and Seidmann (1993) argue that when negotiators are accountable to their managers or the membership they represent, it may be difficult to accept a deal which leads to a worse outcome than what one could have gotten by accepting an offer earlier. Thus there is endogenous commitment to reject such offers. By combining this intuitive idea with the existence of a deadline, they show that delay necessarily arises in equilibrium. Perry and Reny (1993) illustrated how efficiency and relative symmetry of the agreements in Rubinstein (1982) are influenced by the commitment power provided by reaction and response times and thus even the Rubinstein model can be perceived as a specific commitment model.

These main developments of the commitment literature before the turn of the millennium are well summarized in Muthoo

(1999, Chapter 8). In this chapter, I will focus on the complete information non-cooperative literature on commitment following the publication of Muthoo's book. I *define pre-commitment as an explicit choice to restrict one's future action space.* I will thus not consider the endogenous commitment literature where commitment arises as a byproduct of past actions.[3] I will also not address reputational bargaining nor dynamic incomplete information bargaining which are covered in the chapters by Fanning and Wolitzky and by Skrypacz and Fuchs, respectively, in this volume.[4]

The key finding is that costly strategic pre-commitments which are uncertain to succeed may unavoidably lead to inefficiency—a finding challenging the received wisdom that complete information bilateral bargaining is necessarily efficient. These models thus suggest an alternative to incomplete information in explaining the empirically observed delay and inefficiency in bargaining and conflict. I summarize the theoretical developments in the following section. In the final section, I discuss the applied future directions, the empirical evidence, and the limitations of the approach.

2.2 Theoretical Literature

2.2.1 Stochastic Success and Inefficiency

Consider a potentially dynamic $n-$player bargaining game B where players 1 to n bargain on how to divide a continuously divisible pie of size one, and they have to agree unanimously. Suppose the outcome of B is unique and efficient. Let us denote the share of player i at the outcome

---

[3] For studies beyond Muthoo's (1999) comprehensive overview, see Calabuig et al. (2002, 2004, 2006), Cunyat (2004), Compte and Jehiel (2003, 2004), Mauleon and Vannetelbosch (2004), Li (2007), Caruana et al. (2007) Caruana and Einav (2008), Miettinen (2010), Driesen et al. (2012), Hyndman (2011), and Kara et al. (2021).

[4] Neither will I consider endogenous recognition in multilateral bargaining where prior moves could be perceived as tying a particular player to the proposer role, or the status quo literature where commitments concern the current fallback option. See Agranov et al. (2020) and Baron et al. (2017), respectively.

by y_i where by efficiency $y_1+...+y_n = 1$. For example, B could be bilateral and y could coincide with the Nash bargaining solution (Rubinstein 1982; Binmore 1987; Binmore et al. 1987) as in much of the existing applied literature.

Let us now extend B by allowing each player to attempt committing prior to B, or prior to each stage of B. A commitment attempt, if successful, rules out the capacity to accept some proposals in the ensuing interaction. Let us use the notation that player j at time t with commitment status s_j^t cannot accept a deal where she receives a share strictly smaller than s_j^t (player j who did not attempt commitment or who failed has $s_j^t = 0$). If attempts to commit have been made and $s_1^t+...+s_n^t > 1$, then there is disagreement. In this case, if the original B is one-shot or commitments last forever ($s_j^t = s_j^{t'}$ for $t' > t$) the whole pie is lost. If the original B is dynamic and commitments eventually decay, there is delay and the outcome is inefficient for impatient players. If $s_j \leq y_j$ for all j, the pie is shared according to y. If there is i with $s_i > y_i$ and the commitment statuses sum to weakly less than one, then each receives at least the share of the pie equal to her commitment status.

In the bilateral case, Renou (2009) and Bade et al. (2009) show very generally that when the initial pre-commitments are certain to succeed without cost and last forever, any equilibrium of the underlying game B is still an equilibrium outcome of the game with commitments and thus efficient outcomes exist: the argument, when applied to the bargaining context, generalizes the well-known pattern in the Nash-demand game that the just-compatible commitment is a best reply to a given commitment of the other.[5] In particular, committing to y_i is a best reply to the other's commitment y_j and y remains an efficient outcome of the commitment game, much like in Crawford (1982) when commitments are sufficiently likely to succeed.[6]

---

[5] See also Melkonyan and Chakravarty (2020) for some analysis in the general case under uncertain pre-commitments.

[6] Kalai et al. (2010) further strengthen the efficiency result for a general B by showing that by allowing for commitments that condition on commitments made by others, a folk theorem obtains. Other models of conditional commitment include Howard (1971) and Tennenholtz (2004). Karagözoğlu and Keskin (2018) consider a model where players have reference-points

Ellingsen and Miettinen (2008, EM) limit attention to bilateral bargaining but allow commitment to be costly and uncertain to succeed. In line with Schelling's (1960) original intuitions and his ideas on brinkmanship (Schelling 1966), EM predict inefficiencies. They point out that just-compatible commitments to y_1 and y_2 constitute a Nash equilibrium in strategies which are weakly dominated by staying flexible, and a commitment to less than y_i is likewise dominated.[7] In fact, when committing is (infinitesimally) costly, dominance becomes strict and thus any pair of efficient compatible commitments is ruled out. Moreover, when uncertain success of commitment attempts is assumed, staying flexible becomes iteratively strictly dominated by the aggressive commitment to grab the entire pie. Both players attempting such aggressive commitments is the only equilibrium outcome of the game. The key intuition relates to the construction of Zeuthen (1930): the more aggressive is the opponent's commitment, the lower is the gain from avoiding conflict thus incentivizing counter-commitments. Whereas Zeuthen (1930) argued that middle ground obtains when trading off the increasing threat of conflict with a larger share of the pie conditional on deal, in EM costly commitment has already ruled out efficient commitments in the first place. Thus, it is best to aim being the only one to succeed with an extremely aggressive commitment. The commitment game in EM is solvable by iterated elimination of dominated strategies and thus the epistemic requirements for the predictions to arise are weaker than in standard equilibrium analysis (Asheim and Pérea 2019). It is perhaps counterintuitive that the *uncertain* success of pre-commitments uncovers the full force of Schelling's intuitive conflict logic. In fact, the probability of a bargaining impasse can be infinitely close to one in the model if commitments are almost sure to succeed and the cost of attempting commitment is infinitesimally small. Such almost perfect commitment power seems just as unlikely as perfect commitment power. In fact, Schelling (1960) himself criticized Nash (1953) model for

---

which are ex-ante strategically chosen. This is as if bargaining parties choose aspirations and suffer a cost if their aspirations are not met.

[7] EM assume that if only one of the players, say i, fails or chooses to be flexible, she can sign off to player j's commitment s_j by proposing s_j and thus receiving $1 - s_j$ herself. Yet, the assumption that y yields when it is feasible is sufficient for their results.

the capacity to fully commit not to carry on negotiating and his further analysis of armed conflict devotes a whole chapter on understanding the role of the uncertainty of commitment power on outcomes (Schelling 1966, Chapter 3).

Li (2011) and Chung and Wood (2019) investigate the limits of the inefficiency result of EM. They make alternative assumptions about the sequence of commitment choices and their observability. Both papers point out that if a player's commitment attempt is made observable to the other player before the latter strategically commits, the first-mover optimally adjusts her commitment downward. The first-mover leaves the second-mover a sufficient share of the pie to undermine the latter's incentives for attempting commitment. The second-mover does not want to risk destroying the valuable share of the surplus by attempting a potentially mutually incompatible aggressive commitment. Thus, efficiency is restored by a small change in the observation structure (see also Perry and Reny 1993). The papers clarify that the success of commitment of the first-mover does not need to be observable to the second-mover for efficiency to arise, merely an attempt needs to be observed. The result requires, however, that the exact level of commitment is observable. In fact, applying the proposition in Bagwell (1995), one reaches a corollary that if the level of commitment is observed with full-support noise, then the strong inefficiency result is restored. More generally, these ideas are closely related to the debate on observation structures and commitment in games when commitments are certain to succeed (see Van Damme and Hurkens 1996).

Ellingsen and Miettinen (2014) depart from the random proposer infinite horizon bargaining game B and introduce a commitment stage *prior to each bargaining stage* of each round. Strategic pre-commitment with stochastic exogenous decay of commitments is investigated. In this setup where negotiators cannot commit not to carry on negotiating when commitments no longer bind,[8] the inefficiencies are no longer as drastic as in EM. Rather there is delay in the unique symmetric Markov perfect equilibrium. The length of delay depends on the arrival rate of decay of the commitments. Moreover, neither

[8] See Schelling (1960) for the original criticism on Nash (1953) and Rubinstein (1982).

party no longer walks away from the bargaining table with the entire pie conditional on agreement. Rather the division of the surplus is more equal depending on how patient each player is as compared to the rate of decay of commitments. The study can be interpreted as generalizing the bargaining outcome of Rubinstein (1982) and shows how commitment tactics can undermine the gains from trade and influence the division of the surplus. Letting the length of time period tend to zero yields an inefficient bargaining solution relating to the contributions of Muthoo (1992, 1996), Binmore (1987), or Binmore et al. (1986).

Miettinen and Vanberg (2020, MV) assume that B is the multilateral random proposer bargaining game à la Baron and Ferejohn (1989), with no status quo.[9] As in Ellingsen and Miettinen (2014) a commitment stage precedes the random draw of the proposer in each round but unlike in EM 2014, any commitment lasts for one round only.[10] The study compares the efficiency and the equality of outcomes under various voting rules and finds that, under unanimity, inefficiency and delay are unavoidable for a range of parameter values: in any stationary subgame perfect equilibrium, each party optimally resorts to an aggressive commitment tactic. In fact, delay is longer in all equilibria as the number of parties grows larger. Yet, under any majority rule, agreement is immediate and outcomes coincide with those predicted by the original Baron–Ferejohn model. The intuitive reason is that under majority, there is competition between responders to be included in the winning coalition and the most aggressively committed will never be included. The results contrast with models of concessions costs (Cardona-Coll 2003; Caruana et al. 2007) where outcomes are efficient or with Eraslan and Merlo (2002) who show in bargaining with a stochastic surplus, but without commitment, that unanimity rule is always efficient but majority rule may lead to inefficiencies. Relatedly, Merlo and Wilson (1995, 1998) show that efficient delay and inefficient immediate agreements may arise due to fluctuations over time in the total surplus which is being shared. The close analogy to Ali's (2006)

[9] See Ma (2018) for a related three-player model on majoritarian reputational bargaining in the Abreu and Gul (2000) tradition.

[10] The proposer's commitment is assumed to automatically lose strength and thus the proposer is free to propose any deal.

analysis of voting rules and conflict, however, uncovers a connection between strategic pre-commitment and stubbornness driven by excessive optimism thus providing a potential avenue to relate inefficiency due to pre-commitment to incomplete information (with biased beliefs).

The analysis of MV illustrates how the simple complete information pre-commitment setup extends to the multilateral case. The modeling framework also easily lends itself to attempts to understand delay patterns observed in the international arenas of the Doha round of WTO, of UNFCCC climate change negotiations, or among the EU 28 on important issues regarding taxation or refugee policy, for instance. It also shows how the results in the bilateral case are in fact driven by the implicit unanimity requirement in bilateral bargaining. Competition cannot be used to eliminate inefficiencies due to the unanimity requirement.

2.2.2 Models with Deterministic Success

2.2.2.1 Applied Models of Delegation

Schelling (1960) presents delegation as a key method for credible pre-commitment. Delegation has been explicitly analyzed in several (applied) bargaining settings (Jones 1989; Chari et al. 1997; Bester and Sakovics 2001; Jackson and Morelli 2007, 2011).[11] To see the analogy to commitment, consider a principal j who, in addition to a fixed compensation c, pays the delegate a bonus proportional to $x_j - s_j$ conditional on agreement, where x_j is the share received by the principal in and agreement made by the delegate and s_j is a threshold below which the delegate receives no bonus. This commits the delegate to reject any offer below the threshold. The incentives of the delegate essentially implement the

[11] See also Fershtman and Judd (1987) for a seminal paper analyzing delegation and agency in the realm of industrial organization. Frank (1987) argues that a conscientious individual, or more generally emotions, could likewise be perceived as an agent of the selfish gene in the pursuit of evolutionary fitness. Konrad and Thum (2020) study the optimal degree of uncertainty about delegate's preferences when the expectation must nevertheless reflect the principal's outside option.

outcomes of B extended by the commitment stage, and c reflects the cost of pre-commitment featuring in EM. To my knowledge, none of the delegation models have considered the stochastic success of commitment, however.

Jackson and Morelli (2007, Section D) consider a model of endogenous political bias and the implications for emergence of war.[12] At the delegation stage, a representative citizen decides on the bias of the politician who decides whether to negotiate efficient transfers or engage in risky inefficient conflict. Inefficiency is never unavoidable since commitment success is not uncertain. Thus, there are always efficient equilibria alongside the potential inefficient equilibria with war. Harstad (2008, 2010) applies delegation to environmental negotiations and shows how hiring delegates with favorably biased preferences can be privately beneficial but detrimental for efficiency. As in Jackson and Morelli (2007), this is the case only when transfers are allowed and thus pie is perfectly divisible. These types of applied models introduce a richer set of institutional variables than the pre-commitment models.

Another closely related approach in applied work is that of partial commitment driven by the audience or revoking costs. Leventoğlu and Tarar (2005) analyze the case where B is as in Rubinstein (1982), there is a unique commitment stage prior to B, and there is a cost of revoking proportional to the size of the concession that is made.[13] They find, just as Muthoo (1992), that the way in which the pie gets shared depends on the relative cost of revoking the commitment. A higher relative cost is advantageous and associated with a higher share of the pie in equilibrium. Yet, unlike in Muthoo's work and as in Crawford (1982), mutually incompatible commitments are conceivable thus leading to inefficiency—the agreement is immediate but the costs of revoking commitment must be paid to resolve the impasse. Whether there is an impasse or not depends on how symmetric or asymmetric the players are.

---

[12] Jackson and Morelli (2011) offer five explanations of rational armed conflict including asymmetric information and the *lack* of capacity to enforce. Baliga and Sjöström (2013) review game-theoretic studies of armed conflict and factors explaining inefficiency.

[13] See Leventoğlu & Tarar (2009) for a similar applied model where impasse leads to a war.

2.2.2.2 Pre-commitment

There are further models in the pre-commitment tradition where the success of commitment is certain. Closest to the models of Sect. 2.1 are Dutta (2012, 2021) and Miettinen and Perea (2015). Dutta (2012) considers an extension of Muthoo's (1992, 1996) model allowing for arbitrary, convex or concave, costs of revoking commitments, and thus generalizes the Nash bargaining solution results of Muthoo. Dutta (2021) discovers sequential concessions as the key force which restricts the set of subgame perfect equilibria: A subgame-perfect equilibrium may be destabilized by a deviation which does not lead to an immediate deal but leads to a position where the deviating player will have a dominant strategy not to concede (given the mutual equilibrium expectations) and thereby triggers a concession by the opponent.

Miettinen and Perea (2015) consider a variant where B is the deterministic alternating-offer game of Rubinstein (1982). Prior to each round, each player can pre-commit to any share of the pie. Commitments are costly and last for one round only. It is shown that Rubinstein's original result about first-mover advantage is perfectly reversed: the unique and efficient equilibrium features a second-mover advantage which depends on players' time preferences. The basic intuition is that the alternating order structure provides implicit commitment power to the first-mover's role who thus prefers not to make any explicit commitment. The second-mover best-responds by committing to the residual of what is left when the first-mover is kept at her continuation value and thus becomes de-facto first-mover. Amorós and Moreno (2006) study a simple four-stage model of commitments and concessions where commitments fade over time deterministically. The exogenous alternating decision structure implies that the unique SPE is either efficient or inefficient depending on the discount factors and rates of decay.

Britz (2013) shares with Li (2007) the approach that players are committed to present-value payoffs rather than shares of the pie. Thus, if both are committed and discount future, there is a time when commitments become mutually incompatible. And it is at this time, Britz assumes in line with the criticism of Schelling (1960) and Rubinstein

(1982), that commitments lose their power. Britz shows that unilateral capacity to commit allows reaping surplus from the player with proposer power. Britz also considers simultaneous commitments and shows that the Nash-demand-game-like multiplicity of efficient equilibria is greatly reduced: each party's current commitment is constrained by the opponent's option of waiting for the payoff received at the time when commitments eventually become mutually incompatible.

Britz (2018) considers a model of multilateral bargaining under unanimity where the proposer can endogenously commit to delay the agreement at a pre-specified length if the agreement is not reached at a given period. The cost of committing is proportional to the lapse of time between rounds, however. In optimum, the proposer trades off the effect of delay on effective discounting, which is a convex function of time, with the explicit linear cost of delay. When players are not too patient or too impatient, it is optimal for the proposer to inefficiently commit.

2.3 Relevance and Future

Evidence indicates that bargaining is inefficient. There are more than 10 million battle casualties across the globe since the second world war (Lacina and Gleditsch 2005); in year 2000 in U.S. State courts alone, about 20 million cases were filed of which about 3–4% ended up in trial leaving the courts with a workload of about million cases yearly (Ostrom et al. 2003); strikes and labor unrest have a negative impact on productivity and product quality (Krueger and Mas 2004; Mas 2008) and Gruber and Kleiner (2012) show that nurses' strikes increased in hospital mortality by 18.3 percent in the state of New York. In U.S. legislature, filibusters and threats of government shutdown are the new normal. In international arenas, WTO Doha round, UN climate change negotiations, and many negotiations in the sensitive areas of the European Union have stalled. In all cases since conflict is inefficient, rational parties should negotiate a treaty and avoid conflict. This is the thrust of the Coase theorem. So why does bargaining fail? Commitment tactics is just one potential explanation. In the realm of economics, inefficiencies are mainly explained by incomplete information. Yet, not all observed conflict is consistent with incomplete information. In this section, I will discuss various applied contexts and cover some experimental and other empirical evidence.

2.3.1 Experiments

Crawford (1997, p. 207) argues that experimentation informed by theoretical developments and theoretical developments informed by empirical studies is the recipe for advancement of the study of bargaining. Laboratory experiments provide a means of causally testing whether the mechanisms proposed in the theoretical models are borne out in data. Whether thus identified mechanisms are at work in the field requires field experiments and other empirical research with happenstance data.

Neither strategic pre-commitment nor comprehensive strategic delegation models have been cleanly tested in the laboratory. There are a few relevant experimental studies, however. Fershtman and Gneezy (2001) experimentally test a one-sided model of delegation where bargaining outcomes in standard ultimatum game setups are compared with those where one party can send a delegate to bargain instead of the principal. Moreover, the observability of the incentive contracts with the delegates is varied across treatments; only when contracts are observable to the opponent can they be used as a commitment device.[14] The results show that the option to delegate influences outcomes as predicted by theory: the payoff of the side who delegates increases. The delegates are incentivized to reject offers below the equal split and the proposers make efficient proposals in response. Contrary to what theory predicts, delegation equalizes sharing even when contracts are unobservable. Croson et al. (2003) study an ultimatum game where the responder can lie about the value of her outside option, effectively threaten about opting out

[14] There is a short step from this design to designs with an inefficiency prediction where each side could delegate and observability is stochastic.

if offer is too low, before the proposer's move. Threats are just cheap-talk, thus the experiment is not really about pre-commitment. Threats are found to influence bargaining outcomes.[15]

The results from numerous ultimatum bargaining and dictator game experiments (Camerer 2003; Güth and Kocher 2014) show that fairness matters and positive offers are rejected when self-interest dictates that the offer should be accepted. Roth (1985) and Crawford (1997, p. 223) thoughtfully summarize the evidence from unstructured bargaining game experiments arguing that fairness norms provide focal points of equilibrium selection and that, to a large extent, disagreements can be understood as coordination failures. But the fair divisions also provide moral justification for commitment, and the induced intrinsic or reputational moral costs from backing up provide the needed commitment power for such commitments. Strategic mimicking of fair types may explain why self-serving biased demands and delay are commonplace in strategic bargaining experiments but self-serving biases are less commonly observed in non-strategic settings (Luhan et al. 2019; Cappelen et al. 2011). Multiple fairness ideals open the door for conflicting demands, each committing to a demand coinciding with the fairness-ideal which better serves one's private interest. Indeed, many experimental dynamic bargaining studies in such settings exhibit delay (Gächter and Riedl 2005, 2006; Karagözoğlu and Riedl 2015; Embrey et al. 2015; Fanning and Kloosterman, 2019; Luhan et al. 2019).[16]

2.3.2 Field Evidence

There are some relevant field negotiation contexts where the observed delay patterns are more in line with the strategic pre-commitment models than incomplete information models. Kiefer (1988, p. 661) finds that constant hazard rate describes the duration and termination of

[15] In his doctoral dissertation, Giwa (2010) reports results supporting the predictions of Ellingsen and Miettinen (2008).

[16] See also Karagözoğlu (2012) for a review article on experimental bargaining on jointly produced surplus.

American labor disputes. This is in line with the complete information pre-commitment (Ellingsen and Miettinen 2014), and contrary to dynamic incomplete information models predicting that the hazard rate of termination of conflict is increasing over time and/or conflict does not last very long.[17] In the domain of settlement of legal disputes, Kessler (1996) finds that empirical hazard rates of the settlement of automobile bodily injury insurance claims are non-increasing. Fenn and Rickman (1999), however, find that hazard rate in the settlement of health insurance claims in Britain is increasing. This suggests that various alternative conflict models may be effective in explaining empirical conflicts, and combination of theoretical and empirical research is needed to increase our understanding of how these various factors play out in various contexts.

2.3.3 Steps Forward

Prescriptive theory is valuable for deriving benchmarks. It identifies fixed points of the best-reply correspondences reflecting outcomes where every opportunity for reconsideration of bad practices, habits, false beliefs, ill-conceived strategies, misunderstandings have been exhausted, and all slippery slopes toward self-interested opportunism have been slid. As such, it constitutes a central tool for the logical practice of practical and philosophical analysis of economic and societal institutions. To derive transparent rational solutions, indeed, to model complex bargaining interaction, one often needs to make a series of simplifying abstractions. Each rationality assumption serves such a simplifying purpose asserting that a principle of choice holds generally and independent of context. When trading off simplicity and explanatory power, however, a more descriptive approach needs to allow dependence on institutions, individual heterogeneity, and selection, all of which may influence outcomes. If these complications did not generate systematic bias, the heterogeneity in these dimensions could be modeled as noise around the rational

[17] Theory suggests that there must be two-dimensional asymmetric information for longer delay to arise (Abreu et al. 2015; Fanning 2018). See also Powell (2006) and Baliga and Sjöström (2013).

prediction. Yet, often these complications generate a systematic bias which must be modeled explicitly if one wishes to reach higher explanatory power. In bargaining, inefficiency is the central domain of variation which calls for understanding. A good descriptive model accounts for its rational, institutional, and behavioral sources.

To provide example, in fresh haggling or conflict or after drastic institutional changes, for example, there may be non-equilibrium expectations about the incentives or choices of the opposing party. Such expectations complicate matters and require understanding (Crawford et al. 2013). Simsek and Yildiz (2016) and Yildiz (2011) provide examples of how optimism can be incorporated into equilibrium analysis as a source of conflict in the medium run in a rich institutional setting. In the longer run, negotiators who are commonly known to be experienced and operate in recurrent circumstances are more likely to have converged to equilibrium behavior. Nevertheless, the theory also suggests that in tough conflict, payoffs can be low and fairly independent of one's choices, and thus the learning gradient can be quite flat. Other-regrading concerns, either driven by strategic, political or status considerations, or genuine intrinsic preference, will further complicate the logic. Moreover, while many dynamic theoretical models of bargaining focus on simple stationary or Markov perfect strategies, existing experimental studies feature non-stationary strategies (Baranski and Morton 2021, 2020; Agranov et al. 2020), especially strategies reflecting both instrumental and intrinsic reciprocity (Sobel 2005; Cabral et al. 2014), in setups where commitment plays no role. In descriptive models, equilibrium refinements should perhaps be motivated by empirical consistency rather than stationarity or other simplifying refinements. We need to understand to which extent this mismatch between bargaining theory and experiments also holds for the analysis of commitment tactics as the first experimental studies on the topic will be rolled out. Once these mechanisms are well understood both theoretically and in the laboratory, they should be taken to the field.

Future applied work of pre-commitment and delegation should consider uncertain and costly commitment in rich institutional settings. This holds a promise of providing unique comparative statics predictions of agreement and conflict also capturing the moderating role of institutions. This approach could complement the incomplete information explanation and yield a more comprehensive account of bargaining inefficiencies. Section 2.2 of this review shows that uncertain success is a key prerequisite and thus a transparent account of why commitment success might be stochastic is needed in each applied context. Schelling, (1960, p. 149) suggests that this could amount to understanding why communication of commitments might sometimes fail and sometimes succeed. Moreover, descriptively relevant moderators discovered in experimental research should be incorporated into the analysis. In order to make progress, there is a genuine need for theorists, structural and reduced-form field empiricists, and experimentalists to join forces.

References

Abreu, D., & Gul, F. (2000). Bargaining and reputation. *Econometrica, 68*(1), 85–117.

Abreu, D., Pearce, D., & Stacchetti, E. (2015). One-sided uncertainty and delay in reputational bargaining. *Theoretical Economics, 10*(3), 719–773.

Agranov, M., Cotton, C., & Tergiman, C. (2021). Persistence of power: Repeated multilateral bargaining with endogenous agenda setting authority. *Journal of Public Economics, 184*, 104–126.

Agranov, M., & Elliott, M. (2017). Commitment and (in)efficiency: A bargaining experiment. *Journal of the European Economic Association, 19*(2), 790–838.

Ali, S. N. M. (2006). Waiting to settle: Multilateral bargaining with subjective biases. *Journal of Economic Theory, 130*(1), 109–137.

Amorós, P., & Moreno, B. (2006). Bargaining and waning commitments. *Economics Letters, 92*(3), 417–422.

Asheim, G., & Pérea, A. (2019). Algorithms for cautious reasoning in games. *International Journal of Game Theory, 48*, 1241–1275.

Bade, S., Haeringer, G., & Renou, L. (2009). Bilateral commitment. *Journal of Economic Theory, 144*(4), 1817–1831.

Bagwell, K. (1995). Commitment and observability in games. *Games and Economic Behavior, 8*(2), 271–280.

Baliga, S., & Sjöström, T. (2013). Bargaining and war: A review of some formal models. *Korean Economic Review, 29*(2), 235–266.

Baliga, S., & Sjöström, T. (2020). The strategy and technology of conflict. *Journal of Political Economy, 128*(8), 3186–3219.

Baranski, A., & Morton, R. (2021). The Determinants of Multilateral Bargaining: A Comprehensive Analysis of Baron and Ferejohn Majoritarian Bargaining Experiments. Experimental Economics, forthcoming.

Baron, D. P., Bowen, T. R., & Nunnari, S. (2017). Durable coalitions and communication: Public versus private negotiations. *Journal of Public Economics, 156*, 1–13.

Baron, D. P., & Ferejohn, J. A. (1989). Bargaining in legislatures. *American Political Science Review, 83*(4), 1181–1206.

Bester, H., & Sakovics, J. (2001). Delegated bargaining and renegotiation. *Journal of Economic Behavior & Organization, 45*(4), 459–473.

Binmore, K. (1987). Nash bargaining theory II. In K. Binmore & P. Dasgupta (Eds.), *The Economics of Bargaining*. Oxford, UK: Basil Blackwell.

Binmore, K., Rubinstein, A., & Wolinsky, A. (1986). The Nash bargaining solution in economic modelling. *The RAND Journal of Economics, 17*(2), 176–188.

Britz, V. (2013). Optimal value commitment in bilateral bargaining. *Games and Economic Behavior, 77*(1), 345–351.

Britz, V. (2018). Rent-seeking and surplus destruction in unanimity bargaining. *Games and Economic Behavior, 109,* 1–20.

Cabral, L., Ozbay, E. Y., & Schotter, A. (2014). Intrinsic and instrumental reciprocity: An experimental study. *Games and Economic Behavior, 87,* 100–121.

Calabuig, V., Cunyat, A., & Olcina, G. (2002). Bargaining with partially revocable commitments: A simple model. *Economics Bulletin, 3*(30), 1–7.

Calabuig, V., Cunyat, A., & Olcina, G. (2004). Partially revocable commitments in a negotiation with a deadline. *Research in Economics, 58*(4), 371–380.

Calabuig, V., Cunyat, A., & Olcina, G. (2006). Bargaining with commitment under an uncertain deadline. *International Game Theory Review, 8*(04), 525–532.

Camerer, C. F. (2003). *Behavioral game theory: Experiments in strategic interaction.* Princeton university press.

Cappelen, A. W., Hole, A. D., Sørensen, E. Ø., & Tungodden, B. (2011). The importance of moral reflection and self-reported data in a dictator game with production. *Social Choice and Welfare, 36*(1), 105–120.

Cardona-Coll, D. (2003). Bargaining and strategic demand commitment. *Theory and decision, 54*(4), 357–374.

Caruana, G., & Einav, L. (2008). A theory of endogenous commitment. *The Review of Economic Studies, 75*(1), 99–116.
Caruana, G., Einav, L., & Quint, D. (2007). Multilateral bargaining with concession costs. *Journal of Economic Theory, 132*(1), 147–166.
Chari, V. V., Jones, L. E., & Marimon, R. (1997). The economics of split-ticket voting in representative democracies. *The American Economic Review, 87*(5), 957–976.
Chung, B. W., & Wood, D. H. (2019). Threats and promises in bargaining. *Journal of Economic Behavior & Organization, 165*, 37–50.
Compte, O., & Jehiel, P. (2003). *Bargaining with reference dependent preferences.* Unpublished manuscript, University College London.
Compte, O., & Jehiel, P. (2004). Gradualism in bargaining and contribution games. *The Review of Economic Studies, 71*(4), 975–1000.
Crawford, V. P. (1982). A theory of disagreement in bargaining. *Econometrica, 50*(3), 607–637.
Crawford, V. P. (1997). Theory and experiment in the analysis of strategic interaction. *Econometric Society Monographs, 26*, 206–242.
Crawford, V. P., Costa-Gomes, M. A., & Iriberri, N. (2013). Structural models of nonequilibrium strategic thinking: Theory, evidence, and applications. *Journal of Economic Literature, 51*(1), 5–62.
Cunyat, A. (2004). The optimal degree of commitment in a negotiation with a deadline. *Economic Theory, 23*(2), 455–465.
Croson, R., Boles, T., & Murnighan, J. K. (2003). Cheap-talk in bargaining experiments: Lying and threats in ultimatum games. *Journal of Economic Behavior & Organization, 51*(2), 143–159.
Driesen, B., Perea, A., & Peters, H. (2012). Alternating offers bargaining with loss aversion. *Mathematical Social Sciences, 64*(2), 103–118.
Dutta, R. (2012). Bargaining with revoking costs. *Games and Economic Behavior, 74*(1), 144–153.
Dutta, R. (2021). *Bargaining as a struggle between competing attempts at commitment*. Manuscript, McGill University.
Edgeworth, F. Y. (1881). *Mathematical Psychics: An Essay on the Application of Mathematics to the Moral Sciences* (Vol. 10). Kegan Paul.
Ellingsen, T., & Miettinen, T. (2008). Commitment and conflict in bilateral bargaining. *American Economic Review, 98*(4), 1629–35.
Ellingsen, T., & Miettinen, T. (2014). Tough negotiations: Bilateral bargaining with durable commitments. *Games and Economic Behavior, 87*, 353–366.

Ellsberg, D. (1959). The Theory and Practice of Blackmail: Lecture at the Lowell Institute, Boston, March 10. (Published in *Bargaining: Formal Theories of Negotiation*, Young, O. R. (ed.) 1975. University of Illinois Press).

Embrey, M., Fréchette, G. R., & Lehrer, S. F. (2015). Bargaining and reputation: An experiment on bargaining in the presence of behavioural types. *The Review of Economic Studies, 82*(2), 608–631.

Eraslan, H., & Merlo, A. (2002). Majority rule in a stochastic model of bargaining. *Journal of Economic Theory, 103*(1), 31–48.

Fanning, J. (2018). No compromise: Uncertain costs in reputational bargaining. *Journal of Economic Theory, 175*, 518–555.

Fanning, J., & Kloosterman, A. (2019). *A simple experimental test of the coase conjecture: Fairness in dynamic bargaining*. Manuscript, Brown University.

Fenn, P., & Rickman, N. (1999). Delay and settlement in litigation. *The Economic Journal, 109*(457), 476–491.

Fershtman, C., & Gneezy, U. (2001). Strategic delegation: An experiment. *RAND Journal of Economics, 32*(2), 352–368.

Fershtman, C., & Judd, K. L. (1987). Equilibrium incentives in oligopoly. *The American Economic Review, 77*(5), 927–940.

Fershtman, C., & Seidmann, D. J. (1993). Deadline effects and inefficient delay in bargaining with endogenous commitment. *Journal of Economic Theory, 60*(2), 306–321.

Frank, R. H. (1987). If homo economicus could choose his own utility function, would he want one with a conscience? *The American Economic Review, 77*(4), 593–604.

Gächter, S., & Riedl, A. (2005). Moral property rights in bargaining with infeasible claims. *Management Science, 51*(2), 249–263.

Gächter, S., & Riedl, A. (2006). Dividing justly in bargaining problems with claims. *Social Choice and Welfare, 27*(3), 571–594.

Giwa, S. E. (2010). Commitment and Impasses in Negotiation. Chapter 3 of a PhD dissertation entitled Procedural Justice, Social Norms and Conflict, Human Behavior in Resource Allocation. Stockholm School of Economics.

Güth, W., & Kocher, M. G. (2014). More than thirty years of ultimatum bargaining experiments: Motives, variations, and a survey of the recent literature. *Journal of Economic Behavior & Organization, 108*, 396-409.

Güth, W., Levati, M. V., & Maciejovsky, B. (2005). Deadline Effects in Sequential Bargaining—An Experimental Study. *International Game Theory Review, 7*(02), 117–135.

Gruber, J., & Kleiner, S. A. (2012). Do strikes kill? Evidence from New York state. *American Economic Journal: Economic Policy, 4*(1), 127–57.

Harsanyi, J. C. (1956). Approaches to the bargaining problem before and after the theory of games: A critical discussion of Zeuthen's, Hicks', and Nash's theories. *Econometrica*, 144–157.
Harstad, B. (2008). Do side payments help? Collective decisions and strategic delegation. *Journal of the European Economic Association, 6*(2–3), 468–477.
Harstad, B. (2010). Strategic delegation and voting rules. *Journal of Public Economics, 94*(1–2), 102–113.
Hicks, J. R. (1935). Annual survey of economic theory: The theory of monopoly. *Econometrica, 35*(1), 1–20.
Howard, N. (1971). *Paradoxes of Rationality: Theory of Metagames and Political Behavior*. Cambridge: The MIT Press.
Hyndman, K. (2011). Repeated bargaining with reference-dependent preferences. *International Journal of Game Theory, 40*(3), 527–549.
Jackson, M. O., & Morelli, M. (2007). Political bias and war. *American Economic Review, 97*(4), 1353–1373.
Jackson, M. O., & Morelli, M. (2011). The reasons for wars: An updated survey. *The Handbook on the Political Economy of War*, 34.
Jones, S. R. (1989). Have your lawyer call my lawyer: Bilateral delegation in bargaining situations. *Journal of Economic Behavior & Organization, 11*(2), 159–174.
Kalai, A. T., Kalai, E., Lehrer, E., & Samet, D. (2010). A commitment folk theorem. *Games and Economic Behavior, 69*(1), 127–137.
Kara, T., Karagözoğlu, E., & Özcan-Tok, E. (2021). Bargaining, reference points, and limited influence. *Dynamic Games and Applications, 11*(2), 326–362.
Karagözoğlu, E. (2012). Bargaining games with joint production. In G. E. Bolton & R. T. A. Croson (Eds.), *Oxford Handbook of Economic Conflict Resolution*, (Ch. 24, 359–372). Oxford University Press.
Karagözoğlu, E., & Keskin, K. (2018). Endogenous reference points in bargaining. *Mathematical Methods of Operations Research, 88*(2), 283–295.
Karagözoğlu, E., & Riedl, A. (2015). Performance information, production uncertainty, and subjective entitlements in bargaining. *Management Science, 61*(11), 2611–2626.
Kessler, D. (1996). Institutional causes of delay in the settlement of legal disputes. *The Journal of Law, Economics, and Organization, 12*(2), 432–460.
Kiefer, N. M. (1988). Economic duration data and hazard functions. *Journal of economic literature, 26*(2), 646–679.
Konrad, K. A., & Thum, M. (2020). Equilibrium opacity in ultimatum-offer bargaining. *Journal of Public Economic Theory, 22*(5), 1515–1529.

Krueger, A. B., & Mas, A. (2004). Strikes, scabs, and tread separations: Labor strife and the production of defective Bridgestone/Firestone tires. *Journal of political Economy, 112*(2), 253–289.

Lacina, B., & Gleditsch, N. P. (2005). Monitoring trends in global combat: A new dataset of battle deaths. *European Journal of Population, 21,* 145–166.

Li, D. (2007). Bargaining with history-dependent preferences. *Journal of Economic Theory, 136*(1), 695–708.

Li, D. (2011). Commitment and compromise in bargaining. *Journal of Economic Behavior & Organization, 77*(2), 203–211.

Luhan, W. J., Poulsen, O., & Roos, M. W. (2019). Money or morality: Fairness ideals in unstructured bargaining. *Social Choice and Welfare*, 1–21.

Leventoğlu, B., & Tarar, A. (2005). Prenegotiation public commitment in domestic and international bargaining. *American Political Science Review, 99*(3), 419–433.

Ma, Z. (2018). Efficiency and Surplus Distribution in Majoritarian Reputational Bargaining. Wuhan University Working Paper.

Mas, A. (2008). Labour unrest and the quality of production: Evidence from the construction equipment resale market. *The Review of Economic Studies, 75*(1), 229–258.

Mauleon, A., & Vannetelbosch, V. (2004). Bargaining with endogenous deadlines. *Journal of Economic Behavior & Organization, 54*(3), 321–335.

Melkonyan, T. & Chakravarty, S. (2020). *Pre-play agreements with partial credibility*. Manuscript.

Merlo, A., & Wilson, C. (1995). A stochastic model of sequential bargaining with complete information. *Econometrica, 63*(2), 371–399.

Merlo, A., & Wilson, C. (1998). Efficient delays in a stochastic model of bargaining. *Economic Theory, 11*(1), 39–55.

Miettinen, T. (2010). History-dependent reciprocity in alternating offer bargaining. *Finnish Economic Papers, 23*(1), 15.

Miettinen, T., & Perea, A. (2015). Commitment in alternating offers bargaining. *Mathematical Social Sciences, 76,* 12–18.

Miettinen, T. & Vanberg, C. (2020). Commitment and Conflict in Multilateral Bargaining. Helsinki Graduate School of Economics, manuscript.

Muthoo, A. (1992). Revocable commitment and sequential bargaining. *The Economic Journal, 102*(411), 378–387.

Muthoo, A. (1996). A bargaining model based on the commitment tactic. *Journal of Economic theory, 69*(1), 134–152.

Muthoo, A. (1999). *Bargaining Theory with Applications.* Cambridge University Press.

Myerson, R. B., & Satterthwaite, M. A. (1983). Efficient mechanisms for bilateral trading. *Journal of Economic Theory, 29*(2), 265–281.
Myerson, R. B. (1991). *Game Theory*. Harvard University Press.
Nash, J. F. (1950). The bargaining problem. *Econometrica, 18*(2), 155–162.
Nash, J. F. (1953). Two-person cooperative games. *Econometrica, 21*(1), 128–140.
Ostrom, B.J., Kauder, N., B., & LaFountain, R. C. (2003). Examining the Work of State Courts, 2002: A National Perspective From the Court Statistics Project, National Center for State Courts, Williamsburg, VA, USA.
Perry, M., & Reny, P. J. (1993). A non-cooperative bargaining model with strategically timed offers. *Journal of Economic Theory, 59*(1), 50–77.
Powell, R. (2006). War as a commitment problem. *International organization, 60*(1), 169–203.
Renou, L. (2009). Commitment games. *Games and Economic Behavior, 66*(1), 488–505.
Roth, A. E. (1985). Toward a focal point theory of bargaining. In A. Roth (Ed.), *Game-Theoretic Models of Bargaining* (pp. 259–268).
Rubinstein, A. (1982). Perfect equilibrium in a bargaining model. *Econometrica, 50*(1), 97–109.
Schelling, T. C. (1956). An essay on bargaining. *The American Economic Review, 46*(3), 281–306.
Schelling, T. C. (1960). *Strategy of Conflict*. Harvard University Press.
Schelling, T. C. (1966). *Arms and Influence*. Yale University Press.
Serrano, R. (2008). Bargaining. In *The New Palgrave Dictionary of Economics* (Vols. 1–8, 370–380).
Simsek, A., & Yildiz, M. (2016). Durability, deadline, and election effects in bargaining (No. w22284). National Bureau of Economic Research.
Sobel, J. (2005). Interdependent preferences and reciprocity. *Journal of Economic Literature, 43*(2), 392–436.
Tarar, A., & Leventoğlu, B. (2009). Public commitment in crisis bargaining. *International Studies Quarterly, 53*(3), 817–839.
Tennenholtz, M. (2004). Program equilibrium. *Games and Economic Behavior, 49*(2), 363–373.
Van Damme, E., & Hurkens, S. (1996). Commitment robust equilibria and endogenous timing. *Games and Economic Behavior, 15*(2), 290–311.
Yildiz, M. (2011). Bargaining with optimism. *Annual Review of Economics.*
Zeuthen, F. (1930). Problems of Monopoly and Social Welfare.

3

Reputational Bargaining

Jack Fanning and Alexander Wolitzky

3.1 Introduction

In their 1992 survey of noncooperative bargaining theory, Binmore, Osborne, and Rubinstein observe that "Schelling's (1960) view of bargaining as a 'struggle to establish commitments to favorable bargaining positions' remains largely unexplored as regards formal modeling" [11, p. 200]. A generation later, this is no longer true. One

We thank Mehmet Ekmekci, Deepal Basak, Drew Fudenberg, David Pearce, the editors, and an anonymous reviewer for helpful comments.

J. Fanning
Brown University, Providence, RI, USA
e-mail: jack_fanning@brown.edu

A. Wolitzky (✉)
Massachusetts Institute of Technology, Cambridge, MA, USA
e-mail: wolitzky@mit.edu

E. Karagözoğlu and K. B. Hyndman (eds.), *Bargaining*,
https://doi.org/10.1007/978-3-030-76666-5_3

branch of the literature has modeled attempts to establish commitment as explicit moves in a complete-information bargaining game; it is surveyed in the current volume by Miettinen. A second branch considers simple bargaining games with only offers and accept/reject decisions, but introduces incomplete-information about whether a bargainer is a "type" committed to obtaining a large share of the surplus; uncommitted bargainers then have incentives to imitate these types to develop a tough reputation. This is the literature on "reputational bargaining." Such models have proved remarkably tractable and often provide clear predictions that are independent of details such as the bargaining procedure and the distribution of commitment types. They have also delivered new insights in settings beyond bilateral bargaining, such as repeated games and search markets.

The predictions of complete-information bargaining models following Rubinstein [42] have been criticized for depending on unobserved details of the extensive form, such as whether one party can make offers more frequently than the other, or whether offers are sequential or simultaneous [46, 28].[1] The reputational bargaining literature's eschewal of explicit extensive-form modeling of commitment thus reflects an ambition to predict the outcome of negotiations on the basis of players' preferences and beliefs alone, rather than on how bargaining is assumed to proceed.

The first hint that such procedure-independent predictions might be possible comes from the classical Coase conjecture ([21], [23]; see [8] for a survey). Loosely speaking, this result states that in bargaining with one-sided private information about valuations for a good, the informed party's equilibrium payoff is no less than it would be if she were known to have her most favorable valuation (e.g., a seller with a known cost immediately proposes a price that all buyer value types accept). However, extending this model to two-sided private information about valuations produces less compelling predictions. An inevitable feature of such environments is that a player's offers signal her information, typically leading

[1] Perry and Reny [39] provide support for Rubinstein's predictions in a continuous-time model with endogenously timed offers. Cooperative bargaining solutions offer an alternative, procedure-free approach.

to vast equilibrium multiplicity: signaling allows a player to be "punished with beliefs" for deviating from a proposed equilibrium path (e.g., she is identified as the weakest possible type and given a low continuation payoff), and the threat of this punishment can support a wide variety of behavior, ranging from no-trade to Myerson and Satterthwaite [35]'s constrained-efficient bounds [9]. While attempts have been made to impose "reasonable" refinements on these equilibria, it is often hard to agree on what is reasonable, particularly when some natural refinements give paradoxical results such as no-trade [8].

The reputational bargaining literature thus starts not from the classical Coase conjecture, but from a "reputational Coase conjecture" established by Myerson [34]. Myerson considers an infinite-horizon, alternating-offers bargaining game, where one player has a small probability of being a "commitment type" who always demands some exogenous, prespecified share α of the surplus and never accepts less. Myerson shows that, when both players are patient, the possibly committed player cannot receive an equilibrium payoff significantly below α, regardless of the players' relative costs of delay. Kreps [28] conjectured the same result, and predicted it would hold regardless of the details of the bargaining protocol.[2]

The seminal reputational bargaining model of Abreu and Gul [1] (henceforth AG) vastly generalizes Myerson's result by introducing general bargaining protocols (rather than alternating offers), multiple commitment types (rather than Myerson's single "α-insistent type"), and two-sided reputation formation (i.e., commitment types on both sides). AG find a unique equilibrium that is independent of the details of the bargaining protocol, so long as both sides can make offers frequently. Punishing with beliefs does not arise despite two-sided incomplete-information, because commitment types are immune to belief punishments: they insistently make their pre-specified demands, forcing this behavior onto the equilibrium path. The equilibrium features a war of attrition structure, with uncommitted players on both sides mimicking commitment types before eventually conceding. This offers a good description of some real-world negotiations and links AG to earlier models of incomplete-information wars of attrition [e.g., 29, 33].

[2] See Chapter 5 of Kreps [28], and also Exercise 9 to Chapter 15 of Kreps [27].

AG provide especially clear predictions when commitment behavior is vanishingly unlikely: under some conditions, payoffs approximate those from complete-information, alternating-offers bargaining. Similarly clear predictions in the complete-information limit arise in many other reputational bargaining models, even those with multiple equilibria.

The rest of this chapter is arranged as follows. Section 3.2 describes AG's model and its predictions. Section 3.3 discusses extensions of the reputational bargaining framework. Section 3.4 presents applications to specific economic environments. Section 3.5 discusses experimental evidence. Section 3.6 concludes by highlighting some open questions.

3.2 The Abreu-Gul (AG) Reputational Bargaining Model

AG's paper has three parts. It first analyzes a simple concession game with a single commitment type on each side. The game is then generalized to allow multiple commitment types, with a focus on the complete-information limit. Finally, AG show that equilibria in a large class of discrete-time reputational bargaining games converge to the unique equilibrium of the concession game as offers become frequent.

3.2.1 The Concession Game with a Single Commitment Type

Two players must divide a dollar at some point in continuous time. Each player $i \in \{1, 2\}$ is a "commitment type" with independent probability z_i (alternatively, a "behavioral," "inflexible," "insistent," "obstinate," or "irrational" type) and otherwise is rational. A commitment type always demands some fixed share $\alpha_i \in (0, 1)$, where the commitment demands are incompatible: $\alpha_1 + \alpha_2 > 1$. At any moment each player i can "concede" (accept), obtaining share $1 - \alpha_j$ and giving her opponent α_j. Commitment types never concede. Each player i discounts payoffs exponentially at rate $r_i > 0$, so that if she obtains share x_i at time t, she receives payoff $e^{-r_i t} x_i$.

Each player i's strategy is conveniently described by a distribution F_i over concession times, where $F_i(t)$ is the probability that player i concedes by time t. Because commitment types never concede, player i's reputation for being committed at time t (absent agreement) is

$$z_i(t) = \frac{z_i}{1 - F_i(t)}.$$

This concession game has a unique Nash equilibrium, in which play follows a war of attrition. It is characterized by three properties:

a. Both players' reputations reach probability 1 at the same time T^*.
b. At most one player concedes with positive probability at time 0.
c. On the interval $(0, T^*)$, each player i concedes at the constant rate that keeps her opponent indifferent between waiting and conceding.

These properties are not difficult to establish. Property (a) must hold, because if rational player i were ever certain that she faced committed player j, she would concede immediately. If property (b) did not hold, a player could profitably wait until an instant after time 0 before conceding, to see if her opponent concedes first. By similar reasoning, concession must be continuous after time 0, which implies that each player must always be indifferent between waiting and conceding. For i to be indifferent, j must concede at the constant rate λ_j given by

$$r_i(1 - \alpha_j) = \lambda_j(\alpha_i + \alpha_j - 1) \Leftrightarrow \lambda_j = \frac{r_i(1 - \alpha_j)}{\alpha_i + \alpha_j - 1}. \quad (3.1)$$

This equates i's flow cost of delaying concession (the lost interest on j's offer, $1 - \alpha_j$) and her flow benefit of delay (the probability that j concedes multiplied by i's payoff gain when that happens, $\alpha_i - (1 - \alpha_j)$).

Equation (3.1) implies that for $t \leq T^*$, we have

$$1 - F_j(t) = (1 - F_j(0))e^{-\lambda_j t},$$

where $F_j(0)$ is the probability that j concedes at time 0. Since both players' reputations reach 1 at time T^*, we have

$$z_j(T^*) = \frac{z_j e^{\lambda_j T^*}}{1 - F_j(0)} = 1.$$

If i does not concede with positive probability at time 0, her reputation reaches 1 at time

$$T_i = -\frac{\ln z_i}{\lambda_i}.$$

Because at most one player concedes at time 0, the equilibrium characterization is completed by setting

$$T^* = \min\{T_1, T_2\} \qquad \text{and}$$

$$F_j(0) = 1 - z_j e^{\lambda_j T^*} = \max\left\{0, 1 - z_j z_i^{-\lambda_j/\lambda_i}\right\}. \qquad (3.2)$$

A useful way to understand the equilibrium is to first ask which player would win a "race" to reach reputation 1 absent concession at time 0: that is, which player has the smaller T_i. The losing player (the one with the larger T_i) must then concede at time 0 to give her reputation a sufficient "head start" to reach 1 at the same time as her opponent's. Note that because each player i is indifferent to conceding an instant after time 0, her equilibrium payoff is

$$F_j(0)\alpha_i + (1 - F_j(0))(1 - \alpha_j),$$

which exceeds her payoff from immediately conceding only if she wins the reputational race.

So, which player wins the race? Note that $T_i < T_j$ if and only if

$$\frac{\ln z_i}{\ln z_j} \frac{r_i}{r_j} \frac{1 - \alpha_j}{1 - \alpha_i} < 1.$$

Therefore, i is better-positioned to win the race when her initial reputation is larger, when she is more patient, and when her demand is smaller. This last comparison—smaller demands increase bargaining strength—plays a major role in the expanded model with multiple commitment types, because it incentivizes rational players to make moderate demands.

It is also important to note that players' initial reputations z_i, z_j enter bargaining strength through the ratio of their logarithms, unlike the concession rates λ_i, λ_j. This has dramatic implications for the complete-information limit, where commitment types become vanishingly unlikely. Consider a sequence of concesssion games where initial reputations converge to zero at the same rate, $z_i^n, z_j^n \to 0$ with $z_i^n/z_j^n \in [1/K, K]$ for some $K \geq 1$, with all other parameters fixed. If $\lambda_i > \lambda_j$ then j must concede at time 0 with probability approaching 1 along the corresponding sequence of equilibria. This is immediate from examining equation (3.2), which shows that j's time 0 concession satisfies $F_j(0) \geq 1 - K z_i^{1-\lambda_j/\lambda_i}$ when $z_j \leq K z_i$, and noting that this lower bound on $F_j(0)$ is close to 1 when $z_i \approx 0$ and $\lambda_i > \lambda_j$. To see the intuition, notice that to reach a probability 1 reputation when the initial reputations are small, players must concede with probability close to 1. Since after time 0 players concede at constant rates (which are independent of the initial reputations), the reputational race must continue for a long time. During this long race i's reputation grows exponentially faster than j's, $(dz_i(t)/dt)/z_i(t) = \lambda_i > \lambda_j$, which overwhelms any fixed proportional advantage for j in the initial reputations.

3.2.2 The Concession Game with Multiple Commitment Types

Now suppose for each player i there is a finite set of commitment types $C_i \subset (0, 1)$, where each type is identified with its demand. The (exogenous) probability that i demands $\alpha_i \in C_i$ conditional on being committed is $\pi_i(\alpha_i)$, while the total probability that she is committed remains z_i. At time 0, first player 1 publicly announces a demand $\alpha_1 \in C_1$, and then player 2 announces a counterdemand $\alpha_2 \in C_2$, whence play continues into a concession game. Denote the (endogenous, equilibrium) probability that rational player 1 demands α_1 by $\mu_1(\alpha_1)$, and denote the probability that rational player 2 counterdemands α_2 by $\mu_2^{\alpha_1}(\alpha_2)$. Players' reputations at the start of the concession game with demands α_1, α_2 are

$$\bar{z}_1^{\alpha_1} = \frac{z_1\pi_1(\alpha_1)}{z_1\pi_1(\alpha_1) + (1 - z_1)\mu_1(\alpha_1)},$$
$$\bar{z}_2^{\alpha_1,\alpha_2} = \frac{z_2\pi_2(\alpha_2)}{z_2\pi_2(\alpha_2) + (1 - z_2)\mu_2^{\alpha_1}(\alpha_2)}.$$

AG show there is still an essentially unique equilibrium after incorporating this demand-choice stage. The basic intuition is that when rational player i becomes more likely to mimic type α_i, this reduces her posterior reputation after announcing α_i, which reduces her continuation payoff and makes mimicking α_i less appealing. This "strategic substitutability" pushes toward a unique equilibrium.

What happens in the complete-information limit of this richer game? AG show that, along a sequence of concession games where initial reputations converge to zero at the same rate, each player i can guarantee a limiting payoff of at least

$$\underline{\alpha}_i = \max\left\{\alpha_i \in C_i : \alpha_i \leq \frac{r_j}{r_i + r_j}\right\}.$$

To see this for $i = 1$, note that if player 2 counterdemands $\alpha_2 > 1 - \underline{\alpha}_1$, then $r_2/(r_1 + r_2) \geq \underline{\alpha}_1 > 1 - \alpha_2$, and therefore

$$r_1(1 - \alpha_2) < \frac{r_1 r_2}{r_1 + r_2} \leq r_2(1 - \underline{\alpha}_1),$$

so $\lambda_2 < \lambda_1$. As we have seen, this implies that player 2 concedes at time 0 with probability 1 in the complete-information limit.

Given the above result, if the space of commitment types is sufficiently rich, player i's payoff must be approximately $r_j/(r_i + r_j)$, which is also her payoff in Rubinstein [42]'s complete-information, alternating-offers game when offers are frequent. Types who demand exactly $\alpha_i^* = r_j/(r_i+$

r_j) are sometimes called "cannonical" types. When they are present, we can precisely identify equilibrium outcomes in the complete-information limit. The independence of this prediction to the distribution of commitment types, π_i, is a crucial robustness property. It is similar to Fudenberg and Levine [22]'s finding that, in the presence of a type that always plays a Stackelberg action, a patient long-run player facing short-run opponents obtains approximately her Stackelberg payoff.

3.2.3 Convergence of Discrete-Time Bargaining to the Concession Game

The final part of AG's paper considers discrete-time reputational bargaining games. The only assumption made about the bargaining protocol is that each player can make at least one offer in every length-$\Delta > 0$ interval of real time. AG show that all perfect Bayesian equilibrium outcome distributions of all such games converge to the unique equilibrium of the concession game as offers become frequent ($\Delta \to 0$). This crucial result shows that the preceding analysis (of concession games where players cannot change their demands) applies equally to any bargaining game with frequent offers, independently of the details of the bargaining protocol. It is the basis of much of the subsequent literature, which often directly adopts AG's tractable continuous-time concession game structure.

To understand AG's convergence result, suppose we knew that if a player takes an action inconsistent with any of her commitment types ("reveals rationality") before her opponent does, then she must immediately concede. We would then be back to a (discrete-time) concession game: after making her initial demand, a player's only remaining choice is whether to keep mimicking her chosen commitment type or to reveal rationality and concede. Convergence to continuous time would then be a technical exercise.

The key part of AG's result is therefore that, with frequent offers, revealing rationality is essentially the same as conceding, and in particular gives approximately the same continuation payoffs. This follows from a generalization of Myerson's reputational Coase conjecture, discussed above. It remains to explain the logic of Myerson's result.

Suppose player 1 is possibly committed, while player 2 is known to be rational. Note first that there exists a finite time T such that, if player 1 always demands α and never accepts less, then player 2 concedes by T. The argument is similar to ones in the literature on reputation in repeated games (e.g., [22], see [32] for a survey): If player 2 does not immediately accept, she must believe that 1 will cease commitment behavior soon with positive probability. So, if 1 does not cease, 2's belief that 1 is committed must increase. Iterating this argument, 2 must eventually become certain that 1 is committed, and so accept.

This argument implies that at any time $t < T$ rational player 1 can guarantee a continuation payoff of $e^{-r_1(T-t)}\alpha_1$ by insisting on α until T. To complete the proof, we argue that T converges to 0 as offers become frequent. Suppose toward a contradiction that T remains bounded away from 0, and suppose 1 insists on α_1 until time $T - \varepsilon$ for some small $\varepsilon > 0$. From this point forward player 2 can expect at most $1-e^{-r_1\varepsilon}\alpha_1$ in any agreement. Fixing another small number $\eta > 0$, agreements reached after time $T-\eta\varepsilon$ must be worth even less to player 2 from the perspective of time $T-\varepsilon$: at most $e^{-r_2(1-\eta)\varepsilon}(1-e^{-r_1\eta\varepsilon}\alpha_1) < 1-\alpha_1$. Hence, for 2 to delay acceptance from $T-\varepsilon$ to $T-\eta\varepsilon$, she must believe 1 will cease commitment behavior before $T-\eta\varepsilon$ with high probability. Iterating this argument for $k \in \mathbb{N}$, if time $T-\eta^k\varepsilon$ is reached, 1 must cease commitment behavior before $T-\eta^{k+1}\varepsilon$ with high probability.[3] But these repeated expected deviations from commitment behavior eventually exhaust the probability that 1 is rational before time T, a contradiction.

[3] Frequent offers guarantee that 2 has an opportunity to accept 1's demand within each such interval.

3.3 Extensions

3.3.1 Endogenous Commitment Demands

In AG, the interpretation of the distribution over commitment types π_i is somewhat ambiguous. Certainly, real-world bargainers may not have a very precise sense of the probabilities with which their opponents can be committed to various bargaining positions. One of AG's key messages is that the details of π_i are often irrelevant in the complete-information limit, but they do assume that the relative probabilities of different commitment types do not blow up, and π_i also matters away from the limit. These considerations have led some researchers to consider models where the distribution of commitment demands is endogenous.

The first paper in this area—written shortly after AG's paper was first circulated—is due to Kambe [25]. Kambe considers an elegant variant of AG, where each player i is initially rational for sure, but after making any initial demand α_i becomes committed to it with some probability z_i. (Thus, a player is parameterized by a single number z_i rather than a distribution π_i.) A player does not observe whether the opponent becomes committed; moreover, the initial demands cannot signal commitment, because they are made before commitment arises.[4] Once players make their initial demands (and potentially become committed), play proceeds as in AG's concession game.

Kambe shows that in equilibrium players make the unique just-compatible demands α_i, α_j that lead to a tie in AG's reputational race:[5] that is, demands satisfy the system of equations

$$\frac{\ln z_i}{\ln z_j}\frac{r_i}{r_j}\frac{1-\alpha_j}{1-\alpha_i} = 1, \quad \alpha_i + \alpha_j = 1,$$

[4] These assumptions mirror those of the complete-information bargaining model of Crawford [13].

[5] More precisely, these demands arise in the unique equilibrium without randomization over initial demands, and payoffs in equilibria with randomization are similar.

which has solution

$$\alpha_i = \frac{r_j \ln z_i}{r_i \ln z_i + r_j \ln z_j}.$$

If player i's demand is more aggressive than this, she loses the reputational race and ends up conceding; while if she is less aggressive, she gets a smaller share when her opponent accepts.

Kambe's model thus predicts immediate agreement, even when z_i is large (unlike AG). However, $\alpha_i \to r_j/(r_i + r_j)$ when z_i and z_j go to 0 at the same rate, so Kambe's model coincides with AG in the complete-information limit. It can thus be viewed as a reinterpretation of AG where the exogenous commitment type distribution is replaced by endogenous bargaining postures.[6]

3.3.2 Nonstationary Types and Payoffs-as-You-Go

In the models considered so far, the play of commitment types takes a very simple form: always demand some fixed share α_i, and never accept less. There is no obvious reason to restrict attention to such stationary types, and indeed it seems plausible that a player could be committed to richer behaviors, such as making tougher or weaker demands over time, or responding aggressively to certain opposing actions.[7] Such *nonstationary* types are considered by Abreu and Pearce [2] (henceforth AP). AP also analyze "bargaining with payoffs-as-you-go," a hybrid between the pure bargaining model considered so far and a repeated game: players first announce potentially nonstationary commitment types (where all commitment types announce truthfully), and then repeatedly play a stage game and receive payoffs, while simultaneously offering each other binding contracts to govern the future play of the game.

---

[6] Sanktjohanser [44] considers a hybrid of Kambe and AG, where each player knows at time 0 whether she is a "stubborn type," all types are free to make any initial demand, and stubborn types become committed to any initial demand they make. This model reintroduces signaling concerns, which allow almost any equilibrium payoffs; however, the paper also characterizes behavioral properties that hold across all symmetric equilibria.

[7] Richer types also let us avoid AG's somewhat counterfactual "no-haggling" prediction that a player who changes her offer immediately concedes.

In this rich and complex model, the authors establish a remarkable result: in the complete-information limit, payoffs converge to the Nash bargaining with threats (NBWT) payoffs identified by Nash [36], so long as there is a type on each side that always plays the corresponding NBWT action and insistently demands the NBWT payoff. Thus, the stationary NBWT type is canonical, while nonstationary types have no effect.[8]

Intuition for the result comes from first generalizing AG's model with only stationary types to a setting with arbitrary flow/disagreement payoffs and feasible agreements corresponding to the stage game payoffs. With equal patience, a type demanding her Nash bargaining payoff is canonical: it ensures that a player concedes faster than her opponent in the war of attrition. Now allow players to first choose mixed actions in the stage game to determine the flow payoffs. Anticipating that they will agree on Nash bargaining payoffs relative to the flow payoffs, the players will choose their Nash threat actions. Finally, AP show that a war of attrition structure is preserved when nonstationary types are introduced, although now concession rates are determined by equilibrium continuation payoffs rather than current offers. While a player imitating the NBWT type may concede with lower probability than her opponent at certain times, she concedes with higher probability over the long run and so still wins the reputational race.[9]

Wolitzky [47] notes a caveat to AP's powerful equilibrium selection result: it relies on the assumption that commitment types are "transparent," in that they truthfully announce their future behavior at the beginning of the game. Suppose there is instead a positive probability of a "weak" commitment type that initially claims to be the NBWT threat type and mimics its behavior for a long time, before eventually conceding to any demand. If this type is more likely than the true NBWT type, a player will wait when her opponent claims to be the NBWT type, hoping

[8] Recall that given a stage game with action sets A_i and utility functions u_i, the NBWT solution is the Nash equilibrium of the game where players choose "threats" $\beta_i \in \Delta(A_i)$ and payoffs are given by the Nash bargaining solution for the feasible payoff set of the stage game with disagreement point $u(\beta_1, \beta_2)$.

[9] A related paper by Atakan and Ekmekci [7] obtains a war of attrition structure in a class of repeated games with two-sided reputation. In recent work, Abreu and Pearce [3] extend their NBWT prediction to settings without binding contracts, by imposing a form of renegotiation proofness.

that he is actually the weak type. Thus, when commitment types are both nonstationary and nontransparent, equilibrium selection depends on the relative frequency of different types.[10]

3.3.3 Nonequilibrium Analysis

The complexity of the equilibrium reasoning involved in reputational bargaining models raises the question of what predictions are robust to letting players hold more permissive, nonequilibrium beliefs about the opponent's behavior. Wolitzky [48] investigates this issue in a bargaining model where players can announce any (potentially nonstationary) path of bargaining demands, before become committed to the announced path with probability z_i (as in Kambe's variant of AG). He asks what predictions can be made assuming only that players' strategies can be rationalized by some belief, and what path of demands a player must announce to guarantee her largest possible payoff. It turns out that a player with ex-ante commitment probability z_i can guarantee a "minmax" payoff of $\alpha_i^* = 1/(1 - \ln z_i)$ against an uncommitted opponent, which is substantial even for relatively small z_i. The announcement which guarantees this payoff initially demands α_i^* and subsequently demands compensation for any delay: more precisely, it demands $\min\{e^{r_i t}\alpha_i^*, 1\}$ at each time t. The intuition is that a demand path that increases slower than this leaves the player with a payoff below α_i^* when the opponent accepts after some delay; while a path that increases faster fails to convince the opponent that the player is committed by the time her demand reaches 1, and thus could lead to a permanent impasse.

10 If all types are stationary then transparency is irrelevant, because initial play reveals the entire strategy.

3.3.4 Nonstationary Environments

Fanning [15] extends AG's model to a nonstationary environment where players must agree before a random deadline that is continuously distributed on a finite interval $[0, T]$. When commitment is vanishingly unlikely, outcomes differ markedly depending on whether or not commitment types are stationary, unlike in AP. With a rich set of stationary types, players can approximately guarantee their Nash bargaining payoff regardless of their impatience. This occurs because small initial reputations cause bargaining to continue until close to T, when the cost of delay explodes. A Nash demand player concedes much faster than her opponent at that point, and so wins the reputational race. With nonstationary types, the type that adopts the time-varying, complete-information, alternating-offers strategy for this environment is canonical. The intuition is that alternating offers give players equal opportunities to use the threat of costly delay to extract surplus, so if agreement were ever delayed this would be equally costly to both players. Therefore, in reputational bargaining, a player who demands more than her alternating-offers share faces higher delay costs than an opponent imitating an alternating-offers type, and so concedes slower and loses the reputational race.

When commitment types are stationary, the model also predicts "deadline effects" similar to those observed empirically [e.g., 41]. There is frequent agreement at time 0 and close to the deadline but not in between, and some disagreement. Here the time 0 agreements reflect initial concessions as in AG, while the subsequent lull in agreement followed by a spike at the deadline occurs because war of attrition concession rates are proportional to delay costs.

Fanning [16] considers a different nonstationary extension of AG, where now players' costs of delay can change at some "revelation time" $R > 0$, with both players initially uncertain about the direction of such changes. For instance, an election at time R may determine political parties' costs of resisting an agreement in a divided legislature. The main result shows that there is often delay, even in the complete-information limit with a rich set of stationary commitment types. Rational players make aggressive, incompatible demands and then wait until time R in the hope that the opponent will turn out to have a large delay cost, and so concede. Mutually beneficial compromises exist; however, a player who proposes one increases her opponent's option value of waiting, so the opponent still waits.

3.3.5 Incomplete Information About Preferences

A final extension combines commitment types with incomplete-information about preferences. One interpretation of AG's results is that perturbing a complete-information bargaining model with a rich set of commitment types selects a unique equilibrium outcome. Abreu et al. [4] ask the same question for the incomplete-information model of Rubinstein [43], where one player's preferences are known while the other can have one of two possible discount rates. The authors show that perturbing this model with a rich set of stationary commitment types and taking the limit as those types become vanishingly unlikely supports a "Coasean" prediction: the outcome is the same as if the informed player were known to be patient. The intuition is that, since the patient rational type concedes at a slower rate in the war of attribution, in the limit the outcome of the reputational race is solely determined by this type's behavior. By contrast, allowing nonstationary types that can delay making their initial offer yields a non-Coasean equilibrium where the rational informed player no longer receives the payoff corresponding to her patient type. The problem is that the patient type has an incentive to separate by delaying her initial demand, which breaks the pooling equilibrium.[11]

[11] Pęski [40] studies multi-issue reputational bargaining with incomplete-information about players' weights on different issues, where bargainers can offer menus of alternative agreements. With one-sided preference uncertainty, the uninformed party gets half the total surplus by offering a menu consisting of all allocations that give her that payoff.

3.4 Applications

3.4.1 Outside Options and Search Markets

In an early critique of AG, Compte and Jehiel [12] investigate the effect of outside options on reputational bargaining. Their main point can be seen when each player i has a single commitment type, which demands α_i. Assume an alternating-offers bargaining protocol, which gives complete-information payoffs $v_1^* = 1 - v_2^* = (1 - \delta_2)/(1 - \delta_1\delta_2)$. Further, assume that each player can opt out of bargaining at any time, yielding payoffs v_i^{out}, v_j^{out}, and that player i prefers her commitment demand, over her complete-information payoff, over opting out, over a committed opponent's offer: that is, $\alpha_i > v_i^* > v_i^{out} > 1 - \alpha_j$.

Compte and Jehiel show that in the unique equilibrium play proceeds exactly as in the model without outside options or commitment types: the players immediately agree to the complete-information payoffs. The intuition is that since each player will opt out if she becomes convinced her opponent is committed, players have no incentive to build reputations, but instead reveal rationality and bargain under complete-information.

This analysis suggests that much depends on whether outside options are sufficiently attractive relative to the commitment types' offers. With a rich set of commitment types (or in Kambe's endogenous demand model) players make moderate equilibrium demands, and in the complete-information limit we have $\alpha_i + \alpha_j = 1$, which violates the assumption $\alpha_i > v_i^* > v_i^{out} > 1 - \alpha_j$. Thus, Compte and Jehiel's critique is most significant when there is only a small number of relatively aggressive commitment types.

Atakan and Ekmekci [6] consider reputational bargaining with outside options endogenously determined by a search market. Firms and workers flow into the market and are randomly matched to bargain. They exit the market after reaching an agreement that generates a unit of surplus (or randomly dying). Players are rational or committed. Player i's single commitment type always demands α_i, but also stops bargaining and returns to the market if convinced that her opponent is committed. On returning to the market, players must wait time $\tau \geq 0$ before being rematched.

The paper derives several results concerning steady-state equilibria. A headline result is that when search costs are minimal ($\tau \approx 0$) and firms and workers enter the market at the same rate, bargaining involves no initial concessions, so the outcome is inefficient with total payoffs $2 - \alpha_1 - \alpha_2 < 1$ (in contrast with AG, where initial concessions lead to efficiency in the complete-information limit). The reason why initial concessions cannot occur is that this would give players on the other side of the market outside options that are greater than their payoffs from conceding, which is inconsistent with equilibrium. However, it is unclear whether a richer set of commitment types would constrain this inefficiency.

Endogenous outside options are also central to Özyurt [38], who shows that even vanishingly small reputational concerns allow a wide range of prices in a Bertrand-like setting. This occurs because buyers who observe a seller undercutting her rival's posted price use the lower price as an outside option in bargaining with the high price rival.[12]

3.4.2 Mediation

Fanning [17, 18] investigates how an uninformed mediator can improve efficiency in AG's model. The first paper considers a simple form of mediation often used by professional mediators: publicly suggesting a deal only when both parties accept it in private. This can be effective, but only if the mediator sometimes fails to suggest the deal even when both parties accept. The second paper characterizes the equilibrium with mediation that maximizes rational players' payoffs in symmetric games. Mediation improves on unmediated bargaining if and only if commitment demands are larger than the probability of commitment types. The mediator suggests agreements with reduced delay between self-reported pairs of rational agents (compared to unmediated bargaining),

[12] Özyurt [37] introduces commitment types into Fearon [20]'s "crisis bargaining" model, where in addition to waiting or conceding, bargainers can end the game by "attacking"; this is another type of outside option.

while not suggesting any agreements involving a reported commitment type on some initial interval in order to incentivize truthful reporting of rationality.

3.5 Experimental Evidence

Behavior resembling reputational bargaining was observed even in early unstructured bargaining experiments. For example, Roth and Malouf [41] had subjects divide the probability of winning a monetary prize before a deadline by sending proposals and free-form messages over a computer. When the prize was worth three times as much to one player, agreements clustered around two focal points: equal probability of winning a prize (the Nash solution) and equal expected payoffs (75% probability for the low-prize subject). Agreements occurred close to the deadline, although some subjects never agreed. These focal divisions correspond to two notions of fairness that may motivate commitment behavior. By contrast, when each subject could win the same prize, they always split the probability equally, again suggesting that commitment to a demand may depend on its perceived fairness and/or focality.

One feature of behavior in these experiments that does not align with AG's predictions is that small demand changes do not precipitate immediate agreement. Nonetheless, Fanning and Kloosterman [19] provide support for the basic Coasean underpinnings of reputational bargaining when there is only one fair/focal division: in an infinite-horizon bargaining experiment where one subject makes all the offers, outcomes were close to immediate agreement on an equal division (in contrast to relatively unequal divisions in one-shot ultimatum bargaining).

Other experiments have sought to test reputational bargaining predictions more directly. Embrey et al. [14] allow a simultaneous initial demand stage followed by a continuous-time concession stage with fixed demands. When subjects faced either another subject or a computer committed to a fixed demand (without knowing which), they made the computer's demands more frequently than in a control treatment in which they always faced another subject. This suggests that subjects understood the benefit of mimicking a tough computer bargainer. However, many subjects still demanded an equal split instead of the computer demand, and there was more delay than predicted by AG. Heggedal et al. [24] test Compte and Jehiel [12]'s predictions by adding treatments with outside options to the above experimental setup. Outside options reduce imitation of aggressive computer demands but do not improve bargaining efficiency, because they are used too often.

3.6 Open Questions

3.6.1 Foundations for Commitment Behavior

A key feature of reputational bargaining models is that commitment behavior is exogenous. This has the advantage of limiting signaling and equilibrium multiplicity. But it also raises important questions of where commitment behavior comes from, and what forms of commitment behavior are most likely to be observed.

Abreu and Sethi [5] address these questions using evolutionary game theory. They consider a population of commitment and rational types who are randomly matched and then bargain. All players have the same preferences over agreements, but rational types incur an extra cost reflecting their more sophisticated behavior. This cost ensures that commitment types always exist in every evolutionary stable equilibrium.[13] The main result is that whenever there is a commitment type demanding α there must also be a complementary type demanding $1-\alpha$. Complementary types ensure that invading types demanding more than α are incompatible with the complementary type, and so earn lower profits. For any $\alpha > 0.5$, an equilibrium exists with only two complementary types demanding α and $1 - \alpha$ (in addition to rational types, when the cost of rationality is sufficiently small). The equilibrium is efficient when $\alpha \to 0.5$.

[13] Abreu and Sethi's notion of evolutionary stability requires that all types in the population obtain the same expected payoffs, and obtain strictly higher payoffs than the population average after introducing a small fraction of invading types.

Basak [10] provides a simple foundation for commitment in an alternating-offers model where players have private "reservation values." Each player's reservation value ω_i is drawn from a binary distribution, where the high value exceeds her complete-information payoff but is compatible with the opponent's low value. A player receives utility x_i for obtaining a dollar share $x_i \geq \omega_i$, but receives negative utility for a lower share. The unique equilibrium matches AG's war of attrition: high types always demand their reservation value, and low types imitate them before eventually conceding. Uniqueness arises because reservation values do not affect players' intertemporal preferences for dollar shares larger than that value.[14]

Weinstein and Yildiz [45] show that any (stationary or nonstationary) commitment type's behavior in a repeated game is the unique rationalizable strategy of a utility-maximizing type with different payoffs and information about the stage game. Rational players face the same strategic situation as in the original game with commitment types, while the commitment-behavior types sometimes face types that were absent in the original game (in particular, values may be interdependent, so commitment-behavior types may not know their own payoffs). The permissiveness of this result provides some support for AP's approach of flooding the game with a wide variety of types when commitment is vanishingly unlikely.

3.6.2 Other Directions

Further open questions include: What is a tractable model of multilateral reputational bargaining?[15] Can reputational bargaining's powerful equilibrium selection results be further extended in general dynamic

[14] Basak also considers the effect of releasing information about the reservation values. Fully informative signals ensure immediate agreement, but partially informative signals may reduce efficiency.

[15] Kambe [26] analyzes a multilateral, incomplete-information war of attrition with some similarities to reputational bargaining. Ma [31] shows that in majoritarian bargaining, an agent may benefit from having a lower reputation, because this leads to her inclusion in more winning coalitions.

games, such as repeated games?[16] How does repeated reputational bargaining unfold?[17] What are the effects of allowing players to gain and lose commitment over time? Does considering commitment types who randomize their behavior or behave nontransparently deliver new insights?

Finally, we began this survey by discussing the overarching ambition of reputational bargaining models to make predictions on the basis of putatively observably factors like players' beliefs about each other's commitment behavior, rather than the details of the bargaining protocol. A crucial question is thus whether these models can predict and explain bargaining field data better than competing models. Such empirical application of reputational bargaining models is currently a wide open area.

References

1. Dilip Abreu and Faruk Gul. Bargaining and reputation. *Econometrica*, 68(1):85–117, 2000. ISSN 00129682. URL http://www.jstor.org/stable/2999476.
2. Dilip Abreu and David Pearce. Bargaining, reputation, and equilibrium selection in repeated games with contracts. *Econometrica*, 75(3):653–710, 2007. URL http://www.jstor.org/stable/4502007.
3. Dilip Abreu and David Pearce. Bargaining, reputation, and equilibrium selection in repeated games without contracts. *Unpublished Manuscript*, 2019.
4. Dilip Abreu, David Pearce, and Ennio Stacchetti. One sided uncertainty and delay in reputational bargaining. *Theoretical Economics*, 10:719–773, 2015. 10.3982/TE1564. URL http://dx.doi.org/10.3982/TE1564.
5. Dilip Abreu and Rajiv Sethi. Evolutionary stability in a reputational model of bargaining. *Games and Economic Behavior*, 44(2):195–216, 2003. URL http://www.sciencedirect.com/science/article/pii/S0899825603000290.

[16] As in Abreu and Pearce [2], Atakan and Ekmekci [7], and more broadly the literate on reputation in repeated games surveyed by Mailath and Samuelson [32].

[17] Lee and Liu [30] consider an incomplete-information repeated bargaining model with some features of reputational bargaining.

6. Alp E. Atakan and Mehmet Ekmekci. Bargaining and reputation in search markets. *The Review of Economic Studies*, 81(1):1–29, 08 2013a. ISSN 0034-6527. URL https://doi.org/10.1093/restud/rdt021.
7. Alp E. Atakan and Mehmet Ekmekci. A two-sided reputation result with long-run players. *Journal of Economic Theory*, 148(1):376–392, 2013b. ISSN 0022-0531. https://doi.org/10.1016/j.jet.2012.12.007. URL http://www.sciencedirect.com/science/article/pii/S0022053112001226.
8. Lawrence M. Ausubel, Peter Cramton, and Raymond J. Deneckere. Bargaining with incomplete information. In Robert J. Aumann and Sergiu Hart, editors, *Handbook of Game Theory with Economic Applications*, volume 3, chapter 50. Elsevier, 2002.
9. Lawrence M. Ausubel and Raymond J. Deneckere. Efficient sequential bargaining. *The Review of Economic Studies*, 60(2):435–461, 04 1993. ISSN 0034-6527. 10.2307/2298066. URL https://doi.org/10.2307/2298066.
10. Deepal Basak. Fact-finding and bargaining. *Unpublished manuscript*, 2019.
11. Ken Binmore, Martin J. Osborne, and Ariel Rubinstein. Noncooperative models of bargaining. *Handbook of Game Theory with Economic Applications*, 1:179–225, 1992.
12. Olivier Compte and Philippe Jehiel. On the role of outside options in bargaining with obstinate parties. *Econometrica*, 70(4):1477–1517, 2002. URL http://onlinelibrary.wiley.com/doi/10.1111/1468-0262.00339/full.
13. Vincent P. Crawford. A theory of disagreement in bargaining. *Econometrica*, 50(3):607–637, 1982. ISSN 00129682, 14680262. URL http://www.jstor.org/stable/1912604.
14. Matthew Embrey, Guillaume R. Fréchette, and Steven F. Lehrer. Bargaining and reputation: An experiment on bargaining in the presence of behavioural types. *The Review of Economic Studies*, 82(2):608–631, 09 2014. ISSN 0034-6527. URL https://doi.org/10.1093/restud/rdu029.
15. Jack Fanning. Reputational bargaining and deadlines. *Econometrica*, 84(3):1131–1179, 2016. URL https://onlinelibrary.wiley.com/doi/abs/10.3982/ECTA12628.
16. Jack Fanning. No compromise: Uncertain costs in reputational bargaining. *Journal of Economic Theory*, 175:518–555, 2018. ISSN 0022-0531. https://doi.org/10.1016/j.jet.2018.02.001. URL http://www.sciencedirect.com/science/article/pii/S0022053118300358.
17. Jack Fanning. Mediation in reputational bargaining. *American Economic Review*, 111(8): 2444–2472, 2021. https://doi.org/10.1257/aer.20191321.

18. Jack Fanning. Optimal dynamic mediation. *Unpublished Manuscript*, 2021.
19. Jack Fanning and Andrew Kloosterman. An experimental test of the coase conjecture: fairness in dynamic bargaining. *The RAND Jorunal of Economics* (forthcoming), 2021.
20. James D. Fearon. Domestic political audiences and the escalation of international disputes. *American Political Science Review*, 88(3):577–592, 1994. https://doi.org/10.2307/2944796.
21. Drew Fudenberg, David Levine, and Jean Tirole. Infinite horizon models of bargaining with one-sided uncertainty. In *Game Theoretic Models of Bargaining*, volume 73, page 79. Cambridge University Press, 1985.
22. Drew Fudenberg and David K Levine. Reputation and equilibrium selection in games with a patient player. *Econometrica: Journal of the Econometric Society*, 57(4):759–778, July 1989.
23. Faruk Gul, Hugo Sonnenschein, and Robert Wilson. Foundations of dynamic monopoly and the coase conjecture. *Journal of Economic Theory*, 39(1):155–190, 1986.
24. Tom-Reiel Heggedal, Leif Hellandy, and Magnus Våge Knutsenz. The power of outside options in the presence of obstinate types. *Unpublished Manuscript*, 2020.
25. Shinsuke Kambe. Bargaining with imperfect commitment. *Games and Economic Behavior*, 28(2):217–237, August 1999. URL https://doi.org/10.1006/game.1998.0700.
26. Shinsuke Kambe. An n-person war of attrition with the possibility of a non-compromising type. *Theoretical Economics*, 14(3):849–886, 2019. URL https://econtheory.org/ojs/index.php/te/article/view/20190849/0.
27. David M. Kreps. *A Course in Microeconomic Theory*. Princeton University Press, 1990a.
28. David M. Kreps. *Game Theory and Economic Modelling*. Clarendon Press, 1990b.
29. David M. Kreps and Robert Wilson. Reputation and imperfect information. *Journal of Economic Theory*, 27(2):253–279, 1982. URL http://www.sciencedirect.com/science/article/pii/0022053182900308.
30. Jihong Lee and Qingmin Liu. Gambling reputation: Repeated bargaining with outside options. *Econometrica*, 81(4):1601–1672, 2013. URL https://onlinelibrary.wiley.com/doi/abs/10.3982/ECTA9200.
31. Zizhen Ma. Efficiency and surplus distribution in majoritarian reputational bargaining. *Unpublished manuscript*, 2020.

32. George J. Mailath and Larry Samuelson. *Repeated Games and Reputations: Long-Run Relationships*. Oxford University Press, 2006.
33. Paul Milgrom and John Roberts. Predation, reputation, and entry deterrence. *Journal of Economic Theory*, 27(2):280–312, 1982.
34. R. Myerson. *Game Theory: Analysis of Conflict*. Cambridge, MA: Harvard University Press, 1991.
35. Roger B. Myerson and Mark A. Satterthwaite. Efficient mechanisms for bilateral trading. *Journal of Economic Theory*, 29(2):265–281, 1983. ISSN 0022-0531. https://doi.org/10.1016/0022-0531(83)90048-0. URL http://www.sciencedirect.com/science/article/pii/0022053183900480.
36. John F. Nash. Two-Person Cooperative Games. *Econometrica*, 21(1):128–140, January 1953.
37. Selçuk Özyurt. Audience costs and reputation in crisis bargaining. *Games and Economic Behavior*, 88:250–259, 2014. ISSN 0899-8256. https://doi.org/10.1016/j.geb.2014.09.008. URL http://www.sciencedirect.com/science/article/pii/S0899825614001420.
38. Selçuk Özyurt. Bargaining, reputation and competition. *Journal of Economic Behavior & Organization*, 119:1–17, 2015. ISSN 0167-2681. https://doi.org/10.1016/j.jebo.2015.07.010. URL http://www.sciencedirect.com/science/article/pii/S0167268115002012.
39. Motty Perry and Philip J. Reny. A non-cooperative bargaining model with strategically timed offers. *Journal of Economic Theory*, 59(1):50–77, 1993. ISSN 0022-0531. https://doi.org/10.1006/jeth.1993.1004. URL http://www.sciencedirect.com/science/article/pii/S0022053183710045.
40. Marcin Pęski. Reputational Bargaining with Incomplete Information about Preferences. *Unpublished manuscript*, 2021.
41. A. E. Roth and M. W. Malouf. Game-theoretic models and the role of information in bargaining. *Psychological Review*, 86(6):574–594, 1979. URL http://dx.doi.org/10.1037/0033-295X.86.6.574.
42. Ariel Rubinstein. Perfect equilibrium in a bargaining model. *Econometrica*, 50(1):97–109, 1982. ISSN 00129682. URL http://www.jstor.org/stable/1912531.
43. Ariel Rubinstein. Choice of conjectures in a bargaining game with incomplete information. In *Game-Theoretic Models of Bargaining*. Cambridge University Press, 1985.
44. Anna Sanktjohanser. Optimally stubborn. *Unpublished Manuscript*, 2020.
45. Jonathan Weinstein and Muhamet Yildiz. Reputation without commitment in finitely repeated games. *Theoretical Economics*, 11(1):157–185,

2016. 10.3982/TE1893. URL https://onlinelibrary.wiley.com/doi/abs/10.3982/TE1893.

46. Robert Wilson. Game theoretic analysis of trading processes. *Advances in Economic Theory*, 1987.
47. Alexander Wolitzky. Indeterminacy of reputation effects in repeated games with contracts. *Games and Economic Behavior*, 73(2):595–607, 2011. URL http://www.sciencedirect.com/science/article/pii/S0899825611000492.
48. Alexander Wolitzky. Reputational bargaining with minimal knowledge of rationality. *Econometrica*, 80(5):2047–2087, September 2012. URL http://dx.doi.org/10.3982/ECTA9865.

4

Dynamic Bargaining with Private Information

William Fuchs and Andrzej Skrzypacz

4.1 Introduction

In this chapter, we discuss a few recent theoretical papers studying the dynamics of negotiations. This is not a comprehensive review of the field. First, our focus is on recent papers, with the previous literature excellently reviewed in Ausubel et al. (2001). Second, our focus is on papers that describe bargaining "outside the void." That is papers that model

W. Fuchs
University of Texas at Austin, Austin, TX, USA
e-mail: William.Fuchs@mccombs.utexas.edu

A. Skrzypacz (✉)
Stanford University, Stanford, CA, USA
e-mail: skrz@stanford.edu

W. Fuchs
Universidad Carlos III Madrid, Madrid, Spain

E. Karagözoğlu and K. B. Hyndman (eds.), *Bargaining*,
https://doi.org/10.1007/978-3-030-76666-5_4

negotiations between two parties that are influenced by the outside environment: for example, by the possibility of entry of new trading parties, the existence of a deadline, the possibility of arrival of information, or new outside options materializing. Finally, in most of this survey, we focus on highlighting the economic intuitions in the continuous-time limit.

Dynamic bargaining problems have historically been modeled in discrete time, with some important results (like the Coase conjecture we start with) derived as a limit of the equilibria when the discount factor converges to one. As we show, many complex bargaining games are particularly tractable in continuous time. The key observation is that the HJB equation describing the problem of the uninformed player is linear in the speed of trade. This linearity is what lies behind the Coasean forces. Importantly, it provides for a simple algorithm to find equilibria since, in any smooth equilibrium, the linear terms must add up to 0. This condition provides almost immediate implications for the value of the uninformed player and equilibrium prices with clear economic intuition. We will highlight the power of this approach throughout this survey.

The benefits of continuous time do not come without cost. Game-theoretic models in continuous time often create technical problems. We do not discuss any of those problems here. In the literature there are two main approaches. One is to write the game in discrete time and analyze the limit of equilibria as periods get short. The second is to write the game directly in continuous time and propose an appropriate equilibrium notion for that model. Our goal here is to highlight the economic intuition of the results, side-stepping the technical issues. Thus, some of our constructions in this survey may seem incomplete. They should all be read as having a preface "suppose the equilibrium is nice, then here is how it must look like." We direct readers interested in this methodology to the original papers. We hope that a less technical survey, focused on connecting several of the underlying ideas, will serve as a complement to the existing work be an accessible introduction to readers interested in this literature.

4.2 Dynamic Bargaining with (Endogenously) Interdependent Values

A classical result in the bargaining literature, the Coase Conjecture (Coase 1972), establishes that despite market power and asymmetric information, trade would be immediate without inefficient delay if the seller were unable to commit not to revise her prices in the future. Coase argued that the seller's future self would be tempted to lower its price to satisfy the remaining demand and in doing so, create competition for its current self, leading to a competitive outcome with immediate trade. In contrast to these predictions, delays are common in practice. As a result, the literature that followed tried to augment the basic setting of Coase to obtain more realistic results.[1]

In this chapter, we discuss a new set of papers that considers models of bargaining with interdependent values/costs or bargaining in the shadow of new entry, new information, or deadlines. The goal is to illustrate common themes in those papers: if the seller's cost (either physical cost or opportunity cost) of serving a particular type of a client is increasing in the client's willingness to pay, then we will observe a delay in equilibrium. Despite this delay, we argue that a generalized form of the Coase conjecture still often survives.

In the model proposed by Coase and formally analyzed by Stokey (1981), Bulow (1982), Gul et al. (1986)[GSW] and Fudenberg et al. (1985)[FLT] the seller's cost is independent of the valuation of the buyers. As we show, this assumption is crucial for attaining immediate trade. Furthermore, we believe that this assumption naturally often fails in practice. The interdependence of values can be exogenous or arise endogenously. By exogenous, we mean situations in which there is a form of adverse selection. A natural example is an insurance firm bargaining with a potential client. If the client's willingness to pay for insurance is

[1] Examples include: models with two-sided private information about fundamentals and overlapping values (e.g., Cramton 1984; Chatterjee and Samuelson 1987; Cho 1990, among others); irrational players (Abreu and Gul 2000); higher-order beliefs (Feinberg and Skrzypacz 2005); disagreement about continuation play (Yildiz 2004); externalities (Jehiel and Moldovanu 1995); reputation/non-stationary equilibria (Ausubel and Deneckere 1989).

increasing in its privately known risk, the cost of serving this client is also increasing in its type. If we flip the model so that the seller is privately informed (and the buyer makes offers), we can naturally capture situations like the sale of a firm. The better the firm, the more costly it is for the seller to part with it, and the more valuable it is to the buyer. Evans (1989), Vincent (1989), Olsen (1992), and Deneckere and Liang (2006)[DL] have studied bargaining with exogenously interdependent values.

Values can also be endogenously interdependent if there is a correlation between the value of the buyer and the opportunity cost of trading with that type at a given point in time. For example, if new traders or new information can arrive as in Fuchs and Skrzypacz (2010)[FS1], then trading with the buyer now implies forgoing the value to trade with that buyer later, when information arrives, or the value that could be attained from an auction when more buyers arrive in the market.[2] Similarly, when there are deadlines, as modeled by Sobel and Takahashi (1983) and Fuchs and Skrzypacz (2013b)[FS3], trading today has an endogenous opportunity cost of not waiting to trade at the deadline, and that cost is correlated with the type of the buyer who trades today.

4.2.1 Revisiting the "Classic" Coase Conjecture

Consider a seller (she) facing a buyer (he) who has private information about his value of the good, v. Assume $v \in [1, 2]$ is distributed according to an atomless distribution with full support, $F(v)$. The seller has cost $c \geq 0$ to serve the buyer. Every period of an infinite horizon game, the uninformed seller makes an offer p_t. If p_t is accepted, the game ends with payoffs $(v - p_t)$ for the buyer and $(p_t - c)$ for the seller. If the offer is rejected, the seller makes another offer at time $t + \Delta$. Thus, Δ can be thought of as the commitment power of the seller. Both buyer and seller discount future payoffs with a common, continuously compounded, interest rate r.

[2] See also Daley and Green (2019) for a combination of exogenous interdependence and news.

Since higher-value buyers lose more from delay, in any equilibrium the Skimming Property holds. That is, if type v is willing to accept an offer p_t, then all higher types strictly prefer to accept this offer. This property helps characterize equilibria because it means that in every equilibrium, after any history, the remaining distribution of types is given by a truncation of the original distribution. We denote by k_t the highest type remaining before the offer at time t is made, i.e., the seller beliefs at time t are that $v \in [1, k_t]$ with truncated distribution $F(v)/F(k_t)$ (with $k_0 = 2$).

An important distinction arises whether there is common knowledge of strict gains from trade, $c < 1$ (the gap case), or not, $c = 1$ (the no-gap case). As shown by FLT and GSW, in the gap case the game must end in a finite number of rounds (uniformly bounded for all Δ). Intuitively, what happens is that when $(k_t - 1)$ is very small relative to $(1 - c)$ the possible gain from screening the remaining types is small relative to the cost of not realizing the gain of $(1 - c)$ with all remaining types immediately. This gain can be realized by setting $p_t = 1$. Thus, in the gap case, once k_t is close enough to 1, in every equilibrium, the seller offers $p_t = 1$, and there is immediate trade. That allows to apply backward induction (in types) and to show that equilibrium must be unique (up to seller's randomization at time 0). These equilibria have the property that the seller value depends only on the state of the game, k_t, a property called "stationarity" that is similar to the equilibria being Markov. Stationary equilibria continue to exist when $c = 1$ but, besides, as shown by Ausubel and Deneckere (1989), other nonstationary equilibria can be constructed. In these reputation-like equilibria the seller is supposed to start with a high price and lower the prices at a very slow rate. This is sustained with the threat that if the seller ever lowered prices faster, the buyer would believe that the continuation play would revert to a stationary equilibrium with prices dropping quickly to $p = 1$ (for small Δ). In what follows, we do not discuss such reputational equilibria and focus instead on the stationary ones.

The Coase conjecture states that as $\Delta \to 0$, i.e., when the seller loses all ability to commit to prices, prices fall to the lowest buyer valuation, $p_0 \to 1$, and there is no inefficient delay. Our intuition is as follows. Suppose that in a stationary equilibrium the buyer has a simple reservation-price strategy: accept prices below $P(v;\Delta)$ and reject prices above. Taking the limit as $\Delta \to 0$, and defining $P(v) \equiv \lim_{\Delta\to 0} P(v;\Delta)$, we argue that the buyer's reservation price cannot be captured by a downward slopping (demand) function strictly above 1. If such were the case, as illustrated in Fig. 4.1, the seller's optimal response would be to charge the reservation price of the highest type first and then lower its prices continuously to trade with each type at its reservation price. The contradiction arises because the seller would want to run through these prices infinitely fast so as not to suffer from inefficient delays and capture all the available surplus immediately. Since buyers are forward-looking, their reservation prices would fall. Indeed, in equilibrium (in the limit) they must drop all the way to 1. Given these reservation values, the offer made by the seller converges to $p_0 = 1$ as $\Delta \to 0$. In the limit, trade is immediate and the uninformed party, despite making all the offers, effectively does not screen. There are still positive profits since $c < 1$, but these disappear as we shrink the gap $(1 - c)$ by taking $c \to 1$.

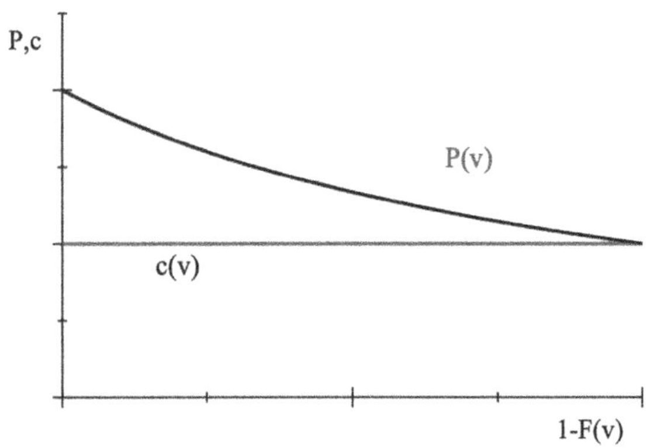

Fig. 4.1 In the limit, if $P(v)$ were strictly above $c(v)$, the seller would want to lower the price infinitely fast to immediately capture all the profits. Therefore, in equilibrium $P(v)$ must be lower

4.2.2 Exogenously Interdependent Values

Consider now a variant of the model with interdependent values, so that the cost of selling to type v is an increasing function of the buyer's type, $c(v)$ with $c'(v) > 0$. We continue to assume that immediate trade is strictly efficient for all $v \in (1, 2]$, $c(v) < v$. In this case, the equilibrium dynamics depend on the degree of adverse selection. If there is little adverse selection, i.e., $E[c(v)] \leq 1$ then, as in the constant-cost case, the continuous-time limit of the unique stationary equilibrium has immediate trade (as shown in DL). If there is more adverse selection, $E[c(v)] > 1$, the seller would prefer not to trade at all rather than offering $p_0 = 1$ and trading with all types, so trade cannot be efficient in equilibrium. No trade cannot be an equilibrium either. For no trade to be an equilibrium, prices would always have to be above 2. If the price were ever lower, a mass of buyers $(2-\varepsilon, 2]$ would accept this price. If, on the other hand, prices were always above 2, there would be a profitable deviation for the seller. The seller could offer $p_0 = c(2) < 2$ and then offer a sequence of prices that would lead to no losses. In the continuation equilibrium, there would either be no more trade (which would make it optimal for types around 2 to accept) or there would be even more trade, on which the seller would not make losses on average (since otherwise, the seller could deviate to asking for $c(2)$ in every period). What then do equilibria look like?

Toward building intuition, heuristically, suppose the continuous-time limit equilibrium strategy of the buyer is characterized by a continuous downward-sloping demand function, $P(v)$. Then the seller's best response problem is to choose the speed at which to trade to maximize her expected value given the history of the game (summarized by k_t):

$$rV(k_t) = \max_{\dot{k}_t \in [0,\infty]} (P(k_t) - c(k_t) - V(k_t))(-\dot{k}_t)\frac{f(k_t)}{F(k_t)} + V'(k_t)\dot{k}_t$$

In this formulation, k_t is the evolution of the cutoff type induced by the sequence of prices chosen by the seller and $\dot{k}_t$ is the time right-derivative

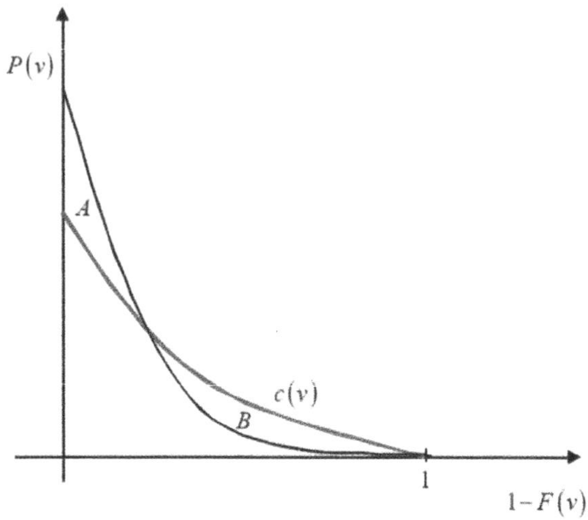

Fig. 4.2 Graphical explanation of the equilibrium reservation prices

of this function.[3] The interpretation of this equation is that in equilibrium, the seller's value comes from trade. When trade happens, the seller collects $P(k_t) - c(k_t)$ and the game ends. Trade happens with a probability flow $\left(-\dot{k}_t\right)\frac{f(k_t)}{F(k_t)}$. If the trade does not happen, the seller becomes a bit more pessimistic, and his continuation payoff drops by $V'(k_t)\dot{k}_t$.

Note that this optimality condition is linear in the chosen speed of trade, $\dot{k}_t$. Therefore, if the seller chooses an interior speed of trade, it must be that all the coefficients multiplying $\dot{k}_t$ add up to zero. In turn, that implies $V(k_t) = 0$ for all k_t and $P(k_t) = c(k_t)$ is the unique candidate for such an equilibrium. The characterization of the equilibrium is completed by pinning down k_t.

The economic intuition for why in equilibrium $P(k_t) = c(k_t)$ is similar to what we described above for constant $c(v)$. If in the limit $P(v)$ were above $c(v)$ (region A in Fig. 4.2), the seller would like to collect the surplus infinitely fast, dropping prices immediately, but then buyers would not be optimizing if they did not wait for the lower offers.

[3] If the seller chooses a continuous price path p_t then the process k_t can be obtained by inverting $P(v)$. If $P(v)$ is strictly downward sloping, it is optimal for the seller to choose a price process such that k_t is continuous.

In turn, if $P(v)$ were below $c(v)$ (region B in Fig. 4.2), the seller would be better off not trading at all, again making the buyers not optimizing. Only when $P(v) = c(v)$ we can have the seller smoothly screen types over time. The economic consequence of $P(v) = c(v)$ is that Coase's idea that even a monopolistic seller would behave competitively (i.e., trade at its marginal cost) survives in this more general setting. However, trade takes place with delay.[4]

We want to highlight two aspects of the linearity of the seller's problem. From the economic perspective, this linearity reflects the Coasean forces. The idea is that the uninformed party must be indifferent regarding the speed at which it screens. Therefore, in the limit, equilibrium demand curves depicted in Figs. 4.1 and 4.2 can never be above the marginal cost curves. From a technical perspective, the fact that we can first (and quite easily) solve for $V(k_t)$ and $P(k_t)$ without solving for the whole equilibrium makes it much easier to solve for the equilibrium. This advantage has been exploited by several related papers such as DeMarzo and Urosevic (2006), Daley and Green (2019), Chaves (2019), and DeMarzo and He (2020) that work directly in continuous time.

To complete the construction of the equilibrium, note that since the seller makes no profits on any trade, she is indifferent over the speed at which she decreases prices. Yet, prices need to drop in equilibrium at the right speed so that the buyers choose optimally to trade when they are supposed to. In particular, a marginal type has to be indifferent between making profit $v - p_t$ today and waiting a little bit, suffering from delay, but benefiting from a lower price. Denote the time-derivative of prices by $\dot{p}_t$. Then, the IC constraint of the buyer is:

$$r(v - p_t) = -\dot{p}_t.$$

Combining this constraint with the reservation price $P(v) = c(v)$ we obtain the differential equation that completes the characterization of the

[4] Olsen (1992) studies a model with "learning by doing" that is a seller whose production costs decrease with past sales. This is an alternative way to motivate exogenously interdependent values. He was the first to show that in the $\Delta \to 0$ limit equilibrium trade is gradual, and pricing is competitive (price equals current cost).

equilibrium:

$$r(k_t - c(k_t)) = -c'(k_t)\dot{k}_t$$
$$k_0 = 2$$

This equation does not depend on the distribution of v, can be often solved explicitly, and allows one to better understand the nature of the equilibrium.

For example, consider what happens as $c(v)$ gets steeper (i.e., as we move away from the independent-values case). As we make $c(v)$ steeper (point-wise, keeping $c(1) = 1$), when the current offer is rejected, the cost of serving the remaining types changes by a larger amount. As a result, the seller would lower the prices at a faster rate. But if prices were to decrease faster, then buyers would want to trade later than when they are supposed to. Thus, in equilibrium, the seller must go through buyers at a lower rate. Therefore, trade speeds up as $c(v)$ gets flatter. If $c(v)$ becomes flat, we get the original Coase conjecture.

Is the equilibrium indeed smooth in the limit as $\Delta \to 0$? It turns out that this hinges on whether there is a gap or not. For the formal analysis of equilibria for $\Delta > 0$, it is easier to solve for equilibria in the gap case. This is done in DL. They show that for $c(1) < 1$, in the limit as $\Delta \to 0$, the equilibrium is characterized by periods with a strictly positive probability of trade and quiet times in between. The seller makes positive profits in its initial offer but, after the initial trade, the seller makes 0 expected profits from all future offers. This last point is crucial since, as discussed above, it leaves the seller indifferent about how fast it drops its prices and the speed can be adjusted such that the different buyer types trade when they are supposed to be in equilibrium. Importantly, this is a robust feature of the equilibria. Yet, since in the gap case trade is lumpy, the equations that describe the equilibrium depend on the distributional assumption and do not lend themselves easily to comparative statics or interpretations.

However, as we have shown in FS2, if we remove the gap by taking the limit as $(1 - c(1)) \to 0$, the equilibrium conditions in DL change so that the lumpy trading converges to smooth trading with no quiet periods (along the sequence, the atoms get smaller and smaller and so do the quiet periods). In the limit, as $\Delta \to 0$ there is perfect separation, with each type trading at a different moment in time. Thus, our characterization above with the HJB, is formally characterizing that limit of equilibria.

4.2.3 Endogenously Interdependent Values: Bargaining with Arrivals

In FS1 we considered a bargaining game where over time information or additional traders can arrive. In that model, the physical cost of serving every type is constant, but the true cost of trading is the opportunity cost of ending the game, which is endogenous. By ending the game, the seller gives up her option to wait for the arrival.

Denote this opportunity cost by $C(v)$, and for contrast, assume a constant exogenous cost of serving all types, $c(v) = c = 1$. For example, suppose that while the seller and buyer bargain, a competing buyer or seller can arrive with Poisson intensities λ_b and λ_s, respectively. The new buyer has the same value as the current buyer, and the new seller has the same cost as the current seller. Upon arrival, the short side of the market captures all the rents.[5]

In that game, $C(v) = \frac{\lambda_b}{\lambda_b+\lambda_s+r}(v - c)$ and $C'(v) = \frac{\lambda_b}{\lambda_b+\lambda_s+r}$. Analogous reasoning to what we discussed in the exogenous case implies that the equilibrium speed of trade decreases as the seller expects to have other interested buyers arrive more frequently (i.e., as λ_b increases) and increases when she expects competing sellers to arrive sooner (i.e., as λ_s increases).

Alternatively, suppose fully revealing information arrives at rate λ and upon revelation, the seller and buyer split the surplus with a fraction α going to the seller and $(1 - \alpha)$ to the buyer. That implies an endogenous opportunity cost of trading today of $C(v) = \frac{\lambda}{\lambda+r}\alpha(v - c)$. Again, the faster the information arrives, the slower the equilibrium trade (conditional on no arrival). Similarly, as the fraction of the surplus captured by

[5] This can be easily generalized to capture other payoffs (and games) upon arrival.

the seller upon information arrival increases, the equilibrium trade slows down.

Define $V_A(k_t) \equiv E[C(v)|v \leq k_t]$. That is the expected payoff of the seller upon arrival of the information (or another trader) conditional on the remaining types being below the cutoff k_t. Heuristically, in equilibrium the seller solves:

$$\begin{aligned} rV(k_t) =& \lambda(V_A(k_t) - V(k_t)) \\ &+ \max_{\dot{k}_t \in [0,\infty]} (P(k_t) - c - V(k_t))\left(-\dot{k}_t\right)\frac{f(k_t)}{F(k_t)} + V'(k_t)\dot{k}_t. \end{aligned} \tag{4.1}$$

The first term comes from the possibility of arrival, the second from the possibility of trade, and the last one from the seller becoming less pessimistic if the trade does not happen.

For the seller to choose an interior speed, we must have again that all the terms that multiply $\dot{k}_t$ add up to zero. That implies that the equilibrium payoff of the seller is

$$V(k_t) = \frac{\lambda}{\lambda + r} V_A(k_t).$$

That is, just like in the Coase conjecture the seller cannot make positive profits from the gradual screening of types that she does in equilibrium: her equilibrium payoff is the same as if she just waited for the arrival of the information (or another trader if we let $\lambda = \lambda_b + \lambda_s$ and $C(v) = \frac{\lambda_b}{\lambda_b+\lambda_s+r}(v - c)$). Moreover, for the coefficients that multiply $\dot{k}_t$ to add up to zero, prices have to satisfy:

$$(P(k_t) - c) f(k_t) = \frac{d}{dk_t}[V(k_t)F(k_t)]$$

Since in equilibrium

$$V(k_t) = \frac{\lambda}{\lambda + r} \int_1^{k_t} \frac{C(v) f(v)}{F(k_t)} dv.$$

we get that the equilibrium prices have to satisfy

$$P(k_t) = c + \frac{\lambda}{\lambda + r} C(k_t).$$

This is again related to the Coase conjecture: the seller prices competitively in the sense that every type pays the full marginal cost of serving them: $c + \frac{\lambda}{\lambda+r} C(k_t)$, where $\frac{\lambda}{\lambda+r} C(k_t)$ is the expected profit the seller would get from waiting for the arrival in case the buyer had type k_t.

The tractability gained by looking at the continuous-time limit allows us to do a series of interesting comparative static exercises. For example, one can show that: (1) when the buyer valuations fall (in a first-order-stochastic-dominance sense) then, time in the market increases and transaction prices fall. (2) When allowing for the arrival of competing buyers λ_b and competing sellers λ_s we can capture the notion of a seller's market or buyer's market by the relative intensity of arrival of additional buyers or competing sellers $\frac{\lambda_b}{\lambda_s}$. (3) One can also extend the model to allow for different time preferences r_s and r_b and compare the relative impatience that stems from facing competition and losing out on the trade vis a vis time discounting. Comparing to Rubinstein (1982) we see that the arrival of competition captured by λ_s generates an additional sense of impatience and that the seller's two sources of impatience (r_s and λ_s) have almost identical effects on prices. Furthermore, when the arrival rates are high relative to the discount rates (which is natural in many settings), then the prices paid by the different buyer types depend mostly on the arrival rates and not on the discount rates.

$$P(v) = c + \frac{\lambda_b}{\lambda_b + \lambda_s + r_s} v.$$

4.2.4 Endogenously Interdependent Values: Bargaining with Deadlines

Deadlines can also imply an endogenous opportunity cost of trading today, albeit one that changes with the time remaining to the deadline,

$C(v, \tau)$. Let T denote the real time by which the players have to reach an agreement. Assume that at T the seller gets to make the last take-it-or-leave-it offer to the buyer. The optimal offer at T can be found using the standard static monopoly approach: given k_T the seller can calculate the marginal revenue of the truncated distribution, $F_T(v) \equiv \frac{F(v)}{F(k_T)}$, as $MR(v) \equiv v - \frac{1-F_T(v)}{f_T(v)}$ (virtual valuation in Myerson 1981) and set it equal to the exogenous marginal cost, c. Let that optimal price be $P_T(k_T)$. Given the commitment power at the deadline, the seller expects some positive profits at $t = T$, which we denote by $\Pi(k_T)$. This means that at any time s, the seller could, by making very high offers until T, guarantee itself a payoff of $e^{-r(T-s)}\Pi(k_s)$. A deadline thus provides the seller with a lower payoff bound that she can achieve by making unacceptable offers until the deadline. Since this final payoff depends on the buyer's type, there is an endogenous interdependence of the buyer's value and the seller's opportunity cost. This model was first studied by Sobel and Takahashi (1983) and later in FS3, we studied its properties in the continuous-time limit.

The first main result is that as commitment disappears ($\Delta \rightarrow 0$), the seller's equilibrium payoff converges to this lower bound: she obtains a payoff equal to the outside option of just waiting for the deadline. However, trade and prices do not converge to the standard Coase conjecture outcome (immediate trade and all types trading at one price) or the outside option (trade only at the deadline). Instead, trade happens gradually over time with an atom at the deadline. The price paid by each type is equal to the discounted price that this type would pay at the deadline if the seller adopted the wait-till-deadline strategy. This is the opportunity cost from serving this type before the deadline. This property of prices is important to satisfy equilibrium conditions: as before, if prices were higher, the seller would like to speed up trade; if they were lower, she would prefer to wait for the deadline. Finally, the speed at which equilibrium prices drop over time (which is one-to-one related to the speed at which the seller screens the types) assures that no buyer type wants to delay or speed up trade.

Heuristically, if in the continuous-time limit the buyer equilibrium strategy is described by a family of functions $P(v, t)$ that are continuous in time and continuous and strictly increasing in v, then the seller's best response problem can be stated as:

$$\begin{aligned} rV(k,t) =& \max_{\dot{k}_t \in [0,\infty]} (P(k_t,t) - c - V(k,t))\left(-\dot{k}_t\right)\frac{f(k_t)}{F(k_t)} \\ &+ \frac{\partial V(k,t)}{\partial k}\dot{k}_t + \frac{\partial V(k,t)}{\partial t} \\ V(k,T) =& \Pi(k). \end{aligned}$$

As above, the optimization problem is linear in the speed of trade. Hence, if the seller chooses in equilibrium an interior speed of trading, all the terms multiplying $\dot{k}_t$ must add up to zero. That yields that any such equilibrium must satisfy:

$$V(k,t) = e^{-r(T-t)}V(k,T) = e^{-r(T-t)}\Pi(k).$$

In turn, equilibrium reservation prices must be:

$$(P(k,t) - c)f(k) = \frac{\partial}{\partial k}(V(k,t)F(k)) = e^{-r(T-t)}\frac{d}{dk}(\Pi(k)F(k)).$$

At the deadline, the seller chooses the final price $P(k,T)$ to induce trade with types between k and $k' = P(k,T)$. The optimization problem at that time is:

$$\Pi(k) = \max_{k'} \frac{F(k) - F\left(k'\right)}{F(k)}\left(k' - c\right).$$

Therefore, by the envelope theorem:

$$\frac{d}{dk}(\Pi(k)F(k)) = f(k)(P(k,T) - c).$$

Plugging it into the expression for equilibrium prices we get

$$P(k,t) = c + e^{-r(T-t)}(P(k,T) - c).$$

In words, every type that trades before the deadline has to pay the physical cost of the good plus the marginal opportunity cost that the seller could have waited for the deadline to trade with that type and make NPV profit of $e^{-r(T-t)}(P(k, T) - c)$ from that type.

The main difference in the trading patterns with respect to the model with arrivals is that there will be an atom of trade at the deadline. We illustrate that in Fig. 4.3. This concentration of agreements at the "eleventh hour" is referred to as the "deadline effect" in the empirical literature. Such effect has been documented by Cramton and Tracy (1992) in the context of labor negotiations, and by Williams (1983) in the context of pre-trial negotiations. Similar findings also arise in lab experiments e.g., Roth et al. (1988), or Güth et al. (2005).

The clean characterization of the continuous-time limit enables us to carry out a series of comparative statics. This generates additional

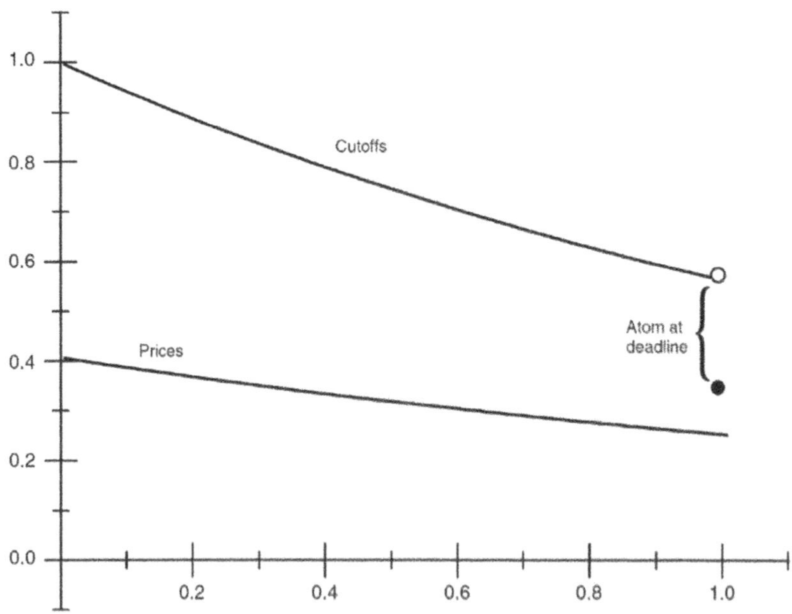

Fig. 4.3 Equilibrium path for Prices and Cutoffs and agreement atom at the deadline normalized to $T = 1$

testable predictions which are in line with some of the available empirical work. For example, as the cost of disagreement rise, more agreements are reached in equilibrium and the deadline effect becomes more pronounced. In the context of labor negotiations, Gunderson et al. (1986) show that the likelihood that the talks fail, and a strike materializes is decreasing in the efficiency loss from a strike.

The model also implies that parties entering a negotiation might purposely subject themselves to costly disagreement payoffs to increase the likelihood of an agreement. This was very prominently featured in the 2011 US budget negotiations. The parties agreed to automatic across-the-board sequestrations which were seen as very painful and undesirable. One can also show that such threats can be welfare enhancing from an ex-ante perspective even though there is no guarantee an agreement will be reached, and agreements may be additionally delayed to the deadline.

4.3 Privacy in Bargaining and Endogenous Entry

As we argued above, bargaining often does not happen in a vacuum, but in the shadow of possible entry or other players and events. For example, in 2017, AT&T approached Straight Path (a publicly traded company) to negotiate an acquisition. After months of negotiations, AT&T announced a negotiated agreement to acquire Straight Path for $1.25 billion. The transaction was supposed to close within 12 months. However, before it closed, Verizon entered the competition to acquire Straight Path, resulting in a bidding war and a final price of $3.1 billion.[6]

This example raises a natural question, studied in Chaves (2019), how transparency of negotiations affects equilibrium outcomes.[7] In that model, there is a Poisson arrival of potential new entrants. Entrants are

[6] See Chaves (2019).

[7] In addition to the economic results we discuss here, Chaves (2019) also contains a technical contribution. Building on the approaches in Ortner (2017) and Daley and Green (2019), he defines and studies regular Markov equilibria directly in continuous time.

short-lived (cannot delay entry) and each draws an independent entry cost. Given beliefs about the remaining types of the incumbent buyer, entrants decide whether to enter. Because as k changes expected profit from entry changes, entry rate is state-dependent, $\Lambda(k)$. If entrants are encouraged by learning they face a weak competition (low k), then $\Lambda(k)$ is decreasing.[8]

Let $\Pi(k)$ be the expected seller profit upon entry of the competing buyer. Assume that in equilibrium the seller screens the incumbent types smoothly. Then her expected payoff is:

$$\begin{aligned} rV(k) = \max_{\dot{k}}(P(k) - V(k) - c)\left(-\dot{k}\right)\frac{f(k)}{F(k)} \\ + \Lambda(k)(\Pi(k) - V(k)) + V'(k)\dot{k}. \end{aligned}$$

As before, linearity in $\dot{k}$ implies that the seller's equilibrium payoff is:

$$V(k) = \frac{\Lambda(k)}{\Lambda(k) + r}\Pi(k).$$

That is, even though in equilibrium the arrival rate changes as the cutoff type k changes, the equilibrium payoff is the same as if the seller stopped screening and just waited for arrival, analogously to our previous results. Interestingly (and in contrast to all the previous results we discussed), prices are more complex in this equilibrium. As before, since seller's equilibrium payoff is linear in the speed of screening all the coefficients on $\dot{k}$ have to add up to zero which requires:

$$P(k) = c + \frac{\frac{\partial}{\partial k}[V(k)F(k)]}{f(k)}.$$

However, now $V'(k)$ is more complex because $\Lambda(k)$ improves as k decreases: screening types today creates an additional benefit in equilibrium, higher arrival rates in the future. Letting $D(k) = \frac{\Lambda(k)}{\Lambda(k)+r}$ and

[8] If entrants are discouraged as k decreases, for example, because the value of the entrant is proportional to the value of the incumbent, then $\Lambda(k)$ can be increasing. Chaves (2019) analyzes both cases, we focus on decreasing $\Lambda(k)$.

$\pi(k)$ be the expected profit upon arrival if the incumbent type is k (so that $\Pi(k) = E[\pi(v)|v \leq k]$), equilibrium prices are

$$P(k) = c + D(k)\pi(k) + \underbrace{D'(k)\Pi(k)\frac{F(k)}{f(k)}}_{<0}. \tag{4.2}$$

The gain from future arrivals (that $D'(k) < 0$) implies lower prices than if Λ were constant. Moreover, equilibrium prices no longer have the no-regret property. When the buyer accepts p_t, the seller regrets making that offer. She realizes at that point that she would have been better off asking for more and waiting for the arrival $(D(k)\pi(k) > P(k) - c)$.

Chaves (2019) considers next a game where rejected offers are not observable by the potential entrants. The potential entrants are aware of when the negotiations started, so they update their beliefs about the value of entry based on the time passed. In equilibrium, high incumbent types trade quickly and low types delay . Therefore, as time progresses, the entrant beliefs become more optimistic, and the arrival rate, λ_t, increases.

The arrival rate grows over time with both private and public offers. However, with private offers it is only a function of time. This distinction does not matter on the equilibrium path since the entrants have correct beliefs about k_t. However, it matters for the incentives to deviate to different prices. In the public-offers game, entrants observe seller deviations and the cutoff and arrival rate adjust. In particular, if the seller deviates to a higher price, no trade takes place and $\Lambda(k_t)$ remains constant after such a deviation. When offers are private, deviations do not affect λ_s $(s \geq t)$.

These observations lead to an important difference in the equilibrium payoffs of the seller. Chaves (2019) shows that in the private offers equilibrium trade is smooth (i.e., k_t changes continuously on the equilibrium path) and hence the equilibrium payoff satisfies:

$$rV^{priv}(k,t) = \max_{\dot{k}} \Big(P^{priv}(k) - V^{priv}(k,t) - c\Big)\big(-\dot{k}\big)\frac{f(k)}{F(k)}$$
$$+ \lambda_t\Big(\Pi(k) - V^{priv}(k,t)\Big)$$

$$+ \frac{\partial}{\partial k} V^{priv}(k,t)\dot{k} + \frac{\partial}{\partial t} V^{priv}(k,t).$$

The solution is

$$V^{priv}(k,t) = D^{priv}(t)\Pi(k),$$

where

$$D^{priv}(t) \equiv \int_t^{\infty} \lambda_s e^{-\int_t^s (\lambda_\tau + r)d\tau} ds$$

is the time-t present value of a dollar that arrives according to the Poisson process of equilibrium entry.

Finally, note that:

$$D(k_0) < D^{priv}(0)$$

because $D(k_0)$ in the public-offers case assumes constant arrival rate (if the seller deviates), while the $D^{priv}(0)$ in the private-offers case has an increasing arrival rate of entry. That implies that the seller prefers to bargain with private offers than with public offers:

$$V(k) < V^{priv}(k,t).$$

4.3.1 Bargaining in the Presence of Outsiders

A different aspect of bargaining in the presence of outsiders is analyzed in Perlroth (2019). He points out that in many bargaining situations, third parties are interested in observing the negotiation process because they want to make informed decisions. For example, when countries negotiate a trade agreement or the UK and the EU negotiate Brexit, producers in those countries would like to infer possible agreements from the offers made (and decide in which country to locate). Similarly, voters can be influenced by the news from the negotiations. In turn, the negotiating parties may want to influence the decisions of those outsiders by making strategic offers.

Motivated by this observation, Perlroth (2019) models a bargaining game between two parties in the shadow of a decision by an outsider. There is a state of the world that affects the possible set of agreements. The two negotiators know the state, but the outsider does not. The outsider's optimal action depends on the beliefs about the state. It can act now, or it can delay (with some discounting cost) in the hope of obtaining additional information from the outcomes of the bargaining. The negotiators care about splitting the bargaining surplus and about the actions of the outsider. Their preferences over the outsider actions are misaligned: one party wants the outsider to believe that the state is high while the other that the state is low.

Perlroth (2019) shows that this situation can lead to posturing in equilibrium: despite the negotiators knowing the state of the world, they may delay reaching an agreement until after the outsider acts. Alternatively, a war of attrition can break out with both the outsider and the negotiators mixing between delaying or not. Moreover, he shows that making the negotiations private (and only revealing the eventual agreement) could solve the problem: posturing behavior disappears, and the negotiations end quickly with the outsider taking action right after a deal is reached.

Drugov (2007, 2018) are related papers that study the informational externalities that might naturally arise between two bargaining pairs when there is correlation in the private values of the bargaining parties.

4.3.2 Effect of Privacy of Offers with a Sequence of Traders

Another tension between privacy and publicity of rejected offers appears in models of sequential bargaining between a single long-lived player negotiating with a sequence of traders on the other side of the market. For example, in Kaya and Liu (2015) one buyer with privately known value bargains with a sequence of homogenous sellers. In a transparent-offers game, when a new seller arrives in the market, he can see all the past offers made. In a private-offers game, the arriving seller observes only that the buyer is still looking for a good but does not observe past rejected offers. Their main result is that equilibria of the private-offers game have lower prices and more trade. Intuitively, rejecting an offer today signals to the market that the buyer value is low. The lower is the rejected offer, the stronger is that signal. While on the equilibrium path sellers anticipate past prices correctly, observability of rejected offers changes the elasticity of demand with respect to price reductions. When offers are private, a price reduction does not change the buyer's continuation payoff. Instead, when offers are public, it increases the buyer's continuation payoff. So, demand is more price-sensitive with private offers, leading to the result. The difference in the outcomes can be dramatic. In a 2-period example with a buyer value distributed uniformly between 0 and 1 and zero cost, for large discount factors trade is approximately efficient with nontransparent offers and bounded from efficiency with public offers. More complicated dynamics appear in a model with interdependent values, as shown in Hörner and Vieille (2009) and the welfare rankings are more ambiguous than in Kaya and Liu (2015). Still, there is a tendency for the equilibrium of the private-offers game to be more efficient for high discount factors.

4.4 Avenues for Future Research

There are several interesting questions we did not have the space to address in this survey. In particular, we focus on the importance of the seller's outside options, while Board and Pycia (2014) focus on the buyer's outside options. Moreover, we assume constant costs, while Ortner (2017, 2019) allow them to change. In the working paper version of this survey we describe these papers and connect them to the general formulation.

Understanding endogenous outside options is an important building block for what we think is a promising avenue for future research. Given that the continuous-time bargaining models are both tractable and amenable to comparative statics, we believe they could be integrated into richer models with endogenous search and matching. Most commonly, for tractability purposes, these models use Nash bargaining to determine how the surplus is split when two parties meet. As highlighted by Hall and Milgrom (2008) in a labor market setting, departing from the Nash bargaining solution can be important to capture certain features of the data. In addition, using these richer models could lead to different policy implications, particularly when policies would affect players' outside options.

Finally, on the technical side, we expect that the continuous-time methods will continue to be developed and that their applications will spread to other areas (for a recent example, see DeMarzo and He 2020).

Acknowledgements Fuchs: University of Texas, Austin and Universidad Carlos III Madrid. Skrzypacz: Stanford University, Graduate School of Business, 518 Memorial Way, Stanford, CA 94305. Our understanding of bargaining has been greatly enlightened and influenced by productive conversations with many colleagues, students, and seminar participants. We are indebted to them. We also thank Isa Chavez, Juan Ortner, and an anonymous referee for specific comments on this survey. Fuchs gratefully acknowledges support from the ERC grant # 681575.

References

Abreu, Dilip and Faruk Gul (2000): "Bargaining and Reputation." *Econometrica* 68, 85–117.

Ausubel, Lawrence, Peter Cramton, and Raymond Deneckere (2001): "Bargaining with Incomplete Information." *Handbook of Game Theory*, Volume 3 by Robert. Aumann and Sergiu Hart.

Ausubel, Lawrence and Raymond J. Deneckere (1989): "Reputation in Bargaining and Durable Goods Monopoly." *Econometrica* 57, 511–531.

Board, Simon and Marek Pycia (2014): "Outside Options and the Failure of the Coase Conjecture." *American Economic Review* 104, 656–671.

Bulow, Jeremy (1982): "Durable-Goods Monopolists." *Journal of Political Economy* 90, 314–332.

Chatterjee, Kalyan and Larry Samuelson (1987): "Bargaining with Two-sided Incomplete Information: An Infinite Horizon Model with Alternating Offers." *Review of Economic Studies* 54, 175–192.

Chaves, Isaias (2019): "Privacy in Bargaining: The Case of Endogenous Entry." Working paper.

Cho, In-Koo (1990): "Uncertainty and Delay in Bargaining." *Review of Economic Studies* 57, 575–596.

Coase, Ronald H. (1972): "Durability and Monopoly." *Journal of Law and Economics* 15, 143–149.

Cramton, Peter (1984): "Bargaining with Incomplete Information: An Infinite-Horizon Model with Two-Sided Uncertainty." *Review of Economic Studies* 51, 579–593.

Cramton, Peter and Joseph Tracy (1992): "Strikes and Holdouts in Wage Bargaining:Theory and Data." *American Economic Review* 82, 100–121.

Daley, Brendan and Brett Green (2019): "Bargaining and News." *American Economic Review*, forthcoming.

DeMarzo, Peter M. and Branko Urosevic (2006): "Ownership Dynamics and Asset Pricing with a Large Shareholder." *Journal of Political Economy* 114, 774–815.

DeMarzo, Peter M. and Zhiguo He (2020): "Leverage Dynamics Without Commitment." *Journal of Finance*, forthcoming.

Deneckere, Raymond J. and Meng-Yu Liang (2006): "Bargaining with Interdependent Values." *Econometrica* 74(5), 1309–1364.

Drugov, Mikhail (2007): "Contracts with Informational Externalities." Working paper.

Drugov, Mikhail (2018): "Bargaining with Informational and Payoff Externalities." Working paper.

Evans, Robert (1989): "Sequential Bargaining with Correlated Values." *Review of Economic Studies* 56, 499–510.

Feinberg, Yossi and Andrzej Skrzypacz (2005): "Uncertainty About Uncertainty and Delay in Bargaining." *Econometrica* 73, 69–91.

Fuchs, William and Andrzej Skrzypacz (2010): "Bargaining with Arrival of New Traders." *American Economic Review* 100, 802–836.

Fuchs, William and Andrzej Skrzypacz (2013a): "Bridging the Gap: Bargaining with Interdependent Values." *Journal of Economic Theory* 148, 1226–1236.

Fuchs, William and Andrzej Skrzypacz (2013b): "Bargaining with Deadlines and Private Information." *American Economic Journal: Microeconomics* 5, 219–43.

Fudenberg, Drew, David Levine, and Jean Tirole (1985): "Infinite-Horizon Models of Bargaining with One-Sided Incomplete Information." In A. Roth, ed., *Game Theoretic Models of Bargaining*, Cambridge University Press, 73–98.

Gul, Faruk, Hugo Sonnenschein, and Robert Wilson (1986): "Foundations of Dynamic Monopoly and the Coase Conjecture." *Journal of Economic Theory* 39, 155–190.

Gunderson, Morley, John Kervin, and Frank Reid (1986): "Logit Estimates of Strike Incidence from Canadian Contract Data." *Journal of Labor Economics* 4, 257–276

Güth, Werner., M. Vittoria Levati, and Boris Maciejovsky (2005): "Deadline Effects in Sequential Bargaining - An Experimental Study." *International Game Theory Review* 7, 117–135.

Hall, Robert E. and Paul R. Milgrom (2008). "The Limited Influence of Unemployment on the Wage Bargaining." *American Economic Review* 98, 1653–1674.

Hörner, Johannes and Nicolas Vieille (2009): "Public vs. Private Offers in the Market for Lemons." *Econometrica* 77, 29–69.

Jehiel, Philippe, and Benny Moldovanu (1995): "Negative Externalities May Cause Delay in Negotiation." *Econometrica* 63, 1321–1335.

Kaya, Ayca and Qingmin Liu (2015): "Transparency and Price Formation." *Theoretical Economics* 10, 341–383.

Olsen, Trend E. (1992): "Durable Goods Monopoly, Learning by Doing and the Coase Conjecture." *European Economic Review* 36, 157–177.

Ortner, Juan (2017): "Durable Goods Monopoly with Stochastic Costs." *Theoretical Economics* 12, 817–861.

Ortner, Juan (2019): "Bargaining with Persistent Private Information." Working paper.

Perlroth, Andres (2019): "Posturing in Bargaining to Influence Outsiders." Working paper.

Roth, Alvin E., J. Keith Murnighan, and Francoise Schoumaker (1988): "The Deadline Effect in Bargaining: Some Experimental Evidence." *American Economic Review* 78, 806–823.

Rubinstein, Ariel (1982): "Perfect Equilibrium in a Bargaining Model." *Econometrica* 50, 97–109.

Sobel, Joel and Ichiro Takahashi (1983): "A Multistage Model of Bargaining." *The Review of Economic Studies* 50, 411–426.

Stokey, Nancy L. (1981): "Rational Expectations and Durable Goods Pricing." *Bell Journal of Economics* 12, 112–128.

Vincent, Daniel R. (1989): “Bargaining with Common Values.” *Journal of Economic Theory* 48, 47–62.
Williams, Gerald. R. (1983): “Legal Negotiations and Settlement.” West Publishing, St. Paul, MN.
Yildiz, Muhamet (2004): “Waiting to Persuade.” *Quarterly Journal of Economics* 119, 223–248.

5

Reference Dependence in Bargaining Models

Kerim Keskin

5.1 Introduction

It is often observed in real-life bargaining encounters and in bargaining experiments that individuals might reach a belated agreement (i.e., delay) or leave the table completely empty-handed (i.e., disagreement) (see Roth et al. 1988; Babcock et al. 1995; Gächter and Riedl 2005; Karagözoğlu and Keskin 2015; among others). Since the classical bargaining models provide little help in explaining such observed behavior,[1] one can utilize the models of behavioral economics in order to have a better understanding of the qualitative aspects of the observed

[1] It is worth noting that those bargaining models are more helpful in this regard under the assumptions of incomplete or asymmetric information.

K. Keskin (✉)
ADA University, Baku, Azerbaijan
e-mail: kkeskin@ada.edu.az

E. Karagözoğlu and K. B. Hyndman (eds.), *Bargaining*,
https://doi.org/10.1007/978-3-030-76666-5_5

bargaining outcomes. Furthermore, since most behavioral models have additional degrees of freedom (compared to the models with standard preferences), they might be of help in explaining the quantitative aspects of the observed outcomes as well. The latter would be important especially when the distributional properties (e.g., equal and/or fair division) of the bargaining outcome are of concern. One of the behavioral models used in bargaining theory is *reference dependence*. This chapter surveys the literature on reference dependence in bargaining models, with a particular focus on theoretical contributions in both cooperative and non-cooperative bargaining theory.

The idea behind reference dependence in bargaining is that there exists a *reference point* that affects the bargaining outcome implemented by an arbitrator or agreed on by bargainers. A reference point can be influenced by norms (e.g., equal division), historical data (e.g., previous agreements), fairness judgments, or it can even be determined endogenously during the bargaining process. Additionally, as defined in some non-cooperative bargaining models, reference points can directly affect the agents' utilities at any division, so that the influence of a reference point on the bargaining outcome is even more intensified. Such studies utilize what is commonly referred to as *reference-dependent preferences*, introduced by Kahneman and Tversky (1979) as a part of *prospect theory*. The theory stipulates that an individual's preferences can be represented by a pair of functions: a value function and a probability weighting function. The value function replaces the utility function in expected utility theory[2] and takes an earning amount and a reference point as its arguments. Reference dependence is generally coupled with *loss aversion*, another important dimension of prospect theory. Accordingly, an individual evaluates his/her earning with respect to a reference point such that losses (earnings below the reference point) loom larger than gains (earnings above the reference point).

Although the first incorporation of reference points into cooperative bargaining problems dates back to the late 1970s and into non-cooperative bargaining problems dates back to the early 2000s, it would

[2] Throughout this chapter, we use the term 'utility function' whenever we mean a 'value function.'

be fair to say that reference dependence in bargaining is still an understudied topic. First, Brito et al. (1977) and Thomson (1981) investigate new approaches to the Nash solution in a cooperative bargaining model in the presence of an allocation that can be regarded as a reference point. Later, Gupta and Livne (1988) extend the standard model by incorporating an exogenously given reference point into the problem and present a new bargaining solution for that extended model, and Shalev (2002) changes the interpretation of reference points in cooperative bargaining by considering agents with reference-dependent preferences and transforming the bargaining set into a set of reference-dependent utility pairs. On the other side, Shalev (2002) and Compte and Jehiel (2003) are the first to incorporate reference dependence into non-cooperative bargaining theory. Afterward, building on the standard alternating-offers bargaining model, Driesen et al. (2012) and Kara et al. (2021) also investigate the equilibrium behavior of agents with reference-dependent preferences. Thanks to the sequential nature of the non-cooperative models utilized in those papers, the authors define reference points endogenously as functions of the offers received in the past. On top of these, there are studies analyzing reference dependence in other bargaining models (see Butler 2007; Hyndman 2011) as well as studies analyzing concepts such as commitment, envy, or fairness (which can be considered as special cases of reference-dependent preferences) in standard bargaining models (see Kohler 2013, Miettinen and Perea 2015, Karagözoğlu and Keskin 2018b; among others).

In this chapter, following a survey of the theoretical contributions on reference dependence in both cooperative (see Sect. 5.2) and non-cooperative (see Sect. 5.3) bargaining theory, we discuss the existing shortcomings in the analysis and suggest possible directions for future research (see Sect. 5.4).

5.2 Reference Dependence in Cooperative Bargaining Models

Consider an n-person bargaining problem (S, d), where $S \subset \mathbb{R}^n$ denotes the bargaining set, including all possible utility n-tuples, and

$d \in S$ represents the *disagreement point*, describing what agents would get in case negotiations break off. The bargaining set is assumed to be convex and compact.[3] The set of all such bargaining problems is denoted by Σ^n. A bargaining solution $F : \Sigma^n \to \mathbb{R}^n$ proposes for any given bargaining problem an allocation from its bargaining set. In the following, for expositional simplicity, we mostly focus on two-person bargaining problems.

When Nash (1950) lays the foundations of cooperative bargaining theory, introducing the setting described above, he also presents a systematic way of determining the bargaining outcome. The Nash solution proposes an allocation such that the product of agents' utility gains over their disagreement utilities is maximized; and the solution is characterized by the axioms of weak Pareto optimality, symmetry, invariance to positive affine transformations, and independence of irrelevant alternatives. Next, Kalai and Smorodinsky (1975) point out some problems with independence of irrelevant alternatives and argue that the axiom of individual monotonicity might be more relevant in a context of cooperative bargaining. Accordingly, for each bargaining problem, the authors define an *ideal point* representing the most optimistic aspiration for every agent; and they present a new solution concept, later called the Kalai–Smorodinsky solution, proposing an allocation at the intersection of the bargaining frontier and the line segment connecting the disagreement and ideal points.

As for the incorporation of reference dependence, it can be argued that Brito et al. (1977) is the first to implement such an idea into cooperative bargaining models. These authors provide a new approach to Nash's bargaining problem by defining a solution concept that uses a threat point (similar to the disagreement point) and an initial allocation (can be regarded as the reference point). The authors formulate a class of bargaining solutions and show that there exists a *Nash fiber* for every initial allocation, which is defined as the set of all threat points that yield a bargaining outcome same as the one proposed by the Nash solution. They also derive a 'Slutsky-like' equation relating the derivatives

[3] The convexity assumption indicates that each agent's payoff from a coin toss between two outcomes is the average of his/her payoffs from those outcomes. The compactness assumption implies that the set of agreements is closed and bounded from above.

of the final allocation with respect to the threat point and to the initial allocation.

Thomson (1981) defines a *reference function* that associates to every bargaining problem $(S, d) \in \Sigma^2$ a utility pair $g(S, d) \in \mathbb{R}^2$. As written by the author, it is a 'reference point' to which agents find it natural to compare any proposed compromise (see pg. 434). Defining $a(S)$ as the most favorable Pareto-optimal point of the bargaining set for agent 1 and $b(S)$ as the same for agent 2, an example of a reference function might be $m(S) = (b_1(S), a_2(S))$, labeled as the point of minimal expectations.[4] Another example might be the middle of the line segment connecting $a(S)$ and $b(S)$, labeled as the point of minimal compromise; or it might be the center of gravity of the bargaining set, which depends on the whole set but not only on some features of its boundary. It is shown that reformulating the axiom of independence of irrelevant alternatives with respect to $g(S, d)$ yields an axiomatization for a modified version of the Nash solution that uses the reference function rather than the disagreement point.[5]

Differently from the studies mentioned above, Vartiainen (2007) and Bozbay et al. (2012) investigate a *collective choice problem*, i.e., a bargaining problem without the disagreement point. In these papers, the authors extend the Nash solution and the Kalai–Smorodinsky solution, respectively, in such a way that the extended solution determines an endogenous disagreement point while proposing an allocation from the bargaining set. To be more precise, the extended Nash solution presented by Vartiainen (2007) chooses a pair $(s, r) \in \mathbb{R}^2 \times \mathbb{R}^2$, where s is called a solution and r is called a reference point , such that the product of agents' utility gains from the solution over the reference point is maximized; whereas the extended Kalai–Smorodinsky solution presented by Bozbay et al. (2012) chooses a similar pair such that s would be proposed by the Kalai–Smorodinsky solution for the bargaining problem (S, r) and r would be the same for the reverse bargaining problem $(-S, -s)$. As

[4] This point is originally used by Roth (1977).

[5] Anbarcı (1995) normalizes the disagreement point to the origin, and defines a class of solutions such that whichever reference function agents adopt, the ratio of their utilities from the bargaining outcome is identical to the ratio of their reference point utilities.

specified by Bozbay et al. (2012), the endogenously formed disagreement point serves as a 'mental reference point' for the agents (see pg. 409).

Gupta and Livne (1988) extend the classical bargaining problem by introducing an exogenously given *reference point* into the problem: (S, d, r). The reference point r is defined in such a way that $r \in S$ and $r > d$. It is effective especially when agents "realize that the existence of such an outcome increases the likelihood that no party exercises its threat to break-off" (see pg. 1304). Some examples are the last period's agreement in wage negotiations, 'toss of a coin' in some division problems, and so on. The authors present a new solution concept, namely the Gupta–Livne solution, which proposes an allocation at the intersection of the bargaining frontier and the line segment connecting the reference and ideal points. They also provide an axiomatic characterization for their bargaining solution, keeping the first three axioms of Nash (1950) and replacing independence of irrelevant alternatives with the axioms of restricted monotonicity and limited sensitivity to changes in the conflict point. Later, Gupta and Livne (1990) present some experimental evidence, supporting the hypotheses that a previous agreement would emerge as a reference outcome and that the agreed bargaining outcome would be close to the prediction of the Gupta–Livne solution.

Similarly, Balakrishnan et al. (2011) study a bargaining problem with a reference point, however, instead of utilizing the reference point directly, they argue that "the salience of the reference point mutes or tempers the negotiators' aspirations" (see pg. 144). Accordingly, the authors define the *tempered aspirations point* representing each agent's maximum utility when the other agent is guaranteed to receive his/her reference point utility. Their analysis continues with the introduction of the tempered aspirations solution, which proposes an allocation at the intersection of the bargaining frontier and the line segment connecting the disagreement and tempered aspirations points. This new solution concept is *dual* to the Gupta–Livne solution in the sense that "it exchanges the roles played by the reference and disagreement points" (see pg. 145). Furthermore, the two solutions coincide in two-person bargaining problems with a linear frontier, however, this result fails to hold for $n \geq 3$.

The fact that the Gupta–Livne solution and the tempered aspirations solution are defined in a similar context, rather by using different interpretations for a reference point, raises the question of which solution concept is *more efficient* than the other. To answer this question, Karagözoğlu and Keskin (2015) perform an efficiency comparison between the two solution concepts in a bargaining problem with a pre-investment stage.[6] The authors implicitly characterize the cases under which each solution concept turns out to be more efficient than the other. The respective condition depends on multiple model parameters, especially on the weights assigned to the disagreement and reference points by the two solution concepts. In another work, also utilizing the similar-context observation above, Karagözoğlu et al. (2019) introduce a two-parameter family of bargaining solutions, where $\alpha \in [0, 1]$ represents the effectiveness of the reference point in determining the anchor point and $\beta \in [0, 1]$ represents the effectiveness of the reference point in shaping agents' aspirations. Using these parameters, the authors argue that the respective convex combinations of the disagreement and reference points would be effective in determining the bargaining outcome. Accordingly, the solution concept that proposes an allocation at the intersection of the bargaining frontier and the line segment connecting the effective anchor and aspiration points constitutes a member of the (α, β)-family, which encompasses the Kalai–Smorodinsky solution, the Gupta–Livne solution, and the tempered aspirations solution as special cases for extreme values of α and β. This clearly indicates that these three solution concepts are similar in essence.

Along similar lines, Alós-Ferrer et al. (2018) define the negotiated aspirations solution for which an endogenous reference point is obtained utilizing the ideal point and a vector of bargaining powers. This new solution concept is quite similar to the Gupta–Livne solution, in terms of how reference point is utilized to determine the bargaining outcome,

[6] Notice that each bargaining solution already proposes a Pareto-optimal outcome, by definition. To perform an efficiency comparison, a pre-investment game is considered such that two agents make costly investments in guns aiming to increase their disagreement point utilities, but at the cost of reducing the size of the pie to be shared. Accordingly, a bargaining solution is said to be more efficient if it leads to a larger pie size in equilibrium.

The two-stage framework is an extension to the model introduced by Anbarcı et al. (2002), who compare three bargaining solutions in terms of efficiency in a similar setting. These authors find that the *equal sacrifice solution* Pareto-dominates the other solutions, since it puts the least weight on the disagreement point.

however, since it does not require an exogenously given reference point, it is still well-defined in a standard bargaining problem (S, d). As written by the authors, "the negotiated aspirations solutions has a natural procedural description in terms of intuitive concepts: bargaining power and maximal aspirations" (see pg. 153).

In all studies mentioned so far, reference points influence the bargaining outcome, hence the utilities received by agents at the end of bargaining. However, an agent's reference point is never assumed to be an argument in his/her utility function. This is a major difference from reference-dependent preferences (as in prospect theory); which is an issue first addressed by Shalev (2002). This author changes the interpretation of reference points in cooperative bargaining theory, when he considers two loss-averse agents trying to agree on an outcome from a set of possible outcomes, X. A reference-dependent utility from an outcome $x \in X$ is defined as

$$U_i(x, r_i) = \begin{cases} u_i(x) & \text{if } u_i(x) \geq r_i \\ u_i(x) - \lambda_i(r_i - u_i(x)) & \text{if } u_i(x) < r_i \end{cases} \tag{5.1}$$

where $u_i(x)$ denotes agent i's material utility, $r_i \in \mathbb{R}$ denotes agent i's reference point, and $\lambda_i \geq 0$ represents agent i's loss aversion parameter. We can see that agent i simply collects his/her utility if that utility is no less than his/her reference point; but if otherwise, evaluating the respective outcome as a *loss*, agent i experiences a decrease in his/her utility in the amount of $\lambda_i(r_i - u_i(x))$. Utilizing (5.1) to obtain a set of reference-dependent utility pairs, Shalev (2002) transforms the current setting into an extended bargaining problem: (S, d, λ, r). He then studies the Nash solution and investigates endogeneity by studying *self-supporting* reference points such that the reference point pair is also the solution to the extended problem, as well as *stable* reference points such that no agent prefers the solution of a problem differing only in his/her opponent's reference point to the solution of the original problem.

Driesen et al. (2011) start with a Shalev-like transformation that incorporates reference-dependent preferences into a cooperative bargaining model. Differently, however, they employ the following utility function:

$$U_i(x_i, r_i) = \begin{cases} x_i & \text{if } x_i \geq r_i \\ x_i - \lambda_i(r_i - x_i) & \text{if } x_i < r_i \end{cases} \tag{5.2}$$

where $x_i \in \mathbb{R}$ denotes agent *i*'s share from the outcome and $r_i \in \mathbb{R}$ denotes agent *i*'s reference point. This is a special case of the utility function used by Shalev (2002) in the sense that the two functions coincide if one considers $u_i(x) = u_i((x_1, x_2)) = x_i$ in (5.1). Concentrating on *n*-player bargaining problems, these authors study the Kalai–Smorodinsky solution and establish that bargaining problems with loss-averse agents have exactly one self-supporting outcome.

Finally, Karagözoğlu and Keskin (2018a) utilize reference-dependent preferences in bargaining problems with a reference point (as defined by Gupta and Livne 1988). This is the first attempt to combine two different reference point interpretations from the existing literature. The authors define a pre-bargaining stage in which agents choose their reference points strategically, such that those reference points determine the set of reference-dependent utility pairs over which agents will bargain.[7] Using the same utility function as (5.2), the authors perform a Shalev-like transformation to obtain the respective bargaining set. They analyze the Gupta–Livne solution in this setting and find that, mostly because the bargaining outcome proposed by the employed solution concept turns out to be convex in the reference point, agents choose either the disagreement point or a particular element from the bargaining frontier as their reference points. It is also worth noting that the paper presents the first attempt to endogenize reference points in the sense of the Gupta–Livne solution in cooperative bargaining models.

[7] The idea is similar to the use of revocable commitment in bargaining, for instance, studied by Muthoo (1992) in a sequential bargaining model. In particular, it is as if each agent commits to an amount in a pre-bargaining stage, and if an agent gets less than what he/she committed to, the agent experiences a decrease in utility.

5.3 Reference Dependence in Non-cooperative Bargaining Models

In non-cooperative bargaining models, multiple economic agents strategically interact with each other in order to determine how to divide a pie. Here we mostly focus on sequential-move games, especially on the alternating-offers bargaining game (see Rubinstein 1982), since reference-dependent preferences have been commonly utilized in such bargaining problems.

In a two-player ultimatum game (see Güth et al. 1982), the bargaining protocol is as follows: One agent proposes a division, and the other agent chooses whether to accept or reject that proposal. If he/she accepts, then the proposed division is implemented; whereas if otherwise, both agents end up with nothing. The alternating-offers bargaining game can be interpreted as a multi-period version of the ultimatum game in that, now, if the responder does not accept an offer, then the game proceeds to the next period in which the responder becomes the proposer, and vice versa. In case agents do not reach an agreement, how the game ends can be defined in several ways: it might end in $T \in \mathbb{N}$ periods, it might end after any period with a certain probability, or it might never end. The first case corresponds to a finite-horizon game, whereas the other two correspond to infinite-horizon games.

The incorporation of reference dependence into non-cooperative bargaining models is mostly through reference-dependent preferences in the existing literature. In that regard, the first attempt is made by Shalev (2002) who analyzes subgame perfect Nash equilibrium in an alternating-offers bargaining model with two loss averse agents such that an agent's reference point is defined as the utility received from the outcome in the previous period. The author shows that the equilibrium outcome is equal to the unique stable self-supporting outcome of the corresponding extended bargaining problem studied in the same paper, if one employs the same utility function, (5.1) (see Sect. 5.2).

Compte and Jehiel (2003) present a similar analysis in a rather different model with possibly several bargaining stages. At the beginning of a phase, an agent is selected randomly with equal probabilities to become the proposer. The rest follows as in the standard alternating-offers bargaining model unless negotiations break down with an exogenous probability, in which case a new bargaining phase starts. In this new phase, a new proposer is selected and everything follows similarly. The novelty lies in the incorporation of reference points, denoted by $r_i \in \mathbb{R}$ for any agent $i \in \{1, 2\}$, which are defined as a joint function of the previous reference point and the largest offer received in the previous phase. The utility function is

$$U_i(x, r_i) = x_i - r_i, \tag{5.3}$$

where x_i denotes agent i's share from $x \in X$. This indicates that the reference point, being fixed in a given bargaining phase, has the same influence on the utilities independent of whether an agent receives an amount higher or lower than his/her reference point.[8] The authors construct a subgame perfect Nash equilibrium and argue that delayed agreements might be observed in equilibrium, which would lead to efficiency losses.

Later, Driesen et al. (2012) incorporate reference points into the standard alternating-offers bargaining model, following the footsteps of Shalev (2002). The initial reference point for each agent is assumed to be zero; and when an agent rejects a proposal, his/her reference point is updated in such a way that it becomes the highest previous offer rejected by the agent.[9] This sets the stage for the analysis of *endogenously determined* reference points. Utilizing the idea that a proposal by an agent should make the other agent indifferent between that proposal and the other agent's proposal in the next round, the authors manage to characterize a subgame perfect Nash equilibrium that satisfies three assumptions. In particular, they prove the existence of an equilibrium, considering stationary Markov strategies only and characterizing the

[8] Note that there is no loss aversion in this functional form.

[9] As written by the authors: "At some moment t, ... all the offers made to player i by the other player j... represent all the shares of the pie that player i could have obtained up to this moment with certainty. Then, it is natural to assume that the maximum of those shares is player i's reference point, since this is what he could have obtained" (see pg. 105).

equilibrium behavior in nine regions for the (r_1, r_2) pair. The equilibrium is such that there is an immediate agreement and being loss averse has a negative effect on an agent's equilibrium share. Due to the former implication, a new reference point never emerges endogenously on the equilibrium path.

Kara et al. (2021) extend the bargaining framework studied by Driesen et al. (2012) in the sense that reference points are updated in a similar manner, but now, the previous offers can have only a *limited influence* such that an offer made to an agent has the potential to influence his/her reference point for a *finite* number of periods. This assumption is inspired by the availability heuristic or retrievability bias in decision-making (see Kahneman and Tversky 1974) and the recency effect in belief updating and intertemporal decision-making (see Hogarth and Einhorn 1992). The authors employ the following utility function:

$$U_i(x_i, r_i) = \begin{cases} x_i + \gamma_i(x_i - r_i) & \text{if } x_i \geq r_i \\ x_i - \lambda_i(r_i - x_i) & \text{if } x_i < r_i \end{cases} \tag{5.4}$$

such that $\lambda_i \geq \gamma_i \geq 0$, where $x_i \in \mathbb{R}$ denotes agent i's share of the outcome and $r_i \in \mathbb{R}$ denotes agent i's reference point. This is a generalized form of (5.2) in that there is an additional γ_i parameter in the gains frame (i.e., for earnings above the reference point), with a similar interpretation to the loss aversion parameter, λ_i. The equilibrium analysis reveals a subgame perfect Nash equilibrium with an immediate agreement, but the agreed bargaining outcome is different from those reported in earlier work. Furthermore, the authors construct an example that illustrates an equilibrium with a delayed agreement under finite expiration length and positive initial reference points.[10]

From a certain perspective, it can be argued that Li (2007) also implements reference dependence into the standard alternating-offers bargaining model. Although the author chooses to label his modeling as 'history dependence,' as he mentions later in the paper, his formalization can be interpreted as reference-dependent preferences (see pg. 696).

[10] It is also shown that a delayed agreement is not possible if one of these assumptions is dropped.

In particular, agent i evaluates his/her earning, $x_i \in \mathbb{R}$, with respect to a reference point , $r_i \in \mathbb{R}$, which is defined in such a way that it yields a utility level equal to the highest discounted utility that could have been received by the agent in case he/she accepted an earlier offer. The following utility function is employed in the analysis:

$$U_i(x, r_i) = \begin{cases} u_i(x_i) & \text{if } x_i \geq r_i \\ -\varepsilon & \text{if } x_i < r_i \end{cases} \tag{5.5}$$

where $\varepsilon > 0$ is some constant and $u_i(x_i)$ represents agent i's material utility. According to this functional form, an agent receives the same disutility as long as he/she earns an amount less than his/her reference point.[11] The equilibrium analysis reveals an essentially unique subgame perfect equilibrium path, which consists of gradual concessions. For instance, it is shown that if agents are sufficiently patient, there is a delayed agreement in equilibrium. This leads to inefficiencies; for example, if agents are infinitely patient, half of the pie would be wasted due to delay.

All studies above explicitly make a reference dependence argument in their analysis. One should note, however, that there are several papers in the literature that model concepts such as commitment, envy, or fairness by employing utility functions with similar mathematical properties to the reference-dependent utility functions provided above. Based on this observation, and given that it is a matter of interpretation, here we mention some examples of those studies. Muthoo (1992) studies a two-stage framework such that in the first stage each agent i commits not to accept a share of the pie which is strictly less than an amount, $z_i \in \mathbb{R}$. In the second stage, agents play an alternating-offers bargaining game, where an agent's commitment can be revoked, but at some cost to the agent. The author employs the utility function (5.2), such that the reference point is interpreted as the commitment level and the loss aversion parameter is replaced by the revoking cost. It is shown that there is

[11] This cannot be captured by any of the alternative utility functions mentioned above. However, if one uses an infinitely large loss aversion parameter in those functions, agent i would always end up with a negative utility in the loss frame and the corresponding equilibrium analysis would follow similarly.

a unique subgame perfect Nash equilibrium, where the agents' equilibrium shares depend on the relative magnitudes of the costs of revoking a commitment. Later, Miettinen and Perea (2015) analyze commitment in a finite-horizon alternating-offers bargaining model where agents can update their commitment levels before each period. It is assumed that commitments are costly and irrevocable and that an agent cannot accept a share lower than his/her commitment level. The authors characterize a subgame perfect Nash equilibrium with an immediate agreement and show that there is a second-mover advantage in the equilibrium if commitment costs are sufficiently small.

Kohler (2013) studies envy in the standard alternating-offer bargaining model, by employing the utility function $U_i(x_i, x_j) = x_i - \alpha_j \max\{x_j - x_i, 0\}$ where $\alpha_j \geq 0$ is the envy parameter. Accordingly, an agent receives only the material utility when earning more than the other agent, but he/she experiences a disutility if otherwise (due to envy). Notice that the function coincides with (5.2) when $\lambda_i = 2\alpha_j$ and the reference point is set to be equal to the equal division. The equilibrium suggests an immediate agreement, and an increase in each agent's envy parameter causes an increase in his/her share. Kohler and Schlag (2018) study inequality aversion in a similar setting, but now in addition to envy, they assume a guilt component in the utility function such that an agent experiences a disutility even when he/she earns more than the other agent: $U_i(x_i, x_j) = x_i - \alpha \max\{x_j - x_i, 0\} - \beta \max\{x_i - x_j, 0\}$ where $\alpha, \beta \geq 0$ are envy and guilt parameters. Notice that the function is similar to (5.4), with an important difference in the signs of the additional utilities in the gains frame. Similarly, the equilibrium suggests an immediate agreement; and in case $\beta > 1/2$, the unique bargaining outcome turns out to be the equal division. More recently, Karagözoğlu and Keskin (2018b) introduce *time-varying* fairness concerns into the finite-horizon alternating-offer bargaining model. This indicates that the weight an agent attaches to his/her fairness ideals decreases over time as the bargaining deadline approaches. The following utility function is utilized: $U_i(x_i) = x_i - \alpha_i(t) \max\{\varphi_i - x_i, 0\}$ for any period $t \in \mathbb{N}$, where $\alpha_i(t) \geq 0$ is the weight attached to fairness and φ_i denotes the amount what agent i believes to be fair. The authors show that an immediate agreement, delayed agreements, and disagreement are all possible in the equilibrium. This is the first theoretical result in the literature showing delayed agreements in the finite-horizon alternating-offers bargaining model under complete information.

Finally, there are studies studying reference dependence in other bargaining models. We complete this section by mentioning two of such examples. Butler (2007) studies a version of the ultimatum game where agents have an outside option to back down or to fight each other. The fighting part is modeled as a winner-take-all contest, which includes a risk factor; and this allows the author to fully utilize prospect-theoretic preferences, also incorporating subjective probability weighting into his analysis. Borrowing a utility function from Tversky and Kahneman (1992), the author considers different types of reference points and shows how those reference points produce different bargaining behavior. It is also shown that bargaining failure is possible for this model. Hyndman (2011) analyzes reference-dependent preferences in a repeated bargaining framework such that a proposer is randomly selected in each period; if the offer is accepted, then the pie in that period is divided accordingly; but if otherwise, then both players receive nothing in that period. In either case, there is a new pie to be divided in the following period. Each player prefers disagreement to receiving something less than his/her reference point. The reference points are either fixed or downward adjusted such that the latter occurs in period $t + 1$ if there is disagreement in period t. It is shown that fixed reference points do not lead to disagreement in equilibrium, but they influence how the pie is divided; and if reference points are adjusted, disagreement might arise as agents try to manipulate the reference point of their opponent.

5.4 Discussion

In this chapter, we have provided a survey of the existing theoretical contributions on reference dependence in bargaining models, starting with the incorporation of reference points into cooperative bargaining problems (dating back to the late 1970s) and into non-cooperative bargaining problems (dating back to the early 2000s). In this section, we discuss the existing shortcomings in the analysis and suggest possible directions for future research.

In cooperative bargaining theory, there are several approaches to the analysis of reference dependence. In one of these approaches, there exists an exogenously given allocation that serves as a reference point, as in Brito et al. (1977) or Gupta and Livne (1988). In other works, Thomson (1981) utilizes a pre-defined reference function and Alós-Ferrer et al. (2018) utilize a vector of bargaining powers, which help them derive a reference point in any given bargaining problem. Although these studies are based on similar ideas, they mostly differ in the way they utilize reference points in determining the bargaining outcome. In another approach, Vartiainen (2007) and Bozbay et al. (2012) investigate a bargaining problem without a disagreement point in which a 'mental reference point' endogenously emerges while a given solution concept determines the bargaining outcome. In a third approach, Shalev (2002) uses a different reference point interpretation in cooperative bargaining, when he introduces reference-dependent preferences into the standard framework. This requires a transformation of the bargaining set into a set of reference-dependent utility pairs via the use of a value function as proposed in prospect theory. Now, a possible problem is that although each approach includes important aspects of its own and provides new insights to the analysis of reference dependence in bargaining, it is still not established which approach is more relevant than the others. Indeed, arguably, it might be better if these approaches are somehow integrated, as attempted by Karagözoğlu and Keskin (2018a) when they utilize a Shalev-like transformation in a bargaining problem with a reference point (as defined by Gupta and Livne 1988). This might provide a unifying framework for future work in this literature. Future research may address this issue.

The same issue does not appear in non-cooperative bargaining theory, since most studies investigate reference-dependent preferences as in prospect theory. These studies also define an endogenous reference point as a certain function of the previous offers received by the agent. However, the main issue in non-cooperative bargaining theory is that the equilibrium analysis and characterization turns out to be a difficult task due to intractability problems. For example, this is particularly the case in Driesen et al. (2012) and Kara et al. (2021), as these authors have to identify nine and sixteen different regions for the reference point pairs, respectively. The models studied by Compte and Jehiel (2003) and Li (2007) are arguably more tractable in that sense, possibly because of the simplifications in the respective utility functions. It can be claimed that this issue is a result of how reference-dependent preferences are formulated (as outlined in prospect theory), however, given that the intractability problems also depend on the bargaining model in question and how reference points are defined, it might be possible to form a more tractable model while preserving the important aspects of reference-dependent preferences. Future research may address this issue.

In the behavioral economics literature, there have been criticisms challenging the scientific value of the models that use exogenously given reference points to explain observed individual behavior: almost any behavioral phenomenon can be explained by appropriate selections of exogenous reference points. Since similar concerns would also arise in bargaining models, endogenizing reference points should be considered an important subject in the bargaining literature. As summarized above, although there are attempts to endogenize reference points in cooperative bargaining theory, it is difficult to claim that there is a well-established model with an endogenous reference point at the time. In non-cooperative bargaining theory, endogenous reference points are more commonly used, however, those studies utilize specific definitions for how reference points evolve over time, which have not yet been tested in the experimental literature. To our understanding, it seems that both strands of literature would benefit from a more generalized approach to the utilization of endogenous reference points. Such a generalized approach might even build a strong bridge between cooperative and non-cooperative bargaining models with reference dependence.

Along similar lines, the so-called *Nash program* aims to provide strategic foundations for solution concepts in cooperative bargaining, thereby bridging the gap between cooperative and non-cooperative bargaining theory. The main idea is to formulate a non-cooperative game and to demonstrate that the outcome proposed by a cooperative bargaining solution results in an equilibrium play of that game. In the bargaining literature, it is already known that the prominent solution concepts under standard preferences can be strategically supported, however, such an analysis remains to be an open question under reference-dependent preferences, especially when reference points are endogenously determined.

Finally, although the classical bargaining models predict an immediate agreement in equilibrium, it is often observed in the experimental literature that delayed agreements and disagreements are quite possible.[12] Furthermore, in case of an agreement, there may be numerous types of bargaining outcomes with different distributional properties (see Roth et al. 1988; Babcock et al. 1995; Gächter and Riedl 2005; Herweg and Schmidt 2015; Karagözoğlu and Keskin 2015; Bolton and Karagözoğlu 2016; Anbarcı and Feltovich 2018; among others). However, to the best of our knowledge, the existing bargaining experiments are not particularly designed to elicit reference-dependent preferences in the standard bargaining models (with one exception: Brekke et al. 2018). Therefore, there is still room for experimental analyses that would provide experimental evidence for the theoretical findings summarized above. Future research may also address this issue.

References

Alós-Ferrer C, García-Segarra J, Ginés-Vilar M (2018) Anchoring on Utopia: A generalization of the Kalai-Smorodinsky solution. *Economic Theory Bulletin* 6: 141–155.

Anbarcı N (1995) Reference functions and balanced concessions in bargaining. *Canadian Journal of Economics* 28: 675–682.

Anbarcı N, Feltovich N (2018) How fully do people exploit their bargaining position? The effects of bargaining institution and the 50–50 norm. *Journal of Economic Behavior and Organization* 145: 320–334.

[12] Delayed agreements and disagreements are ubiquitous features of real-life bargaining encounters as well.

Anbarcı N, Skaperdas S, Syropoulos C (2002) Comparing bargaining solutions in the shadow of conflict: How norms against threats can have real effects? *Journal of Economic Theory* 106: 1–16.

Babcock L, Loewenstein G, Issacharoff S, Camerer C (1995) Biased judgments of fairness in bargaining. *American Economic Review* 85(5): 1337–1343.

Balakrishnan PV, Gómez JC, Vohra RV (2011) The tempered aspirations solution for bargaining problems with a reference point. *Mathematical Social Sciences* 62: 144–150.

Bolton GE, Karagözoğlu E (2016) On the influence of hard leverage in a soft leverage bargaining game: The importance of credible claims. *Games and Economic Behavior* 99: 164–179.

Brekke KA, Ciccone A, Heggedal T, Helland L (2018) Reference points in sequential bargaining: Theory and experiment. *Working Paper*.

Butler CK (2007) Prospect theory and coercive bargaining. *Journal of Conflict Resolution* 51(2): 227–250.

Bozbay I, Dietrich F, Peters H (2012) Bargaining with endogenous disagreement: The extended Kalai-Smorodinsky solution. *Games and Economic Behavior* 74: 407–417.

Birkeland S, Tungodden B (2014) Fairness motivation in bargaining: A matter of principle. *Theory and Decision* 77: 125–151.

Brito DL, Buoncristiani A, Intriligator MD (1977) A new approach to the Nash bargaining problem. *Econometrica* 45: 1163–1172.

Compte O, Jehiel P (2003) Bargaining with reference dependent preferences. *Working Paper*.

Driesen B, Perea A, Peters H (2011) The Kalai-Smorodinsky bargaining solution with loss aversion. *Mathematical Social Sciences* 61: 58–64

Driesen B, Perea A, Peters H (2012) Alternating offers bargaining with loss aversion. *Mathematical Social Sciences* 64: 103–118.

Gächter S, Riedl A (2005) Moral property rights in bargaining with infeasible claims. *Management Science* 51: 249–263.

Gupta S, Livne ZA (1988) Resolving a conflict situation with a reference outcome: An axiomatic model. *Management Science* 34: 1303–1314.

Gupta S, Livne ZA (1990) Testing the emergence and effect of the reference outcome in an integrative bargaining situation. *Marketing Letters* 1: 103–112.

Güth W, Schmittberger R, Schwarze B (1982) An experimental analysis of ultimatum bargaining. *Journal of Economic Behavior and Organization* 3(4): 367–388.

Herweg F, Schmidt KM (2015) Loss aversion and inefficient renegotiation. *Review of Economic Studies* 82: 297–332.
Hogarth RM, Einhorn HJ (1992) Order effects in belief updating: The belief-adjustment model. *Cognitive Psychology* 24(1): 1–55.
Hyndman K (2011) Repeated bargaining with reference-dependent preferences. *International Journal of Game Theory* 40: 527–549.
Kahneman D, Tversky A (1974) Judgment under uncertainty: Heuristics and biases. *Science* 185: 1124–1131.
Kahneman D, Tversky A (1979) Prospect theory: An analysis of decision under risk. *Econometrica* 47(2): 263–291.
Kalai E, Smorodinsky M (1975) Other solutions to Nash's bargaining problem. *Econometrica* 43: 513–518.
Kara T, Karagözoğlu E, Özcan-Tok (2021) Bargaining, reference points, and limited influence. *Dynamic Games and Applications* 11(2): 326–362.
Karagözoğlu E, Keskin K (2015) A tale of two bargaining solutions. *Games* 6: 161–174.
Karagözoğlu E, Keskin K (2018a) Endogenous reference points in bargaining. *Mathematical Methods of Operations Research* 88: 283–295.
Karagözoğlu E, Keskin K (2018b) Time-varying fairness concerns, delay, and disagreement in bargaining. *Journal of Economic Behavior and Organization* 147: 115–128.
Karagözoğlu E, Keskin K, Özcan-Tok (2019) Between anchors and aspirations: A new family of bargaining solutions. *Review of Economic Design* 23(1-2): 53–73.
Karagözoğlu E, Riedl A (2015) Performance information, production uncertainty, and subjective entitlements in bargaining. *Management Science* 61: 2611–2626.
Kohler S (2013) Envy can promote more equal division in alternating-offer bargaining. *Journal of Neuroscience, Psychology, and Economics* 6: 31–41.
Kohler S, Schlag KH (2018) Inequality aversion causes equal or unequal division in alternating-offer bargaining. *Bulletin of Economic Research* 71: 47–57.
Li D (2007) Bargaining with history-dependent preferences. *Journal of Economic Theory* 136(1): 695–708.
Miettinen T, Perea A (2015) Commitment in alternating offers bargaining. *Mathematical Social Sciences* 76: 12–18.
Muthoo A (1992) Revocable commitment and sequential bargaining. *The Economic Journal* 102: 378–387.
Nash JF (1950) The bargaining problem. *Econometrica* 18: 155–162.

Nash JF (1953) Two-person cooperative games. *Econometrica* 21: 128–140.
Roth AE (1977) Independence of irrelevant alternatives and solutions to Nash's bargaining problem. *Journal of Economic Theory* 16: 247–251.
Roth AE, Murnighan JK, Schoumaker F (1988) The deadline effect in bargaining: Some experimental evidence. *American Economic Review* 78(4): 806–823.
Rubinstein A (1982) Perfect equilibrium in a bargaining model. *Econometrica* 50(1): 97–110.
Shalev J (2002) Loss aversion and bargaining. *Theory and Decision* 52: 201–232.
Thomson W (1981) A class of solutions to bargaining problems. *Journal of Economic Theory* 25: 431–441.
Tversky A, Kahneman D (1992) Advances in prospect theory: Cumulative representation of uncertainty. *Journal of Risk and Uncertainty* 5: 297–323.
Vartiainen H (2007) Collective choice with endogenous reference outcome. *Games and Economic Behavior* 58(1): 172–180.

6

Focal Points in Experimental Bargaining Games

Andrea Isoni, Robert Sugden, and Jiwei Zheng

> Most situations [...] provide some clue for coordinating behavior, some focal point for each person's expectation of what the other expects him to be expected to do. (Schelling, 1960, p. 57)

The experimental literature on bargaining games is vast and growing. The common thread is the investigation of games in which bargainers reach an agreement that results in some allocation of resources between

A. Isoni (✉)
University of Warwick, Coventry, UK
e-mail: a.isoni@warwick.ac.uk

R. Sugden
University of East Anglia, Norwich, UK
e-mail: r.sugden@uea.ac.uk

J. Zheng
Lancaster University, Lancaster, UK
e-mail: j.zheng18@lancaster.ac.uk

E. Karagözoğlu and K. B. Hyndman (eds.), *Bargaining*,
https://doi.org/10.1007/978-3-030-76666-5_6

them. Unlike real-world bargaining, in which negotiations are often multi-dimensional and therefore rather complex, in most experiments outcomes are defined in terms of monetary payoffs to the bargainers, providing participants with real incentives to pursue their interests in a way that is intelligible to researchers.

Beyond the major and subtle differences between specific bargaining protocols, most experimental bargaining games have in common the most distinctive feature of bargaining: the multiplicity of alternative agreements (including the possibility of disagreement). The bargainers typically have conflicting preferences over alternative agreements, but a common interest in avoiding costly disagreement. This multiplicity of conflicting alternatives will be the focus of this chapter.

Bargaining problems can be usefully represented as games with multiple pure-strategy Nash equilibria.[1] Such games pose an equilibrium selection problem, which has been approached by imposing axioms that relate the solution to bargainers' utilities (e.g., Nash 1950). An alternative route—and the one that will be the focus of this chapter—is through some form of focal-point reasoning, as first proposed by Schelling (1960).

6.1 Focal Points in Bargaining

The Strategy of Conflict (1960) was Schelling's response to the inadequacy of contemporary game theory for the analysis of the 'mixture of mutual dependence and conflict' that characterise 'bargaining' or 'mixed motive' games (p. 89). One of his main contributions is the hypothesis that, in such games, 'rational' players will often be able to reach an agreement, even without communication, by using their shared knowledge of 'incidental details' of the game.

In a famous example, Schelling considers how two army commanders can decide to stop their advance without engaging in costly warfare. Some 'prominent' features of the surrounding environment (e.g., water

[1] Because we are interested in coordination, unless otherwise stated, when we talk about 'equilibria' we will mean pure-strategy equilibria.

courses, ridges) could 'suggest themselves' as obvious points of arrest, their prominence making communication between the commanders unnecessary: the 'power of suggestion' would make them the 'obvious' or 'natural' 'place to compromise' (pp. 68–69). The arbitrariness of such *cues* may result in one army occupying more territory or securing more valuable resources. Schelling proposes that rational players would recognise that, even if these details discriminate against them, the mutual expectation of the resulting agreement would leave them no choice but to submit to it. He uses the term *focal point* to indicate an equilibrium that is selected through such a process of 'meeting of minds' based on *commonly known* cues that *discriminate* between the available equilibria.

This process is best illustrated by pure coordination games, in which all equilibria give the same payoff to all players. Because any equilibrium is as good as any other, what matters is 'finding the key, or rather finding *a* key—any key that is mutually recognised as the key becomes *the* key' (p. 57, emphasis in original). Schelling reports some evidence from informal experiments on very simple coordination games that confirms his belief (pp. 54–57). Starting from Mehta et al. (1994), these early results have been widely replicated and extended, establishing that focal points are easily identified in pure coordination games (see also Bardsley et al. 2010).

In Schelling's analysis, pure coordination games are used to illustrate the principles by which *tacit* (i.e., without communication) bargaining problems may be solved. He hypothesises that the 'power of suggestion' of the incidental details extends to games with communication, which he refers to as *explicit* bargaining games. His argument is based on backward induction, and applies to games with a pre-set deadline. If it is commonly known that a certain agreement would be salient in a *tacit* game, then it can also be expected to be salient in the explicit game, because this 'necessarily gives way, at some definite penultimate moment, to a *tacit* (noncooperative) bargaining game' (p. 271, emphasis in original).

What counts as a cue in the identification of a focal point? Undoubtedly, some agreements may stand out because of properties of the resulting distribution of payoffs. For instance, when sharing a fixed-size pie, the equal split may be particularly salient. If the sum of payoffs differs between agreements, maximising total payoff may stand out.

We will call equilibria selected following principles such as equality or efficiency *payoff-based* focal points. However, there is no reason for bargainers to limit the search for cues to properties of the payoffs. Many of Schelling's incidental details would be treated by game theory as *labelling* of either the players (e.g., 'who are the parties and what they know about each other'), or the strategies (e.g., 'precedent, accidental agreement, ...'). We call equilibria selected using such cues *label-based* focal points.

This distinction is crucial for testing hypotheses about focal-point reasoning. Certain payoff configurations may be attractive for reasons other than equilibrium selection—e.g., players' preference for equality or efficiency. It is much less credible that bargainers pick certain labels because they like them more than others. Because changing labels does not alter the game as viewed by standard theory, most experimental tests of focal points have manipulated labelling cues.

For similar reasons of experimental control, experiments have often used one-shot simultaneous games with limited communication. As recognised by Schelling himself, focal points can be based on precedent—e.g., 'entitlements' based on previous agreements (Gächter and Riedl 2005, 2006; Karagözoğlu and Reidl 2015)—and so inducing an equilibrium can have persistent effects (e.g., Roth and Schoumaker 1983; Binmore et al. 1993). But like payoff-based cues, precedents and entitlements may be related to players' normative judgments.

Our discussion will start with selected examples of payoff-based focal points, in recognition of their real-world relevance (see also Pope et al. 2015), with the proviso that their emergence may be driven by reasons beyond the essential goal of equilibrium selection.

6.2 Bargaining with Payoff-Based Focal Points

Because the players of an experimental bargaining game care about their monetary payoffs, their search for cues may start from the payoffs. We consider selected experiments mostly not intended as tests of hypotheses about focal points in which *equal* or *efficient* allocations emerged particularly frequently. 'Focality' may be a reason for this, but not the only one.

6.2.1 Equality as Focal Point

In many bargaining games, the players' objective is to reach an agreement on the division of some surplus or resource. In such games, dividing *equally* may be a strong payoff-based cue. We will offer two paradigmatic cases: the binary lottery games studied by Roth and colleagues and the ultimatum game.[2]

In a binary lottery game, two players bargain for a fixed time over the division of 100 points, which represent the probability of winning a subject-specific monetary prize. If no agreement is reached within the allotted time, both players get nothing. The Nash (1950) bargaining solution entails a 50:50 split of the points regardless of the values of the monetary prizes. Roth and Malouf (1979) found that the 50:50 split was particularly common when each player only knew her own prize value, but agreements often equalised the players' expected earnings when both prize values were known. Roth et al. (1981) found that, when the monetary values of the prizes were unknown and payoffs were expressed in terms of an intermediate commodity (chips), players tended to equalise expected earnings in chips. Roth and Murnighan (1982) varied whether one or both players knew both prize values (both always knew their own) and found that agreements tended to the 50:50 split of points whenever the player with the low monetary prize did not know both prizes, otherwise tending towards equal expected earnings. These experiments illustrate that notions of equality are often very attractive, but also that when there are conflicting focal points players compromise between them.

In the ultimatum game (Güth et al. 1982), two players—a *proposer* and a *responder*—bargain over the division of a pie (usually a fixed sum of money). The proposer proposes a division that can be either accepted

---

[2] Recent studies in which an equal split has been interpreted as a focal point include Herreiner and Puppe (2010), Bolton and Karagözoğlu (2016) and Camerer et al. (2019).

or rejected by the responder. If the responder accepts, each player receives the share specified by the offer, otherwise both players receive nothing. The game has quickly become one of the most widely studied games in behavioural game theory (e.g., Güth and Kocher 2013). Although any allowable division of the pie is a potential equilibrium of the game, repeated elimination of weakly dominated strategies entails that the proposer should offer the smallest possible amount and the responder should accept it. Contrary to this prediction, most experiments find that offers are much larger than the minimum, often averaging between 40 and 50% of the pie. Offers below 20% of the pie are often rejected. More importantly for our purposes, the 50:50 split is often the *modal* offer.

It is likely that the focality of the equal split may be contributing to its prevalence in these sets of experimental results. However, focality is only one of the possible factors. Alternative explanations may be that players derive disutility from unequal payoff distributions (e.g., Fehr and Schmidt 1999), that they have reciprocal tendencies and low offers may be seen as unkind (e.g., Rabin 1993), that they feel guilty if they let others down (e.g., Battigalli and Dufwenberg 2007), or that sharing equally is a social norm the violation of which causes disutility (Bicchieri 2006). This illustrates two important points. First, the appeal of equality may derive from these other factors. Second, if one is interested in identifying pure focality, experiments that use payoff-based cues are not ideal.

6.2.2 Efficiency as Focal Point

In games with multiple equilibria, outcomes that give players as a whole a higher total payoff may stand out for this payoff-related reason. Pareto-dominant equilibria are often chosen in coordination games without conflicts of interest (e.g., Bacharach 2006; Isoni et al. 2019). Pareto dominance has also been found to be a strong cue in bargaining games with mild conflict of interest.

To illustrate, consider a two-player game with two Nash equilibria giving positive payoffs to both players; all other payoffs are zero. For efficiency to be a discriminating cue independent of equality, it must be that

(i) the sum of the two players' payoffs is higher in one equilibrium and that (ii), in the efficient equilibrium, one of the payoffs is larger (otherwise there would also be an equality cue). Conflict of interest requires that at least one player has a strict preference for one of the equilibria. For example, in a game in which the two equilibria have payoffs [7, 6] and [6, 6], under standard assumptions Player 1 has a strict preference for the first equilibrium and Player 2 is indifferent. In this case, [7, 6] is (weakly) Pareto dominant. Bett et al. (2016) report that, in games of this kind, 60% of players in both roles chose (simultaneously and without communication) the [7, 6] allocation, while the remaining 40% chose the [6, 6] allocation. With strong Pareto dominance—i.e., when the [7, 6] allocation was pitted against various [X, X] allocations with $X < 6$—the overwhelming majority of players chose the efficient and Pareto-dominant allocation, but these are hardly bargaining games, as the conflict of interest is absent.[3]

The question of whether efficiency is a strong cue when it does not correspond with Pareto dominance is an interesting one. Suppose the two allocations were [9, 5] and [6, 7], resulting in a more obvious conflict of interest. We are not aware of experiments that investigated games of this kind, but it must be noted that in these games the inefficient equilibrium is less unequal, creating conflicting cues.[4] For the study of focality, this adds to the complications arising from players deriving utility from certain payoff configurations.

[3] Bett et al. (2016) also considered games with three allocations, e.g. [7, 6], [6, 7], [5, 5]. Such games have conflict of interest, but efficiency is not a discriminating cue. Similar games studied by Faillo et al. (2017) kept the sum of the two payoffs in each equilibrium constant, also excluding efficiency as a cue.

[4] Some of the games studied by López-Pérez et al. (2015) had this structure, but there were also non-trivial differences between the payoffs in the non-equilibrium cells, making risk dominance considerations relevant. Luhan et al. (2017) considered the focality of total payoff efficiency in real-time tacit bargaining games in which payoffs were determined by the time spent on different allocations, but their results do not suggest that maximising efficiency was a priority.

6.3 Bargaining with Label-Based Focal Points

We now turn to experiments that investigated bargaining games with labelling cues. Because labels are generally taken to play no role in standard game-theoretic analyses, finding that they systematically affect bargaining provides more compelling evidence for their use as coordination devices.

The investigation of the effects of labelling is one that benefits from reducing the bargaining problem to its most essential elements. The simplest game with multiple equilibria and conflict of interest is a battle-of-the-sexes (BoS) game played simultaneously with no communication. It can be seen as a stripped-down version of the Nash demand game with just two possible splits, one favouring each player, as in the game below.

		Column	
		S_1	S_2
Row	S_1	L, S	0,0
	S_2	0,0	S, L

Two players, Row and Column, choose between two strategies, S_1 and S_2. The payoffs from the strategy combination $\{S_1, S_1\}$ are L for Row and S for Column, indicated as $[L, S]$, $\{S_2, S_2\}$ resulting in $[S, L]$, $0 < S < L$. Any other strategy combination yields payoffs $[0, 0]$. In this representation, Row and Column are placeholders for player labels. S_1 and S_2 are placeholders for strategy labels. We will only consider cases in which the two strategy labels are the same for the two players and all labels are common knowledge. This makes labels potential discriminating cues.

If labels are ignored, the two equilibria are perfectly symmetrical, and so are the player roles. Thus, swapping the players, the strategies, or both, results in essentially the same game. The *isomorphism* of the equilibria poses a coordination problem unsolvable through standard best-response reasoning.

Labels can break the symmetry between the equilibria. One of the players may be salient, suggesting their favourite equilibrium is selected—e.g., if the player labels are *King* and *Duke*, knowing that kings are more important than dukes may suggest the equilibrium that favours *King*. Or one of the labels may be salient—e.g., if the strategies are *Heads* and *Tails*, players may recognise that 'heads and tails' occurs in speech more often than 'tails and heads' and choose *Heads*.

In the remainder of this section, we will discuss research on the effects of player or strategy labels in experimental bargaining games.

6.3.1 Player Labels as Focal Points

Early evidence for the use of player labels in BoS games can be found in Cooper et al.'s (1993) study of forward induction in a BoS game with $S = 200$ points and $L = 600$, in which Row had an outside option that would result in a payoff $O = 300$ to both players without the BoS game being played. As long as $O > S$, forward induction predicts that the players will coordinate on Row's favourite equilibrium.

Cooper et al. compared this game (BoS-300) with the same game without outside option (BoS), and the normal-form version of BoS-300 (BoS-300-NF), in which the predicted outcome after iterated elimination of dominated strategies was the same as that of forward induction in BoS-300. Players could not coordinate in BoS, but were much better in BoS-300. In BoS-300-NF, coordination was not as good, questioning the forward induction argument and suggesting the outside option made Row the *focal* player. This possibility was investigated with three variants of the game: one with a dominated outside option $O = 100$ (BoS-100); one in which Row moved first but her choice was not communicated to Column (BoS-Seq); one in which Row could send a non-binding message to Column about her strategy choice (BoS-1W). Row's favourite equilibrium was played 19% of the cases in BoS, 63% in BoS-100, 62% in BoS-Seq and 96% in BoS-1W, suggesting that a great deal of coordination success could be attributed to the focality of Row.

Holm (2000) investigated whether knowing the gender of one's opponent could provide cues for coordination. In a first experiment, conducted in Sweden, gender was communicated by handing questionnaires with the text 'female student' or 'male student' to participants of the corresponding gender, and using that information prior to the elicitation of choices in the BoS game. The headline result is that both female and male participants played more aggressively (choosing their favourite equilibrium) when matched with females, improving overall coordination success relative to the mixed-strategy equilibrium. A second study in which gender was communicated using fictitious Swedish names replicated this result. A third study with a US sample found the effect for females but not for males. Holm interpreted his results as an instance of 'gender-based' focal points. However, while this story works for mixed-gender games, in the case of females facing females, going for the better equilibrium induces discoordination. Moreover, given that the experiment used the participants' real gender, their behaviour may reflect their attitudes to gender. The identification of the pure labelling effect of gender requires common knowledge that the gender information provided in the experiment is unrelated to the real gender of the players.

6.3.2 Strategy Labels as Focal Points

One of the first investigations of label-based focal points in bargaining games was reported by Mehta et al. (1992). They studied a version of the Nash demand game in which two players decided how to divide £10. Each player was handed four random cards from a set containing four aces and four twos. The four aces together were worth £10. Any other combination was worthless. Unless a player had the four aces, the two players could bargain about how to divide the £10 deriving from pooling their cards. There was an agreement if the sum of the two players' demands did not exceed £10. So, the number of aces contributed by each player provided a cue for the division of the surplus, a 3:1 split suggesting £7.50–£2:50, a 2:2 split £5–£5 and a 1:3 split £2.50–£7:50. The equal split was expected to be the most salient (see Section 2.1), but its use was systematically affected by the distribution of aces, with 48% of players owning one ace, 95% of players owning two and 52% of players owning three demanding £5. Players owning one ace demanded £2.50 in 33% of the cases, while those owning three demanded £7.50 only in 12% of the cases. In the latter case, 24% demanded £6, the closest round number between the two focal solutions of £5 and £7.50. Overall, the distribution of aces clearly influenced how much players demanded, with the player having three aces playing conservatively.

6.3.2.1 Tacit Bargaining Games Framed as Matching Games

Crawford et al. (2008) studied a number of BoS games framed as a choice between options describing different payoff distributions for the two players. Coordination success occurred when players made the same choice, hence the label *matching* games. Crawford et al. (2008) varied the differences between the equilibrium payoffs and whether one of the strategy labels was salient. In their setup, *S* was always equal to \$5, while *L* could be either \$5.10, \$6 or \$10. In the 'unlabelled' treatments, the options were described in text form (e.g., 'P1 receives \$*b* and P2 receives \$*a*'), while in the 'labelled' versions the text options were also called '*X*' and '*Y*'. The expectation that *X* would be salient was confirmed using pure coordination games with the same labels and all payoffs equal to \$5, in which *X* was chosen by 76% of participants, resulting in an expected coordination rate (i.e., the likelihood that two players, chosen at random, coordinate with each other) of 64%. In the BoS games, the salient strategy was chosen by 52%, 48% and 48% of players when *L* was \$5.10, \$6 and \$10 respectively, resulting in expected coordination rates of 38%, 46% and 47%. Interestingly, when *L* was \$5.10, X was chosen *less* often by the players favoured by the labelling cue, whereas when *L* was \$6 or \$10, the majority of both players chose the strategy with a higher own payoff. But both patterns induced discoordination.

These results were broadly replicated by Parravano and Poulsen (2015), who varied the stake size by adding a *small* stake condition (all payoffs divided by ten), and a *large* stake condition (all payoffs tripled). Their hypothesis that larger stakes would encourage focal-point reasoning was not supported for BoS games (although larger stakes increased salient choices in pure coordination games).

Crawford et al. (2008) also reported a series of three-allocation games, which can be seen as extensions of BoS games that add a third equilibrium to the two isomorphic ones ([L, S] and [S, L]). The third equilibrium was of the form [S, S], [L, S], [G, S] or [L, K], with $K < S < L < G$. In some cases, coordination success exceeded the random benchmark because the label-salient option was chosen with high frequencies. But this was particularly the case when the payoffs of the label-salient equilibrium were [S, S], suggesting that an equality cue might have been at work.

Three-option games with the same broad structure were studied by Jackson and Xing (2014), who used the labels 'Purple', 'Orange' and 'Green' for the three strategies. Coordination on Purple resulted in payoffs [S, L], Orange in [L, S], Green in [M, M], with $S < M < L$. Jackson and Xing manipulated whether or not the two players were from the same country (either US or India) and whether one label was made salient. [M, M] was the modal choice without label salience. When one of the unequal equilibria was made salient, Indian participants were more likely than Americans to follow the prompt, whereas Americans responded more markedly when the equal equilibrium was made label-salient.

6.3.2.2 The Bargaining Table Design

Schelling's hypotheses about the role of strategy labels in bargaining were addressed directly by Isoni et al. (2013), who developed the new *bargaining table* design to construct an environment that could be seen as a bargaining situation by both experimenters and participants. Two of their games are shown in Figure 6.1.

The bargaining game is represented by a 9 × 9 grid of squares with a red and a blue 'base' identifying the two players. Valuable objects, represented as 'discs' with a monetary value, are scattered on the table. The players' objective is to 'agree on a division of the discs'. Each player separately records which disc(s) she wants to 'claim', knowing that the other player will be doing the same. It is common knowledge that there is an agreement if, and only if, no disc is claimed by both players. Agreements

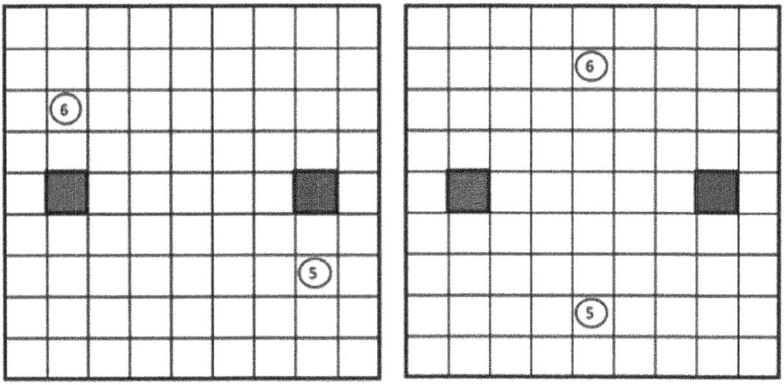

Fig. 6.1 Two bargaining table games from Isoni et al. (2013)

result in each player earning a payoff equal to the sum of the values of the disc(s) she claimed. If any disc is claimed by both players, there is no agreement, and both receive a payoff of zero.

Claiming no disc is a dominated strategy, as it guarantees a payoff of zero. Then, claiming both discs is dominated. So, after iterated elimination of dominated strategies, both games in Figure 6.1 reduce to a BoS game.[5] Participants could construe the game in Figure 6.1(a) as a choice between the *close* and the *far* disc. The game in Figure 6.1(b) could be either a choice between the *top* and the *bottom* disc, or between the disc more to the *left* and the one more to the *right*. That is, the distinction between the two games is only a matter of labelling. The bargaining table design is based on the verifiable premise that the 'closeness' rule applicable to *closeness* games like that in Figure 6.1(a) is more salient than rules that can be used in *spatially neutral* games like that in Figure 6.1(b). Thus, agreements should be more likely in *closeness* games than in *spatially neutral* games.

[5] Performing iterated elimination of dominated strategies is not always straightforward for experimental participants (e.g., Cooper et al. 1993). However, in Isoni et al.'s setup, dominated claims occurred extremely rarely.

Isoni et al. (2013) studied three simple BoS games, with *L*:*S* payoffs 6:5, 8:3 and 10:1. The percentages of left (respectively, right) players claiming the disc closer to their base for different *L*:*S* combinations were 76% (78%) for 6:5, 66% (62%) for 8:3, and 66% (52%), resulting in standardised efficiency (i.e., the ratio of the sum of the players' expected payoffs and the total surplus available) of 64.8%, 51.4% and 36.9%. In the former two cases, these were significant improvements over the corresponding spatially neutral efficiency levels of 48.6% and 45.7%, but not in the latter (35.0%). Unlike matching games, labelling exerted an important influence on BoS games framed as bargaining problems with claims, but the extent of the conflict of interest hampered the effect of closeness: in the corresponding pure coordination game standardised efficiency was 46.7% in the spatially neutral and 84.4% in the closeness version.

Isoni et al. (2013) also considered games with four and eight discs. These were either *equality-compatible* games, in which the *least unequal efficient* (LUE) division was 5:5, or *equality-incompatible* games, in which the LUE was 6:5. In the latter, the principles of closeness and *accession* (treating groups of discs as indivisible units when two or more discs were close to each other to form coherent groups—see Mehta et al. 1994) always suggested an LUE split. Although with more discs the number of strategies increases exponentially, the closeness and accession rules do not necessarily become less obvious. Correspondingly, with more discs, efficiency and agreement rates were substantially higher in closeness and accession games than in their spatially neutral counterparts. With more discs, participants could play more conservatively by claiming less often the discs nearer the middle column.

6.3.2.3 Other Applications of the Bargaining Table Design

The bargaining table design captures important features of real-world bargaining: bargainers make claims on valuable resources; ostensibly payoff-irrelevant 'relational' cues (closeness) assign parts of the surplus to individual players; part of the surplus can be left unclaimed. These features make the design particularly well-suited to test Schelling's hypotheses about the role of payoff-irrelevant cues in bargaining. A central question has been why such cues are weakened by conflicts of interest.

Isoni et al. (2019) noted that, by establishing common knowledge that agreements favour one player, most experimental designs overemphasise conflicts of interest relative to real-world scenarios in which payoffs are imperfectly known. They extended the bargaining table design to allow each disc to have different values for different players, using two-disc games in which, for each player, one of the discs was worth L and the other S. Depending on the disc values, with $L > S$ the game could be either a BoS or a Hi-Lo game, i.e., a game with two equilibria with payoffs $[L, L]$ and $[S, S]$ respectively. There were three conditions. *Full information*: participants knew all disc values, and so knew whether the game was BoS or Hi-Lo. *Own information*: each player knew L and S but only her own disc values. *No information*: neither player knew which disc was worth $L(S)$ to either player (but knew L and S). The results do not support the hypothesis that focal-point reasoning is more likely when conflicts of interest are merely potential. In the partial information games, the close disc was claimed significantly less often than in the corresponding BoS games, and in the no information game, the close disc was claimed significantly less often than in an equivalent pure coordination game. Uncertainty about payoffs may have additional hindering effects on focal-point reasoning.

Isoni et al. (2020) addressed the difference between BoS and pure coordination games noting that they differ in two important respects: conflict of interest and payoff inequality. Coordinating in BoS requires one of the players to accept her less preferred equilibrium (conflict of interest), but it also means that one player receives a lower material payoff than the other (payoff inequality). To disentangle the effects of these two factors, Isoni et al. (2020) devised the new *pizza night* game, which features payoff inequality but not conflict of interest. The pizza night game is a coordination game with two equilibria—both resulting in the payoffs $[L, S]$—in which it is common knowledge that one player is favoured by both equilibria.[6] Though not as likely as in pure coordination games, agreements were more likely in pizza night games than in BoS games, even with extreme payoff inequality (i.e., $L = 17$ and $S = 4$). So, while both payoff inequality and conflict of interest matter for focal-point reasoning, conflict of interest is the main disrupting factor.

Sitzia and Zheng (2019) adopted the bargaining table design to investigate whether, when the players of a BoS game are groups of two people, focal points can be identified more easily. If one thinks about the focal solution as some 'truth' needing to be 'discovered', it seems intuitive to expect that two people may have better chances of finding the solution than individuals. Sitzia and Zheng (2019) used some of Isoni et al.'s (2013) games (and some of Crawford et al.'s [2008] three-allocation games) played by individuals or groups. Groups chose the focal strategy more often than individuals, especially for smaller payoff differences. This may be relevant in the context of Schelling's analysis, as many of his real-world examples involve decisions made by teams or committees.

So far, we have focused on 'tacit' bargaining games. However, Schelling suggested that the same cues would work in 'explicit' bargaining. This hypothesis was tested by Isoni et al. (2014), who extended the bargaining table design by allowing the two players to bargain over a period of 90 seconds in which both players' claims were shown on each player's screen, effectively allowing players to make proposals and counter-proposals. The real-time nature of the game changed the expected differences between closeness and spatially neutral games, and the relationship between payoff-based and label-based cues. Isoni et al. (2014) studied closeness games in which closeness was pitted against a variety of payoff-relevant principles. Their main findings are summarised by the title of their paper: efficiency, equality and labelling. Players were mostly concerned with efficiency, and rarely left discs unclaimed. Subject to

[6] The name 'pizza night game' derives from the cover story used by Isoni et al. (2020). This is a variant of the BoS story, in which husband and wife must meet for dinner downtown but cannot communicate. They prefer eating together to eating on their own. In the BoS version, the spouses choose between pizza and steak, the wife preferring pizza, the husband steak. In the pizza night game, the choice is between two pizza places (the spouses are meeting on 'pizza night'), so it is common knowledge that, wherever they meet, she will enjoy the meal more than he does.

efficiency being maximised, they tried to minimise inequality. When efficient and least unequal agreements could be achieved in multiple ways, labelling cues influenced who got the larger share. Contrary to Schelling's hypothesis, labelling cues may have only second-order effects on the outcome of explicit bargaining.

6.4 Discussion and Conclusion

The organising principle of our selected survey has been the distinction between payoff-based and label-based focal points, because we see the essence of Schelling's intuition to be the players' recognition that conflicts of interest should be set aside in the search for a discriminating cue. In this respect, label-based focal points are better suited to identify pure focal-point reasoning. But because of the power of suggestion, even payoff-irrelevant cues may derive their salience from associations with real-world concepts of value. Many conventions involve strategies that are in some sense focal (Sugden 1986) and may be applied by extension to other situations thanks to the power of suggestion. It is unclear whether focality is the source of conventions or the reverse.

Focal points often appear in the discussion of bargaining as a result of the empirical prevalence of equal splits. Besides the credible possibility that people have a preference for equality, there are bargaining protocols in which equality emerges as a result of rational behaviour (e.g., the 'smoothed Nash demand game' discussed by Binmore 1987). Isolating the role of focality in the prominence of equal splits is a challenging task for future research; so is the task of identifying the focal attraction of efficiency separately from equality.

The evidence points to a differential effectiveness of player and strategy labels. Beyond the ambiguities in the use of real, as opposed to arbitrary, gender labels to identify the players, player labels seem to be more conducive to focal-point reasoning than strategy labels, whose effects appear to be more fragile in Battle-of-the-Sexes games. The pizza night game suggests this is mostly caused by conflicts of interest. It is an interesting open question whether player labels may solve conflicts of interest more easily because they directly identify who gets more, whereas labelling cues do that indirectly through a strategy that favours one player.

Given that most existing research has focused on illustrating the power of focal points, there is limited evidence about conflicting cues. In binary lottery experiments, whether equality is applied to chips or expected earnings depends on the knowledge of the disadvantaged player (Roth and Murnighan 1982). In Mehta et al.'s (1992) game, participants sometimes compromise between the equal and the 3:1 splits. In the bargaining table design, payoff cues take precedence over labelling (Isoni et al. 2014), but labelling can interfere with payoffs when the cues are incongruent (Isoni et al. 2019). An intriguing topic for future research is the possibility that sophisticated players may try to strategically and self-servingly (e.g., Babcock and Loewenstein 1997) steer bargaining towards cues that favour them.

Given our primary focus on experimental evidence, we have deliberately avoided the debate surrounding the theoretical explanations of how and when focal points emerge. The two leading explanations—*team reasoning* (e.g., Sugden 1993; Bacharach 2006) and *level-k* reasoning (e.g., Crawford et al. 2008)—do not appear to be mutually exclusive (Faillo et al. 2017), with people liable to use different reasoning in different games (Isoni et al. 2019). But which of the two modes of reasoning is the 'default' is unclear, with some suggesting that 'focality is intuitive' (Poulsen et al. 2019) and others reaching the opposite conclusion (van Elten and Penczynsky 2020). Explaining when and how focal-point reasoning works and understanding its psychological underpinnings remain the greatest challenges lying ahead of us.

Acknowledgments This project has received funding from the European Research Council (ERC) under the European Union's Horizon 2020 research and innovation programme (grant agreement No. 670103), and from the Economic and Social Research Council of the UK (award No. ES/P008976/1). The funders had no other involvement in the conduct of the research.

References

Babcock, Linda and George Loewenstein (1997). Explaining Bargaining impasse: The role of self-serving biases. *Journal of Economic Perspectives* 11(1): 109–126.

Bacharach, Michael (2006). *Beyond individual choice: Teams and frames in game theory*. Edited by Natalie Gold and Robert Sugden. Princeton, NJ: Princeton University Press.

Bardsley, Nicholas, Judith Mehta, Chris Starmer and Robert Sugden (2010). Explaining focal points: Cognitive hierarchy theory versus team reasoning. *Economic Journal* 20(March): 40–79.

Battigalli, Pierpaolo and Martin Dufwenberg (2007). Guilt in games. *American Economic Review: Papers and Proceedings* 97(2): 171–176.

Bett, Zoe, Anders Poulsen and Odile Poulsen (2016). The focality of dominated compromises in tacit coordination situations: Experimental evidence. *Journal of Behavioral and Experimental Economics* 60: 29–34.

Bicchieri, Cristina (2006). *The grammar of society: The nature and dynamics of social norms*. Cambridge: Cambridge University Press.

Binmore, Ken (1987). Nash bargaining theory II. In Ken Binmore and Partha Dasgupta (Eds.), *The economics of bargaining*. Ch. 4. Oxford: Blackwell.

Binmore, Ken, Joe Swierzbinksi, Steven Hsu and Chris Parloux (1993). Focal points and bargaining. *International Journal of Game Theory* 22: 381–409.

Bolton, Gary E. and Emin Karagözoğlu (2016). On the influence of hard leverage in a soft leverage bargaining game: The importance of credible claims. *Games and Economic Behavior* 99: 164–179.

Camerer, Colin F., Gideon Nave and Alec Smith (2019). Dynamic unstructured bargaining with private information: Theory, experiment, and outcome prediction via machine learning. *Management Science* 65(4): 1867–1890.

Charness, Gary and Matthew Rabin (2002). Understanding social preference with simple tests. *Quarterly Journal of Economics* 117(3): 817–869.

Cooper, Russell, Douglas V. DeJong, Robert Forsythe and Thomas W. Ross (1993). Forward induction in the battle-of-the-sexes games. *American Economic Review* 83(5): 1303–1316.

Crawford, Vincent P., Uri Gneezy and Yuval Rottenstreich (2008). The power of focal points is limited: Even minute payoff asymmetry may yield large coordination failures. *American Economic Review* 98(4): 1443–1458.

Faillo, Marco, Alessandra Smerilli and Robert Sugden (2017). Bounded best-response and collective-optimality reasoning in coordination games. *Journal of Economic Behavior and Organization* 140: 317–335.

Fehr, Ernst and Klaus M. Schmidt (1999). A theory of fairness, competition, and cooperation. *Quarterly Journal of Economics* 114(3): 817–868.

Gächter, Simon and Arno Riedl (2005). Moral property rights in bargaining with infeasible claims. *Management Science* 51: 249–263.

Gächter, Simon and Arno Riedl (2006). Dividing justly in bargaining problems with claims. *Social Choice and Welfare* 27: 571–594.

Güth, Werner, Rolf Schmittberger and Bernd Schwarze (1982). An experimental analysis of ultimatum bargaining. *Journal of Economic Behavior and Organization* 3: 367–388.

Güth, Werner and Martin G. Kocher (2013). More than thirty years of ultimatum bargaining experiments: Motives, variations and a survey of the recent literature. *Journal of Economic Behavior and Organization* 108: 396–409.

Herreiner, Dorothea K. and Clemens Puppe (2010). Inequality aversion and efficiency with ordinal and cardinal social preferences—An experimental study. *Journal of Economic Behavior and Organization* 76(2): 238–253.

Holm, Hakan J. (2000). Gender-based focal points. *Games and Economic Behavior* 32(2): 292–314.

Isoni, Andrea, Anders Poulsen, Robert Sugden and Kei Tsutsui (2013). Focal points in tacit bargaining problems: Experimental evidence. *European Economic Review* 59: 167–188.

Isoni, Andrea, Anders Poulsen, Robert Sugden and Kei Tsutsui (2014). Efficiency, equality and labelling: An experimental investigation of focal points in explicit bargaining. *American Economic Review* 104(10): 3256–3287.

Isoni, Andrea, Anders Poulsen, Robert Sugden and Kei Tsutsui (2019). Focal points and payoff information in tacit bargaining. *Games and Economic Behavior* 114: 193–214.

Isoni, Andrea, Robert Sugden and Jiwei Zheng (2020). The pizza night game: Efficiency, conflict and inequality in tacit bargaining games with focal points. *European Economic Review* 127, article 103428.

Jackson, Matthew O. and Yiqing Xing (2014). Culture-dependent strategies in coordination games. *Proceedings of the National Academy of Sciences of the United States of America* 111(3): 10889–10896.

Karagözoğlu, Emin and Arno Reidl (2015). Performance information, production uncertainty, and subjective entitlements in bargaining. *Management Science* 61(11): 2611–2626.

López-Pérez, Raúl, Ágnes Pintér and Hubert J. Kiss (2015). Does payoff equity facilitate coordination? A test of Schelling's conjecture. *Journal of Economic Behavior and Organization* 117: 209–222.

Luhan, Wolfang J., Anders Poulsen and Michael W. M. Roos (2017). Real-time tacit bargaining, payoff focality, and coordination complexity: Experimental evidence. *Games and Economic Behavior* 102: 687–699.

Mehta, Judith, Chris Starmer and Robert Sugden (1992). An experimental investigation of focal points in coordination and bargaining: Some preliminary results. In John Geweke (Ed.) *Decision making under risk and uncertainty: New models and empirical findings*, 211–219. Dordrecht: Kluwer.

Mehta, Judith, Chris Starmer and Robert Sugden (1994). The nature of salience: An experimental investigation of pure coordination games. *American Economic Review* 84(3): 658–673.

Nash, John (1950). The Bargaining problem. *Econometrica* 18(2): 155–162.

Parravano, Melanie and Odile Poulsen (2015). Stake size and the power of focal points in coordination games: Experimental evidence. *Games and Economic Behavior* 94: 191–199.

Pope, Devin G., Jaren C. Pope and Justin R. Sydnor (2015). Focal points and bargaining in housing markets. *Games and Economic Behavior* 93: 89–107.

Poulsen, Anders and Axel Sonntag (2019). Focality is intuitive—Experimental evidence on the effects of time pressure in coordination games. CBESS Discussion Paper 2019–01.

Rabin, Matthew (1993). Incorporating fairness into game theory and economics. *American Economic Review* 83(5): 1281–1302.

Roth, Alvin E. and Michael W. K. Malouf (1979). Game-theoretic models and the role of information in bargaining. *Psychological Review* 86(6): 574–594.

Roth, Alvin E., Michael W. K. Malouf and J. Keith Murnighan (1981). Sociological versus strategic factors in bargaining. *Journal of Economic Behavior and Organization* 2: 153–177.

Roth, Alvin E. and J. Keith Murnighan (1982). The role of information in bargaining: An experimental study. *Econometrica* 50(5): 1123–1142.

Roth, Alvin E. and Francoise Schoumaker (1983). Expectations and reputations in bargaining: An experimental study. *American Economic Review* 73(3): 362–372.

Schelling, Thomas C. (1960). *The strategy of conflict*. Cambridge, MA: Harvard University Press.

Sitzia, Stefania and Jiwei Zheng (2019). Group behaviour in tacit coordination games with focal points—An experimental investigation. *Games and Economic Behavior* 117: 461–478.

Sugden, Robert (1986). *The economics of rights, cooperation and welfare*. Oxford: Blackwell.

Sugden, Robert (1993). Thinking as a team: Toward an explanation of nonselfish behaviour. *Social Philosophy and Policy* 10: 69–89.

van Elten, Jonas and Stephan Penczynski (2020). Coordination games with asymmetric payoffs: An experimental study with intra-group communication. *Journal of Economic Behavior and Organization* 169: 158–188.

7

Between Utilitarianism and Egalitarianism: Some Ethical Aspects of the Nash Bargaining Solution

Shiran Rachmilevitch

7.1 Introduction

In a classic paper, Nash (1950) formalized a bargaining problem as consisting of two elements, S and d. The former is a set of feasible utility allocations out of which one allocation needs to be selected, the latter is a particular point of S that specifies the players' utilities in the event of disagreement. The model has two interpretations. In the first, S is understood as describing the utilities that are obtainable in some underlying strategic bargaining procedure in which the players are engaged, and d specifies the utilities the players can secure unilaterally (i.e., their maxmin payoffs). In the second, the reality underlying the model involves an

S. Rachmilevitch (✉)
Department of Economics, University of Haifa, Haifa, Israel
e-mail: shiranrach@econ.haifa.ac.il

E. Karagözoğlu and K. B. Hyndman (eds.), *Bargaining*,
https://doi.org/10.1007/978-3-030-76666-5_7

impartial arbitrator who needs to choose an allocation from S, and d specifies the players' utilities if the arbitrator makes no choice.[1]

Utilitarianism and egalitarianism—the two classical notions of distributive justice—are relevant to the model under either of its interpretations. In the arbitrator-based interpretation this relevance stems from the fact that the arbitrator would like to choose a fair compromise, and the quest for fairness involves utilitarian and/or egalitarian considerations. From the strategic perspective, this relevance presents itself in the form of arguments that the players may invoke through the play of the underlying game. For example, a player may complain that "it is not fair that I will gain only this much when you gain that much," thereby resorting to egalitarian reasoning; his opponent may reply by "do me a favor, it will only cost you a little but will help me a lot," thereby invoking a utilitarian principle.

Utilitarianism and egalitarianism pool in different directions: when one recommends increasing the payoff of some player i at the expense of some other player j, the other makes the opposite recommendation. More specifically, utilitarianism shifts resources to where they produce high levels of utilities, hence it favors agents who are efficient "utility production machines." Egalitarianism, by contrast, tends to shift resources towards less capable agents. These opposing forces are taken into account by the Nash bargaining solution, which creates a compromise between them. In this chapter I survey the various ways in which this solution offers a "golden path" between utilitarianism and egalitarianism, as well as related ethical aspects of this solution.

After the presentation of preliminaries in Sects. 7.2 and 7.3 starts off by presenting the pioneering work of Shapley (1969) regarding the relation between the Nash solution on the one hand, and utilitarianism and egalitarianism on the other hand. Next, each of Sects. 7.4–7.6 concentrates on a different ethical property which is related to utilitarianism and egalitarianism. Sections 7.7–7.9 present models, different from the canonical bargaining model that serves as the framework for the earlier sections, in which either the ethical aspects of the Nash solution

[1] The arbitrator's choice can be viewed either as a recommendation, or as a binding outcome that he can enforce on the players.

or its connections to utilitarianism and egalitarianism are illustrated. Section 7.10 concludes. For brevity, proofs—all of which can be found in the cited papers—are omitted.

7.2 Preliminaries

I consider the following basic version of Nash's (1950) bargaining model. A *bargaining problem* (problem, for short) is a compact, convex and comprehensive set $S \subset \mathbb{R}^2_+$, that contains $d \equiv \mathbf{0} \equiv (0, 0)$ and satisfies $S \cap \mathbb{R}^2_{++} \neq \emptyset$. That is, the disagreement point is normalized to the origin and it is assumed that non-individually rational alternatives (alternatives under which some player obtains a payoff below his disagreement payoff), if they at all exist, can be ignored. The existence of utility allocations that strictly Pareto dominate the disagreement point guarantees that there is a reason to bargain. Compactness is the combination of closedness and boundedness. The former says, for example, that if it is feasible to give a player 2.99999... utility units, then providing him with 3 utils is also feasible; the latter expresses resource-scarcity. Convexity is a consequence of the assumption that the players are expected utility maximizers and randomization over agreements is feasible.[2] Comprehensiveness means that S contains any vector $v \in \mathbb{R}^2_+$ for which there is some $s \in S$ with $v \leq s$;[3] that is, utility can be freely disposed in the region above the disagreement point.

The *weak Pareto frontier* of S consists of those $x \in S$ for which there is no $y \in S$ that satisfies $y > x$. The *strong Pareto frontier* of S consists of those $x \in S$ for which there is no $y \in S$ that satisfies $y \gneq x$. These frontiers are denoted by $WP(S)$ and $P(S)$, respectively. A bargaining problem S is *smooth* if $WP(S) = P(S)$ and this set equals

[2] There is no shortage of natural economic settings that give rise to a convex utility set without assuming expected utility; for example, if bargaining is over a perfectly divisible resource and the players' utilities from consumption are concave. However, some of the properties to be discussed in the sequel require the expected utility assumption (e.g., the property MD, to be discussed in Section 7.6). Therefore, it is convenient to assume expected utility.

[3] Vector inequalities: xRy iff $x_i R y_i$ for both i, for each $R \in \{>, \geq\}$; $x \gneq y$ iff $x \geq y$ and $x \neq y$.

$\{(t, f(t)) : 0 \leq t \leq M\}$, where $M > 0$ is some number and f is a decreasing, strictly concave, differentiable function. This function f is called S's *boundary function.* The best that player i can hope for in S—his *ideal payoff in* S—is $a_i(S) \equiv \max\{s_i : s \in S\}$; $a(S)$ is called S's *ideal point*.[4] A bargaining problem S is *normalized* if $a(S) = (1, 1)$.

A *solution* is a function μ that assigns a unique feasible point for every problem S, namely $\mu(S) \in S$. The *Nash solution* N (Nash 1950) assigns to each S the maximizer of $x_1 \cdot x_2$ over $x \in S$. The *egalitarian solution* E (Kalai 1977) assigns to each S the point $(e(S), e(S))$ where $e(S) \equiv \max\{e' : (e', e') \in S\}$. In other words, E selects for each S the maximizer of the *Rawlsian objective* $R(x) \equiv \min\{x_1, x_2\}$over $x \in S$.[5] Let $\mathcal{U}(S)$ denote the set of utilitarian points in S: those that maximize the *utilitarian objective* $\Sigma(x) \equiv x_1 + x_2$ over $x \in S$.[6] A solution is *utilitarian* if it always makes its selection out of $\mathcal{U}$. For any domain on which $\mathcal{U}$ is single-valued, it is convenient to simply talk about *the* utilitarian solution. The domain of smooth problems has this property.

7.2.1 Axioms

Throughout the chapter I refer to the following axioms, in the statements of which S and T are arbitrary problems.

Weak Pareto optimality (WPO): $\mu(S) \in WP(S)$.[7]

Symmetry (SY): $S = \{(s_2, s_1) : (s_1, s_2) \in S\} \Rightarrow \mu_1(S) = \mu_2(S)$.

Independence of irrelevant alternatives (IIA): $\mu(T) \in S \subset T \Rightarrow \mu(S) = \mu(T)$.

---

[4] The ideal point (sometimes called the utopia point) plays an important role in bargaining theory; it first appeared in a seminal paper by Kalai and Smorodinsky (1975).

[5] The name comes from the Rawlsian principle of maximizing the well-being of society's least better-off individual (Rawls 1971).

[6] More generally, one could use the term "utilitarian objective" to refer to any expression of the form $\alpha x_1 + \beta x_2$, for some positive α and β. I will briefly make use of this more permissive definition in the next section, and I will be explicit when I do that; otherwise, in any other place in the sequel, "utilitarian objective" means the above-mentioned definition from the text, namely the one corresponding to $\alpha = \beta = 1$.

[7] A stronger version of this axiom is *Pareto optimality*, that requires $\mu(S) \in P(S)$.

Scale covariance (SC): $\mu(l \circ S) = l \circ \mu(S)$ for every pair of positive linear transformations l.[8]

Nash's (1950) original characterization of his solution is based on these axioms. Two other axioms I consider are the following:

Strong individual rationality (SIR): $\mu(S) > \mathbf{0}$.

Conflict-freeness (CF): $a(S) \in S \Rightarrow \mu(S) = a(S)$.

7.3 Shapley's Result

Shapley (1969) was the first to highlight the strategic role that utilitarian and egalitarian arguments can play in bilateral bargaining, and he proposed an ingenious way to combine them. His key point is that arguments of the type mentioned in the Introduction—e.g., "it is not fair that I will gain only this much when you gain that much"—are expressions of *interpersonal utility comparisons*. These comparisons take into account efficiency and equity, and these, in turn, are related to two *weights*, in the following sense. Let S be a problem and suppose, for convenience, that it is smooth. Suppose that the selected point for S is $\mu(S) = x > \mathbf{0}$. Then, the payoff-proportion is well-defined, and is given by:

$$p \equiv \frac{x_2}{x_1}. \tag{7.1}$$

If x is "fair," that is if each player obtained what he deserves, then the relative weight p is an expression of this fairness: the right thing to do is to give player 2 a payoff that is p times that of player 1. Thus, p expresses the weight given to player 2, relative to player 1, in the fairness consideration.

But there is another weight associated with x, which is derived not from an exercise that compares x and the worst possible outcome—the disagreement point—but rather compares x with nearby efficient points.[9] When we decrease x_1 by an arbitrarily small amount and stay

[8] A solution that satisfies this property is called *scale covariant*.

[9] The payoff x_i is player i's *gain relatively to disagreement*; hence, disagreement is implicitly involved in the weight p.

on the Pareto frontier, the resulting increment in player 2's payoff is approximately q, where:

$$q \equiv -f'(x_1). \tag{7.2}$$

This is a weight that describes the substitutability between the individual utilities. It is the efficiency weight in the following sense. Suppose that one unit of player 2's utility equals θ units of player 1's utility. If our objective is utilitarian (in the sense of footnote 6), then we should have moved away from any point on the frontier as long as the conversion rate between the individual utilities is different from θ, because doing so would increase the objective's value. That x is a point from which there is no such movement implies that $\theta = q$.

A conflict between the fairness consideration and the utilitarian consideration does not arise if, and only if, the two weights agree, namely if $q = p$. Substituting the expressions for the weights gives:

$$-f'(x_1) = \frac{x_2}{x_1},$$

which is the first-order-condition associated with the Nash solution. Thus, a Pareto optimal utility allocation induces a common fairness/efficiency weight if, and only if, it is the Nash solution point.

Since the Nash solution is scale covariant, it follows that it maximizes both the utilitarian and the Rawlsian objectives for some rescaling of the individual utilities. To see why, start with the abovementioned first-order-condition:

$$-f'(N_1(S)) = \frac{N_2(S)}{N_1(S)},$$

rescale player 2's utility by λ and leave player 1's utility intact, where $\lambda \equiv \frac{N_1(S)}{N_2(S)}$. Denote the rescaled problem by $\tilde{S}$ and its boundary function by $\tilde{f}$; note that $\tilde{f} = \lambda f$. Since $N(\tilde{S}) = (N_1(S), N_1(S))$, the Nash solution maximizes the Rawlsian objective over $\tilde{S}$. Since $-\tilde{f}'(N_1(S)) = -\lambda f'(N_1(S)) = \frac{N_1(S)}{N_2(S)} \cdot \frac{N_2(S)}{N_1(S)} = 1$, it also maximizes the utilitarian objective.

Now, let us look at our solution μ, which induces the fairness and efficiency weights given by (7.1) and (7.2). Suppose that μ is scale covariant, and that it maximizes both the utilitarian and Rawlsian the objectives for *some* rescaling of the individual utilities: c_1 of player 1's utility and c_2 of player 2's. Since the utilitarian and Rawlsian objectives are homogeneous of degree one, it can be assumed that $c_1 = 1$. Then $c_2 x_2 = x_1$ and $-c_2 f'(x_1) = 1$, which implies $-f'(x_1) = \frac{x_2}{x_1}$. Therefore, $x = \mu(S) = N(S)$.

The foregoing analysis is summarized in Shapley's result:

Proposition 1 The Nash solution is the unique scale covariant solution that maximizes simultaneously the utilitarian and Rawlsian objectives for some rescaling of the individual utilities.

Two remarks are in order. The first considers a technicality: it has been implicitly assumed above that the discussion is confined to WPO and SIR solutions, but there is actually no need to *assume* this. As for WPO, note that it is implied by the combination of SC and the fact that the solution maximizes the utilitarian and Rawlsian objectives for some rescaling of the individual utilities. Specifically, if $\mu(S) \notin WP(S)$, then no matter how S is rescaled, the solution point of the resulting problem will not maximize the utilitarian objective. If SIR is violated in S, then no matter how S is rescaled, the solution point of the resulting problem will not maximize the Rawlsian objective.

The second remark is historical: Shapley was not the first to note the connections between the Nash solution and utilitarianism and egalitarianism. The first paper to mention them is probably Harsanyi (1959). However, Shapley's work is the first systematic analysis of these connections that emphasizes the interpersonal comparisons aspect. A detailed account of Shapley's approach can be found in Yaari (1981).

7.4 Bounds

In Rachmilevitch (2015) I showed that the Nash solution is the unique scale covariant solution μ that has the following property: for every problem S and player $i \in \{1, 2\}$:

$$\min\{E_i(S), U_i(S)\} \leq \mu_i(S) \leq \max\{E_i(S), U_i(S)\},$$

for some $U(S) \in \mathcal{U}(S)$. Namely, the solution is "sandwiched" between egalitarianism and utilitarianism. Therefore, in particular:

$$\min\{E_i(S), U_i(S)\} \leq N_i(S) \leq \max\{E_i(S), U_i(S)\}, \tag{7.3}$$

for some $U(S) \in \mathcal{U}(S)$. For convenience, I will maintain in the present section—as I did in the previous one—that S is smooth. Among other things, it assures the uniqueness of the utilitarian point, hence renders the qualification "for some $U(S) \in \mathcal{U}(S)$" unnecessary.

The inequalities described in (7.3) follow from Proposition 1. To see how, consider an arbitrary problem S and scale it so that the resulting problem, S', satisfies $E(S') = U(S') = N(S')$.[10] Let l be a rescaling such that $S' = l \circ S$ and now scale back the problem S' to S, namely apply to it l^{-1}; w.l.o.g., suppose that l^{-1} is the transformation that leaves player 1's utility intact and scales player 2's utility by $c \in \mathbb{R}_{++} \setminus \{1\}$. Note that the rescaling has no impact on player 1's Nash solution payoff, $N_1(S) = N_1(S')$. If $c > 1$—i.e., the rescaling makes player 2 more capable in utility production—then the utilitarian point will move to the north-west, because utilitarianism rewards such higher productivity; the egalitarian point will move to the east, hence the new Nash point will be sandwiched between the two. If $c < 1$, the analogous pattern applies.

The bounds-result is implied by Proposition 1, and is therefore logically weaker. However, the bounds-approach can be used to obtain results that say more than what Proposition 1 does. Specifically, in Rachmilevitch (2015) I showed that for normalized smooth problems S, the bounds in (7.3) can be improved to:

$$\min\{A_i(S), U_i(S)\} \leq N_i(S) \leq \max\{A_i(S), U_i(S)\}, \tag{7.4}$$

[10] The existence of such a rescaling was established in the previous section.

where:

$$A(S) \equiv \text{argmax}_{x \in S} \frac{1}{2} \Sigma(x) + \frac{1}{2} R(x).$$

Since A is sandwiched in between U and E, (7.4) implies that whenever $U(S) \neq E(S)$, $A(S)$ divides the range between $U(S)$ and $E(S)$ into two parts, and $N(S)$ lies in the part that is closer to $U(S)$. Thus, if the average A is viewed as a "midpoint" between utilitarianism and egalitarianism, then the Nash solution is closer to utilitarianism than it is to egalitarianism. With the required adjustments, this result can be stated more generally, in a way applicable to non-normalized problems.[11] Further bounds-type results, as well as alternative senses in which the Nash solution is close to utilitarianism, appear in Rachmilevitch (2016).

7.5 Suppes-Sen Dominance and Mariotti's Result

An appealing property of E, U, and N is that they all satisfy *Suppes-Sen dominance* (SSD), which is defined as follows. A vector x SS-dominates another vector y if either $x > y$ or $\pi x \equiv (x_2, x_1) > y$,[12] and SSD is the requirement that the bargaining solution never selects an SS-dominated point. The idea behind SSD is that it does not matter which person enjoys what payoff, it only matters what payoffs are being distributed; in particular, there is no ethical distinction between x and πx, so excluding y as a possible solution point on the grounds that it is Pareto dominated by some other feasible alternative implies that it should also be excluded if it is Pareto dominated by a permutation of a feasible alternative.

Mariotti (1999) proved the following result:

Proposition 2 A solution satisfies scale covariance and Suppes-Sen dominance if and only if it is the Nash solution.

[11] The details can be found in Rachmilevitch (2015).

[12] This notion of dominance is due to Suppes (1966) and Sen (1970).

The permutation-component of SSD can be viewed as saying that both individuals are "the same," and this "sameness" can be taken to mean that interpersonal utility comparisons are legitimate. The combination of this idea with scale covariance can be interpreted as follows: while interpersonal utility comparisons are acceptable *in principle*, conducting them *in practice* may not be doable. More specifically, it may very well be that there is some objectively correct conversion rate between the individual utilities, but it is, unfortunately, unknown. Since it is unknown, there is no reason to confine oneself to the specific scales in which the bargaining problem is happened to be given, which is where scale covariance comes into the picture.[13]

Anbarcı and Sun (2011) showed that Mariotti's result can be improved by weakening SSD to an axiom called *weak SSD*, which requires that there be no feasible point that dominates the solution point both in the SS-sense and in an additional sense, called *E-dominance*. Given two vectors $x, y \in \mathbb{R}^2_+ \setminus \{\mathbf{0}\}$, x E-dominates y if $\frac{\min\{x_1,x_2\}}{\max\{x_1,x_2\}} \geq \frac{\min\{y_1,y_2\}}{\max\{y_1,y_2\}}$. That is, E-dominance ranks utility allocations according to their equity.

A concept related to SSD is *egalitarian-utilitarian monotonicity* (EUM). A solution μ satisfies EUM if the following holds for every pair of nested problems $S \subset T$:

- $R(\mu(T)) < R(\mu(S)) \Rightarrow \Sigma(\mu(T)) > \Sigma(\mu(S))$,
  and
- $\Sigma(\mu(T)) < \Sigma(\mu(S)) \Rightarrow R(\mu(T)) > R(\mu(S))$.

That is, when utility-opportunities expand, a decrease in the value of the objective of either utilitarianism or egalitarianism is accompanied by an increase in the value of the other objective. The rationale is that since each of these ethical principles has its merit, it would be unjustified to make the supporters of both views unhappy when an opportunity for improvement presents itself. In Rachmilevitch (2019) I showed that the combination of conflict-freeness and EUM implies SSD. Therefore, the following is a consequence of Mariotti's result:

[13] It is interesting to contrast this view with the one from Section 7.3: there, the correct rate is not unknown—rather, it is the one under which utilitarianism and egalitarianism coincide.

Proposition 3 A solution satisfies scale covariance, conflict-freeness and egalitarian-utilitarian monotonicity if and only if it is the Nash solution.

7.6 Midpoint Domination

Utilitarianism and egalitarianism also suffer from drawbacks. Consider the problem of splitting a perfectly divisible good between two players, each of whom has a constant marginal utility from consumption: that of player 1 is 1, that of player 2 is $k > 1$. Thus, player 2 is a more productive "utility production machine." In the utility space, this problem is $S_k \equiv \text{conv}\{(0, 0), (1, 0), (0, k)\}$, and it is easy to check that $E(S_k) = (\frac{k}{k+1}, \frac{k}{k+1})$ and $U(S_k) = (0, k)$. The unattractiveness of these solutions is clear when one considers parameter values that are either very low or very high: with low values ($k \sim 1$) the players are almost symmetric yet player 2 obtains the entire surplus under utilitarianism while player 1 gets nothing; under high values ($k \to \infty$), if egalitarianism is applied then player 2 gets no chance to utilize his ability to enjoy arbitrarily high levels of utility—his utility is bounded by one, simply because his partner is the unfortunate player 1, whose capability of enjoyment is limited.

The Nash solution prevents this extremism by selecting the frontier's midpoint, $(\frac{1}{2}, \frac{k}{2})$. Anbarcı (1998) called this property *midpoint outcome on a linear frontier* (MOLF) and showed that its combination with IIA characterizes the Nash solution:[14]

Proposition 4 A solution satisfies midpoint outcome on a linear frontier and independence of irrelevant alternatives if and only if it is the Nash solution.

It is easy to check that every solution that satisfies {WPO, SY, SC} satisfies MOLF. Hence, Proposition 4 is an improvement of Nash's original characterization of his solution, as the latter involves the axioms

[14] MOLF is stated as an axiom in the utility space (that is, the story about splitting a resource between players with constant marginal utilities is merely illustrative).

{WPO, SY, SC, IIA}. It is also an improvement of a result by Moulin (1983), who characterized the Nash solution by IIA and *midpoint domination* (MD), the latter being the requirement that in every problem each player obtains at least half of his ideal payoff.[15]

In the context of the division problem from the beginning of the section, there is a simple actual procedure corresponding to MOLF: a fair coin toss determines who will win the surplus, and the corresponding pair of expected utilities is the midpoint. The more general MD corresponds to the requirement that the solution point Pareto dominate the utility image of the coin toss. Another related procedure is the well-known *divide-and-choose*: one player splits the good into two, and the other player chooses one of the parts, leaving the remaining part for the divider.[16] It is clear that the (subgame perfect) equilibrium of this procedure result in the equal split, with utility image $(\frac{1}{2}, \frac{k}{2})$.[17]

A property similar to MD/MOLF is *symmetry based compromise*, which requires that for every weakly Pareto optimal x such that πx is also feasible and weakly Pareto optimal, there be some $t \in (0, 1)$ such that $\mu(S) \geq tx + (1-t)\pi x$. As opposed to MD/MOLF, the points in the convex combination are not confined to $\{(a_1(S), 0), (0, a_2(S))\}$, but can be any $\{x, \pi x\} \subset WP(S)$;[18] at the same time, the weight in this combination is not restricted to be $\frac{1}{2}$. Xu (2012) proved the following:

Proposition 5 A solution satisfies weak Pareto optimality, scale covariance and symmetry based compromise if and only if it is the Nash solution.

---

[15] Another two-axiom characterization of the Nash solution in which one of the axioms is MD has been obtained by De Clippel (2007) in a model with a variable disagreement point.

[16] For a detailed discussion about this mechanism, see Brams and Taylor (1996).

[17] When the players' utility functions are not linear, the utility allocation resulting from divide-and-choose satisfies MD, provided that these functions are concave and assume the value zero at 0. To see this, consider such a function u: note that $u(\frac{1}{2}) = u(\frac{1}{2} \cdot 1 + \frac{1}{2} \cdot 0) \geq \frac{1}{2}u(1) + \frac{1}{2}u(0) = \frac{1}{2}u(1)$. The LHS is a player's utility under divide-and-choose, the RHS is half of the player's ideal payoff.

[18] Note that the support of the convex combination in symmetry based compromise is qualitatively different from the one in MD/MOLF: only in the non-generic case of a symmetric S it holds that $(0, a_2(S)) = \pi(a_1(S), 0)$.

To make an interim summary: not only does the Nash solution offer a compromise between utilitarianism and egalitarianism, but there are also circumstances in which the absence of compromise, in the sense of choosing either a utilitarian or an egalitarian recommendation, leads to extreme (perhaps even absurd) outcomes.

In the following sections I revisit the Nash solution in several alternative models. In these models, too, the Nash solution exhibits attractive ethical features and creates a compromise between utilitarian and egalitarian principles.

7.7 Indivisible Goods

Recent years have seen much development in the economics-and-computer-science community regarding fairness questions related to the allocation of indivisible objects. Below I present a couple of results from an important paper from this literature, Caragiannis et al. (2016), in which the Nash solution in studied in the indivisibilities context.

There are m indivisible goods to be allocated between two players.[19] When player i is allocated a subset A of the goods, his utility is $\sum_{g \in A} v_i(\{g\})$, where v_i is non-negative valued, and the utility from not obtaining any item is normalized to zero. Call this the *AIG model*.[20] In this model, "Nash solution" means any allocation-selection that maximizes the utilities-product.

In the AIG model, the notion of egalitarianism becomes irrelevant—at least in the way that it is stated in the classical bargaining model—because a weakly Pareto optimal allocation in which the players' utilities coincide typically does not exist. An alternative fairness criterion, one which is trivially implied by egalitarianism, is *envy-freeness*: every player should weakly prefer his own bundle to that of the other player. However, even this weaker requirement is too much to ask for in the realm of

[19] Caragiannis et al. (2016) consider n players. I restrict my attention to $n = 2$ in order to present (some of) their results in the simplest possible way, and also in order to be consistent with the rest of this chapter, in which I have focused on the 2-person case exclusively.

[20] AIG stands for Allocating Indivisible Goods. This is my terminology; it is not used in Caragiannis et al. (2016).

indivisible goods: for example, think of one indivisible good which is valued positively by either player—no matter how the good is allocated, someone is going to envy. This motivates the following milder version of envy-freeness, *envy-freeness up to one good*, which does not result in non-existence: For every player i there is a good g, such that if g is removed from j's bundle, then i does not envy j. Caragiannis et al. (2016) proved the following:

Proposition 6 In the AIG model, the Nash solution satisfies Pareto optimality and envy-freeness up to one good.

Indivisibilities dictate further adjustments relative to the classical model, not just the one concerning egalitarianism. Another example is given by the divide-and-choose protocol mentioned in the previous section. There, any division of the good was feasible, and the divider could secure for himself half of the good. In the AIG model, by contrast, there are only finitely many ways to divide the goods between the players, and it is less clear what the divider can secure for himself. This number, called the *maxmin share*, is given by:

$$\text{MMS}_i = \max_{(A_1,A_2)\in\Pi}\min_{k\in\{1,2\}} v_i(A_k),$$

where Π is the set of partitions. It is of course desirable that a solution assigns each player i a payoff no smaller than MMS_i, but this is too much to ask for. Instead, a weaker demand is that each player obtains at least some fraction out of his MMS_i. Formally, a solution satisfies α*-MSS* if each i's solution-payoff is at least $\alpha \cdot \text{MMS}_i$.

Caragiannis et al. (2016) proved the following:

Proposition 7 In the AIG model, the Nash solution satisfies φ-MMS, where $\varphi \equiv \frac{-1+\sqrt{5}}{2}$ is the golden ratio conjugate.

Proposition 7 can be viewed as establishing a property similar to MD, in the sense that both are minimal utility guarantees.

As we see, the Nash solution's impressive fairness properties are not confined to the classical domain over which it is defined, but present themselves in other areas too; in particular, they present themselves in the important and practical context of allocating indivisible goods.

I now turn to a model that allows for both divisibility and indivisibility.

7.8 "Utility Production" and the Nash Product

Let $F \subset \mathbb{R}^2_{++}$ be a general non-empty set of feasible utility allocations. It is allowed to be finite, or some other non-convex set. The elements of F are called the *primitive utility pairs*. In addition, there are other feasible utility allocations, which are generated as follows: given a probability $p \in (0, 1)$, let F^p denote the utility pairs of the form $p * u \equiv (pu_1, (1 - p)u_2)$, for some $u = (u_1, u_2) \in F$. The elements of F^p—*non-primitive utility pairs*—are obtained by the following operation on the primitive ones: with probability p player 1 obtains his u-payoff and player 2 obtains nothing, and with the complementary probability player 2 obtains his u-payoff and player 1 obtains nothing. The parameter p measures the relative abilities of the players to "produce utility" out of primitive pairs: large p's imply that player 1 is more productive than player 2, small p's imply the opposite. This model is due to Mariotti (2000).

Consider choice functions on $F \cup \{F^p : 0 < p < 1\}$. As utilitarian choices favor the more productive player and egalitarian choices go in the opposite direction, striking a balance between them can be expressed by ignoring this productivity. Mariotti formalized this by the following requirement: if u is selected out of F then $p * u$ should be selected out of F^p, *for any* $p \in (0, 1)$. Additionally, he required choices to be made in a *permutation optimal* way, which is the following version of SSD: if $u = (u_1, u_2)$ is a feasible non-primitive utility pair and $\pi u = (u_2, u_1)$ is Pareto dominated by some other feasible pair, then u should not be selected. The two requirements—productivity-blindness and permutation optimality—characterize "Nash choices": any choice function that satisfies them maximizes the utilities-product on F.

7.9 A Probabilistic View on Bargaining

In a recent paper, Bastianello and LiCalzi (2019) take a novel approach to bargaining, in which the center of attention is the probability that an agreement will be reached. The basic ingredient in their model is a set of alternatives, A, and every alternative $a \in A$ is mapped into a pair of individual acceptance probabilities, $(p_1(a), p_2(a))$, where $p_i(a)$ is the probability that player i will agree to a, if it were the alternative on the table. Next, each such pair is mapped, or aggregated, into a single probability number, the probability of agreement. In probabilistic terms, such an aggregation is represented by a copula. Several copulas are axiomatized, each representing a different bargaining solution. The egalitarian solution corresponds the copula $M(p, q) = \min\{p, q\}$, which is the Fréchet lower bound, associated with the strongest possible positive dependence between two marginal distributions. The relative utilitarian solution corresponds to the copula $W(p, q) = \max\{p + q - 1, 0\}$, which is the Fréchet upper bound, associated with the strongest possible negative dependence between two marginal distributions.[21] The Nash solution corresponds to the copula $\Pi(p, q) = p \cdot q$, which expresses stochastic independence. Hence, the Nash solution is in between the egalitarian and utilitarian solutions not only in the utility-based definitions surveyed above, but also in a probabilistic sense.

7.10 Conclusion

I have surveyed ethical properties of the 2-person Nash bargaining solution, with an emphasis on its connections to utilitarianism and egalitarianism. While most of the results can be extended to n players, Proposition 3 is an exception. Specifically, there does not exist an n-person solution (for $n \geq 3$) that satisfies conflict-freeness, scale covariance, and egalitarian-utilitarian monotonicity (EUM).[22] This gives rise

[21] The *relative utilitarian solution* (Dhillon and Mertens 1999; Sobel 2001; Pivato 2009) maximizes the normalized sum of utilities $\frac{x_1}{a_1(S)} + \frac{x_2}{a_2(S)}$ over $x \in S$.

[22] See Theorem 1 in Rachmilevitch (2019).

to the following questions: Is there an EUM-type property which is consistent with conflict-freeness and scale covariance in the n-person case? If there is, what is its relation to the Nash solution? Answering them remains, at present, a goal for future research.

I will end the chapter with a brief discussion about the implicit assumption, that the framework within which I have worked is suitable for a study in distributive justice. Roemer (1986) argues to the contrary, since an ethical discussion involves concepts such as freedom, rights, and needs—all of which live out of the utility space. Since he clearly has a point, why discuss utilitarian-egalitarian trade-offs, and ethics more generally, in the utility space? Here is an answer.

First, let us distinguish between *thick bargaining problems* and *thin bargaining problems*.[23] Problems of the former kind are those that involve essential non-utility information. To take the simplest example, consider division of a pie between two players, one of whom is the pie's owner. Property rights are not expressible in the utility space, but they are clearly relevant in this situation. Hence, this situation is a thick bargaining problem. Problems of the latter kind are those in which there is no such non-utility information. For example, division of a pie between two players who have the same ownership status regarding the pie, none of them is particularly deprived, none of them needs the pie for medical reasons, and so forth.

My first claim is that there are thick problems to which a utilitarian-versus-egalitarian approach can be fruitful. For example, division problems in which the names of the goods matter, e.g., water and whiskey.[24] It seems perfectly reasonable to insist that each individual be allocated at least some minimal quantity of water, but make no such demand for whiskey. In such a setting is seems reasonable to divide the water according to an egalitarian principle (e.g., *resource egalitarianism*, under which physical quantities are equated) and treat the whiskey separately, allocating it in a utilitarian fashion. More generally, different goods can

[23] This terminology is inspired by Avishai Margalit's distinction between thick and thin relations (Margalit 2002, 2017).

[24] The idea of including the goods' names in the model is Roemer's.

be treated differently on a "utilitarian-to-egalitarian" scale, depending on their nature.[25]

My second claim is that it is appropriate to resort to ethical considerations also in thin problems. These, despite their thinness, may present real challenges: even if nobody had any special status or needs, and even in the absence of danger that some freedom will be compromised—even then, bargaining situations can be quite non-trivial; there is no reason to exclude ethics from the set of considerations intended to resolve these non-trivialities.

Acknowledgements I am grateful to Emin Karagözoğlu and an anonymous reviewer for helpful comments and suggestions.

References

Anbarcı, N. (1998). Simple characterizations of the Nash and Kalai/Smorodinsky solutions, *Theory and Decision*, **45**, 255–261.

Anbarcı, N. and Sun, C.J. (2011). Distributive justice and the Nash Bargaining solution, *Social Choice and Welfare*, **37**, 453–470.

Bastianello, L. and LiCalzi, M. (2019). The probability to reach an agreement as a foundation for axiomatic Bargaining, *Econometrica*, **87**, 837–865.

Brams, S.J. and Taylor, A.D. (1996). *Fair division: From cake-cutting to dispute resolution.* Cambridge University Press.

Caragiannis, I., Kurokawa, D., Moulin, H., Procaccia, A.D., Shah, N. and Wang, J. (2016). *The unreasonable fairness of maximum Nash welfare.* In Proceedings of the 2016 ACM Conference on Economics and Computation (pp. 305–322). ACM.

De Clippel, G. (2007). An axiomatization of the Nash Bargaining solution, *Social Choice and Welfare*, **29**, 201–210.

[25] Assigning each good the "right location" on the scale is itself an interesting task. It can be approached either as a philosophical question or as a formal social choice problem. Philosophically, it can be viewed as related to the question "which goods should be allocated by the market?" (Walzer 2008).

Dhillon, A. and Mertens, J.F. (1999). Relative utilitarianism, *Econometrica*, **67**, 471–498.
Harsanyi, J.C. (1959). *A Bargaining model for the cooperative n-person games. Contributions to the theory of Games IV*. Princeton: Princeton University Press, pp. 325–355.
Kalai, E. (1977). Proportional solutions to Bargaining situations: Interpersonal utility comparisons, *Econometrica*, **45**, 1623–1630.
Kalai, E. and Smorodinsky, M. (1975). Other solutions to Nash's Bargaining problem, *Econometrica*, **43**, 513–518.
Margalit, A. (2002). *The ethics of memory*. Harvard University Press.
Margalit, A. (2017). *On betrayal*. Harvard University Press.
Mariotti, M. (1999). Fair Bargains: Distributive justice and Nash Bargaining theory, *The Review of Economic Studies*, **66**, 733–741.
Mariotti, M. (2000). An ethical interpretation of the Nash choice rule. *Theory and Decision*, **49**, 151–157.
Moulin, H. (1983). Le choix social utilitariste. Ecole Politechnique DP.
Nash, J.F. (1950). The Bargaining problem, *Econometrica*, **18**, 155–162.
Pivato, M. (2009). Twofold optimality of the relative utilitarian Bargaining solution, *Social Choice and Welfare*, **32**, 79–92.
Rachmilevitch, S. (2015). The Nash solution is more utilitarian than egalitarian, *Theory and Decision*, **79**, 463–478.
Rachmilevitch, S. (2016). Egalitarian-utilitarian bounds in Nash's Bargaining problem, *Theory and Decision*, **80**, 427–442.
Rachmilevitch, S. (2019). Egalitarianism, utilitarianism, and the Nash Bargaining solution, *Social Choice and Welfare*, **52**, 741–751.
Rawls, J. (1971). *A theory of justice*. Harvard university press.
Roemer, J. (1986). The mismarriage of Bargaining theory and distributive justice, *Ethics*, **97**, 88–110.
Sen, A. (1970). *Collective choice and social welfare*. San-Francisco: Holden-Day.
Shapley, L.S. (1969). Utility comparison and the theory of games, in: *La Décision: Agrégation et Dynamique des Ordres de Préf'erence*, Editions du CNRS, Paris, 251–263.
Sobel, J. (2001). Manipulation of preferences and relative utilitarianism, *Games and Economic Behavior*, **37**, 196–215.
Suppes, P. (1966). Some formal models of grading principles, *Synthese*, **6**, 284–306.

Walzer, M. (2008). *Spheres of justice: A defense of pluralism and equality*. Basic books.
Xu, Y. (2012). Symmetry-based compromise and the Nash solution to convex bargaining problems, *Economics Letters*, **115**, 484–486.
Yaari, M.E. (1981). Rawls, Edgeworth, Shapley, Nash: Theories of distributive justice re-examined, *Journal of Economic Theory*, **24**, 1–39.

8

Dynamic Legislative Bargaining

Hülya Eraslan, Kirill S. Evdokimov, and Jan Zápal

8.1 Introduction

In this paper, we survey the literature on legislative bargaining with endogenous status-quo. Since the term "endogenous status-quo" is used to express different things by different authors, we start by proposing a typology to distinguish "endogenous status-quo" from "evolving

This survey was prepared for the book "Bargaining: Current Research and Future Directions", Emin Karagözoğlu and Kyle Hyndman (eds.), Palgrave Macmillan. We thank the editors for their invitation and an anonymous referee for insightful feedback on an earlier version. Due to space limitations, we do not discuss or even cite a number of related works. A longer version with a more comprehensive references can be found at Eraslan et al. (47).
Eraslan: Department of Economics, Rice University and Institute of Social and Economic Research, Osaka University, eraslan@rice.edu. Evdokimov: Department of Economics, Rice University, kirill.evdokimov@rice.edu. Zápal: CERGE-EI, j.zapal@cerge-ei.cz.

H. Eraslan (✉) · K. S. Evdokimov
Rice University, Houston, TX, USA
e-mail: eraslan@rice.edu

E. Karagözoğlu and K. B. Hyndman (eds.), *Bargaining*,
https://doi.org/10.1007/978-3-030-76666-5_8

status-quo."[1] Bargaining with endogenous status-quo is dynamic bargaining where *in each period a new policy is decided* and the policy implemented if there is no agreement is endogenously determined by the outcome of bargaining in the previous period. Bargaining with evolving status-quo is dynamic bargaining where *a single policy is decided* during the entire bargaining time horizon, the status-quo policy in each round depends on the history up to that round, and in the final round, if there is no agreement, the status-quo in that round is implemented.

As in Eraslan and Evdokimov [46], by "legislative bargaining" we mean multilateral bargaining where agreement requires less than unanimous consent and agreement on a proposal binds all parties. They survey the literature on *legislative bargaining with exogenous status-quo* where players decide on a policy through voting between an exogenously given status-quo and a proposal offered by a proposer. This protocol is repeated until an agreement is reached. Here we survey the literature on *legislative bargaining with endogenous status-quo.*

Baron [13] is typically credited as the first paper in the literature. Two important early precursors are Ingberman [52] and Epple and Riordan [45] who study spatial and redistributive bargaining respectively. Unlike the subsequent work, these early papers focus on deterministic proposer recognitions, and in the case of the latter paper, on subgame-perfect equilibria (SPE).

We start by introducing a general framework that incorporates two main strands of the literature we discuss in detail: bargaining over distributive policy and bargaining over spatial policy. After discussing the

K. S. Evdokimov
e-mail: kirill.evdokimov@rice.edu

J. Zápal
CERGE-EI, a joint workplace of Charles University and the Economics Institute of the Czech Academy of Sciences, Prague, Czech Republic
e-mail: j.zapal@cerge-ei.cz

[1] Anesi and Seidmann [8] discuss some of the literature using these two concepts without introducing new terminology.

equilibrium existence, we use this framework to study the many interesting questions the literature has raised: How does the endogeneity of the status-quo affect incentives? What are the equilibrium dynamics of policies? Do the policies converge? If so, to which policy? If not, what is their long-run behavior? What is the appropriate efficiency concept? Are equilibrium policies (Pareto) efficient? We end our survey by discussing avenues for future research.

The general framework we study incorporates related political economy models with bilateral bargaining, bargaining with evolving status-quo, random proposal models, costly policy change, and models in which either a dictator or median chooses policy. We do not review these papers due to space limitations. We also ignore other related literature on elections, dynamic linkages via macro variables or power structures, and coalitional bargaining.

8.2 General Framework

In a typical model, legislators in set $N = \{1, \ldots, n\}$ choose a policy x_t in each period $t = 0, 1, \ldots, T$, where T is finite or infinite. The policy space is X. When $X \subseteq \mathbb{R}$, bargaining is over a one-dimensional spatial policy. When X is the $(n-1)$-dimensional simplex, bargaining is over distributive policy.

The game in each period t proceeds as follows. First, period t starts with a publicly observed state denoted by s_t. The state s_t is a vector whose components include x_{t-1} but it can include other (potentially stochastic) variables as well. Player $\kappa(s_t)$ is the proposer and she makes a proposal $x \in X(s_t)$ where $X(s_t) \subseteq X$ is the set of feasible policies in state s_t. All players vote to accept or reject x. If the set of players who accept x is in $\mathcal{W}(s_t)$, which is the collection of winning coalitions in state s_t, policy x_t implemented at time t is x. Otherwise, x_t is $\zeta(s_t)$, the status-quo in period t when the state is s_t, where ζ is some known function.

Stage utility of player i from policy x in state s is $u_i(x, s)$. Player i's discounts rate is δ_i, thus the utility of player i from a sequence of policies

$(x_t)_{t=0}^{T}$ and states $(s_t)_{t=0}^{T}$ is

$$(1-\delta_i)\sum_{t=0}^{T}\delta_i^t u_i(x_t, s_t).$$

The papers we survey fit this framework. For example, Baron [13] and Kalandrakis [53] study, respectively, spatial and distributive settings with simple majority and random proposer recognitions. Under our notation, they assume that s_t includes the policy x_{t-1} from the previous period and identity of the proposer in the current period, and, for any state s_t, $X(s_t) = X$, $\mathcal{W}(s_t) = \{C \subseteq N : |C| \geq \frac{n+1}{2}\}$, and $\zeta(s_t) = x_{t-1}$. The framework naturally incorporates more complex models with state-dependent stage utilities [e.g., 67, 43, 26], models in which the status-quo in period t equals the $(t-1)$-period policy with some noise [e.g., 41], models in which players distribute pie with size that stochastically changes over time (as in the stochastic bargaining models in the spirit of [61]), or models with state-dependent winning coalitions and policy spaces [e.g., 31].

Histories, strategies and SPE can be defined in the standard way. The papers we survey restrict attention to (stationary) Markov strategies and equilibria. A Markov (behavioral) *proposal* strategy of player i specifies a distribution of proposals $\pi_i(s,t)$ over $X(s)$ for each period t and state s in which i is the proposer. A Markov (behavioral) *voting* strategy of player i specifies the probability $\alpha_i(x,s,t)$ that player i accepts proposal x in period t when the state is s. Infinite horizon models further restrict attention to stationary strategies, which do not depend on t. Moreover, strategies are usually allowed to depend only on certain (payoff relevant) components of the state, e.g., the previous-period policy or preference shocks, but not allowed to depend on others, e.g., the identity of the proposer.

A Markov strategy of player i is $\sigma_i = (\pi_i, \alpha_i)$. A profile of strategies $\sigma = (\sigma_i)_{i\in N}$ induces a dynamic utility $V_i^{\sigma}(x,s,t)$ from policy x implemented in period t when the state is s, which satisfies the following recursive relation

$$V_i^\sigma(x,s,t) = (1-\delta_i)u_i(x,s) + \delta_i \int V_i^\sigma(x',s',t+1)dP^\sigma(x',s'|x,s,t) \quad (8.1)$$

where $P^\sigma(x',s'|x,s,t)$ is the probability measure over period $(t+1)$ policies and states induced by profile σ and period t policy and state. Let

$$\alpha(x,s,t) = \sum_{C \in \mathcal{W}(s)} \prod_{i \in C} \alpha_i(x,s,t) \prod_{i \in N \backslash C} (1-\alpha_i(x,s,t)) \quad (8.2)$$

be the probability that proposal x is accepted in period t when the state is s.

A profile of strategies σ constitutes a Markov Perfect equilibrium (MPE) if

(i) for each i, s in which i is the proposer, t and p in the support of $\pi_i(s,t)$,

$$p \in \text{argmax}_{x \in X(s)} \alpha(x,s,t)V_i^\sigma(x,s,t) + (1-\alpha(x,s,t))V_i^\sigma(\zeta(s),s,t),$$

(ii) for each i, x, s and t, if $V_i^\sigma(x,s,t) > V_i^\sigma(\zeta(s),s,t)$, then $\alpha_i(x,s,t) = 1$, and if $V_i^\sigma(x,s,t) < V_i^\sigma(\zeta(s),s,t)$, then $\alpha_i(x,s,t) = 0$.

A profile of strategies σ is a stationary MPE (SMPE) if it is an MPE and σ_i is independent of t for each player i.

The two condition in the definition of MPE require, respectively, that the proposal strategies and the voting strategies are optimal. As is standard in the literature, the definition of MPE uses the one-stage deviation principle, and hence implicitly assumes that it holds. The voting strategies in the definition assume that players vote *as if* pivotal. This rules out implausible equilibria that support arbitrary outcomes because no voter is pivotal. Some work further focuses on voting strategies with indifferent players voting for the proposal. This implies that any proposal is either accepted or rejected with probability one, and hence allows one to focus on proposal strategies that generate proposals that are always accepted.[2]

8.3 Existence of Equilibria

SMPE existence is an open issue, outside special cases represented by finite-horizon models with finite policy spaces, for which MPE existence follows by standard backward induction arguments. The literature studying discounted stochastic games, of which the dynamic legislative bargaining models are a special case, includes numerous conditions for SMPE existence (see [51], for a recent contribution) but also examples of SMPE non-existence (see [57, 58]). Moreover, none of the known conditions for SMPE existence applies to legislative bargaining models (see [39], for further discussion).

Difficulties typically arise in models where the status-quo in period t equals the policy in period $t - 1$. One approach is then to work with models where x_{t-1} induces a distribution over $\zeta(s_t)$ that changes smoothly when x_{t-1} changes. This is how Duggan and Kalandrakis [41] prove general SMPE existence result for dynamic legislative bargaining models; they require shocks to status-quo transitions and players' preferences. Similarly, Duggan [37] assumes smooth transitions from a continuous policy space to a countable state space. An alternative strategy is to assume finite policy space [3, 35].

Because SMPE is not guaranteed to exist, most papers in the literature construct an equilibrium and study its properties. In the next two sections we display such constructions, in distributive and spatial settings.

[2] If the voting strategies are pure and $\zeta(s) \in X(s)$ for each state s, it is without loss of generality to assume that proposers choose policies *only* from the set of policies that would be accepted. This is because proposing a policy that would be rejected is equivalent to proposing the default outcome $\zeta(s)$.

8.4 Distributive Policy

In this section, we review the results for bargaining over distributive policies. This type of model raises many interesting questions regarding equilibrium strategies and outcomes in addition to the questions raised in the introduction. Specifically, what is the structure of winning coalitions? Does the size principle of Riker [69][3] hold? Is the entire surplus shared or is there waste? More generally, are equilibria inefficient?

As we will see, this model admits multiple equilibria, some of which differ drastically in their answer to the above questions. To emphasize this, we focus on two equilibrium constructions that have been influential: Kalandrakis [53] (henceforth K04) which is an early paper that features an intuitive construction, and Anesi and Seidmann [9] (henceforth AS15) which is a thorough investigation of a more general model.[4]

K04 is the first to describe an SMPE in a game in which three players bargain over distribution of a surplus of size 1. The policy space is the two-dimensional simplex $X = \{x \in \mathbb{R}^3_+ : \sum_{i=1}^3 x_i = 1\}$. Under our earlier notation, s_t includes policy x_{t-1} from the previous period, and, for any state s_t, $X(s_t) = X$, $\mathcal{W}(s_t) = \{C \subseteq N : |C| \geq 2\}$, and $\zeta(s_t) = x_{t-1}$. Player i's utility from policy x is $u_i(x) = x_i$ and players have a common discount rate δ.

We describe the equilibrium constructed by K04 with the help of Figure 8.1. The figure shows an equilateral triangle with each vertex designated for one player. Each edge has length $\frac{2}{\sqrt{3}}$, and therefore the distances between an arbitrary point inside the triangle and the edges sum to unity.[5] For example, x represents the equal allocation $(\frac{1}{3}, \frac{1}{3}, \frac{1}{3})$, x' and x'' represent allocations in which player 3 and player 2 respectively receive zero share, and x''' represent the unequal allocation $(1, 0, 0)$ favorable to player 1.

---

[3] Riker's size principle states that only minimum winning coalitions can occur.

[4] The earliest paper we know of is Epple and Riordan [45] which characterizes SPE in a three-player game to show that a wide range of outcomes can be sustained in equilibrium using punishment strategies.

[5] This is known as Viviani's theorem.

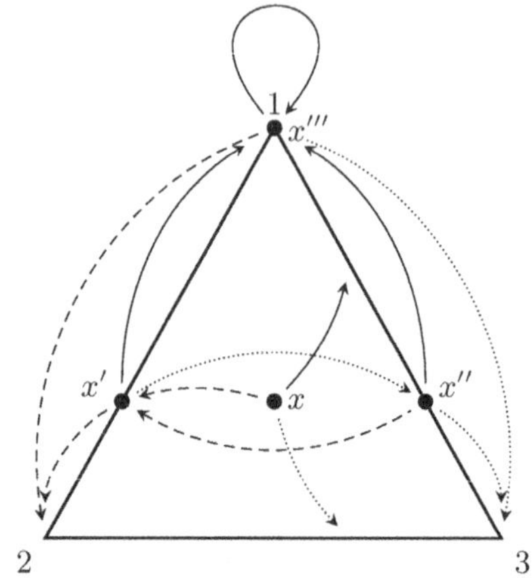

Fig. 8.1 Equilibrium dynamics in the distributive model

The figure represents the equilibrium dynamics. For four different status-quo policies x, x', x'' and x''', the arrows point to the policy proposed by player 1 (solid line), player 2 (dashed line) and player 3 (dotted line).[6] The germane feature of the equilibrium is the dynamics that moves policies from strictly inside the triangle to its edges and from the edges to its vertices. That is, the equilibrium dynamics moves over allocations that differ in the number of players who receive zero share: starting with no, then with one and then with two players receiving zero share. Eventually, the equilibrium reaches a state in which the proposer receives the entire resource. The literature has dubbed this a *rotating dictator* equilibrium.

The equilibrium dynamics arises from the nature of winning coalitions. We explain the intuition with the help of Figure 8.2. All four figures show indifference curves of the equilibrium dynamic utility. The left column is for player 1 and the right column is for player 3 (higher

[6] The equilibrium shown is symmetric, which allows one to work out the entire equilibrium policy dynamics starting from x. In particular, given a status-quo at the vertex, all players allocate the entire pie to themselves. And given a status-quo at the edge close to one of the vertices, both players with non-zero status-quo share allocate the entire pie to themselves and the player with zero status-quo share allocates zero share to the player with the largest status-quo share.

utility levels closer to the player's vertex). The top row is for $\delta = 0$ and the bottom row is for $\delta = \frac{6}{10}$.

Start with the case when $\delta = 0$, so that the model is an infinitely-repeated one-shot ultimatum game with three players and simple majority. Consider player 1's proposer problem assuming she seeks the approval of player 3, given some status-quo utility level of player 3. Using top row of Figure 8.2, player 1's optimal proposal is a policy at the north-eastern edge of the policy space that gives player 3 the same utility as the status-quo, allocates zero share to player 2 and allocates the rest to player 1. When, in addition, the status-quo is located at the north-western edge of the policy space, the status-quo utility of player 3 is zero and player 1 proposes a policy in which she obtains the entire pie. That is, the equilibrium dynamics moves policies from within the policy space to its edges and from the edges to the vertices. Inspection

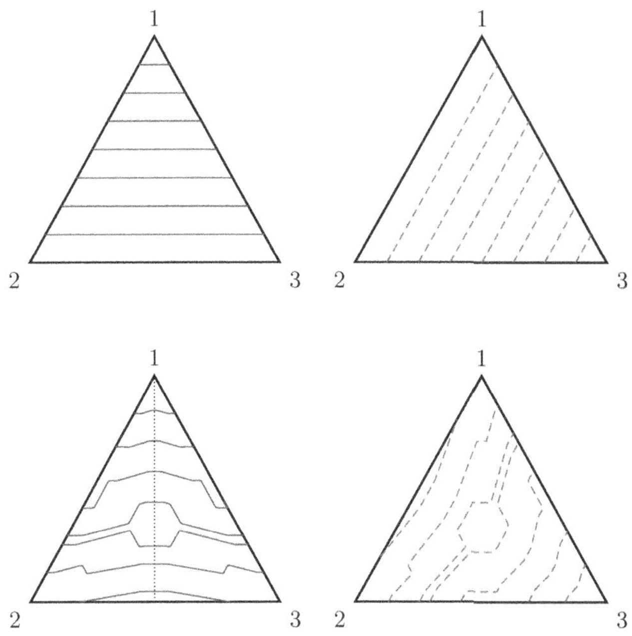

Fig. 8.2 Indifference curves of the dynamic utility in the rotating dictator equilibrium

of the bottom row of Figure 8.2 shows that similar forces operate when $\delta = \frac{6}{10}$, although now the equilibrium is considerably more complex and its construction significantly more involved.

The rotating dictator equilibrium has several interesting properties. First, players prefer policies that maintain their share of the resource but make the other players' shares unequal. For example, in the left bottom part of Figure 8.2, starting on the dotted line and moving horizontally towards the edges of the policy space typically increases player 1's dynamic utility. This preference arises endogenously; the more unequal the other players are, the more accommodating will the disadvantaged of the two players be as a responder and hence the stronger the bargaining position of player 1 as a proposer next period.

Second, in the rotating dictator equilibrium, the dynamic utilities lack quasi-concavity, the acceptance sets might not be convex, and the acceptance correspondence might not be lower hemicontinuous.[7] These results highlight the difficulties in working with the dynamic legislative bargaining games because the endogenous objects are not guaranteed to be well-behaved.

Finally, K04 notes that there are multiple rotating dictator equilibria.[8] The subsequent work finds other equilibria and culminates in AS15 who study a significantly more general model and show that large number of outcomes can be supported by SMPE when players become arbitrarily patient.[9] Their model features general number of players, policy space $X = \{x \in \mathbb{R}^n_+ : \sum_{i \in N} x_i \leq 1\}$ that allows waste, any quota voting rule, and heterogeneous recognition probabilities, discount factors and nonlinear utilities.

[7] Acceptance set is the set of policies that would be accepted given some status-quo. Acceptance correspondence maps status-quos to acceptance sets.

[8] Kalandrakis [54] extends the rotating dictator equilibrium to a more general class of games.

[9] Bowen and Zahran [26] construct a *compromise* equilibrium in which more than a minimum winning coalition is allocated a positive share in each period. Their construction relies on risk-sharing incentives. By additionally allowing waste, Richter [68] constructs an *equal division* equilibrium. Baron and Bowen [16] independently use a construction similar to AS15. Our discussion focuses on the latter since its construction is also applicable to spatial bargaining [7]. Baron [15] simplifies the construction in Baron and Bowen [16] and studies equilibrium coalitions and proposal power.

The argument in AS15 is constructive and we describe its main features for n odd and a threshold voting rule with quota $q \in [\frac{n+1}{2}, n)$. Thus, $\mathcal{W}(s_t) = \{C \subseteq N : |C| \geq q\}$. The key ingredient is a concept called *simple solutions*. A simple solution consists of n policies. For each player i, each of these policies allocates either a bad share b_i or a good share $g_i > b_i$ to i, with policy x^i being a good policy and at least one other policy being a bad policy for i. In addition, each of these policies is a good policy for at least q players. Formally, a simple solution $S = (x^j)_{j \in N}$ consists of n policies such that for all j (i) $x^j \in X$, (ii) $x^i_j \in \{b_j, g_j\}$ for all i, where $b_j < g_j$, with $x^j_j = g_j$ and $x^i_j = b_j$ for some i, and (iii) $|\{i \in N : x^j_i = g_i\}| \geq q$.

Given a simple solution S, let $B_i = \{x \in S : x_i = b_i\}$ and $G_i = \{x \in S : x_i = g_i\}$ be the set of bad and good policies in S for i, and let σ be the following strategy profile. Player i recognized to propose given status-quo x_{t-1} proposes x^i if $x_{t-1} \notin S$ and proposes x_{t-1} if $x_{t-1} \in S$. Player i responding to status-quo x_{t-1} and proposal $x \neq x_{t-1}$ accepts iff either (i) $x_{t-1} \in B_i$, or (ii) $x_{t-1} \notin S$ and $x \in G_i$, or (iii) $x_{t-1}, x \notin S$ and $u_i(x) \geq u_i(x_{t-1})$. Notice the policy dynamics induced by σ: starting from any status-quo, the equilibrium policy reaches S in at most one period and stays constant thereafter. AS15 show that the profile σ constitutes an SMPE for sufficiently patient players.

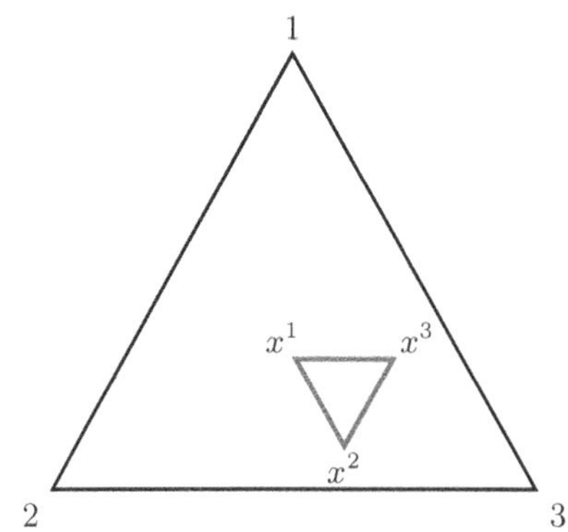

Fig. 8.3 A simple solution in the distributive model

Figure 8.3 draws part of the three-player policy space such that $\{x \in \mathbb{R}^3_+ : \sum_{i=1}^3 x_i = c\}$, where $c \in (0, 1]$, along with a simple solution $S = (x^1, x^2, x^3)$ that corresponds to vertices of an inverted equilateral triangle inscribed into the policy space. With patient players, an SMPE exists with equilibrium dynamics converging on S in at most one period. However, a continuum of simple solutions and hence SMPE outcomes exist. For example, vertices of any inverted equilateral triangle inscribed into the policy space in Figure 8.3 correspond to a simple solution, irrespective of the size of the inscribed triangle and irrespective of the value of c. Thus, any policy in $\{x \in \mathbb{R}^3_+ : \sum_{i=1}^3 x_i \leq 1\}$ can be supported as an equilibrium outcome including policies with strictly positive share allocated to all players or with waste. The only policies that cannot be supported in equilibrium are those that assign zero share to two or three players.[10]

8.5 Spatial Policy

The spatial dynamic legislative bargaining literature starts with Baron [13]. In his model players choose the scale of collective goods from policy space $X = \mathbb{R}_+$ and each player i has a strictly concave utility with bliss-point θ_i. The state s_t includes the policy x_{t-1} from the previous period, and, for any state s_t, $X(s_t) = X$, $\mathcal{W}(s_t) = \{C \subseteq N : |C| \geq \frac{n+1}{2}\}$, and $\zeta(s_t) = x_{t-1}$. Players have a common discount rate δ. Kalandrakis [55] (henceforth K16) and Zápal [72] (henceforth Z16) analyze three-player models similar to Baron [13]. This is the version of the model we study here: three players with quadratic stage utilities, bliss-points $\theta_L = -1$, $\theta_M = 0$ and $\theta_R = 1$ and equal recognition probabilities choose policies from $\mathbb{R}$.[11]

As shown by Z16, this model admits a pure strategy SMPE. We first discuss the asymmetric equilibrium shown in Figure 8.4 and later turn

[10] With n players, the only policies ruled out by equilibrium are those where $n - q + 1$ or more players receive zero share.

[11] Baron [13] assumes existence of a 'dynamic median' voter, which is guaranteed to exist when stage utilities are quadratic [12, 36].

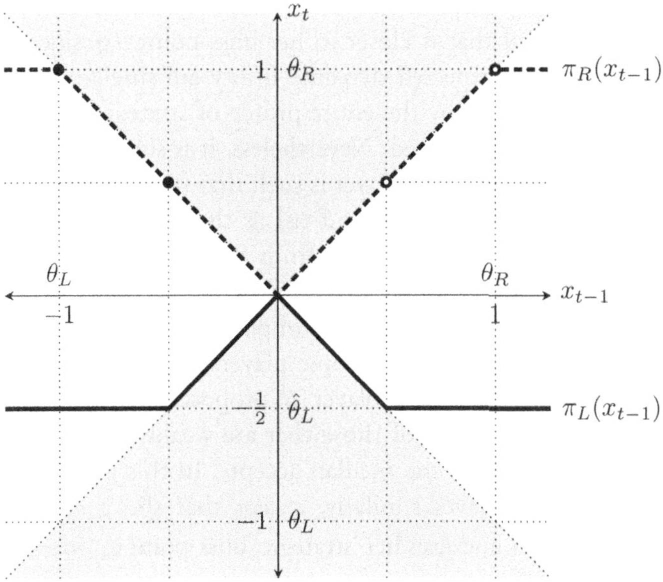

Fig. 8.4 Asymmetric pure strategy equilibrium in the spatial model

to other (symmetric and asymmetric) equilibria.

In Figure 8.4, for relevant subset of the policy space, the white area is the acceptance correspondence induced by the equilibrium voting strategies while the π_L and π_R functions are the equilibrium proposal strategies of players L and R. We do not show the equilibrium proposal strategy of the median player M; for any status-quo, she proposes her bliss-point $\theta_M = 0$ (e.g., given status-quo $x_{t-1} = -1$, a proposal is accepted iff it falls into $[-1, 1]$, and players L, M and R propose $-\frac{1}{2}$, 0 and 1 respectively).

The shape of the acceptance correspondence is identical to the one that would arise with a myopic median player: the median player accepts any proposal that is weakly closer to her bliss-point $\theta_M = 0$ than the status-quo. To see this, first note that the shape of the acceptance correspondence is driven by the dynamic preferences of player M. This follows because under quadratic utilities the decisiveness of player M in voting over deterministic alternatives extends into the decisiveness of player M

in voting over stochastic policy paths [12, 36]. Second, the median player accepts any proposal that is closer to her bliss-point θ_M since both her stage utility and her expected dynamic utility are single-peaked at θ_M. The latter is determined by the entire profile of strategies and its single-peakedness cannot be assumed. Nevertheless, it is single-peaked because the proposal strategy of every player is such that (i) given any status-quo, any proposal made is accepted, and (ii) as the status-quo moves away from θ_M, the proposals move away from θ_M, and hence the expected dynamic utility of the median player decreases.

The shape of the proposal strategies of players L and R are also related to those that would arise with myopic players as in Romer and Rosenthal [70]: for any status-quo, player R proposes the policy closest to his bliss-point $\theta_R = 1$ out of those that are weakly closer to θ_M than the status-quo and hence the median accepts. In this asymmetric equilibrium, player L behaves similarly, except that she is not using her bliss-point $\theta_L = -1$ and uses her 'strategic' bliss-point $\hat{\theta}_L = -\frac{1}{2}$ instead. Because $\hat{\theta}_L = -\frac{1}{2}$ is closer to $\theta_M = 0$, that is, it is more moderate than $\theta_L = -1$, we call this behavior *moderation*.

Why does player L moderate? Her incentive to do so is strategic and is driven by the endogenous status-quo. Consider status-quo $x_{t-1} = -1$. We claim player L proposes $\hat{\theta}_L = -\frac{1}{2}$ in equilibrium. To see this, consider a one-stage deviation to propose $\theta_L = -1$, which is the policy that maximizes L's static utility. Both of these policies are accepted given the status-quo. Player L proposes $\hat{\theta}_L = -\frac{1}{2}$ instead of $\theta_L = -1$ in order to constrain the proposed policy of player R if this player is recognized in the next period: player R's policy will be 1 if player L proposes $\theta_L = -1$ now, while player R's policy will be $\frac{1}{2}$ if player L proposes $\hat{\theta}_L = -\frac{1}{2}$ now (Figure 8.4 highlights these policies by dots in its left half). That is, player L moderates in equilibrium using the acceptance set of the median player M and the endogenous status-quo to constrain the future policies of her opponent player R.

Why does *not* player R moderate? Player R has the same incentive to constrain the policies of player L. Consider status-quo $x_{t-1} = 1$. We claim player R proposes $\theta_R = 1$ in equilibrium. To see this, consider a one-stage deviation to propose $x_t = \frac{1}{2}$. Both of these policies are accepted given the status-quo. However, the only effect of moderating and proposing $x_t = \frac{1}{2}$ rather than $\theta_R = 1$ is for player R to constrain herself if she is recognized next period: player R's policy will be $\frac{1}{2}$ if she proposes $x_t = \frac{1}{2}$ now and will be 1 if she proposes $\theta_R = 1$ (Figure 8.4 highlights these policies by circles in its right half). In order to constrain the policy of player L, player R would have to moderate to some proposal below $\frac{1}{2}$, which is too costly for her in terms of the foregone static utility. That is, the incentive to moderate is a *strategic substitute*: because player L moderates, she is effectively constraining herself and player R has no incentive to moderate. Because player R does not moderate, her strategic bliss-point coincides with her bliss-point.

Equilibrium moderation and its strategic substitute nature are two key insights of the model. But the model delivers additional observations. First, in order to simplify the exposition, we have chosen $\delta = \frac{3}{4}$, identical recognition probabilities and particular bliss-points such that the strategic bliss-point of player L is $\hat{\theta}_L = -\frac{1}{2}$. For general values of these parameters, the strategic bliss-point of a non-median player i is $\theta_i(1 - 2\delta r_{-i})$, where r_{-i} is the recognition probability of player $\{L, R\} \setminus \{i\}$ (Z16). That is, the strategic bliss-point is a point where two forces offset each other. The first force is standard: policies are pushed towards players' bliss-points. The second force is strategic: players moderate in order to constrain their opponents. The second force intensifies moderating the strategic bliss-point of a player when the player becomes more patient and when the probability of recognition of her opponent increases. In fact, when $1 - 2\delta r_{-i} < 0$, player i's incentive to moderate is strong enough for this player to propose $\theta_M = 0$ for any status-quo in equilibrium.

Second, because the game underlying Figure 8.4 is symmetric, it is intuitive that a mirror equilibrium exists in which player L does not moderate and uses a proposal strategy with her bliss-point $\theta_L = 1$, while player R moderates and uses a proposal strategy with strategic bliss-point $\hat{\theta}_R = \frac{1}{2}$. This multiplicity is driven by the strategic substitute nature of moderation: when player L moderates player R has no incentive to do so, while when player L does not moderate player R has incentive to do so. However, this multiplicity is non-generic and restricted to symmetric games [73].

Third, K16 shows that the game underlying Figure 8.4 admits a symmetric mixed strategy SMPE. Figure 8.5 shows key features of this equilibrium. For status-quos outside $X_m = \left[-\frac{3}{2}, -\frac{1}{2}\right] \cup \left[\frac{1}{2}, \frac{3}{2}\right]$, both players L and R use strategies similar to those from Figure 8.4, *except* that both players use strategies with moderate strategic bliss-points $\hat{\theta}_L = -\frac{1}{2}$ and $\hat{\theta}_R = \frac{1}{2}$ respectively. For any status-quo $x_{t-1} \in X_m$, player R mixes over two proposals $|x_{t-1}|$ and $\hat{\theta}_R = \frac{1}{2}$ putting probability $|x_{t-1}| - \frac{1}{2}$ on the latter. Player L mixes in the similar way over $-|x_{t-1}|$ and $\hat{\theta}_L = -\frac{1}{2}$. (Figure 8.5 shows the mixing probabilities for $x_{t-1} \in X_m$.) This equilibrium is symmetric and does not inherit the strategic substitute nature of moderation and, interestingly, features policies outside the set of statically Pareto efficient policies $[-1, 1]$ that are proposed and accepted with strictly positive probability.

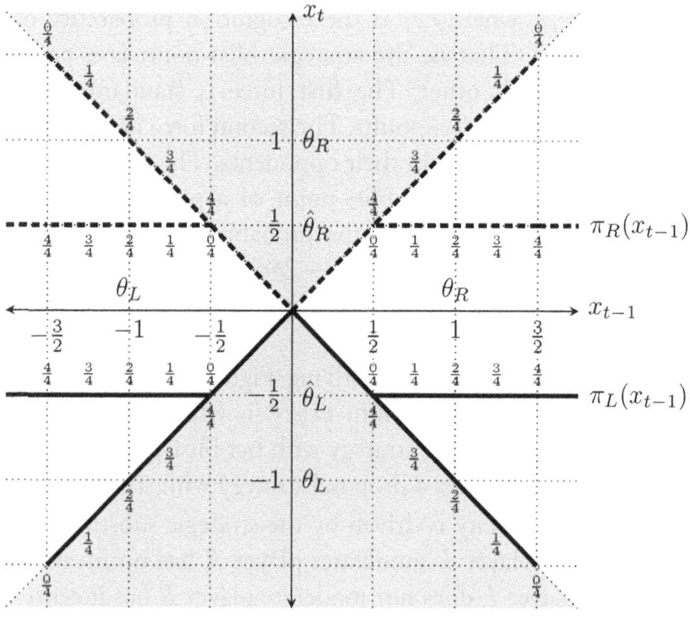

Fig. 8.5 Symmetric mixed strategy equilibrium in the spatial model

The game underlying Figures 8.4 and 8.5 features three symmetric players and admits multiple SMPE. Going beyond this setup opens new questions, some of which has been tackled by existing work. First, generalizations of the model that have been studied include versions with three asymmetric players (Z16), with general number of players [73], and with multi-dimensional policy spaces and general utility functions [18, 71, 7, 14]. No study of the model with general voting rule exists.

Do all equilibria involve moderation driven by strategic incentives? In fact, Dziuda and Loeper [43, 44] highlight that bargaining with an endogenous status-quo leads to strategic polarization in bilateral bargaining. The logic behind the *moderating effect* just discussed and their *polarizing effect* is the same: with an endogenous status-quo a policy determines both the current and future policies. Consider player L and two policies $x < x'$ both in $[\theta_L, \theta_M]$. In the equilibrium described in Figure 8.4, both x and x' are revised when player R proposes, but x is revised to a policy that is worse for L than the policy x' is revised to. Although player L prefers x to x', policy x brings about worse policies than x', and hence L's preference for x becomes moderate or even reverses as a result of an endogenous status-quo. Dziuda and Loeper [43] study equilibria in which policies are unlikely to be revised, because acceptance of a policy requires unanimity. In these equilibria, player L prefers x to x' and x brings about better policies than x', and hence L's preference for x becomes stronger as a result of an endogenous status-quo. An endogenous status-quo thus induces moderation over policies that are revised when they become status-quo and polarization over policies that remain unchanged. The contrast between Dziuda and Loeper [43, 44] and Z16 highlights the importance of voting rule on polarization.

Finally, our understanding of dynamic bargaining models with changing preferences is limited. Several papers partially advanced in this direction: [67] assume fixed proposer; [40] compute equilibria numerically; [43, 44] have two policies in the policy space; [10] have three policies; [26, 27, 28] focus on two-period models. Similarly limited is our understanding of models with a stochastic drift in policies [29, 30], or models with endogenously changing policy spaces [31].

8.6 Efficiency

Are the equilibrium outcomes of the dynamic legislative bargaining models efficient? Answering this requires a framework for thinking about (in)efficiency of political outcomes. One possibility is to follow Besley and Coate [22] who draw a parallel with general equilibrium theory: one defines feasible allocations and uses players' preferences to decide, without reference to the process that determines which allocations arise, whether an allocation is Pareto efficient or not, and, only then, looks at the allocations that arise as a result of an economic or political process.

Let ω_t be the variables included in state s_t apart from x_{t-1}, i.e., $s_t = (x_{t-1}, \omega_t)$, and let $\boldsymbol{\omega} = (\omega_t)_{t=0}^{T} \in \Omega$. An allocation is a contingent sequence of policies $(\mathbf{x}^{\omega})_{\omega\in\Omega} = ((x_t^{\omega})_{t=0}^{T})_{\omega\in\Omega}$ and is feasible if $x_t^{\omega} \in X(x_{t-1}^{\omega}, \omega_t)$ for all t and $\boldsymbol{\omega}$.[12] A feasible allocation $(\mathbf{x}^{\omega})_{\omega\in\Omega}$ is *ex-ante dynamically Pareto efficient* if there is no feasible allocation $(\mathbf{y}^{\omega})_{\omega\in\Omega}$ such that $(1-\delta_i)\mathbb{E}_{\omega}[\sum_{t=0}^{T}\delta_i^t u_i(y_t^{\omega}, (y_{t-1}^{\omega}, \omega_t))] \geq (1-\delta_i)\mathbb{E}_{\omega}[\sum_{t=0}^{T}\delta_i^t u_i(x_t^{\omega}, (x_{t-1}^{\omega}, \omega_t))]$ for all $i \in N$, with at least one inequality strict. For given $\boldsymbol{\omega}$, feasible $\mathbf{x}^{\omega}$ is *ex-post dynamically Pareto efficient in* $\boldsymbol{\omega}$ if there is no feasible $\mathbf{y}^{\omega}$ such that $(1-\delta_i)\sum_{t=0}^{T}\delta_i^t u_i(y_t^{\omega}, (y_{t-1}^{\omega}, \omega_t)) \geq (1-\delta_i)\sum_{t=0}^{T}\delta_i^t u_i(x_t^{\omega}, (x_{t-1}^{\omega}, \omega_t))$ for all $i \in N$, with at least one inequality strict. Looking at a single period t, $x_t \in X(s_t)$ is *statically Pareto efficient in* s_t if there is no $y_t \in X(s_t)$ such that $u_i(y_t, s_t) \geq u_i(x_t, s_t)$ for all $i \in N$, with at least one inequality strict.

General characterization of Pareto efficient policy sequences is an open question.[13] Nevertheless, we make the following general observations. First, in the distributive setting with policy space $\{x \in \mathbb{R}_+^n : \sum_{i\in N} x_i \leq 1\}$, ex-ante dynamic Pareto efficiency in the special case of

---

12 The variable $\boldsymbol{\omega}$ is what [Mas-Colell et al. 60, chapter 19] call a state and should be understood as a 'complete description of a possible outcome of uncertainty' (page 688). Our contingent policy sequences are analogous to (state) contingent commodities, one of the central concepts in general equilibrium under uncertainty.

13 See Anesi and Seidmann [9] for a discussion. Typically, Pareto efficient allocations maximize utility of one player subject to a lower bound on the utilities of the other players. See [Mas-Colell et al. 60, chapter 16] and Duggan [38] for details.

linear preferences and homogeneous discount factors requires that policies do not involve waste, and, otherwise, requires that policy sequences allocate larger shares to more patient players in later periods. The rotating dictator equilibrium of Kalandrakis [53] is thus ex-ante dynamically Pareto efficient, unlike many of the equilibria constructed by Anesi and Seidmann [9], which are efficient only in special cases.

Second, with risk averse players, ex-ante dynamic Pareto efficiency requires that policies track (only) the preference or policy space relevant variables included in the states. Formally, an ex-ante dynamically Pareto efficient$(\mathbf{x}^{\boldsymbol{\omega}})_{\boldsymbol{\omega}\in\Omega}$ needs to satisfy $\mathbf{x}^{\boldsymbol{\omega}} \neq \mathbf{x}^{\boldsymbol{\omega}'}$ iff $\boldsymbol{\omega}$ and $\boldsymbol{\omega}'$ differ in preference and policy space relevant variables. The inefficiency arising when policies are insensitive to relevant variables and are sensitive to irrelevant variables is what Bowen et al. [25] call, respectively, gridlock and political risk. The latter is another source of inefficiency in Anesi and Seidmann [9], while the former is a source of efficiency in Piguillem and Riboni [63, 64], by serving as an (endogenous) commitment.

Third, if $(\mathbf{x}^{\boldsymbol{\omega}})_{\boldsymbol{\omega}\in\Omega}$ is ex-ante dynamically Pareto efficient, then, for each $\boldsymbol{\omega}$, the policy sequence $\mathbf{x}^{\boldsymbol{\omega}}$ is ex-post dynamically Pareto efficient in $\boldsymbol{\omega}$, and $x_t^{\boldsymbol{\omega}}$ is statically Pareto efficient in $(x_{t-1}^{\boldsymbol{\omega}}, \omega_t)$ for each ω_t.[14] This means that the static Pareto inefficiencies noticed by Riboni and Ruge-Murcia [67], Dziuda and Loeper [43, 44] and Kalandrakis [55] imply ex-post and ex-ante dynamic Pareto inefficiencies. The former three papers single out the endogenous status-quo, under which policies determine players' future bargaining position, as the source of the inefficiency. The opposite holds in Bowen et al. [24] where endogenous status-quo improves efficiency , while Bowen et al. [25] suggest that efficiency might be achieved by combining exogenous and endogenous status-quo. These contrasting results show that the link between endogenous status-quo and efficiency is not fully understood.

---

[14] See Mas-Colell et al. [60], chapter 19.D) for sketch of the argument.

8.7 Open Questions

We end with what we deem to be open questions, beyond the ones already mentioned. First, Anesi and Duggan [7] show that the large multiplicity of SMPE observed by Anesi and Seidmann [9] for the distributive model extends to other environments. Their result requires infinite horizon, continuous policy space, patient players, absence of veto players, and strictly positive recognition probabilities and hence does not apply to a number of papers.[15] Nevertheless, their work highlights that the literature lacks an equilibrium refinements that would restore the predictive power of the models it studies. Eraslan and Piazza [48] propose refining MPE to ensure that the property chosen to refine MPE is satisfied in (i) a single player version of the model, and (ii) a finite horizon version of the model. Specifically, they restrict attention to strategies that satisfy a shape restriction that is also satisfied by the optimal policy of a dictator. Remarkably, the refinement allows them to fully characterize equilibria. Gersbach et al. [49] use similar refinement to establish a unique equilibrium.

Second, although the surveyed literature includes a number of applications, further, especially economically relevant ones, should provide novel insights.[16] In particular, the dynamic nature of the surveyed models seems to be well suited to the study of debt (see [65, 23], for headways), dynamic issues of taxation (see [63, 59], for existing work), and should be embedded in realistic macro models (see [50, 11], for early examples).

Third, a study of incomplete information is missing, which is an obvious gap. Possible developments in this spirit include dynamic bargaining with a stochastic pie size (as in [61]), or dynamic bargaining with privately-observed type-dependent preferences (see [4], for an initial contribution).

---

[15] For example, Anesi [3], Diermeier and Fong [34], Dziuda and Loeper [43, 44], Anesi and Duggan [6], Diermeier et al. [33] study models with finite policy spaces, Buisseret and Bernhardt [27, 28], Chen and Eraslan [31] focus on finite horizon, Duggan et al. [42], Diermeier et al. [33], Nunnari [62] include veto players, and Riboni and Ruge-Murcia [67], Riboni [66], Diermeier and Fong [35] feature fixed proposers.

[16] A partial list of applications includes studies of lobbying [56], precedents [2, 32], mandatory versus discretionary public spending [24, 25, 64], environmental policies [10], experimentation [5].

Finally, very little effort has been devoted to testing the predictions of the surveyed models. The limited existing evidence comes from laboratory experiments ([21, 20, 19, 17, 62, 1], see also the chapter on laboratory experiments in this volume by Marina Agranov) and we are not aware of any evidence using observational data.

References

1. Marina Agranov, Christopher Cotton, and Chloe Tergiman. Persistence of power: Repeated multilateral bargaining with endogenous agenda setting authority. *Journal of Public Economics*, 184:104–126, 2020.
2. Luca Anderlini, Leonardo Felli, and Alessandro Riboni. Why stare decisis? *Review of Economic Dynamics*, 17(4): 726–738, 2014.
3. Vincent Anesi. Noncooperative foundations of stable sets in voting games. *Games and Economic Behavior*, 70(2): 488–493, 2010.
4. Vincent Anesi. Dynamic legislative policy making under adverse selection. *NICEP Working Paper Series*, No. 2018-06, 2018.
5. Vincent Anesi and T. Renee Bowen. Policy experimentation in committees: A case against veto rights under redistributive constraints. *American Economic Journal: Microeconomics*, forthcoming. 10.1257/mic.20190023.
6. Vincent Anesi and John Duggan. Dynamic bargaining and stability with veto players. *Games and Economic Behavior*, 103: 30–40, 2017.
7. Vincent Anesi and John Duggan. Existence and indeterminacy of Markovian equilibria in dynamic bargaining games. *Theoretical Economics*, 13(2): 505–525, 2018.
8. Vincent Anesi and Daniel J. Seidmann. Bargaining over an endogenous agenda. *Theoretical Economics*, 9(2): 445–482, 2014.
9. Vincent Anesi and Daniel J. Seidmann. Bargaining in standing committees with an endogenous default. *Review of Economic Studies*, 82(3): 825–867, 2015.
10. David Austen-Smith, Wioletta Dziuda, Bård Harstad, and Antoine Loeper. Gridlock and inefficient policy instruments. *Theoretical Economics*, 14: 1483–1534, 2019.
11. Marina Azzimonti, Laura Karpuska, and Gabriel Mihalache. Bargaining over mandatory spending and entitlements. *Mimeo*, 2020.

12. Jeffrey S. Banks and John Duggan. A social choice lemma on voting over lotteries with applications to a class of dynamic games. *Social Choice and Welfare*, 26(2): 285–304, 2006.
13. David P. Baron. A dynamic theory of collective goods programs. *American Political Science Review*, 90(2): 316–330, 1996.
14. David P. Baron. Elections and durable governments in parliamentary governments. *Journal of Theoretical Politics*, 30(1): 74–118, 2018.
15. David P. Baron. Simple dynamics of legislative bargaining: Coalitions and proposal power. *Economic Theory*, 67(1): 319–344, 2019.
16. David P. Baron and T. Renee Bowen. Dynamic coalitions. *Mimeo*, 2015.
17. David P. Baron, T. Renee Bowen, and Salvatore Nunnari. Durable coalitions and communication: Public versus private negotiations. *Journal of Public Economics*, 156: 1–13, 2017.
18. David P. Baron and Michael C. Herron. A dynamic model of multidimensional collective choice. In Ken Kollman, John H. Miller, and Scott E. Page, eds., *Computational models in political economy*, pp. 13–48. MIT Press, Cambridge, MA, 2003.
19. Marco Battaglini, Salvarore Nunnari, and Thomas R. Palfrey. The political economy of public debt: A laboratory study. *Journal of the European Economic Association*, forthcoming. 10.1093/jeea/jvz031.
20. Marco Battaglini, Salvatore Nunnari, and Thomas R. Palfrey. Legislative Bargaining and the dynamics of public investment. *American Political Science Review*, 106(2): 407–429, 2012.
21. Marco Battaglini and Thomas R. Palfrey. The dynamics of distributive politics. *Economic Theory*, 49(3): 739–777, 2012.
22. Timothy Besley and Stephen Coate. Sources of inefficiency in a representative democracy: A dynamic analysis. *American Economic Review*, 88(1): 139–156, 1998.
23. Laurent Bouton, Alessandro Lizzeri, and Nicola Persico. The political economy of debt and entitlements. *Review of Economic Studies*, forthcoming. 10.1093/restud/rdaa003.
24. T. Renee Bowen, Ying Chen, and Hülya Eraslan. Mandatory versus discretionary spending: The status quo effect. *American Economic Review*, 104(10): 2941–2974, 2014.
25. T. Renee Bowen, Ying Chen, Hülya Eraslan, and Jan Zápal. Efficiency of flexible budgetary institutions. *Journal of Economic Theory*, 167: 148–176, 2017.
26. T. Renee Bowen and Zaki Zahran. On dynamic compromise. *Games and Economic Behavior*, 76(2): 391–419, 2012.

27. Peter Buisseret and Dan Bernhardt. Dynamics of policymaking: Stepping back to leap forward, stepping forward to keep back. *American Journal of Political Science*, 61(4): 820–835, 2017.
28. Peter Buisseret and Dan Bernhardt. Reelection and renegotiation: International agreements in the shadow of the polls. *American Political Science Review*, 112(4): 1016–1035, 2018.
29. Steven Callander and Keith Krehbiel. Gridlock and delegation in a changing world. *American Journal of Political Science*, 58(4): 819–834, 2014.
30. Steven Callander and Gregory J. Martin. Dynamic policymaking with decay. *American Journal of Political Science*, 61(1): 50–67, 2017.
31. Ying Chen and Hülya Eraslan. Dynamic agenda setting. *American Economic Journal: Microeconomics*, 9(2): 1–32, 2017.
32. Ying Chen and Hülya Eraslan. Learning while setting precedents. *RAND Journal of Economics*, forthcoming.
33. Daniel Diermeier, Georgy Egorov, and Konstantin Sonin. Political economy of redistribution. *Econometrica*, 85(3): 851–870, 2017.
34. Daniel Diermeier and Pohan Fong. Legislative Bargaining with reconsideration. *Quarterly Journal of Economics*, 126(2): 947–985, 2011.
35. Daniel Diermeier and Pohan Fong. Characterization of the von Neumann-Morgenstern stable set in a non-cooperative model of dynamic policymaking with a persistent agenda setter. *Games and Economic Behavior*, 76(1): 349–353, 2012.
36. John Duggan. Majority voting over lotteries: Conditions for existence of a decisive voter. *Economics Bulletin*, 34(1): 263–270, 2014.
37. John Duggan. Existence of stationary Bargaining equilibria. *Games and Economic Behavior*, 102: 111–126, 2017a.
38. John Duggan. Notes on optimization and Pareto optimality. *Mimeo*, 2017b.
39. John Duggan and Tasos Kalandrakis. Dynamic legislative policy making. *University of Rochester Wallis Institute of Political Economy Working Paper Series*, No. 45, 2007.
40. John Duggan and Tasos Kalandrakis. A Newton collocation method for solving dynamic Bargaining games. *Social Choice and Welfare*, 36(3–4): 611–650, 2011.
41. John Duggan and Tasos Kalandrakis. Dynamic legislative policy making. *Journal of Economic Theory*, 147(5): 1653–1688, 2012.

42. John Duggan, Tasos Kalandrakis, and Vikram Manjunath. Dynamics of the presidential veto: A computational analysis. *Mathematical and Computer Modelling*, 48(9–10): 1570–1589, 2008.
43. Wioletta Dziuda and Antoine Loeper. Dynamic collective choice with endogenous status quo. *Journal of Political Economy*, 124(4): 1148–1186, 2016.
44. Wioletta Dziuda and Antoine Loeper. Dynamic pivotal politics. *American Political Science Review*, 112(3): 580–601, 2018.
45. Dennis Epple and Michael H. Riordan. Cooperation and punishment under repeated majority voting. *Public Choice*, 55(1): 41–73, 1987.
46. Hülya Eraslan and Kirill S. Evdokimov. Legislative and multilateral bargaining. *Annual Review of Economics*, 11(1): 443–472, 2019.
47. Hülya Eraslan, Kirill S. Evdokimov, and Jan Zápal. Dynamic legislative bargaining. *The Institute of Social and Economic Research Osaka University Discussion Paper Series*, No. 1090, 2020.
48. Hülya Eraslan and Adriana Piazza. Efficiency with political power dynamics and costly policy change. *Mimeo*, 2019.
49. Hans Gersbach, Matthew O. Jackson, Philippe Muller, and Oriol Tejada. Electoral competition with costly policy changes: A dynamic perspective. *Mimeo*, 2020.
50. Daryna Grechyna. Mandatory spending, political polarization, and macroeconomic volatility. *MPRA Working Paper Series*, No. 83452, 2017.
51. Wei He and Yeneng Sun. Stationary Markov perfect equilibria in discounted stochastic games. *Journal of Economic Theory*, 169: 35–61, 2017.
52. Daniel E. Ingberman. Running against the status quo: Institutions for direct democracy referenda and allocations over time. *Public Choice*, 46(1): 19–43, 1985.
53. Anastassios Kalandrakis. A three-player dynamic majoritarian Bargaining game. *Journal of Economic Theory*, 116(2): 294–322, 2004.
54. Tasos Kalandrakis. Minimum winning coalitions and endogenous status quo. *International Journal of Game Theory*, 39(4): 617–643, 2010.
55. Tasos Kalandrakis. Pareto efficiency in the dynamic one-dimensional Bargaining model. *Journal of Theoretical Politics*, 28(4): 525–536, 2016.
56. Gilat Levy and Ronny Razin. Dynamic legislative decision making when interest groups control the agenda. *Journal of Economic Theory*, 148(5):1862–1890, 2013.
57. Yehuda Levy. Dicounted stochastic games with no stationary Nash equilibrium: Two examples. *Econometrica*, 81(5): 1973–2007, 2013.

58. Yehuda John Levy and Andrew McLennan. Corrigendum to: "Discounted stochastic games with no stationary Nash equilibrium: Two examples". *Econometrica*, 83(3): 1237–1252, 2015.
59. Yanlei Ma. Curse or blessing? On the welfare consequences of divided government and policy gridlock. *Mimeo*, 2014.
60. Andreu Mas-Colell, Michael D. Whinston, and Jerry R. Green. *Microeconomic Theory*. Oxford University Press, Oxford, 1995.
61. Antonio Merlo and Charles Wilson. A stochastic model of sequential bargaining with complete information. *Econometrica*, 63(2): 371–399, 1995.
62. Salvarore Nunnari. Dynamic legislative bargaining with veto power: Theory and experiments. *Mimeo*, 2018.
63. Facundo Piguillem and Alessandro Riboni. Dynamic Bargaining over redistribution in legislatures. *Mimeo*, 2013.
64. Facundo Piguillem and Alessandro Riboni. Spending-biased legislators: Discipline through disagreement. *Quarterly Journal of Economics*, 130(2): 901–949, 2015.
65. Facundo Piguillem and Alessandro Riboni. Fiscal rules as Bargaining chips. *Mimeo*, 2018.
66. Alessandro Riboni. Committees as substitutes for commitment. *International Economic Review*, 51(1): 213–236, 2010.
67. Alessandro Riboni and Francisco J. Ruge-Murcia. The dynamic (in)efficiency of monetary policy by committee. *Journal of Money, Credit and Banking*, 40(5): 1001–1032, 2008.
68. Michael Richter. Fully absorbing dynamic compromise. *Journal of Economic Theory*, 152: 92–104, 2014.
69. William H. Riker. *The theory of political coalitions*. Yale University Press, London, 1962.
70. Thomas Romer and Howard Rosenthal. Bureaucrats versus voters: On the political economy of resource allocation by direct democracy. *Quarterly Journal of Economics*, 93(4): 563–587, 1979.
71. Jan Zápal. Simple Markovian equilibria in dynamic spatial legislative Bargaining. *CERGE-EI Working Paper Series*, No. 515, 2014.
72. Jan Zápal. Markovian equilibria in dynamic spatial legislative Bargaining: Existence with three players. *Games and Economic Behavior*, 98: 235–242, 2016.
73. Jan Zápal. Simple Markovian equilibria in dynamic spatial legislative bargaining. *European Journal of Political Economy*, 63: 101816, 2020.

Part II

Applications

9

Legislative Bargaining Experiments

Marina Agranov

9.1 Introduction

In this chapter we survey the experimental literature on legislative bargaining in committees. Legislative committees are typically comprised of three or more members, each representing her own group of constituencies, and are charged with making decisions using a pre-specified set of rules and procedures dictated by institutions in place. The focus of our survey will be on understanding the effects of these rules on policies chosen by committees and bargaining process per se.

M. Agranov (✉)
California Institute of Technology, Pasadena, CA, USA
e-mail: magranov@hss.caltech.edu

E. Karagözoğlu and K. B. Hyndman (eds.), *Bargaining*,
https://doi.org/10.1007/978-3-030-76666-5_9

We will not cover the papers that deal with two-person bargaining games or unstructured bargaining.[1]

From a methodological point of view, we focus on incentivized controlled laboratory experiments, which fall into the economics tradition. The chapter starts with a short description of the methodology used in laboratory experiments. The remainder of the chapter looks at the two main types of committees: ad hoc or temporary committees (one-time decisions) and standing committees (repeated decisions by the same committee). Rather than summarizing every experimental paper on this topic, the chapter will attempt to identify the main insights about the effects of institutional rules on the bargaining process and bargaining outcomes.

9.2 Methodology of Laboratory Experiments

Laboratory experiments in Political Science follow the principles of Experimental Economics developed by Vernon Smith in the early 1970s, and further advanced by Charles Plott, who was one of the first to study the effects of political institutions and rules on policy outcomes in non-market settings such as committees, elections, and juries.[2,3] The approach pioneered by Smith and Plott is the marriage of theory and experimental designs (Plott and Smith 1978).

At the heart of theory-based experiments is the creation of simple yet real economic environments, in which we observe real subjects making decisions with real economic consequences. While the settings studied in these experiments are usually very complex, the objective of the experiments is to provide clean tests of core theories of human behavior; theories that are often hard to test using field data due to the scarcity of

[1] See Roth (1995) and Palfrey (2015) for excellent surveys of two-person bargaining experiments and unstructured bargaining.

[2] See, for instance, the influential paper by Fiorina and Plott (1978) who experimentally test the basic theory of the core in small committees and examines its robustness with respect to the fine details of committee rules.

[3] For the survey of the early history of Experimental Economics see Roth (1993).

such data, unobservability of counterfactuals, endogeneity problems, and other confounding factors that prevent identification of causal effects. If theoretical predictions fail in the simplest and most transparent version of the model, i.e., in the laboratory experiment, that casts serious doubt on the usefulness of the theory as applied to complex settings.

The key features of the laboratory experiments are control, incentives, and replicability. Participants in the experiments operate under a controlled and carefully designed set of institutional rules and are provided monetary incentives that are linked to their behavior and reflect trade-offs captured by theory. These incentives are crucial, as hypothetical behavior may diverge from how participants behave when their decisions have real consequences measured in monetary terms. Finally, most of the experiments frame the task in a neutral way avoiding labels that may influence participants' decisions. The advantages of context-free designs include the ease of replicability and general inferences that one can make about effects of institutions on behavior absent any specific context. For the literature discussing the methodology of controlled laboratory experiments see Davis and Holt (1993), Roth (1988), and Smith (1976, 1989).

9.3 Ad hoc Committees

Experimental literature on legislative multilateral bargaining originated with studies of ad hoc committees that distribute fixed budgets among members with conflicting interests, i.e., the divide-the-dollar game. The conflict of interest between members represents the classical economic problem of scarcity of resources since each member would like to deliver a higher share to her constituencies. The workhorse model in this literature is Baron and Ferejohn (1989). It provides a natural and parsimonious formulation of the bargaining protocol, which lends itself easily to incorporation of various institutional features present in real committees. As a result, it serves as a theoretical benchmark for many experimental papers that investigate the effects of institutional rules on implemented policies.

9.3.1 Overview of Baron and Ferejohn (1989) Model

A committee of size n decides how to allocate a unit of resources among its members; i.e., this is the divide-the-dollar game. Each committee member is a legislator representing constituencies in her district. The game has an infinite-horizon with common discount factor $\delta \in (0, 1]$ applied between bargaining stages. The discounting captures the cost of delay in reaching the agreement. Each member cares about the share allocated to her district only; i.e., the utility of member i when proposal x with share x_i allocated for member i is implemented in stage t is $U_i = \delta^{t-1} x_i$. The bargaining protocol is an extension of the two-person bargaining protocol of Rubinstein (1982) to a multi-person bargaining situation. Specifically, the recognition rule specifies the probability that each member is selected to be the proposer in a bargaining stage, and the voting rule specifies the number of votes required to pass the proposal. At the beginning of each bargaining stage, based on the recognition rule, one member is selected to be the proposer. The proposer submits a budget allocation $x = (x_1, x_2, ..., x_n)$ where $\sum_{i=1}^{n} x_i \leq 1$ and $x_i \geq 0$ for all i. Committee members observe the allocation vector x and vote either to support or to reject it. If the proposal receives the required number of positive votes, then the allocation is implemented and the game is over. If, however, the proposal fails, then the committee moves on to the next bargaining stage, in which again one of the members is selected to serve as the proposer based on the recognition rule and she proposes an allocation, which is then put to a vote. The process repeats itself until one of the proposals obtains the required number of votes; otherwise, all members receive zero payoffs.

This game admits a plethora of subgame-perfect equilibria: for sufficiently high δ and n any allocation can be maintained as part of a subgame perfect equilibrium. To increase the predictive power of this model, the literature has focused on the stationary equilibria (SSPE), which restrict attention to memoryless strategies.[4] The unique symmetric SSPE in the case of a uniformly random recognition rule prescribes the

[4] See Baron and Kalai (1993) who argue that a stationary subgame-perfect equilibrium is the simplest and therefore most likely subgame-perfect equilibrium.

proposer to allocate positive shares to a minimum winning coalition and appropriate the remainder of resources. Specifically, if $q \leq n$ votes are required to pass the proposal, then $q - 1$ randomly selected members are invited into a coalition and receive $x^{\text{Coalition}} = \frac{\delta}{n}$, while the proposer gets a larger share of $x^{\text{AS}} = 1 - (q - 1)\frac{\delta}{n}$; the remaining members get nothing. The coalition partners vote in favor of the proposal, which guarantees that agreement occurs immediately without any delay.

In the remainder of this section, we survey experimental papers that address many variants of this basic game focusing on games with an infinite horizon. Palfrey (2015) surveys the finite-horizon lab implementations of the Baron-Ferejohn model.

9.3.2 Bargaining Protocol

The first laboratory experiment to investigate the infinite-horizon model of Baron-Ferejohn is Frechette, Kagel, and Lehrer (2003).[5] The experiment compares two types of amendment rules: the closed one, in which submitted proposals are immediately put to a vote, and the open one, in which submitted proposals are subject to possible amendment by a randomly selected committee member. The theory predicts that the equilibrium in the game with the open amendment rule might feature delays in agreements, larger than minimum winning coalitions, and smaller proposers' shares compared with the game with the closed amendment rule.

Frechette et al. (2003) test these predictions using five-member committees and observe that the main theoretical predictions regarding the effects of amendment rules are borne out in the data. Specifically, the closed rule produces no delays, while there is considerable delay in the open rule committees. Proposers enjoy higher shares than any other committee members in both rules, with the closed rule featuring higher proposers' shares than the open rule. However, in both treatments, proposers appropriate a much smaller fraction of resources than the theory predicts even after subjects play the game many times. Finally,

[5] For the very first test of Baron-Ferejohn model see McKelvey (1991) who implements the finite-horizon version of the game.

despite the fact that parameters of the game were chosen so that only minimum winning coalitions should arise in both treatments, larger than minimum winning coalitions are frequent in the open rule committees, while the most common coalition size is minimum winning in the closed rule committees.

What determines bargaining power of players in multilateral bargaining games? Frechette et al. (2005a, b) design a series of experiments to separate out two natural suspects: the voting power, i.e., the number of votes controlled by each member and the recognition power, i.e., the likelihood of being selected to serve as a proposer. The authors conduct experiments, in which they vary voting and recognition powers one at time and contrast predictions of the Baron-Ferejohn model with Gamson's Law, which is the popular competing model of coalition formation in Political Science. According to Gamson's Law, coalition members receive shares of resources proportional to the voting power that they bring to the coalition. The experimental data shows that the Baron-Ferejohn model organizes results better than Gamson's Law; however the fit of the Baron-Ferejohn model is not perfect.[6]

Does the bargaining protocol per se have an effect on what transpires during bargaining sessions and which outcomes are implemented? This is the question studied by Frechette et al. (2005c) who compare two bargaining protocols: the Baron-Ferejohn protocol and the alternative model of bargaining developed by Morelli (1999) called the demand bargaining model. According to the demand bargaining model, committee members are randomly ordered and make sequential demands until a subset of feasible demands emerges that holds a majority share of votes. If there is no feasible winning coalition when all members have had their turn to speak, then the process starts all over again with discounted payoffs. Theoretically, the demand bargaining model predicts allocations which are proportional to voting weights and no first mover advantage.[7]

[6] See also Maaser et al. (2019) who compare three nominally different representations of majority rule in a Baron-Ferejohn game with five players and find that while inexperienced players respond to the framing of the voting rule, effects are weak for experienced players.

[7] Breitmoser and Tan (2013) study experimentally a simultaneous version of the demand bargaining game with three players, in which two non-proposers submit demands to the proposer, who proposes an allocation after observing these demands. If at least one demand

The experiment considers five-member committees without discounting, two bargaining protocols and two sets of parameters: one, in which all voters have equal voting weights, and another, in which one member has three times the voting weight as other members. The data shows that in demand bargaining sessions, proposals are more likely to pass in the first bargaining stage as compared with Baron-Ferejohn sessions. Most of the implemented allocations are minimum winning in both bargaining protocols. In the treatment with equal voting weights, the first-mover appropriates a higher share of resources compared with other coalition members in both protocols; this advantage is stronger in the Baron-Ferejohn sessions. However, in the treatment with unequal voting weights, proposers who control higher numbers of votes appropriate shares comparable to those of other coalition partners, and overall, the outcomes are much more similar between the two bargaining protocols than the theory predicts.

9.3.3 Voting Rules and Continuation Values

The effects of voting rules are explored in Miller and Vanberg (2013, 2015). Miller and Vanberg (2013) compare three-person committees that use majority and unanimity voting rules focusing on delay in bargaining. The theory predicts immediate agreement irrespective of the number of votes required to pass the proposal. In fact, the only differences between the two voting rule treatments should be the number of non-agenda setter players that are included in the coalition and the proposer's share. Consistent with the theory, experimental results show that majority committees feature mostly minimum winning coalitions, while the unanimity committees feature all-inclusive coalitions. However, contrary to the theory, unanimity committees take longer to reach agreements and, moreover, while proposers appropriate higher shares of resources than any other committee member, these shares are below those predicted by the theory. These results speak to the work of Buchanan and Tullock (1962) who argue in favor of approximate

is satisfied by this allocation, then it is implemented and the game ends. Otherwise, the next bargaining round begins.

unanimity rules given that less inclusive voting rules involve higher external costs of collective decisions defined as the cost associated with the coercion of the minority. In a follow-up paper Miller and Vanberg (2015) consider the effect of group size (three-person versus seven-person committees) on the frequency of delay in bargaining under both voting rules. Under the unanimity rule, the delays occur equally often in both large and small committees, while under the majority rule , the delays are more frequent in large than in small committees.

Frechette and Vespa (2017) zoom in on the voting behavior of non-proposers. The authors vary subjects' discount factors to generate substantial variation in their continuation values and uncover the determinants of voting in favor of the proposal. The results show that about 90% of all voting choices are consistent with the equilibrium prediction of voting in favor of a proposal whenever one's own share is higher or equal to the continuation value. This suggests that the equilibrium voting rule formulated based on the continuation value principle organizes data better than alternative behavioral rules which do not take continuation values into account.

Breitmoser and Tan (2017) compare a standard infinite-horizon Baron-Ferejohn game with discount factor $\delta = 0.95$ with a one-period game, in which players are paid their continuation payoffs from the first game if they do not reach agreement in the first period of the game. While the two games are strategically equivalent for payoff-maximizing players, the experimental results show substantial differences, which are best explained by the reference dependent altruism model, according to which a player's degree of altruism is low if her payoff is below the reference point and high otherwise.

9.3.4 Voting Power

Kagel, Sung and Winter (2010) study the effect of granting some members veto power which can inefficiently prolong the process of reaching the agreement and award its holder excessive power. The authors study the three-member committees with and without a veto player and vary costs of delay. While, in theory, no delay should be observed in either treatment, there are more delays in committees with a veto player especially when the cost of delay is low. Most of the difference comes from the inability of non-veto proposers to pass their proposed allocations right away. Results show that veto players obtain significantly higher shares when serving as proposers than both other non-veto proposers and proposers in the control treatment with no veto power; however, these shares of the veto proposers are still below the theoretically predicted ones. Consistent with the theory, the increase in the costs of delay increases the willingness of players without veto power to accept lower shares. Finally, the authors conduct an additional treatment in which they disentangle the proposer power and the veto power and find that veto power trumps proposer power.

Drouvelis, Montero, and Sefton (2010) study changes in voting power driven by adding new committee members holding fixed the budget and the voting rule. The authors find that the addition of a new member has differential effects on the bargaining power of the original members depending on whether the original members had veto power or not.[8]

9.3.5 Communication

Several recent papers have analyzed the effects of cheap-talk communication that precedes formal bargaining. Theoretically, it is not clear why communication should have any effect in the Baron-Ferejohn game, since this is the game with complete information, in which one should be able to compute players' continuation values without talking to each other. Consistent with this intuition, SSPE predictions in the Baron-Ferejohn game do not change when bargainers have access to communication channels.

Agranov and Tergiman (2014) study five-member committees that use the majority voting rule and allow members to send any free-form messages to any subset of the committee before the proposer submits the allocation for the vote. The results show that the introduction of

[8] For the investigation of a vote of confidence procedure, which links the survival of a winning coalition to the successful passage of a bill in a finite-horizon Baron-Ferejohn game see Tergiman (2015).

communication moves outcomes closer to those predicted by SSPE: delays almost never happen, the vast majority of passed allocations feature minimum winning coalitions, and, most importantly, proposers appropriate significantly *higher* shares when communication is allowed. The mechanism that drives these results resembles an auction for a place in the coalition, which occurs between the non-proposers. Given that a simple majority is enough to pass a proposal, non-proposers compete with each other for a place in the coalition by announcing their reservation prices. The proposer exploits this competition and invites into the coalition the 'cheapest' members and appropriates the remaining resources. Baranski and Kagel (2015) confirm these results and the mechanism underlying them with the committees of three members.

The introduction of communication in unanimity committees leads to very different outcomes. Agranov and Tergiman (2019) show that in unanimity committees communication leads to *more* egalitarian outcomes and significantly reduces delay in reaching agreements as documented by Miller and Vanberg (2013) in experiments without communication. The differential effect of communication in unanimity versus majority committees comes from different uses of communication channels in the two voting rules. In the majority committees, most communication is private and contains conversations about amounts non-proposers are willing to support in the voting stage, while in the unanimity committees, most communication is public and contains conversations about fairness, equality and social concerns. These conversations despite being cheap-talk affect the behavior of proposers, especially in the unanimity treatment, in which each member de facto has a veto power.

Merkel and Vanberg (2020) introduce explicit costs to communication: every second of communication increases the probability that the game is terminated before a proposal can be made, in which case each player receives an exogenously fixed value with the sum of values being smaller than the budget size. The results show that the unanimity rule leads to longer communication delays and more frequent breakdowns especially when disagreement values are asymmetric.

9.3.6 Bargaining with Public Goods and Public Policy

Frechette, Kagel and Morelli (2012) study a modification of the Baron-Ferejohn game, in which a budget can be allocated to both public good and private transfers to individual members of the legislature. Members value both a public good and private transfers and the experiment varies the parameter α, which governs the relative weight members attach to private goods in their payoff function. This experiment is based on the theoretical paper by Volden and Wiseman (2007), which predicts full investment in the public good for low values of α and no investment in the public good for high α. For the intermediate values of α, we should observe both public and private goods, with a somewhat counterintuitive prediction that the investment in the public good increases with α, which results in a non-monotonic relationship between α and the proposer's private share.[9] The experimental results are at odds with this last prediction for the intermediate values of α, but track theory closely for low and high values of α. Other characteristics of bargaining outcomes are similar to those observed in previous Baron-Ferejohn games: delays are rare, proposers' shares tend to be higher than those of other coalition partners but lower than predicted and minimum winning coalitions are frequent (in the appropriate region). Overall, consistent with the experimental literature on the voluntary provision of public goods , public good provision is substantially higher than predicted (see the survey of voluntary public good games by Ledyard [1995]).

Christiansen et al. (2014) consider a related but different setting in which a three-person legislature bargains over the public policy with or without the availability of private goods. The experiment is based on the model of Jackson and Moselle (2002). In all treatments, members have a single-peaked preferences over public policy with different ideal policies. In addition, in a treatment with private goods, there is a fixed budget available to be distributed between committee members. The bargaining protocol is standard with an equal recognition rule and no discounting. Theoretically, in games without private goods the median

[9] This prediction is driven by the linearity in preferences and does not hold for more general types of preferences.

preferred policy should emerge. Under the parameterization used in the experiments, in games with private goods, we expect to see the shift in average implemented policy (towards one of the extreme legislators) and positive probability of coalitions that exclude the median legislator and instead consist of two extremists. Experimental results show the shift in location of public policy when private transfers are introduced, which is in line with the theoretical prediction. First stage proposals are much more likely to pass in games with private transfers than in games without private transfers consistent with the "greasing the wheels" interpretation of private transfers. Total welfare of the committees is generally higher when private transfers are available.[10] All this evidence highlights the positive role of private transfers in bargaining in ad hoc committees.

9.3.7 Bargaining over Endogenous Budgets

Several recent papers investigate the Baron-Ferejohn bargaining game augmented by the production stage in which surplus to be divided through bargaining is created. Baranski (2016, 2018) compares the two versions of such a game: the redistributive game, in which the production stage precedes the bargaining stage, and the pre-distribution game, in which the production stage occurs after the bargaining stage. The production of a joint surplus resembles the public good game, i.e., players allocate their endowment between private consumption and investment in the joint project; the sum of contributions into the joint project is scaled up by a factor of two to produce the joint budget. The bargaining stage follows the standard Baron-Ferejohn protocol with equal recognition probabilities, majority voting rule and no discounting. Theoretically, the production stage in the redistribution game is similar to the standard public good game, since shares allocated to subjects in the bargaining stage are independent of their contributions. Thus, the theory predicts no individual investments in the production stage. In the pre-distribution game, the proposer is expected to appropriate the whole budget, and, thus, he is the only one expected to contribute his

[10] Christiansen et al. (2018) study how framing of the bargaining problem affects bargaining outcomes in a similar environment.

whole endowment to the joint production. In the experiment, individual contributions in the two games are different but not consistent with the theory predictions. In the redistribution game, investments rise with experience towards an efficient rather than an equilibrium outcome. In the pre-distribution game, subjects' contributions decline over time and joint budgets converge to zero. Contrary to the theory, many coalitions are all-inclusive rather than minimum winning, which drives down proposers' shares. Finally, in the redistribution game players obtain shares proportional to their individual contributions, while in the pre-distribution game, players free-ride in the production stage, which results in unravelling towards no contributions.

Merkel and Vanberg (2019) compare how claims based on contributions to production affect bargaining behavior under the majority and unanimity rule in a redistribution game, in which the budget to be divided is produced by an individual real effort task. Under both voting rules, observed outcomes constitute a convex combination of equal-splits and splits proportional to relative contributions.[11] Taken together, these studies suggest that distribution of endogenously created budgets are quite different from exogenous ones despite the fact that the same bargaining protocol is used to govern the bargaining process.

9.3.8 Effect of Malapportionment

Vespa (2016) explores legislative committees which consist of members who represent communities of different sizes. He studies two commonly used institutions that introduce malapportionment in voting power in legislative committees, which are meant to protect the rights of minority groups. The two institutions are bicameralism and weighted voting. The bicameralism system requires the approval of a proposal from two chambers, House and Senate, and implements proportional representation in the House and a fixed number of senators in the Senate. Weighted voting has a unicameral committee with higher representation

[11] Gantner et al. (2016) compare different bargaining procedures, all of which require unanimous consent to reach agreement, and also find that fairness judgments reflect individual contributions.

of more populated states. The experiment is concerned with understanding how implemented allocations change in response to the two institutions described above and to changes in the recognition probability of members representing groups of constituencies of different sizes, i.e., states. Several treatments are conducted with variation in the institution used to pass the proposals as well as the recognition probability of members. All treatments use a variant of the Baron-Ferejohn bargaining protocol with a closed amendment rule and no discounting. The results show support for qualitative prediction of the theory, which suggests that proposer power can be used to equalize per-capita allocations under bicameralism, but not under weighted voting. Under bicameralism, final allocations feature no difference across members representing states of different sizes if all members have the same probability of being recognized as the proposer. On the contrary, members representing small states appropriate a higher per-capita share of resources under weighted voting and in case recognition probabilities are malapportioned under bicameralism.

9.4 Standing Committees

Many bargaining situations involve repeated interactions. This is certainly true in legislatures which operate by standing committees that interact repeatedly year after year and bargain over the allocation of scarce resources over the sequence of budget cycles rather than just once. The experimental literature on dynamic bargaining , which we survey below, is still in its infancy and has been developing rapidly over the past few years.

9.4.1 Dynamic Bargaining with Endogenous Status quo

The first studies of dynamic bargaining introduced dynamics by linking decisions of the committee over several budget cycles via endogenous status quo determined by previously implemented outcomes. The game was introduced theoretically by Kalandrakis (2004) and studied experimentally by Battaglini and Palfrey (2012). In the game, the committee with n members must decide in each of an infinite number of periods how to allocate a fixed budget among its members using the majority voting rule. The agenda setter is selected randomly in every period. If the allocation proposed by the agenda setter receives a majority of votes, then this allocation is implemented, the current cycle ends, the committee moves on to the next bargaining cycle and the implemented allocation becomes the status quo for the next cycle. However, if the current proposal fails to achieve the support of the majority, then the status quo policy is implemented. Theoretically, there exists a Markov Perfect Equilibrium in undominated strategies, in which regardless of the initial status quo, the trajectory of implemented allocations converges to a rotating dictatorship with the current proposer appropriating the whole budget and such allocations passing without any delay.

Experiments conducted by Battaglini and Palfrey (2012) consider several versions of this game with three-member committees and discount factor $\delta < 1$. In two of the three treatments, the set of possible allocations was limited, while in the third treatment proposals could be any three-way split of the budget with fine grid. The allocations in the first two treatments were chosen in such a way that the three-way equal split is the Condorcet winner and the absorbing state in the first treatment and a Condorcet loser in the second treatment. The experimental results were quite mixed with the second treatment showing patterns most closely tracked by theoretical predictions. The unconstrained third treatment shows a lot of egalitarian outcomes, which are not predicted by the theory. The authors show that concavity of utility (instead of linearity assumed in the theory) is able to decrease the gap between theoretical predictions and observed outcomes.

9.4.2 The Effects of Communication

Baron, Bowen, and Nunnari (2017) extend the unrestricted treatment of Battaglini and Palfrey (2012) by allowing the committee members to communicate with each other either through a public chat or privately and study the effects of communication on bargaining outcomes and the coalition formation process. Similar to the results obtained by Battaglini and Palfrey (2012), when communication channels are not available, dictatorial outcomes are almost never observed, most outcomes feature all-inclusive coalitions, and less than a third are minimum winning coalitions. Private communication decreases the fraction of all-inclusive coalitions and boosts the number of minimum winning coalitions to nearly half of all outcomes. In contrast, public communication increases the number of all-inclusive coalitions and essentially eliminates minimum winning coalitions. Durable coalitions emerge more frequently and last longer when communication is allowed. The contents of communication logs show patterns similar to the ones observed in the static bargaining games with communication (see Agranov and Tergiman 2014). In particular, public communication by non-proposers is correlated with all-inclusive three-way allocations. Moreover, advocating for fairness increases the fraction of an all-inclusive allocation, while advocating for minimal winning coalitions and one's own allocation decreases this fraction.

9.4.3 Veto Power

The introduction of the veto players in the dynamic bargaining may lead to status quo inertia and even larger leverage of the veto players as compared with the static bargaining games with veto players. Nunnari (2019) investigates experimentally these concerns by studying a dynamic bargaining game with three players and an endogenous status quo . The experiment manipulates the strength of dynamic incentives captured by a variation in the players' degree of patience (discounting) and the presence of a veto player. The empirical investigation of this setting is particularly warranted since even when one focuses on the Markov Perfect Equilibria, theoretical predictions depend strongly on the assumptions about the space of feasible allocations, initial status quo , and discount factors (see Diermeier et al. 2017; Nunnari 2018). Experimental results show that in games with a veto player most outcomes allocate a positive share to the veto player and to at most one non-veto player, and allocations which give most resources to the veto player are stable and absorbing state with share of the veto player gradually increasing over time. Further, the frequency of dictatorial and all-inclusive three-way coalitions does not depend on players' patience, and allocations that give a substantial amount of resources to both non-veto players are more likely to survive when committee members are more patient.

9.4.4 Public Good Accumulation

Several papers have considered the ability of legislatures to provide public goods in dynamic settings. These papers consider a legislature with n members which divides a fixed budget between durable public good and private transfers to individual members over a sequence of periods. Members value both public good and private transfers. The bargaining protocol is the Baron-Ferejohn protocol with a randomly chosen proposer in every period. The passage of a proposal requires obtaining the support of q members. If the proposal fails, then the status-quo policy with no public good investment is implemented.

The first paper of this kind is Battaglini, Nunnari, and Palfrey (2012) who study an infinite-horizon model. Theoretically, Markov Perfect Equilibria feature a monotonic relation between the steady-state provision of public goods and the voting rule: higher q implies higher provision of public goods.[12] Battaglini et al. (2012) test theory predictions with five-member committees, no depreciation, and three different voting treatments: unanimity rule ($q = 5$), majority rule ($q = 3$) and dictatorship rule ($q = 1$). Experimental results confirm the main comparative static predictions of Markov perfect equilibria: a higher q leads to higher investment in the public good. However, similar to the static voluntary provision public good experiments and the public good provision in static legislatures described above, the authors observe significant over-investment in the public good in the early rounds of play

[12] There are two effects at play. First, similar to the static environment, a higher q forces the agenda setter to internalize a larger share of the public good. Second, a higher q reduces the worry about the future proposers' incentives to appropriate the current public good investments, which is only present in dynamic settings.

for all three voting rules. This over-investment is mainly compensated by disinvestments in the later rounds in all three treatments. Within each bargaining round, most of the proposals pass without invoking the status-quo and most feature allocation of private transfers to minimum winning coalitions.

Agranov et al. (2016) design an experiment to empirically estimate relative magnitudes of static and dynamic distortions in a dynamic bargaining game. The experiment utilizes variation in depreciation rates across treatments in order to identify the importance of dynamic linkage between periods, and decomposes dynamic distortions into two types of distortions: crowding-out effect and durability effect. Experimental results show that dynamic inefficiencies can be large and increase with a dynamic link across periods. Among the two types of dynamic distortions, the durability effect is large in magnitude, while the crowding-out effect is less pronounced. The analysis of individual strategies shows that many subjects choose high public good investments in the first periods of the game and then shift towards minimum winning coalitions, excluding members who do not invest enough in the public good in early periods and rewarding those who do by including them in their coalitions.

Finally, Battaglini et al. (2019) modify this game by introducing the possibility of borrowing and lending between periods and uncertainty about the future value of the public good. The theory predicts that the proposer issues too much debt and uses these funds for private transfers to get the support of members of the minimum winning coalition. The amount of debt is decreasing in the size of the required majority and converges to an efficient level for the unanimity rule. For a fixed voting rule, the equilibrium level of debt is decreasing in the probability that the public good has a high value in the future. The treatments vary the voting rules, the distribution of the future public good value, and the presence of commitment. The experimental results show many patterns consistent with the theory. Public policies are inefficient, and efficiency is increasing in the number of votes required to pass the proposals, q. Observed levels of debt are lower when the probability of future negative shocks is higher. When proposers can commit to a policy in early periods, the dynamic distortions are essentially eliminated. However, contrary to the theory, most of the time subjects choose allocations which are budget-balanced in each period of the game, which leads to lower distortions than predicted. In addition, consistent with the insights of the static bargaining experiments, higher q leads to more delays in reaching the agreements.

9.4.5 Agenda Setting Rules

Agranov, Cotton, and Tergiman (2020) consider the dynamic bargaining settings without the status-quo structure, and, instead, focus on the agenda-setting rules. The paper studies both theoretically and experimentally two versions of the infinitely repeated multilateral divide-the-dollar game: the Endogenous Power game and the Random Power game. In the Endogenous Power game, the proposer can hold onto power across bargaining rounds as long as she maintains the support of a majority of other members. In the Random Power game, the proposer is chosen randomly in every bargaining round. Under the standard stationarity refinement, the two games are outcome equivalent, since stationarity rules out the ability of the proposer to reward those who supported her in the past. This eliminates any incentives that players have to keep a proposer in power, and results in high turn-over of proposers and outcome-equivalence in both games. Contrary to the theory, the experimental analysis shows substantial differences in behavior and outcomes across the games. In the Endogenous Power game, proposers use institutional rules to their advantage and remain in power for long stretches of time. This, coupled with the fact that proposers obtain on average higher shares than other members creates a high level of inequality in the long-run payoffs between committee members. Slightly over half of observed coalitions are minimum winning, while the remaining are all inclusive coalitions. In general, the evolution of coalitions across cycles features stability across several dimensions: coalition size, identity of coalition partners and their shares. On the contrary, when rotation in proposers' power is institutionalized as in the Random Power game, persistence of power is not possible by design, which reduces the inequality in members' long-run payoffs. This also affects which types of coalitions are formed and passed within each round. Most outcomes in the Random Power game feature all inclusive coalitions with equal splits among all members. Overall, the experimental data clearly show that in both games, subjects use strategies that involve punishments, reciprocity and history dependence—all properties that contradict the stationarity refinement. This casts serious doubts on the ability of the stationary refinement to organize the data for the dynamic bargaining games despite its very good fit in the one-shot bargaining games.

9.5 Future Directions

As is apparent from this short survey, we have accumulated a much more nuanced understanding of how institutional details of the bargaining process affect bargaining dynamics and outcomes in the ad hoc committees that are dissolved after reaching the agreement. Much less is known about the functioning of standing committees which interact repeatedly. Existing studies of dynamic bargaining paint a clear picture which prevents a simple extrapolation of results from one-shot bargaining environments to the dynamic ones. This makes future studies of dynamic bargaining environments both exciting and complex due to the many forms that dynamic interactions take in legislatures. The progress in this literature will crucially depend on the dialog between two dimensions: (a) the development of appropriate theoretical refinements that can narrow down the set of possible outcomes and bargaining trajectories one can expect to emerge in dynamic environments, and (b) the collection of richer data sets which will be used to evaluate theoretical predictions and inform the theory of missing forces.

References

Agranov, Marina, and Chloe Tergiman (2014) "Communication in Multilateral Bargaining," *Journal of Public Economics* 118: 75–85.

Agranov, Marina, and Chloe Tergiman (2019) "Communication in Bargaining Games with Unanimity," *Experimental Economics*, forthcoming.

Agranov, Marina, Guillaume Frechette, Thomas Palfrey, and Emanuel Vespa (2016) "Static and Dynamic Underinvestment: An Experimental Investigation," *Journal of Public Economics* 14: 125–141.

Agranov, Marina, Christopher Cotton, and Chloe Tergiman (2020) "Persistence of Power: Dynamic Multilateral Bargaining," *Journal of Public Economics* 184.

Baranski, Andrzej, and John H. Kagel (2015) "Communication in Legislative Bargaining," *Journal of the Economic Science Association* 1: 59–71.

Baranski, Andrzej (2016) "Voluntary Contributions and Collective Redistribution," *American Economic Journal: Microeconomics* 8(4): 149–173.

Baranski, Andrzej (2018) "Endogenous Claims and Collective Production: An Experimental Study of the Timing of Profit-Sharing Negotiations," *Experimental Economics*.

Baron, D. P., and J. A. Ferejohn (1989) "Bargaining in Legislatures," *The American Political Science Review* 83(4): 1181–1206.

Baron, David, Renee Bowen, and Salvatore Nunnari (2017) "Durable Coalitions and Communication: Public versus Private Negotiations," *Journal of Public Economics* 156: 1–13.

Baron, David, and Ehud Kalai (1993) "The Simplest Equilibrium of a Majority-rule Division Game," *Journal of Economic Theory* 61: 290–301.

Battaglini, Marco, and Thomas Palfrey (2012) "The Dynamics of Redistributive Politics," *Economic Theory* 49(3): 739–777.

Battaglini, Marco, Salvatore Nunnari, and Thomas Palfrey (2012) "Legislative Bargaining and the Dynamics of Public Investment," *American Political Science Review* 106(2): 407–429.

Battaglini, Marco, Salvatore Nunnari, and Thomas Palfrey (2019) "The Political Economy of Public Debt: A Laboratory Study," *Journal of the European Economic Association*, forthcoming.

Breitmoser, Y., and J. H. Tan (2013) "Reference Dependent Altruism in Demand Bargaining," *Journal of Economic Behavior & Organization* 92: 127–140.

Breitmoser, Y., and J. H. Tan (2017) "Why Should Majority Voting Be Unfair?," *Journal of Economic Behavior & Organization.*

Buchanan, James and Gordon Tullock (1962) *The Calculus of Consent: Logical Foundations of Constitutional Democracy*. Ann Arbor: University of Michigan Press.

Christiansen, N., John Kagel, and Sotiris Georganas (2014) "Coalition Formation in a Legislative Voting Game," *American Economic Journal: Microeconomics* 6.

Christiansen, N., Tanushree Jhunjhunwala, and John Kagel (2018) "Gains versus Costs in Legislative Bargaining," working paper.

Davis, Douglas, and Charles Holt (1993) *Experimental Economics*. Princeton, NJ: Princeton University Press. Chapter 1, Introduction and Overview.

Diermeier, Daniel, Georgy Egorov, and Konstantin Sonin (2017) "Political Economy of Redistribution," *Econometrica* 85(3): 851–870.

Drouvelis, M., M. Montero, and M. Sefton (2010) "Gaining Power Through Enlargement: Strategic Foundations and Experimental Evidence," *Games and Economic Behavior* 69(2): 274–292.

Fiorina, Morris, and Charles R. Plott (1978) "Committee Decisions Under Majority Rule: An Experimental Study," *American Political Science Review* 72: 575–598.

Frechette, Guillaume, John H. Kagel, and Steven F. Lehrer (2003) "Bargaining in Legislatures: An Experimental Investigation of Open versus Closed Amendment Rules," *American Political Science Review* 97: 221–232.

Frechette, Guillaume, John H. Kagel, and Massimo Morelli (2005a) "Gamson's Law versus Non-Cooperative Bargaining Theory," *Games and Economic Behavior* 51: 365–390.

Frechette, Guillaume, John H. Kagel, and Massimo Morelli (2005b) "Nominal Bargaining Power, Selection Protocol, and Discounting in Legislative Bargaining," *Journal of Public Economics* 89: 1497–1517.

Frechette, Guillaume, John H. Kagel, and Massimo Morelli (2005c) "Behavioral Identification in Coalitional Bargaining: An Experimental Analysis of Demand Bargaining and Alternating Offers," *Econometrica* 73: 1893–1937.

Frechette, Guillaume R., John H. Kagel, and Massimo Morelli (2012) "Pork Versus Public Goods: An Experimental Study of Public Good Provision Within a Legislative Bargaining Framework," *Economic Theory* 49(3): 779–800.

Frechette, Guillaume, and Emanuel Vespa (2017) "The Determinants of Voting in Multilateral Bargaining Games," *Journal of the Economic Science Association* 3(1): 26–43.

Gantner, A., K. Horn, and R. Kerschbamer (2016) "Fair and Efficient Division Through Unanimity Bargaining When Claims Are Subjective," *Journal of Economic Psychology* 57: 56–73.

Jackson, Matthew and Boaz Moselle (2002) "Coalition and Party Formation in a Legislative Voting Game," *Journal of Economic Theory* 103(1): 49–87.

Kagel, John H., Hankyoung Sung, and Eyal Winter (2010) "Veto Power in Committees: An Experimental Study," *Experimental Economics* 31(2): 167–188.

Kalandrakis, Tasos (2004) "A Three-player Dynamic Majoritarian Bargaining Game," *Journal of Economic Theory* 116: 294–322.

Ledyard, John O. (1995) "Public Goods Experiments." In J. Kagel and A. Roth (eds.) *Handbook of Experimental Economics*. Princeton: Princeton University Press.

Maaser, N., F. Paetzel, and S. Traub (2019) "Power Illusion in Coalitional Bargaining: An Experimental Analysis," *Games and Economic Behavior* 117: 433–450.

McKelvey, Richard D. (1991) "An Experimental Test of a Stochastic Game Model of Committee Bargaining." In *Contemporary Laboratory Research in Political Economy*. Ann Arbor: University of Michigan Press.

Merkel, Anna, and Christoph Vanberg (2019) "Legislative Bargaining with Joint Production: An Experimental Study," Working Papers 0670, University of Heidelberg.

Merkel, Anna, and Christoph Vanberg (2020) "Legislative Bargaining with Costly Communication," *Public Choice* 183: 3–27.

Miller, Luis, and Christoph Vanberg (2013) "Decision Costs in Legislative Bargaining: An Experimental Analysis," *Public Choice* 155: 373–394.

Miller, Luis, and Christoph Vanberg (2015) "Group Size and Decision Rules in Legislative Bargaining," *European Journal of Political Economy* 37: 288–302.

Morelli, Massimo (1999) "Demand Competition and Policy Compromise in Legislative Bargaining," *American Political Science Review* 93: 809–820.

Nunnari, Salvatore (2018) "Dynamic Legislative Bargaining with Veto Power," working paper.

Nunnari, Salvatore (2019) "Veto Power in Standing Committees: An Experimental Study," working paper.

Palfrey, T. R. (2015) "Experiments in Political Economy". In J. H. Kagel, and A. E. Roth (eds.) *Handbook of Experimental Economics*, Vol. 2. Princeton University Press (in press).

Plott, Charles R., and Vernon L. Smith (1978) "An Experimental Examination of Two Exchange Institutions," *The Review of Economic Studies* 45: 133–153.

Roth, Alvin E. (1988) "Laboratory Experimentation in Economics: A Methodological Overview," *Economic Journal* 98: 974–1031.
Roth, Alvin E. (1995) "Bargaining Experiments." In J. H. Kagel, and A. E. Roth (eds.) *Handbook of Experimental Economics*. Princeton University Press, pp. 253–348.
Roth, Alvin E. (1993) "On the Early History of Experimental Economics," *Journal of the History of Economic Thought* 15: 184–209.
Rubinstein, Ariel (1982) "Perfect Equilibrium in a Bargaining Model," *Econometrica* 50: 97–109.
Smith, Vernon L. (1989) "Theory, Experiment and Economics," *Journal of Economic Perspectives* 3(1): 151–169.
Smith, Vernon L. (1976) "Experimental Economics: Induced Value Theory," *American Economic Review* 66: 274–279.
Tergiman, C. (2015) "Institution Design and Public Good Provision: An Experimental Study of the Vote of Confidence Procedure," *Experimental Economics* 18(4): 718–730.
Vespa, Emanuel (2016) "Malapportionment and Multilateral Bargaining: An Experiment," *Journal of Public Economics* 133: 64–74
Volden, C., and A. E. Wiseman (2007) "Bargaining in Legislatures over Particularistic and Collective Goods," *American Political Science Review* 101(1): 79–92.

10

Market Institutions, Prices and Distribution of Surplus: A Theoretical and Experimental Investigation

Nick Feltovich and Nejat Anbarcı

10.1 Introduction

In this chapter, we use a lab experiment to investigate the effects of the market institution (the rules under which prices are determined) on market outcomes such as prices, efficiency and profits. We exogenously vary the institution under which the good is traded, and we compare the outcomes. While previous studies have experimentally compared market institutions, they have typically assumed financial-market contexts with

---

Electronic supplementary material The online version of this chapter (https://doi.org/10.1007/978-3-030-76666-5_10) contains supplementary material, which is available to authorized users.

N. Feltovich (✉)
Monash University, Melbourne, VIC, Australia
e-mail: nicholas.feltovich@monash.edu

N. Anbarcı
Durham University, Durham, UK
e-mail: nejat.anbarci@durham.ac.uk

E. Karagözoğlu and K. B. Hyndman (eds.), *Bargaining*,
https://doi.org/10.1007/978-3-030-76666-5_10

buyers and sellers meeting in a central location, and emphasising double auctions (e.g., Smith 1964; Cason and Friedman 2008; Van Boening and Wilcox 2008). We instead focus on goods markets, with two primary implications. First, we adapt a decentralised directed-search setting (Montgomery 1991; Burdett et al. 2001), where sellers compete for buyers by posting prices, and buyers direct their search based on the information they receive. Directed search implies a greater role for *frictions*: even though all potential exchanges are mutually profitable, sellers may be visited by too few or too many buyers, meaning there will be both buyers and sellers who are unable to trade. Also, though our markets have equal numbers of buyers and sellers overall (either 2 sellers × 2 buyers or 3 × 3), the realisations of buyers' visit choices mean that some sellers will face *local* excess demand and others will not.

Second, our comparison involves three market institutions more typical of goods markets. Under *non-negotiable price posting* ("posting"), sellers post prices which are observed by buyers prior to the visit choice, and any trade is at the posted price. Under *negotiated prices* ("haggling"), no prices are posted; instead, the price is determined after buyers have made their visit choices, either by bilateral bargaining if the seller faces only one buyer, or by auction if the seller faces multiple buyers. Under *price posting with negotiation* ("flexible pricing"), sellers post prices that are non-binding: negotiable downwards by bargaining or upwards by auction, depending on how many buyers visit the seller. There has been some comparative theoretical analysis of these institutions and related ones (Lu and McAfee 1996; Kultti 1999; Julien et al. 2000, 2001, 2002; Albrecht et al. 2006; Camera and Selcuk 2009), but we are unaware of any previous controlled experimental studies. We also add to a small but growing literature on experiments involving directed-search markets (Cason and Noussair 2007; Anbarci and Feltovich 2013, 2018; Anbarci et al. 2015; Kloosterman 2016; Helland et al. 2017; Kloosterman and Paul 2018). In particular, we are (to our knowledge) the first to consider the possibility that the outcome depends on the number of buyers visiting a seller.

Market outcomes in our experiment are only partly in line with the theory. There are substantial deviations from point predictions, with efficiency lower under haggling and flexible pricing, and sellers' profits lower under haggling and flexible pricing but higher under posting. These deviations affect comparisons of the institutions, with observed seller profit in the 2 × 2 market *higher* under posting than under flexible pricing, the opposite sign of the theoretically predicted effect. These results may be due in part to deviations in the bargaining and auction stages. Bargaining in our haggling treatment favours the seller, who receives roughly 55% of the cake in agreements despite this being a symmetric bargaining setting. Bargaining under flexible pricing is even more skewed towards sellers, with little tendency for even high posted prices to be negotiated downwards. Auction results also favour the seller, though not to the extent implied by the theory. Disagreements are also inconsistent with the theory (though not surprising in experiments); these occur about 10% of the time in bargaining and about 3% in auctions.

10.2 Theory and Experiment

We consider $m \times n$ markets, with $m \geq 2$ sellers and $n \geq 2$ buyers. Sellers produce a single unit of a homogeneous, indivisible, perishable good. Identical buyers each have a valuation of 20 for a single unit. Trading takes place under one of three exogenously imposed market institutions (see Fig. 10.1). Under *posting*, sellers simultaneously post prices in [0, 20]. Buyers observe these prices and each simultaneously chooses a seller to visit. A seller visited by at least one buyer sells at the posted price; in the case of multiple buyers, one is chosen randomly to buy, while the other buyers are unable to buy.

Under *haggling*, sellers do not post prices, so buyers simultaneously choose a seller to visit based on zero information. If exactly one buyer visits a seller, they bargain over the price under Nash's (1953) demand

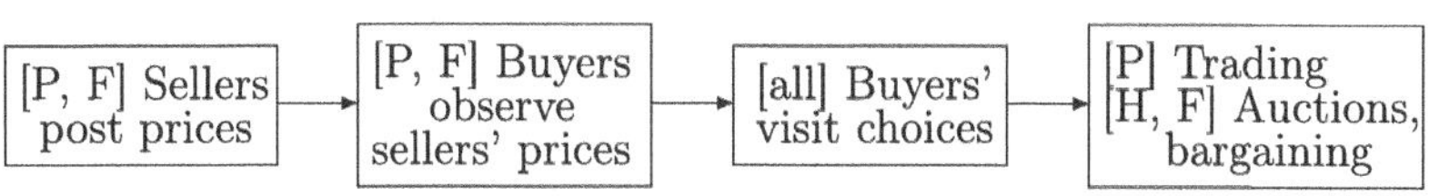

Fig. 10.1 Sequence of decisions in the experiment (P = posting, H = haggling, F = flexible pricing)

game, with buyer and seller each simultaneously proposing a single price in [0, 20]. (This is strategically equivalent to the standard formulation where each bargainer claims a share of the available surplus.) If the buyer's "bid price" is at least as high as the seller's "offer price", they trade at a price halfway between these; otherwise they do not trade. A seller visited by two or more buyers conducts a second-price auction, with buyers' bids and the seller's reserve price chosen simultaneously in [0, 20]. If one or more bids is at least as high as the reserve price, the seller sells to the highest bidder, and the price is the larger of the reserve price and the second-highest bid. If all bids are below the reserve price, the unit is "passed in" (unsold).

Our third institution, *flexible pricing*, combines aspects of the other two. Sellers post prices in [0, 20], after which buyers are informed of these and choose whom to visit. However, these prices are negotiable. If a seller posting price p^P is visited by exactly one buyer, they play a Nash demand game as under haggling, but with the bid and offer prices restricted to $[0, p^P]$. If the seller is visited by multiple buyers, there is an auction with bids and reserve price restricted to $[p^P, 20]$. The initially posted price is therefore not cheap talk, but neither is it completely binding; it can be negotiated downwards in case of a single visiting buyer, or upwards if there are multiple buyers. (The unit may also fail to be traded, as in the case of haggling.)

10.2.1 Theoretical Predictions

In our experiment, there are six combinations of institution (posting, haggling, flexible pricing) and market (2×2 and 3×3).[1] We will often abbreviate our cells as Post2, Hagg2 and Flex2 for the three 2×2 institutions, and with similar notation for the 3×3 institutions. The case of posting is analysed in detail by Burdett et al. (2001); below we discuss the

[1] The 2×2 market is the simplest non-trivial directed-search setting; the 3×3 market is the next-simplest version with no structural excess demand or excess supply, allowing the three possibilities of local excess demand, local excess supply and local market clearing each to occur with substantial frequency.

haggling and flexible-pricing cases, with additional details in the online appendix.

Bargaining/Auction Stage

When multiple buyers visit a seller, there is a second-price sealed-bid auction. All buyers have a known valuation of 20, so they all bid this amount. Then, the unit is traded with certainty at a price of 20—equal to the seller's profit—and each buyer earns zero.

When one buyer visits a seller, they propose prices p_b and p_s, respectively (constrained to be at most the posted price in the flexible-pricing treatment). Payoffs are $20 - (p_b + p_s)/2$ for the buyer and $(p_b + p_s)/2$ for the seller if $p_b \geq p_s$, and zero otherwise. Any pair of equal, feasible bid and offer prices are consistent with Nash equilibrium. To overcome this multiplicity, we impose risk dominance (Harsanyi and Selten 1988), which selects a unique equilibrium, shown in Fig. 10.2.

The unit is traded with certainty. Under flexible pricing with a posted price of p^P, the transaction price is $\min\{p^P, 10\}$, while under haggling (which in the bargaining stage can be thought of as a special case of flexible pricing with $p^P = 20$), the transaction price is 10. This is the "deal me out" outcome (Sutton 1986; Binmore et al. 1998): the available surplus is split equally unless one bargainer can unilaterally guarantee more than half of the surplus, in which case that bargainer receives

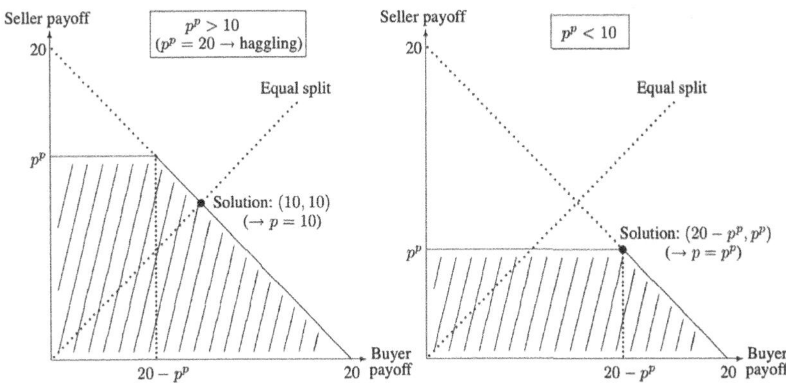

Fig. 10.2 Bargaining set (hatched area) and bargaining solution, haggling and flexible-pricing treatments

		Buyer 2	
		Visit Seller 1	Visit Seller 2
Buyer 1	Visit Seller 1	0, 0	v_1, v_2
	Visit Seller 2	v_2, v_1	0, 0

Fig. 10.3 Normal form of the 2 × 2 market with flexible pricing ($v_i = \max\{20 - p_i^p, 10\}$, with posted prices p_1^p, p_2^p)

exactly the amount she can guarantee, with the remainder going to the other bargainer. This outcome can be thought of as "the" prediction of bargaining theory, as it coincides with many other solutions (e.g., Nash 1950; Carlsson 1991).

Visit-Choice Stage

Suppose Seller i in the flexible-pricing treatment posts price p_i^p. From the discussion above, a buyer earns zero when more than one chooses the same seller, while a sole visitor to Seller i earns $v_i = \max\{20 - p_i^p, 10\}$. Hence buyers in the 2 × 2 market play a symmetric two-player game between themselves (see Fig. 10.3); in the unique symmetric Nash equilibrium, each visits Seller 1 with probability $q = v_1/(v_1 + v_2)$.

In the 3 × 3 market, they play a three-player game, also with a completely mixed symmetric equilibrium (see the online appendix for details).[2]

Since bargaining and auctions always lead to the good being traded (there is no disagreement in bargaining or passing in at an auction), the only predicted source of inefficiency is frictions: the possibility a seller is not matched due to the realisations of buyers' visit choices. In the 2 × 2 market, if each buyer visits Seller i with probability q_i, the expected number of trades is $1 + 2q_1q_2$, so efficiency (normalising to [0, 1]) is $(1 + 2q_1q_2)/2$. In the 3 × 3 market, efficiency is $[2 + 6q_1q_2q_3 - (q_1^3 + q_2^3 + q_3^3)]/3$, given visit probabilities q_1, q_2 and q_3. When all sellers post the same price, and in the special case of haggling,

[2] This is in contrast to posting, where out of equilibrium, buyers may visit the low-priced seller with certainty. Under flexible pricing, being the sole visitor to a high-price seller means bargaining for a lower price than the one posted, while being one of multiple visitors to a low-price seller means a zero profit from the auction. This reduces the importance of sensitivity to the advertised price and raises that of local market tightness (i.e., whether or not there is excess demand for that particular seller's item), compared to posted pricing.

buyers visit each seller with equal probability, so efficiency is 3/4 in the 2×2 market and 19/27 in the 3×3 market.

Price-Posting Stage

Under flexible pricing, Seller i posting price p_i^p earns zero if not visited, $\min\{p_i^p, 10\}$ if exactly one buyer visits, and 20 if two or more visit. Let Φ_1 and Φ_2, respectively, be the probabilities of Seller i being visited by exactly one and at least two buyers, computed from the buyers' equilibrium visit probabilities. Then her profit is

$$\Pi_i = \Phi_1 \cdot \min\{p_i^p, 10\} + \Phi_2 \cdot 20. \tag{10.1}$$

To find a symmetric equilibrium in prices, we first derive the first-order condition assuming all rival sellers post price p^p, then we impose symmetry ($p_i^p = p^p$). In the 2×2 market, this procedure yields a continuum of equilibria; sellers can post any price in [10, 20]. In the 3×3 market, there is a unique equilibrium in seller prices: each chooses $p^p = 20/3$.

10.2.2 Experimental Design and Hypotheses

Table 10.1 summarises the theoretical predictions underlying our hypotheses.

Table 10.1 Theoretical predictions

Cell	Market institution	Market size	Efficiency	Posted price	Transaction price All	Transaction price 1 visit	Transaction price 2+ visits	Profit Sellers	Profit Buyers
Post2	Posting	2×2	0.750	10.00	10.00	10.00	10.00	7.50	7.50
Post3		3×3	0.704	9.33	9.33	9.33	9.33	6.57	7.51
Hagg2	Haggling	2×2	0.750		13.33	10.00	20.00	10.00	5.00
Hagg3		3×3	0.704		13.68	10.00	20.00	9.63	4.44
Flex2	Flexible	2×2	0.750	10.00*	13.33	10.00	20.00	10.00	5.00
Flex3	Pricing	3×3	0.704	6.67	11.58	6.67	20.00	8.15	5.93

Note *: or any higher value up to 20.00

First, as noted above, predicted efficiency depends only on the numbers of buyers and sellers (and hence the likelihood of frictions), not on the institution itself.

Hypothesis 1: For a given market (2 × 2 or 3 × 3), efficiency is the same across all three market institutions.

Second, there are usually unambiguous order relationships for the *transaction price*—the price at which the good is traded (which may differ from the posted price)—in both 2 × 2 and 3 × 3 markets.

Hypothesis 2: Transaction prices in the 2 × 2 market are the same under either haggling or flexible pricing, and lower under posting, while those in the 3 × 3 market are highest under haggling and lowest under posting.

Since expected profits for buyers and sellers depend only on profit per trade (determined by the transaction price) and the probability of trading (determined by efficiency, which does not vary across market institutions), the hypotheses for buyers' and sellers' profits follow immediately from Hypothesis 2.

Hypothesis 3: Sellers' profits in the 2 × 2 market are the same under either haggling or flexible pricing, and lower under posting. In the 3 × 3 market they are highest under haggling and lowest under posting.

Hypothesis 4: Buyers' profits in the 2 × 2 market are the same under either haggling or flexible pricing, and higher under posting. In the 3 × 3 market they are lowest under haggling and highest under posting.

10.2.3 Experimental Procedures

The experiment was conducted at Monash University; the 376 subjects were mainly undergraduates, recruited using ORSEE (Greiner 2015). There were at least ten markets in each of the six cells (see the online appendix for details). Some sessions with large numbers of subjects were partitioned into two "matching groups", each at least twice the size of an individual market, and closed with respect to interaction, allowing two independent observations from the same session. Subjects played 40 market rounds with the cell (Post2, etc.) and role (buyer or seller) fixed, but were randomly re-assigned to markets each round.

All interaction took place via z-Tree (Fischbacher 2007). Subjects were visually isolated and received no identifying information about other subjects, reducing the scope for repeated-game behaviour such as tacit collusion by sellers (by making it impossible to recognise and punish a deviator in future rounds) or dynamic coordination by buyers (such as alternating who visits the low-priced seller). Written instructions were given to subjects before the first round, and read aloud in an attempt to make the rules common knowledge. All price choices (posted prices, bids, etc.) were restricted to multiples of AUD 0.10 (at the time, the Australian dollar varied from roughly 0.70–0.80 USD). End-of-round feedback included all posted prices (when applicable), the number of visits (if a seller) or buyers visiting the same seller (if a buyer), quantity traded and profit for the round, as well as bargaining and auction results when applicable. No information about other markets' results was provided.

After the 40th round, subjects undertook an incentivised Eckel-Grossman (2008) lottery-choice task, and a survey of demographic and attitudinal questions, including an elicitation of what price is "fair" given one, or more than one, buyers visit a seller.[3] After completing these tasks, subjects were paid. Subjects received (exactly) the sum of their profits from four randomly chosen rounds, plus the earnings from the lottery-choice task, plus a show-up fee of $10. Total earnings averaged $42.07, including $26.94 from the market rounds ($31.99 for sellers and $21.89 for buyers), for a session that typically lasted about 90 min.

[3] Subjects' original instructions stated that there would be a Part 2 to the session, but nothing about what would take place. See the online appendix for sample instructions and screen-shots, including those for the post-market tasks. Additional materials including the raw data are available from the corresponding author upon request.

10.3 Results

Aggregate observed market outcomes (Table 10.2) diverge in several ways from the theoretical point predictions (recall Table 10.1).

First, efficiency under haggling and flexible pricing is between 3.4 and 6.5% points below the theoretical prediction. The "fraction matched" column suggests that this is due to bargaining and auction behaviour rather than to frictions (which are captured in the fraction of traders who are matched, while bargaining disagreements and units passed in at auctions—due to all bids being below the seller's reserve price—are not). By contrast, efficiency under posting is exactly at the predicted level in the 2 × 2 market and only 2.5% points below it in the 3 × 3 market.

Second, transaction prices under posting are higher than predicted—due to high posted prices—while those under haggling and flexible pricing are lower than predicted in three of the four cells, by amounts ranging from 31 cents to $1.86. (In the Flex3 cell, transaction prices are above the predicted level, but not enough to offset the below-predicted efficiency.)

Third, sellers' profits are higher than predicted under posting, reflecting the high transaction prices, but lower than predicted under haggling and flexible pricing. This last result reflects the below-predicted efficiency levels in those treatments, along with the (usually) lower-than-predicted transaction prices. Fourth, buyers' profits often, but not always, deviate from theory in the opposite direction to sellers' profits; the exceptions are the Hagg3 and Flex3 cells, where the below-predicted efficiency

Table 10.2 Aggregate observed behaviour (all sessions and rounds)

Cell	Market		Efficiency	Fraction	Posted	Transaction	Profit	
	Institution	Size		matched	price	price	Sellers	Buyers
Post2	Posting	2 × 2	0.750	0.750	11.28	11.03	8.27	6.73
Post3		3 × 3	0.679	0.679	10.64	10.40	7.06	6.52
Hagg2	Haggling	2 × 2	0.716	0.774		12.54	8.98	5.34
Hagg3		3 × 3	0.643	0.702		13.37	8.59	4.27
Flex2	Flexible	2 × 2	0.685	0.752	9.66	11.47	7.86	5.84
Flex3	Pricing	3 × 3	0.657	0.710	10.24	11.97	7.86	5.27

(which reduces profits for both buyers and sellers) outweighs the deviation in transaction prices (which affects buyers and sellers in opposite ways), so that both buyers and sellers earn lower profits than predicted. In the Hagg2 and Flex2 cells, buyers' profits are higher than predicted, while in the two posting cells, they are lower than predicted.

These deviations between predicted and observed profits can be substantial (eight out of twelve represent increases or decreases of more than 10% from the theoretical point prediction), and lead to observed treatment effects that can differ qualitatively from the predicted treatment effects. Seller profits in the 2×2 market are actually higher under posting than under flexible pricing, the opposite of the theoretical prediction. Even when the ordering across treatments is not changed, the magnitudes of treatment effects can be substantially different. For sellers, profits under haggling are predicted to be higher than under posting by \$2.50 in the 2×2 market and by \$3.06 in the 3×3 market, but the actual differences are much smaller: only \$0.71 and \$0.73, respectively.

We further examine treatment effects with probit regressions for efficiency (which is binary at the individual-subject level) and Tobits for transaction price, seller profit and buyer profit. The main explanatory variables are indicators for the Hagg and Post treatments (so Flex is the baseline). We additionally include the round number and its interactions with the treatment indicators, the number of markets in the matching group (as a proxy for incentives for seller collusion) and a constant term. All regressions in this article were estimated by Stata, with standard errors clustered by matching group.

Table 10.3 displays the main results, focusing on treatment effects. Differences between either the Post or Hagg treatments and the Flex treatment are given by the average marginal effects (MEs) of the Post and Hagg indicators, while differences between the Post and Hagg treatments are summarised by the *p*-value for the Post-versus-Hagg comparison immediately below the Hagg treatment indicator. (Corresponding point estimates are approximately given by the difference between the Post- and Hagg-treatment indicators.)

The results reinforce what was seen in the summary statistics. Despite the theoretical prediction of equal efficiency across market institutions,

Table 10.3 Tobit results (average marginal effects, with standard errors in parentheses)

	[1] Efficiency	[2]	[3] Transaction price	[4]	[5] Seller profit	[6]	[7] Buyer profit	[8]
	2 × 2	3 × 3	2 × 2	3 × 3	2 × 2	3 × 3	2 × 2	3 × 3
Post treatment (vs. Flex)	0.073***	0.027*	−0.415	−1.702***	0.594	−0.630**	1.142*	1.302***
	(0.020)	(0.016)	(0.847)	(0.523)	(0.454)	(0.307)	(0.616)	(0.369)
Hagg treatment (vs. Flex)	0.033**	−0.012	1.049*	1.340***	0.996***	0.449*	−0.209	−0.736***
	(0.017)	(0.014)	(0.634)	(0.479)	(0.330)	(0.340)	(0.479)	(0.282)
p-value, Post vs. Hagg	$p \approx 0.020$	$p \approx 0.012$	$p \approx 0.017$	$p < 0.001$	$p \approx 0.35$	$p < 0.001$	$p < 0.001$	$p < 0.001$
Round	0.0030***	0.002***	0.042***	0.041***	0.064***	0.045***	0.002	−0.009
	(0.0004)	(0.001)	(0.009)	(0.005)	(0.007)	(0.006)	(0.008)	(0.006)
Matching group size	−0.015***	−0.025**	−0.134	0.384	−0.287***	−0.082	−0.057	−0.500**
(num. of markets)	(0.006)	(0.012)	(0.213)	(0.376)	(0.108)	(0.256)	(0.162)	(0.250)
Sample	Sellers	Sellers	Sellers	Sellers	Sellers	Sellers	Buyers	Buyers
N	3200	4320	2287	2844	3200	4320	3200	4320
|*ln*(*L*)|	1892.70	2766.74	6009.97	7351.04	8790.49	11471.62	8218.98	10506.17

* (**,***): *Note* Marginal effect significantly different from zero at the 10% (5%, 1%) level

efficiency is significantly higher under posting than in the other treatments (though the difference between Post3 and Flex3 is only significant at the 10% level). While the other three variables are ordered across treatments in the same way as the theoretical predictions in the 3 × 3 market, the 2 × 2 market shows qualitative deviations from the theory, similar to those in the descriptive statistics. Seller profit is significantly higher under haggling than flexible pricing, as is transaction price, whereas the theory predicted both of these to be equal between those cells. Also, seller profits were predicted to be lower under posting than under haggling and flexible pricing, but Table 10.3 shows no significant differences there, and in the case of flexible pricing, the effect is actually in the opposite direction.

10.3.1 Observed Bargaining Behaviour

We move to bargaining and auction behaviour, which may help explain the deviations we observe in the market outcomes. In the Hagg treatment, bargaining is symmetric, which would normally imply a strong tendency towards equal splits, corresponding here to an agreement on a price of $10. However, Fig. 10.4 shows that bargaining actually favours the seller.

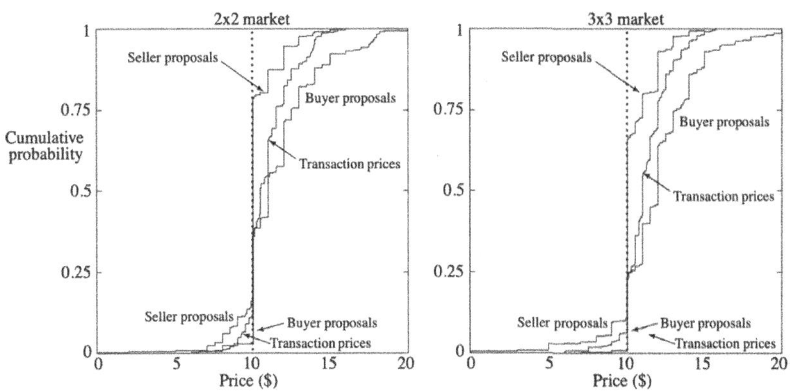

Fig. 10.4 Bargaining results in Hagg treatment—cumulative distribution functions

Mean transaction prices are \$10.97 in 2×2 markets and \$11.24 in 3×3 markets, significantly higher than \$10 (two-tailed Wilcoxon signed-ranks test, pooled Hagg2 and Hagg3 matching-group-level data, $p \approx 0.008$).[4] While seller price proposals, averaging \$10.16 and \$10.33 in 2×2 and 3×3 markets respectively, do not significantly differ from equal splits ($p \approx 0.16$), buyers' proposals averaging \$11.74 and \$12.20 in 2×2 and 3×3 markets, respectively, are significantly higher ($p \approx 0.004$).

Our bargaining environment differs from standard bargaining settings in two ways: (i) framing as a buyer-seller interaction rather than symmetric roles, and (ii) the presence of other components of the market (price posting, auctions, etc.) rather than exclusively bargaining. Either of these could have disrupted the usual pull towards equal splits. Another departure from standard experiments involving the Nash demand game is relatively low, though not negligible, frequency of disagreements: 8.9% in the 2×2 market and 11.7% in the 3×3 market.

In the Flex treatment, there is little tendency for prices to be negotiated downwards from the posted price. Transaction prices determined by bargaining average \$8.83 in the Flex2 cell and \$9.57 in the Flex3 cell, compared to the maximum possible transaction prices of \$9.36 and \$10.09, respectively (i.e., if all transactions were at the posted price).[5]

Figure 10.5 shows scatterplots of the posted and transaction price for all bargaining agreements in the Flex treatment, separately for 2×2 and 3×3 markets. The horizontal and vertical coordinates of the points are both perturbed with uniform$[-0.2, 0.2]$ noise, to minimise observations obscuring one another. Also shown are the 45-degree line and a least-squares line that is piecewise linear with a kink at \$10 (to allow for the deal-me-out solution).

The most striking result in the figure is the lack of any tendency to settle on equal splits, but nor is the typical result similar to that seen in

---

[4] See Siegel and Castellan (1988) for descriptions of the non-parametric tests used here.

[5] Even when the posted price is above \$10, meaning that the equal-split norm ought to nudge prices downwards, average transaction prices are \$10.59 and \$11.32 in the Flex2 and Flex3 cells, respectively, compared to maximum possible prices of \$11.50 and \$12.01. Also, average buyers' proposals—over all posted prices, and irrespective of agreement—are \$9.09 and \$9.88 in the Flex2 and Flex3 cells, respectively, while sellers' average \$8.83 and \$9.57.

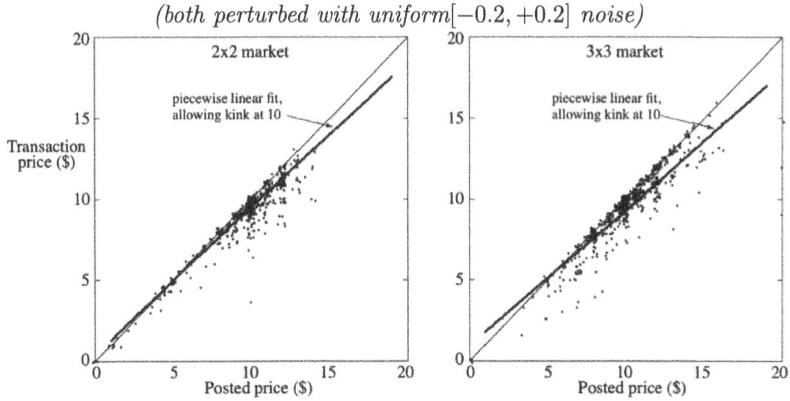

Fig. 10.5 Bargaining results in Flex treatment—scatterplots of posted and transaction price

the Hagg treatment. Instead, sellers in the Flex treatment capture nearly the maximum surplus possible, with transaction prices tending to remain close to the original posted price. This outcome is consistent with deal-me-out when the posted price is below \$10, but not when it is above \$10 (where deal-me-out implies a transaction price of \$10). Disagreement frequencies are comparable to those in the Hagg treatment: 12.4% in Flex2 and 9.4% in Flex3.

Table 10.4 shows results from panel linear regressions with (buyer or seller) price proposal as the dependent variable. Eight models are estimated, corresponding to the possible combinations of Hagg or Flex treatment, buyer or seller price proposals and 2×2 or 3×3 market, so the samples we use are the Hagg2, Hagg3, Flex2 or Flex3 market rounds where the seller is visited by exactly one buyer.[6] Explanatory variables include the posted price on its own and multiplied by a "low price" indicator equal to one if the posted price is less than 10 (again, allowing the deal-me-out bargaining solution to emerge), the low-price indicator on

[6] Here, we drop those observations where either (a) the posted price is 0 and one buyer visits, or it is 20 and multiple buyers visit, in either of which case the subsequent choices by buyer and seller are forced (0 in the former case and 20 in the latter), or (b) the decision-maker does not choose a price before time expires in the bargaining or auction stage (and a default choice is imposed, of the minimum allowable choice for sellers or the maximum for buyers). Combined, these cases make up less than 0.5% of observations in the Hagg and Flex treatments.

Table 10.4 Factors affecting bargaining proposals (average MEs unless noted)

Dep. var.: proposed price	[9]	[10]	[11]	[12]	[13]	[14]	[15]	[16]
Role:	Seller		Buyer		Seller		Buyer	
Cell:	Hagg2	Hagg3	Hagg2	Hagg3	Flex2	Flex3	Flex2	Flex3
Posted price...								
...if > 10					0.758***	0.323**	0.644***	0.712***
					(0.135)	(0.156)	(0.114)	(0.111)
...if < 10					0.932***	1.045***	0.990***	0.996***
					(0.024)	(0.053)	(0.006)	(0.043)
signif. diff. from each other?					$p \approx 0.20$	$p < 0.001$	$p \approx 0.004$	$p \approx 0.004$
Low price ($p^P < 10$)					0.009	0.073	−0.165	−0.024
					(0.185)	(0.140)	(0.145)	(0.114)
Round	−0.006	0.005	−0.018	−0.023	0.013	0.024**	0.018***	0.019***
	(0.015)	(0.007)	(0.016)	(0.022)	(0.008)	(0.011)	(0.005)	(0.005)
Female	−0.282	0.314	0.170	0.166	−0.112	−0.031	0.086	−0.059
	(0.381)	(0.283)	(0.320)	(0.718)	(0.209)	(0.416)	(0.135)	(0.262)
Risk tolerance	−0.051	0.182	−0.755***	−0.106	−0.120**	0.119***	−0.050	−0.079
	(0.085)	(0.177)	(0.112)	(0.309)	(0.053)	(0.036)	(0.042)	(0.051)
Fair price	0.456	0.213	0.627***	0.206	−0.067	0.120	0.020	0.047*
	(0.331)	(0.179)	(0.211)	(0.173)	(0.058)	(0.120)	(0.026)	(0.028)
N	482	471	482	470	644	764	642	762
R^2	0.082	0.052	0.464	0.072	0.799	0.656	0.810	0.801

* (**,***): *Note* Marginal effect significantly different from zero at the 10% (5%, 1%) level

Table 10.5 Auction results, Hagg and Flex treatments

	Hagg			Flex		
	2 × 2	3 × 3, 2 buyers	3 × 3, 3 buyers	2 × 2	3 × 3, 2 buyers	3 × 3, 3 buyers
Mean buyer bid	16.56	17.03	17.06	17.09	16.66	16.95
Fraction of $20 bids	0.261	0.280	0.392	0.404	0.384	0.422
Mean seller reserve price	12.13	12.48	13.41	11.55	12.49	11.71
Mean transaction price	16.14	16.35	18.27	16.29	15.80	17.46

its own, all three of these multiplied by the round number, and the round number on its own, as well as a constant term and subject random effects. As additional controls, we include an indicator for female, the degree of risk tolerance from the lottery-choice task and the elicited fair price.[7]

Models 9–12 add little to what we could see in Fig. 10.4 about bargaining in the Hagg treatment, and we do not elaborate further on the results. The results for the Flex treatment are more noteworthy. Consistent with Fig. 10.5, we observe that deal-me-out does not characterise bargaining well (e.g., proposals significantly increase in the posted price, even for posted prices above $10). There is some evidence of an increase in price proposals (for both buyers and sellers) over time, but there are no systematic effects of gender, risk tolerance or elicited fair price.

10.3.2 Observed Auction Behaviour

In our auctions, the theoretical prediction is for all of the available surplus going to the seller: prices of $20 irrespective of the market and whether there are two buyers or three. Table 10.5 shows that bids at the predicted level of $20 occur less than half the time. Average bids are

[7] Recall from Sect. 10.2.3 that two fair prices were elicited at the end of the experimental session: one for when only one buyer visited a seller, and one for when multiple buyers visited. We use the former for these regressions.

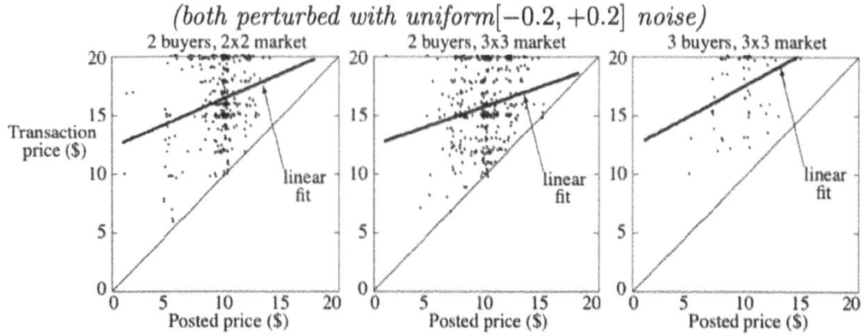

Fig. 10.6 Auction results in Flex treatment—scatterplots of posted and transaction price

roughly \$17, and despite the different frequencies of equilibrium bids, do not vary much across the six cases.

Accordingly, transaction prices are well below \$20 in all cases, though sellers still receive the lion's share of the surplus.[8]

Figure 10.6 shows how auction results in the Flex treatment associate with the posted price.

We see positive associations between posted and transaction prices, in contrast to the theoretical prediction of no systematic relationship between the two.[9] Roughly speaking, average transaction prices tend to lie roughly midway between the posted price and the theoretically predicted price of \$20, though they are higher when there are three bidders than when there are two.

10.4 Discussion

Understanding the performance of pricing mechanisms such as price posting, haggling and flexible pricing is an important step towards understanding why these institutions have survived for so long, how they can

[8] Unsold units are rare here, occurring about 3.23% of the time overall.

[9] Panel regressions, not reported here but similar to those in Table 10.4 (and available from the authors upon request) show that buyers' bids are also increasing in the posted price. Also, bids tend to increase over time, and are lower for more risk-seeking subjects.

co-exist in some markets and when buyers, sellers or social planners may prefer one to another. We find that the standard theory has mixed success in characterising actual market outcomes, both in point predictions and in directional predictions of treatment effects. A potential explanation for the deviations we find lies in the observed bargaining and auction behaviour, which departs from theory in several ways:

1. Agreement in bargaining occurs only about 90% of the time, while the theoretical prediction is full agreement.
2. In symmetric bargaining (the Hagg treatment) conditional on agreement, the seller receives about 55% of the surplus, while the theoretical prediction is an equal split.
3. In auctions in the Hagg treatment, the seller receives about 85% of the surplus, while the theoretical prediction is the entire surplus.
4. In the Flex treatment conditional on bargaining agreement, the transaction price is (approximately) equal to the posted price, while the theoretical prediction is deal-me-out.
5. In auctions in the Flex treatment, the transaction price is roughly halfway between the posted price and buyers' valuation, while the theoretical prediction is the buyers' valuation.

The last four of these deviations act to make bargaining less attractive for buyers relative to auctions (and the opposite for the sellers). This impacts the other decision buyers face: which seller to visit, and in particular, whether to chase the lowest price (and likely participate in an auction) or visit a higher-price seller (and likely bargain). The more buyers benefit from auctions relative to bargaining, the more incentive they have to visit the low-price seller, so the more price-sensitive buyers should be. Therefore, haggling and flexible pricing are behaviourally more similar to price posting than they are in theory, though with the extra complication of disagreements in the former, which make both buyers and sellers worse off.

It is plausible that a behavioural theory that incorporated these stylised facts, instead of standard bargaining and auction theory—combined with equilibrium behaviour in the other stages of the model—would generate predictions for the haggling and flexible-pricing treatments that fit the experimental data better than the predictions we used. This is likely, rather than certain, since the model could fall short in other areas besides bargaining and auctions: buyers may choose out-of-equilibrium visit probabilities (either too much or too little price-responsiveness), or sellers may choose above- or below-equilibrium posted prices.[10]

Our work is in the spirit of other recent work that adapts theoretical models to account for stylised facts observed in the lab. Bolton and Karagözoğlu (2016) and Kloosterman and Paul (2018) develop (quite different) models that incorporate bargaining subgames, and use empirical bargaining regularities in formulating theoretical predictions, rather than relying exclusively on the standard-theory solution. There is much more room for this in economic modelling, however. Bargaining or auction subgames exist in many environments, such as household economics (intra-household bargaining affects incentives to invest in human capital and to marry), professional labour markets (incentives to take on non-promotable tasks depend on current and future employers' hiring, promotion and compensation decisions, which may be determined via bargaining or auction), housing markets (expected sale prices, based on bargaining or auctions, impact on buyers' willingness to expend resources on visiting and assessing properties, as well as sellers' willingness to improve their properties prior to sale), and others. With more realistic behavioural assumptions for bargaining and auction outcomes, the implications of these and other models may change for the better. We encourage more of this kind of work, by both theorists and experimenters.

We also encourage more applications of directed search in theoretical and experimental modelling. There are numerous variations of the institutions we have examined, and particular markets may be better described by one of these rather than the versions we have used. For example, posted prices could be completely cheap talk, rather than constraining transaction prices in one or both directions. Sellers visited by several buyers may use multiple pairwise bargaining rather than an

[10] Evidence presented in an earlier version of this chapter suggests that modifying the assumptions about bargaining and auction behaviour does indeed improve fit with the data from the current experiment, though this still raises the question of whether such a model could predict well out-of-sample.

auction. Failing to agree with a seller might result in visiting another seller at a positive cost, rather than failing to trade entirely. Sellers' products may be differentiated rather than homogeneous, with them announcing not only prices, but possibly other attributes of their items (which may be search, experience or credence attributes) as well. Directed search is theoretically versatile, behaviourally interesting and descriptive of many real-world settings, and we look forward to seeing it used more widely.

References

Albrecht, James, Pieter Gautier and Susan Vroman (2006), "Equilibrium directed search with multiple applications", *Review of Economic Studies* 73, pp. 869–891.

Anbarci, Nejat and Nick Feltovich (2013), "Directed search, coordination failure and seller profits: An experimental comparison of posted pricing with single and multiple prices", *International Economic Review* 54, pp. 873–884.

Anbarci, Nejat and Nick Feltovich (2018), "Pricing in competitive search markets: Experimental evidence of the roles of price information and fairness perceptions", *Management Science* 64, pp. 1101–1120.

Anbarci, Nejat, Richard Dutu and Nick Feltovich (2015), "Inflation tax in the lab: A theoretical and experimental study of competitive search equilibrium with inflation", *Journal of Economic Dynamics and Control* 61, pp. 17–33.

Binmore, Ken, Chris Proulx, Larry Samuelson and Joe Swierzbinski (1998), "Hard bargains and lost opportunities", *Economic Journal* 108, pp. 1279–1298.

Bolton, Gary E. and Emin Karagözoğlu (2016), "On the influence of hard leverage in a soft leverage bargaining game: The importance of credible claims", *Games and Economic Behavior* 99, pp. 164–179.

Burdett, Kenneth, Shouyong Shi and Randall Wright (2001), "Pricing and matching with frictions", *Journal of Political Economy* 109, pp. 1060–1085.

Camera, Gabriele and Cemil Selcuk (2009), "Price dispersion with directed search", *Journal of the European Economic Association* 7, pp. 1193–1224.

Carlsson, Hans (1991), "A bargaining model where parties make errors", *Econometrica* 59, pp. 1487–1496.

Cason, Timothy N. and Charles Noussair (2007), "A market with frictions in the matching process: An experimental study", *International Economic Review* 48, pp. 665–691.
Cason, Timothy N. and Daniel Friedman (2008), "A comparison of market institutions", in Plott, Charles R. and Vernon L. Smith, eds., *Handbook of experimental economics results,* v. 1, North-Holland, Amsterdam, pp. 264–272.
Eckel, Catherine C. and Phillip J. Grossman (2008), "Forecasting risk attitudes: An experimental study of actual and forecast risk attitudes of women and men", *Journal of Economic Behavior & Organization* 68, pp. 1–17.
Fischbacher, Urs (2007), "z-Tree: Zurich toolbox for ready-made economic experiments", *Experimental Economics* 10, pp. 171–178.
Greiner, Ben (2015), "Subject pool recruitment procedures: Organizing experiments with ORSEE", *Journal of the Economic Science Association* 1, pp. 114–125.
Harsayni, John C. and Reinhard Selten (1988), *A general theory of equilibrium selection in games,* MIT Press, Cambridge, MA.
Helland, Leif, Espen Moen and Edgar Preugschat (2017), "Information and coordination frictions in experimental posted offer markets", *Journal of Economic Theory* 167, pp. 53–74.
Julien, Benoit, John Kennes and Ian P. King (2000), "Bidding for labor", *Review of Economic Dynamics* 3, pp. 619–649.
Julien, Benoit, John Kennes and Ian P. King (2001), "Auctions and posted prices in directed search equilibrium", *Topics in Macroeconomics* 1, Article 1.
Julien, Benoit, John Kennes and Ian P. King (2002), "Auctions beat posted prices in a small market", *Journal of Institutional and Theoretical Economics* 158, pp. 548–562.
Kloosterman, Andrew (2016), "Directed search with heterogeneous firms: An experimental study", *Experimental Economics* 19, pp. 51–66.
Kloosterman, Andrew and Stephen Paul (2018), "Ultimatum game bargaining in a partially directed search market", *Journal of Economic Behavior & Organization* 154, pp. 60–74.
Kultti, Klaus (1999), "Equivalence of auctions and posted prices", *Games and Economic Behavior* 27, pp. 106–113.
Lu, Xiaohua and R. Preston McAfee (1996), "The evolutionary stability of auctions over bargaining", *Games and Economic Behavior* 15, pp. 228–254.
Montgomery, James D. (1991), "Equilibrium wage dispersion and interindustry wage differentials", *Quarterly Journal of Economics* 106, pp. 163–179.

Nash, John (1950), "The bargaining problem", *Econometrica* 18, pp. 155–162.
Nash, John (1953), "Two-person cooperative games", *Econometrica* 21, pp. 128–140.
Siegel, Sidney and N. James Castellan Jr. (1988), *Nonparametric statistics for the behavioral sciences*, McGraw-Hill, New York.
Smith, Vernon L. (1964), "Effect of market organization on competitive equilibrium", *Quarterly Journal of Economics* 78, pp. 181–201.
Sutton, John (1986), "Non-cooperative bargaining theory: An introduction", *Review of Economic Studies* 53, pp. 709–724.
Van Boening, Mark and Nathaniel T. Wilcox (2008), "Avoidable cost structures and competitive market institutions", in Plott, Charles R. and Vernon L. Smith, eds., *Handbook of experimental economics results*, v. 1, North-Holland, Amsterdam, pp. 206–212.

11

Empirical Models of Bargaining with Externalities in IO and Trade

Ali Yürükoğlu

11.1 Introduction

This chapter provides an overview of empirical models of situations where a small number of agents interact with each other in pairwise negotiations. The surplus in each pairwise negotiation is partially determined by the terms of other pairwise negotiations. The two leading examples are firm-to-firm negotiations over supply contracts in the context of bilateral oligopoly used in the field of industrial organization and country-to-country negotiations over trade agreements in international trade. In the last fifteen years, an empirical literature has emerged estimating such models and using them for counterfactual analysis in a variety of industries and in the context of tariff negotiations.

The most widely used model in recent work models pairs as engaging in Nash bargaining, and defines an equilibrium to the model as each

A. Yürükoğlu (✉)
Stanford University, Stanford, CA, USA
e-mail: ayurukog@stanford.edu

E. Karagözoğlu and K. B. Hyndman (eds.), *Bargaining*,
https://doi.org/10.1007/978-3-030-76666-5_11

pair solving its Nash bargaining problem given the solutions to the other bargaining problems. This solution concept has been termed a "Nash-in-Nash" equilibrium in recent work, but the idea goes back to the notion of "contract equilibrium" in Cremer and Riordan [11] and was developed further by Horn and Wolinsky [28] and Davidson [13] much before acquiring its "Nash-in-Nash" name. This chapter will generally focus on this formulation which is a hybrid of cooperative and non-cooperative game theoretic concepts, but will touch on advances in providing non-cooperative foundations as well as alternative formulations. The agents' payoff functions that enter the bargaining problems are formulated from a model of oligopoly industry equilibrium or a Ricardian model of international trade.

Most of the work has been in the context of firm-to-firm negotiations over supply contracts. To begin to fix ideas, consider the interaction between Walmart and the Coca-Cola Company. Coca-Cola supplies a number of different brands and package sizes to Walmart. The two parties have to agree on terms of this relationship which would include first and foremost the price schedule, potentially nonlinear, that Walmart pays Coca-Cola. Both firms are extremely large with strong brands so would have some degree of market power. This creates a negotiation problem where both parties would prefer some deal to no deal, but disagree in the sense that Walmart would prefer a lower price schedule and Coca-Cola would prefer a higher price schedule (up until the monopoly price). However, the situation is complicated by the presence of other agents. Walmart faces the same type of negotiation problem with Pepsi. And Coca-Cola faces the same type of problem with Costco. The amount of Coca-Cola that will be sold at Walmart will depend not just on whether Walmart and Pepsi have an agreement, but potentially on the terms of that agreement. Furthermore, Walmart's profits are affected by the existence and terms of Costco's contracts with Coca-Cola and Pepsi because Walmart competes with Costco to bring customers to its stores. The models under consideration in this chapter are rich enough to predict equilibrium prices and contract terms in bilateral oligopoly market such as the Walmart–Costco–Coca-Cola–Pepsi example.

Many industries have a similar structure. The literature has so far focused mostly on media and health care markets. In a leading example of the media case, the downstream firms are cable distributors like Comcast or AT&T. The upstream firms are content producers such as ESPN and HBO. In health care, the most common example has the downstream firms as health insurance carriers like Aetna or Cigna and the upstream firms as hospitals. The media and health care sectors have been the focus of several high-profile antitrust cases where these models have been employed.

The same bargaining model has been applied in the context of tariff negotiations between countries. Consider the United States (US) and European Union (EU) negotiating tariff reductions. Even discriminatory tariff reductions that only alter the two entities' tariffs with each other will affect other countries' welfare because the tariff changes might lead to direct effects of substitution away from Japanese products toward products whose tariffs were reduced in the negotiation or through general equilibrium effects. Furthermore, because post-war tariff negotiations happen predominantly in the context of the World Trade Organization (WTO) which requires non-discrimination outside of free trade agreements, any tariff reductions between the US and EU will translate into tariff reductions for all other WTO members.

The rest of the chapter describes the specification of the model at a level of generality that applies to both the bilateral oligopoly context and the trade agreement context before describing methods for estimating parameters of these models. I will then describe specific examples from the media, health care, and tariff negotiation examples and the types of counterfactual analysis that have been performed. Finally, I will discuss directions for future research.

11.2 Bargaining Equilibrium

Before considering applications, we define and discuss the bargaining equilibrium notion. There are N agents. Each agent has a payoff function $\pi_n(\mathbf{x})$ where $\mathbf{x}$ is the set of all bilateral contracts between all agents. Partition the set of contracts into those which involve agent i and those which don't as $(\mathbf{x_i}, \mathbf{x_{-i}})$ where $\mathbf{x_i}$ consists of $(x_{i1}, x_{i2}, ..., x_{iN})$. Agent i's payoff thus may depend on contracts to which it is not party, as in the example of Pepsi's profits depending on the contractual terms reached between Coca-Cola and Walmart. Each agent can negotiate with some subset M_i of the other agents. Some pairs of agents might be restricted by assumption to not negotiate so that $M_i < N$. For example, in IO settings it is common to not allow competing firms such as Coca-Cola and Pepsi to negotiate over anything in respect of antitrust laws. If $j \notin M_i$ then we say that $x_{ij} = \emptyset$. Null contracts can also be the outcome in a pair which is allowed to negotiate if no contract leads to positive gains from trade for that pair.

Each pair of negotiating agents (i, j) solves the following Nash bargaining problem:

$$\max_{x_{ij}}(\pi_i(x_{ij}, \mathbf{x_{i,-j}}, \mathbf{x_{-i}}) - \pi_i(\emptyset, \mathbf{x^D_{i,-j}}, \mathbf{x^D_{-i}}))^{\zeta_{ij}}(\pi_j(x_{ij}, \mathbf{x_{j,-i}}, \mathbf{x_{-j}}) \\ - \pi_j(\emptyset, \mathbf{x^D_{j,-i}}, \mathbf{x^D_{-j}}))^{1-\zeta_{ij}}$$

The contract vector is spelled out to differentiate between an agent's contract under negotiation, x_{ij}, contracts that the agent is party to but not under negotiation, $\mathbf{x_{i,-j}}$ in agent i's case, and all contracts that the agent is not party to, $\mathbf{x_{-i}}$ in agent i's case.

The maximization is subject to there being gains from trade to both parties, so the values inside each parenthesis must be non-negative. The second term inside each parenthesis is the disagreement value for each agent. x^D denotes a contract that might be different in response to disagreement. As written, the disagreement value allows for other contracts to change in response to agents i and j disagreeing. However, the equilibrium notions we define will put strong restrictions on how these change, and in the leading case hold them fixed. Along the same lines, in the agreement payoff, all other contracts besides the one under negotiation are held fixed. That is, when i and j are evaluating different values for their own contract to maximize their Nash product, they hold fixed all other contracts, including other contracts to which they are party but are not under negotiation.

A bargaining equilibrium consists of contracts $\mathbf{x}$ such that each pair i, j that can negotiate chooses x_{ij} to maximize its Nash product given the other contracts.

A key component in calculating an equilibrium involves defining disagreement values. The most common choice, and one that treats other contracts in disagreement analogously to how the model treats other contracts at non-equilibrium candidate values for the contract under negotiation, is to hold fixed all other contracts at their equilibrium levels. This choice is typically the cheapest computationally. However, it may not serve as a good approximation to the situation under study in some settings. Other options have been explored. One possibility is to eliminate (i, j) from the set of pairs which can negotiate, and recompute the bargaining equilibrium. To do this consistently, this requires computing bargaining equilibria for all sub-coalitions of bargaining pairs, which can be computationally expensive. This setup is described in the appendix to Yurukoglu [37]. Another option that has been explored in Ho and Lee [27] is to set up a mechanism for i and j to form a new agreement with some other non-contracted agent in case of disagreement, but hold all other contracts fixed.

The equilibrium concept employed is a hybrid of cooperative and non-cooperative game theoretic solution concepts. If one thinks of each pair as being a player in a synthetic game, and each Nash product as that "player"'s payoff in that synthetic game, and the contract x_{ij} as the "player"'s action, then the bargaining equilibrium can be thought of as a Nash equilibrium to that synthetic game. From this analogy emerged the terminology of "Nash-in-Nash," the first "Nash" referring to the Nash equilibrium between bargains, and the second referring to each bargain being a Nash bargaining problem.

Many users of this equilibrium notion concede that a fully non-cooperative formulation would be preferable. Such a formulation would eliminate the arbitrariness of specifying what happens in disagreement. Furthermore, a non-cooperative formulation would be more amenable to matching institutional features in actual negotiations as actions, information, and timing would be explicit. Such a formulation has proven difficult, partly because of the intractability of informational issues that arise and the sensitivity of the models to assumptions on timing and ordering. Some progress has been made. Collard-Wexler et al. [8] provide conditions on payoffs and the contract space for existence and uniqueness of a non-cooperative alternative offers game in a setting of bilateral oligopoly leads to prices that converge to Nash-in-Nash prices. The result employs the concept of passive beliefs when necessary to specify what contracts agents who receive out-of-equilibrium contract offers believe other agents have negotiated. Passive beliefs have been explored in a take-it-or-leave-it offer setting by Hart and Tirole [24] and McAfee and Schwartz [30]. Earlier related results are found in Björnerstedt and Stennek [7]. De Fontenay and Gans [14] examines a version with renegotiation of other contracts in case of disagreement and derives a relation to the Myerson-Shapley cooperative solution concept. When all upstream firms have bargaining parameters equal to one, then Nash-in-Nash is a Bertrand-Nash pricing game by the upstream firms that only considers single deviations to support the equilibrium.

The researcher must specify the timing of bargaining relative to the other decisions in the model. In the typical industrial organization case so far, the choice is between whether bargaining is decided simultaneously with downstream prices or prior to downstream prices. This choice is related to the distinction of interim observability in the theoretical literature on vertical relationships. Under the simultaneous specification, prices are taken as given when negotiating which implies, under the usual choice of disagreement specification, that the price of the downstream firms stays the same even if the downstream firm loses the input. For example, the prices of other goods at Walmart would remain constant if Walmart no longer stocks Coca-Cola. Under sequential bargaining then pricing, prices would respond to disagreement. Furthermore, prices adjust when computing the payoffs to candidate (that is, non-equilibrium) contractual terms. In most market settings, price setting and bargaining are staggered and can be triggered endogenously, so little guidance comes from the field. The simultaneous assumption is computationally more tractable and allows for some analytical progress. Both timing assumptions have been employed in the literature.

11.3 Estimation

In all applications of which I am aware, the bargaining model is part of a larger model. In many cases, it is the outer nest with the inner nest being an oligopoly industry equilibrium. It could also be nested inside and generating payoffs for an investment or entry and exit model. Because of this interplay with other parts of the full model, discussion of identification and estimation is difficult to do in a general fashion. Therefore, here I will discuss in loose terms what sorts of data and what patterns in data can help to estimate the bargaining parameters and potentially other objects.

Consider the case where a researcher knows or has estimates of the payoff function for different contracts and a data set of contractual outcomes. The bargaining model can be used to estimate bargaining parameters for each player. In this situation, the researcher can choose the bargaining parameter in each pair to predict the observed contractual outcome for that pair as closely as possible. As one example, consider the case of a bilateral monopoly with linear contracts and price setting by the downstream firm to consumers. Assuming the demand function is known and the linear fee between the upstream and downstream firm is observed. One can solve for the bargaining parameter which induces the observed linear fee. More generally, in a bilateral oligopoly, if each pairwise contract is observed, and the researcher allows for a separate bargaining parameter for each pair, then the researcher can hold all the other contracts fixed, and solve for the pairwise bargaining parameter which induces the observed pairwise contract as closely as possible.

Matters are more complicated in the typical case where the researcher is missing components of the payoff functions or does not have detailed data on contractual outcomes. One strategy is to estimate the contracts using another part of the model. For example, in a bilateral oligopoly with Nash-Bertrand pricing downstream, the researcher could back out from the implied marginal costs of each good from the first order conditions for downstream prices, and regress these marginal costs on product characteristics. If the input being negotiated is one of the product characteristics, then this will provide an estimate of the negotiated wholesale cost. This approach was employed by Villas-Boas [36] in an early empirical paper on wholesale pricing and vertical relationships in the grocery industry. The paper in fact goes further and infers the form of the contracts from how retail prices change with cost shocks to the manufacturers' raw ingredients. A similar idea is to infer what contracts must have looked like to rationalize other observable outcomes than prices. For example, Ho [25] estimates how payments between insurers and hospitals must have looked like to rationalize which hospitals are available on which insurance plans. Relatedly, Mortimer [32] observes contractual form and terms and studies how terms and welfare change after a technological innovation allowed for a richer contractual space.

11.4 Empirical Applications

Applications in IO use the above notion of a bargaining equilibrium by generating profit functions from nested models of consumer demand and firm competition. Researchers also often further restrict the model using institutional features of the industry under study, for example they may restrict the contract space in certain ways. Finally, most studies are ultimately using the bargaining model as part of a larger goal of answering some economic or policy question. The answer to the question is typically provided in the form of counterfactual analysis, that is, the fully estimated model's prediction for what would have happened under alternative scenarios.

All of the applications in IO partition the set of firms into upstream firms, or suppliers, and downstream firms, or distributors or retailers. Downstream firms procure inputs from upstream firms and transform them for sale to consumers. The bargaining equilibrium is used to characterize the market interaction between upstream and downstream firms. Competition between downstream firms and consumer demand typically follows a model of Nash-Bertrand pricing by firms to consumers who follow a differentiated products random coefficients demand system. This setup for downstream demand and pricing is usually from Berry et al. [6] and has become a workhorse in industrial organization. That said, nothing in the bargaining model requires that the payoff functions come from a certain type of oligopoly model. One could just as well plug in a model with Cournot pricing or a different form of demand system to generate the payoffs under different contracts.

We now detail a variety of applications by identifying the specific research question under study, specifying which agents in the system are negotiating with whom, point out any unique features of the implementation, and highlight the main results. At present, this is an active area with new papers using these models appearing frequently. As such, some of the papers I detail are current unpublished working papers whose results may change under revision.

11.4.1 Media Content and Distribution

We consider first the setting of media content and distribution. Specifically, we focus on the US cable television industry during the period of 2000–2010. Models of the sort we will discuss have already been used by agencies in merger analysis and have showed up in high-profile antitrust court cases.

We consider two applications. The first application, studied in Crawford and Yurukoglu [9] asks the research question of what would happen to social welfare if the government were to mandate unbundling of content by downstream cable distributors? The second application, studied in Crawford et al. [10], addresses the research question of what are the effects on social welfare of vertical integration between content and distribution?

Both papers feature a model with three types of agents: consumers, downstream cable and satellite distributors, and upstream content producers. The content producers are conglomerates which own "channels." For example, the Disney owns the channels ABC, ESPN, The Disney Channel, ABC Family, and a host of lesser known channels. Downstream distributors negotiate with conglomerates or channels over the terms of access. Building on knowledge of the industry, the authors assume these contracts are linear and stipulate the payment from the distributor to the channel for every subscriber of that distributor who has access to watch the channel, whether they watch it or not. The distributors sell the channels to consumers. In practice, the distributors package the channels into larger bundles and charge one price per bundle. However, they pay separate linear fees for each channel on the bundle.[1] Distributors are assumed to play a Nash-Bertrand equilibrium when pricing bundles to consumers. Consumers choose which distributor bundle to purchase and subsequently how much time to spend watching each channel. The time spent watching decision allows the authors to use data on viewership patterns to inform the estimates of consumer tastes for channel content, though it does require assuming a parametric model of how consumers value time spent watching content.

The earlier paper, Crawford and Yurukoglu [10], uses the model to counterfactually simulate à la carte pricing regulations at the downstream level. That is, after estimating the demand and bargaining model parameters, they force the downstream firms to offer more flexible options for consumers. They counterfactually simulate equilibria where the distributor's price numbers of channels, and consumers are free to pick and choose which exact channels, and an approximation to à la carte pricing. In all scenarios, accounting for the equilibrium in the wholesale market is important for the welfare results. Without modeling the reaction of wholesale contracts, such pricing regulations are predicted to have large consumer welfare benefits. However, once the bargaining equilibrium is applied in the presence of the pricing regulations, wholesale prices rise by around 100%, offsetting these consumer gains. On net, average consumer surplus increases by just 0.2%, though there are bigger winners and losers among consumers. The estimated bargaining parameters in this application were close to 0.5 for most pairs suggesting that a model of take-it-or-leave-it offers would not have provided as good a fit to the observed outcomes, and potentially less reliable counterfactual predictions.

The latter paper adopts the same framework but makes several improvements and alternative assumptions. It uses a more realistic viewership model and estimates most of the bargaining and demand parameters jointly rather than separately as in the earlier paper. It also models the vertical integration between distributors and channels. Vertically integrated entities value the payoffs to their co-owned segments. For

[1] This industry structure has been eroding recently with more direct-to-consumer (D2C) and over-the-top (OTT) offerings that are billed by the content producers but still must travel over some distributors infrastructure. The structure described above was the dominant paradigm for the sector from about 1985 (when cable began to take off) to 2015.

example, a vertically integrated channel negotiating with a downstream distributor who is rival to its integrated distributor will take into account that when it negotiates a higher input fee, this will raise downstream prices and some benefit will accrue to its downstream distributor. Similarly, when the integrated distributor is pricing its bundle to consumers, it understands that any fee it has to pay to the upstream segment is not a true economic cost, thereby eliminating double marginalization. One modeling difference between these two papers is that Crawford et al. [9] employs the simultaneous bargaining and pricing assumption while Crawford and Yurukoglu [10] employed the sequential bargaining and pricing assumption.

The empirics in Crawford et al. [9] focus on regional sports channels (RSN's) in the US, some of which are vertically integrated and some of which aren't. It counterfactually simulates integrating the unintegrated RSN's and disintegrating the integrated RSN's for the year 2007. The main results are that a full ban on integration would lower welfare, but would be raise welfare in markets where the integrated downstream firm has strong incentives to exclude rivals from the content. Regulations banning exclusive dealing work to reduce the welfare losses in these markets while maintaining the benefits of reduced double marginalization.

These papers did not have data on exact contractual terms between each pair of downstream and upstream firms. They did have access to estimates of average terms by channel, for example the average input fee received by ESPN across its downstream distributors per year. It combined these data with the approach outlined in the previous section for using downstream pricing and packaging behavior to infer pairwise contractual terms.

11.4.2 Health Care

Many exciting applications of bargaining models in industrial organization have been in the health care sector. This is partly because the health care sector is a large portion of the US economy and partly because many markets are highly concentrated which leads to bargaining situations.

Grennan [23] used a bargaining model to make predictions about policies that limit price discrimination among buyers of medical devices. In this application, the upstream firms are manufacturers of coronary stents, a medical device that is implanted by surgery to keep arteries open for blood flow. The downstream firms are doctors in hospitals representing patients. The paper has detailed data on payments from hospitals to manufacturers. The paper documents significant price dispersion across hospitals for the same stent. Motivated by this observation, the author asks the research question of what would happen if price dispersion were eliminated? After estimating the bargaining and doctor choice model jointly, the author implements the counterfactual under a variety of plausible assumptions about how such a regulation might play out. In one case he assumes that all the hospitals negotiate using the average bargaining parameter or the maximum that he estimates across hospitals or when hospitals have a zero bargaining parameter. He finds that requiring uniform pricing in this manner would raise average prices and harm welfare unless the hospitals are able to bargain at the maximum bargaining parameter that he estimates.

The next set of papers focused on local markets where the upstream firms are the hospitals and the downstream firms are insurance companies. This structure is very similar to the cable television structure in that insurers are offering packages of hospitals to consumers for a monthly premium. One important difference is that consumers do pay a copayment when choosing different hospitals whereas in the television example there is no additional charge for watching after subscription. Gowrisankaran et al. [22] used a bargaining model to study the effects of a hospital merger in the market for Northern Virginia. They had detailed contractual data on payments from insurance companies to hospitals. This model abstracted away from the competition between insurance companies for consumers and modeled the insurance companies' payoff function as the consumer value of its enrollees minus the payments made to hospitals. Their main result is that a counterfactual hospital merger, which had been proposed but challenged and aborted, would have raised hospital prices and lowered consumer welfare absent significant efficiencies. This paper also derives, under the assumption of no competition between insurers, an analytical expression for equilibrium negotiated prices in terms of demand, demand elasticities, and bargaining parameters that can be used to facilitate estimation.

Ho and Lee [26] used a bargaining model to study the effects of insurance mergers. The structure is similar Gowrisankaran et al. [22] except that this model allows for competition between insurers, and thus brought the hospital-insurance bargaining models to the same degree of richness of competition as the earlier cable television models discussed above. Their setting is California. They find that insurance mergers typically lead to higher consumer prices and lower welfare, but do also produce off-setting reductions in negotiated prices with hospitals. Having fewer insurers to play off of each other worsens the disagreement values of hospitals leading to worse outcomes for hospitals. Despite these lower input prices, insurers still raise prices to consumers due to a reduction in competition in an already concentrated market.

Ho and Lee [27], Liebman [29], and Ghili [21] all use this framework to study the effects of minimum network policies whereby the government requires health insurers to maintain a minimum number of hospitals in the package it offers consumers. All three papers note difficulty with using the plain vanilla Nash-in-Nash framework to model minimum network policies. First, under the demand and cost models used in previous papers, there are typically gains from trade for any pair of hospital and insurer, thereby making it difficult to generate narrow networks in equilibrium. Secondly, in the case where one does generate a narrow network, and there is a minimum coverage regulation in place, the disagreement point that holds all other contracts fixed is likely not a good approximation to behavior as the insurer would replace the dropped hospital to meet the minimum coverage regulation. To address the first problem, Ho and Lee [27] and Liebman [29] allow insurers to commit to a narrow network before negotiations. Ghili [21] instead assumes there are additional fixed costs to an agreement, and finds the costs that offset the gains from trade from agreements that are not observed. To address the second issue, the papers allow for some form of replacement of hospitals in the case of disagreement. For example, Ho and Lee [27] allows the insurer to make a take-it-or-leave-it offer to a hospital that it does not have a contract within the case that it disagrees with a hospital it does have a contract within equilibrium. This allows the insurers to fulfill their adequacy regulations while threatening to walk away from a negotiation.

Cuesta et al. [12] examine vertical integration between hospitals and health insurers using a bargaining model. Their setting is the Santiago, Chile market which features a segment of privately insured patients whose choice set includes some insurers who own hospitals. In contrast to the cable case in Crawford et al. [9], Cuesta et al. [12] find that disintegrating the integrated entities would raise welfare. Apart from differences in the industry and geographical setting, this paper also employs the sequential timing assumption whereas Crawford et al. [9] employs the simultaneous assumption.

Shifting to pharmaceutical markets, a pair of papers analyzes the bargaining between pharmaceutical manufacturers with retailers in Dubois and Sæthre [18] and with a government purchaser in Dubois et al. [17]. Dubois and Sæthre [18] analyze how parallel trade, that is the ability of retailers to import the same drug from different countries with different regulated prices in the EU, affects the negotiations between manufacturers and retailers. Their downstream model includes an assortment decision by the retailers and quantifies the benefit to manufacturers from banning parallel trade. Dubois et al. [17] consider the possibility of US regulators using Canadian drug prices as a benchmark, and show that this significantly alters the incentives of manufacturers in the bargaining with the Canadian government such that Canadian prices would likely rise without much effect on US prices due to the differences in market size and price elasticities between Canada and the US.

11.4.3 Groceries

Draganska et al. [16] is the one of the earliest empirical papers to use the "Nash-in-Nash" framework. Their application has upstream coffee product manufacturers and downstream grocery stores in the German market. Their goal was to quantify the effect of different observable characteristics on the bargaining parameters of the firms. Noton and Elberg [33] similarly analyze the estimated bargaining parameters of grocery retailers and coffee product manufacturers in the Chilean market, and find that small and large retailers both have bargaining parameters near one-half. These two papers are mostly interested in the bargaining parameters themselves rather than using the model in a counterfactual analysis. Ellickson et al. [20] study the effects of private label brands which are essentially vertically integrated with the grocery retailer. Molina [31] studies the effects of buyer alliances.

11.4.4 Other Sectors

While media, health care, and groceries make up the lion's share of applications, there is much potential for applications to other sectors. Here we mention two working papers. De los Santos et al. [15] examines an important antitrust case involving book publishers, Amazon, and Apple in the e-book market. Book publishers jointly switched their pricing model from wholesale pricing to agency pricing. Under agency pricing, publishers would choose the retail price and the retailer (Amazon or Apple) would take a negotiated percentage of the retail price. Wholesale pricing is the model discussed in all applications above, where the firms negotiate over the input price and the retailer chooses the retail price. De los Santos et al. [15] use data from before and after the change to estimate the parameters of a bargaining model. Robles-Garcia [35] studies the bargaining over commission rates between mortgage brokers and lending banks in the UK market. She finds that banning commissions would hurt consumers despite the incentives for steering induced by the presence of asymmetric commissions. Both of these papers use the bargaining model to improve the realism and fit of the model relative to take-it-or-leave-it offers.

11.4.5 Tariff Determination in International Trade

A smaller number of papers have begun using these bargaining models to study the determination of tariffs in negotiations between large economic entities. Similar to the industrial organization settings, international tariff negotiations feature large entities with market power negotiating over terms of trade that have effects on third parties through competition. The system here is more dense in a certain sense than in the bilateral oligopoly framework because the countries are both buyers and sellers of goods and because tariffs in different product markets can have effects through the general equilibrium conditions of these models. As just one example, the tariff on cars that Japan imposes on the US affects the price of vegetables in the EU through general equilibrium effects.

We focus on negotiations that fall under the "terms-of-trade" rationale for trade agreements. Absent a trade agreement, large countries have an incentive to levy tariffs to exercise monopsony power by depressing world prices in goods for which their purchases make up a large share. All large countries engaging in this non-cooperative tariff setting lead to equilibrium tariffs which are too high from a global perspective. A trade agreement lets all countries cooperate to reduce tariffs to an efficient level. Institutionally, the world trading system since World War II has operated under the auspices of the Generalized Agreement on Trade and Tariffs (GATT) and its successor the World Trade Organization (WTO). Bagwell and Staiger [2] details which institutional features of the GATT/WTO and world trading system lend themselves to reaching multilateral efficiency and which features, such as preferential tariffs, impede reaching global efficiency.

On the empirical front, an important initial contribution was Ossa [34] who took an estimated Ricardian trade model and computed a counterfactual Nash equilibrium in tariffs and counterfactual total welfare maximizing tariffs. The total welfare maximizing tariffs can be considered as emerging from a multiparty negotiation where all parties are at the table in contrast to the interconnected bilateral bargaining detailed in this chapter. One motivation for this is that the WTO is a centralized organization for tariff negotiations, so a joint surplus maximizing procedure is perhaps a decent approximation. In practice, tariff negotiations at the GATT and WTO did proceed bilaterally, with extension to third parties through "Most Favored Nation" treatment. As an example, if the US and Japan came to a bilateral agreement to lower tariffs on some set of products, for example for Japan to lower its tariffs on computers and the US on cars, these new tariffs would apply to any member of the WTO.[2] Tariff negotiations thus typically took place during negotiation rounds where principal suppliers of goods would negotiate effectively on behalf of the other members of the GATT/WTO over certain tariffs. The details of the Torquay round and some analysis of the bargaining patterns there are available in Bagwell et al. [3].

Bagwell et al. [5] model the bilateral bargaining over tariffs with extension through most favored nation status to other GATT members. Their focus is on the Uruguay round of negotiations which occurred between 1986 and 1994. The question of interest is what tariffs would have been were negotiations done without the most favored nation rule. In this discriminatory case, tariffs still have third party effects through competition and general equilibrium conditions. Bagwell et al. [4] derive a sense in which most favored nation rules lead to too little tariffs reductions and discriminatory negotiations lead to over-liberalization, including possibly subsidizing production of foreign goods. Bagwell et al. [5] estimates a Ricardian trade model following Eaton and Kortum [19] and embeds this into a Nash-in-Nash bargaining equilibrium under most favored nation rules to estimate bargaining parameters. The bargaining parameters are then held fixed to simulate discriminatory tariff negotiations. The results suggest the most favored nation rules outperform discriminatory negotiations for total welfare by reducing the incentive for discriminatory tariff reductions that lead to cross-subsidization of imports.

11.5 Conclusion and New Directions

Bilateral bargaining models with externalities are being used more and more in empirical work and even in some high stakes antitrust proceedings. New data sets on firm-to-firm contracts will only increase their usefulness. There is still much scope for future work in this area.

On the theoretical side, more work on the non-cooperative foundations of bargaining with externalities is clearly needed. Despite the

[2] A notable exception to this is if countries are in a free trade agreement across all goods, like NAFTA or Mercosur.

progress that is been made, many questions remain regarding what equilibria of non-cooperative offer-counteroffer games look like under more general contract structures, non-passive beliefs, and alternative timing specifications. To the extent that the state space of such models becomes too large for meaningful analytical results, computational work using approximate dynamic programming or mean field approximations are one avenue for potential progress. On the estimation side, a treatise on identification conditions under different availability conditions of data would be useful. For example, some researchers observe wholesale prices but not marginal costs of production. Some research observes marginal costs of production but not downstream market shares. Some researchers see average wholesale prices and shifters of marginal costs of production, and so on.

In terms of applications, while there has been a proliferation of papers recently, this literature is still likely in its beginning stages. Since complex supply chains are the rule rather than exception [1], most industries have some structure like that studied so far more extensively in media, health care, and groceries. Future work will also likely take into account multiple segments in the supply chain. For example, in media, there are television studios that supply programs to channels that negotiate with distributors. In health care, doctors groups, pharmaceutical manufacturers, hospitals, health insurers, pharmacies, and pharmacy benefits managers are all players with market power whose contractual terms affect one another.

Actual contracts are often much higher dimensional than what researchers have so far modeled. In commercial contracts, in addition to prices, firms often specify a length of time that the contract is in place, quantity and marketing provisions, information-sharing provisions, confidentiality, and potentially exclusive dealing terms. International trade negotiations take place over tariffs and non-tariff barriers such as intellectual property protection. Enriching the scope of the modeled negotiations to include additional terms could be important for some policy-relevant counterfactuals.

Finally, embedding the bargaining models into models of investment or other dynamic processes is of first order importance. How surplus gets split between parties should have first order effects on the investments those parties make. Changes in market structure and product quality from investment and other dynamic decisions likely outweigh static pricing decisions in welfare calculations.

References

1. Antras, P. (2015). *Global production: Firms, contracts, and trade structure*. Princeton University Press.
2. Bagwell, K. and R. W. Staiger (1999). An economic theory of gatt. *American Economic Review 89*(1), 215–248.
3. Bagwell, K., R. W. Staiger, and A. Yurukoglu (2015). Multilateral trade bargaining: A first look at the gatt bargaining records. *American Economic Journal: Applied Economics 12*(3), 72–105.
4. Bagwell, K., R. W. Staiger, and A. Yurukoglu (2020). "Nash-in-Nash" tariff bargaining. *Journal of International Economics* (Vol. 122).
5. Bagwell, K., R. W. Staiger, and A. Yurukoglu (2021). Quantitative analysis of multiparty tariff negotiations. *Econometrica 89*(4), 1595–1631.
6. Berry, S., J. Levinsohn, and A. Pakes (1995). Automobile prices in market equilibrium. *Econometrica 63*(4), 841–890.
7. Björnerstedt, J. and J. Stennek (2007). Bilateral oligopoly—The efficiency of intermediate goods markets. *International Journal of Industrial Organization 25*(5), 884–907.
8. Collard-Wexler, A., G. Gowrisankaran, and R. S. Lee (2019). "Nash-in-Nash" bargaining: A microfoundation for applied work. *Journal of Political Economy 127*(1), 163–195.
9. Crawford, G. S. and A. Yurukoglu (2012). The welfare effects of bundling in multichannel television markets. *American Economic Review 102*(2), 643–685.
10. Crawford, G. S., R. S. Lee, M. D. Whinston, and A. Yurukoglu (2018). The welfare effects of vertical integration in multichannel television markets. *Econometrica 86*(3), 891–954.
11. Cremer, J. and M. H. Riordan (1987). On governing multilateral transactions with bilateral contracts. *The RAND Journal of Economics 18*(3), 436–451.

12. Cuesta, J. I., C. Noton, and B. Vatter (2019). Vertical integration between hospitals and insurers. Available at SSRN 3309218.
13. Davidson, C. (1988). Multiunit bargaining in oligopolistic industries. *Journal of Labor Economics 6*(3), 397–422.
14. De Fontenay, C. C. and J. S. Gans (2014). Bilateral bargaining with externalities. *The Journal of Industrial Economics 62*(4), 756–788.
15. De los Santos, B., D. P. O'Brien, and M. R. Wildenbeest (2018). Agency pricing and bargaining: Evidence from the e-book market. Kelley School of Business Research Paper (18-90).
16. Draganska, M., D. Klapper, and S. B. Villas-Boas (2010). A larger slice or a larger pie? An empirical investigation of bargaining power in the distribution channel. *Marketing Science 29*(1), 57–74.
17. Dubois, P. and M. Sæthre (2020). On the effect of parallel trade on manufacturers' and retailers' profits in the pharmaceutical sector. *Econometrica 88*(6), 2503–2545.
18. Dubois, P., A. Gandhi, and S. Vasserman (2018). Bargaining and international reference pricing in the pharmaceutical industry.
19. Eaton, J. and S. Kortum (2002). Technology, geography, and trade. *Econometrica 70*(5), 1741–1779.
20. Ellickson, P. B., P. Kong, and M. J. Lovett (2018). Private labels and retailer profitability: Bilateral bargaining in the grocery channel. Available at SSRN 3045372.
21. Ghili, S. (2018). Network formation and bargaining in vertical markets: The case of narrow networks in health insurance. Working Paper.
22. Gowrisankaran, G., A. Nevo, and R. Town (2015). Mergers when prices are negotiated: Evidence from the hospital industry. *American Economic Review 105*(1), 172–203.
23. Grennan, M. (2013). Price discrimination and bargaining: Empirical evidence from medical devices. *American Economic Review 103*(1), 145–177.
24. Hart, O. and J. Tirole (1990). Vertical integration and market foreclosure. *Brookings Papers on Economic Activity. Microeconomics*, 205–286.
25. Ho, K. (2009). Insurer-provider networks in the medical care market. *American Economic Review 99*(1), 393–430.
26. Ho, K. and R. S. Lee (2017). Insurer competition in health care markets. *Econometrica 85*(2), 379–417.
27. Ho, K. and R. S. Lee (2019). Equilibrium provider networks: Bargaining and exclusion in health care markets. *American Economic Review 109*(2), 473–522.

28. Horn, H. and A. Wolinsky (1988). Bilateral monopolies and incentives for merger. *The RAND Journal of Economics 19*(3), 408–419.
29. Liebman, E. (2018). Bargaining in markets with exclusion: An analysis of health insurance networks. Working Paper.
30. McAfee, R. P. and M. Schwartz (1994). Opportunism in multilateral vertical contracting: Nondiscrimination, exclusivity, and uniformity. *American Economic Review 84*(1), 210–230.
31. Molina, H. (2019). Buyer alliances in vertically related markets. Available at SSRN 3452497.
32. Mortimer, J. H. (2008). Vertical contracts in the video rental industry. *The Review of Economic Studies 75*(1), 165–199.
33. Noton, C. and A. Elberg (2017). Are supermarkets squeezing small suppliers? Evidence from negotiated wholesale prices. *The Economic Journal 128*(610), 1304–1330.
34. Ossa, R. (2014). Trade wars and trade talks with data. *American Economic Review 104*(12), 4104–4146.
35. Robles-Garcia, C. (2019). Competition and incentives in mortgage markets: The role of brokers.
36. Villas-Boas, S. B. (2007). Vertical relationships between manufacturers and retailers: Inference with limited data. *The Review of Economic Studies 74*(2), 625–652.
37. Yurukoglu, A. (2008). Bundling and vertical relationships in multichannel television. Draft, NYU Stern.

12

Bargaining in Healthcare Markets: Applications of Nash-in-Nash and Extensions

Matthew Grennan and Ashley Swanson

Many prices in healthcare are determined in business-to-business negotiations. Private, self-insured employers negotiate with private insurers over insurance plan characteristics and prices. Insurers in turn negotiate with healthcare providers and pharmaceutical manufacturers/distributors over prices for the goods and services used in providing care. Providers themselves negotiate with suppliers of the medical devices they use to provide services. Combined with the rich data that has become available to healthcare researchers, this has led to a growing body of empirical research on bargaining in healthcare markets, particularly in the development of structural models of bargaining that researchers can estimate

M. Grennan
University of California-Berkeley, Berkeley, CA, USA
e-mail: mgrennan@berkeley.edu

A. Swanson (✉)
Columbia University, New York, NY, USA
e-mail: ats2180@gsb.columbia.edu

E. Karagözoğlu and K. B. Hyndman (eds.), *Bargaining*,
https://doi.org/10.1007/978-3-030-76666-5_12

from data and use to consider counterfactual policies. In this chapter, we review these models and their importance for healthcare and bargaining research more broadly. We also discuss other studies that provide the foundation for this literature or that inform the directions in which this literature could mature in order to better capture bargaining scenarios important to healthcare policy and economics more broadly.

12.1 Bargaining in Healthcare, Upstream, and Downstream

Health economists have for some time analyzed the ex-ante willingness-to-pay for adding a player to an economic exchange—variously referred to as a player's "marginal contribution" or "added value" or "gains from trade"—a fundamental building block to most economic models of bargaining. Pioneering work in Town and Vistnes [65] and Capps et al. [3] characterized healthcare as an *option demand* market, in which intermediaries offer a network of upstream suppliers to downstream consumers, and these networks are valued by consumers' ex-ante willingness-to-pay for expected future treatment needs. Ho [35, 36] connected these ideas to their current use, estimating detailed demand models for hospitals, and then estimating an explicit bargaining game.

To fix ideas, consider the following model. For a trading network $\mathcal{G}$, define the gains for a hospital h trading with partner j (here the model is sufficiently abstract for j to be, for example, an upstream input supplier or a downstream insurer):

$$GFT_{hj}^{H} := \pi_h^H(\mathcal{G}, \{p_{hj}, \mathbf{p_{-hj}}\}, \phi) - \pi_h^H(\mathcal{G} \setminus hj, \mathbf{p_{-hj}}, \phi) \quad (12.1)$$

where p_{hj} denotes the price negotiated between the focal parties, and $\mathbf{p_{-hj}}$ is the vector of prices negotiated by other trading pairs in $\mathcal{G}$. ϕ is a vector of demand and supply parameters governing production, consumption, and bargaining. π_h^H is a functional that maps these primitives ϕ and equilibrium objects $(\mathcal{G}, \mathbf{p})$ into ex-ante expected hospital surplus. Similarly, define gains from trade to partner j trading with the hospital, GFT_{hj}^{J}, by replacing π_h^H with π_j^J in (12.1).

After Ho [36], a series of empirical applications of bargaining in healthcare markets were relatively direct adaptations of the Crawford and Yurukoglu [8] empirical specification of the Horn and Wolinsky [40] "Nash-in-Nash" (NiN) bargaining model. The Grennan [27] study of hospitals bargaining with their suppliers and the Gowrisankaran et al. [25] study of hospitals bargaining with insurers contributed to this new methodology by clarifying the ways in which the model could be identified and estimated. The NiN model specifies that each buyer-supplier pair reaches a solution that maximizes its pairwise Nash Product, and no pair wants to renegotiate, taking the prices negotiated by the other pairs as given, solving:

$$\max_{p_{hj}} \left[GFT_{hj}^{J} \right]^{\phi_j^B(h)} \left[GFT_{hj}^{H} \right]^{\phi_h^B(j)} \forall hj \in \mathcal{G} \tag{12.2}$$

where the parameter $\phi_j^B(h) \geq 0$ represents the bargaining ability of player j negotiating with player h.

This model extends the well-known Nash-Bertrand Equilibrium (NBE) in prices with differentiated substitutes. To see this, consider a case where hospital h procures differentiated medical devices $j \in \mathcal{J}$ used in a particular surgical procedure (e.g., prosthetic knee implants). In this case, the network is the set of the device manufacturers paired with the hospital, $\mathcal{G} = \mathcal{J} \times h$. Further, assume that the quantity sold to this hospital is small relative to any fixed costs of production or distribution, so that $GFT_{hj}^{J} := \pi_j^J(\mathcal{G}, \{p_{hj}, \mathbf{p_{-hj}}\}, \phi) - \pi_j^J(\mathcal{G} \setminus hj, \mathbf{p_{-hj}}, \phi) = q_{hj}(p_{hj} - mc_{hj}) - 0$. Then we can solve for the pricing equation implied by the first-order conditions of this maximization problem:

$$p_{hj} = mc_{hj} + \frac{\phi_j^B(h)}{\phi_j^B(h) + \phi_h^B(j)} \left[\left(1 + \frac{\partial q_{hj}}{\partial p_{hj}} \frac{p_{hj} - mc_{hj}}{q_{hj}} \right) \frac{GFT_{hj}^{H}}{q_{hj}} + \frac{GFT_{hj}^{J}}{q_{hj}} \right]. \tag{12.3}$$

Here the markup of the supplier is a function of the total bilateral gains from trade, the demand elasticity, and the ratio of the supplier bargaining ability relative to that of the hospital $\frac{\phi_j^B(h)}{\phi_j^B(h)+\phi_h^B(j)} \in [0, 1]$. When this ratio is zero, $p_{hj} = mc_{hj}$. When this ratio is one, the equation reduces to the first-order condition for NBE where the manufacturer sets price, $\frac{\partial q_{hj}}{\partial p_{hj}} \frac{p_{hj}-mc_{hj}}{q_{hj}} = -1$.

The elasticity term measures how the total gains from trade shrink as equilibrium quantities respond to a price increase. In studies such as Grennan [27, 28] where physicians are not very price sensitive in their usage of medical devices, it plays a relatively small role.[1] However, elasticities are central in other contexts. For example, Brown [2] studies how New Hampshire's price transparency initiative affects equilibrium prices and quantities for medical imaging services. Transparency makes some consumers more price elastic as they gain information on prices and switch to cheaper providers. This increased elasticity then decreases the gains from trade generated by providers, lowering all prices in equilibrium.

Thus when prices are negotiated, they will be a function of elasticities (as they are when suppliers post prices), but they will also be a function of gains from trade and bargaining ability parameters. Bargaining abilities provide a new source of supply shifters when estimating demand, and a new parameter that may change under counterfactual analysis [27]. Gains from trade depend on the availability of close economic substitutes, and thus are related to market structure (and changes to market structure, such as mergers) in a manner that goes beyond standard cross-elasticity analyses. These three components: elasticities, gains from trade, and bargaining abilities represent the basic channels determining negotiated prices in this literature.

[1] This highlights one reason why bargaining models have been important in healthcare: NBE often implies unreasonably large markups when end users are insensitive to price [25, 27].

12.1.1 Applications to Buyer Power: Purchasing of Medical Devices, Pharmaceuticals, and Hospital Care

The conventional wisdom that "bigger is better" in business-to-business negotiations pervades the policy discussion on topics ranging from insurer mergers to hospital mergers to group purchasing organizations and whether or not the government should negotiate drug prices. For example, this notion has led U.S. policymakers to advocate for more centralized procurement of healthcare products and services by federal and state governments [43], rather than decentralized bilateral bargaining as is the norm.

In spite of conventional wisdom, a "buyer size advantage" is not a given in the economics literature. In a fairly general class of models, larger buyer firms may obtain better prices if and only if the supplier's surplus function is concave (e.g., Chipty and Snyder [5]). However, size may also be associated with differences in bargaining abilities if, for example, larger firms are better managed.[2] Moreover, mechanisms that lead to lower input prices may not improve welfare [4, 33].[3] The impact of these mechanisms may further depend on details such as geography or supplier market structure.[4]

These ambiguities and the multiplicity of mechanisms laid out in theory have prompted a move toward empirical studies. The empirical literature on the effects of buyer power in healthcare has focused on purchasing of healthcare production inputs, drugs, and hospital care.

One strain of the literature focuses on hospital mergers and costs. Hospital systems have consolidated substantially in recent decades [11]. A typical justification for these horizontal mergers is their potential to generate cost synergies. Much of the literature on the effects of

[2] Bloom et al. [1] find that larger hospitals have better management practices.

[3] For example, a merger downstream could lead to decreased innovation or product variety upstream [41].

[4] Geographic proximity may be a success factor for mergers (a common contributor to buyer size increases), economies of scale in supplier distribution, or otherwise. Larger buyers may spur competition among multiple suppliers. These competition effects may be mediated by buyers' demand commitments [12, 41], by suppliers' own tacit collusion [59, 60], or by the presence of transaction costs [22, 48].

hospital mergers on costs has focused on overall hospital costs [14, 56] and on labor costs [10, 54]. This literature generally finds that horizontal hospital mergers lead to cost reductions for at least some types of combinations. However, attributing these findings to changes in bilateral bargaining between hospitals and suppliers presents several difficulties. As noted in Gaynor and Town [23], cost data are usually limited to Medicare Cost Reports and state financial data, which "are not easily adjusted for changes in patient severity, and are subject to the vagaries of accounting methodologies."

One study that explicitly examines the effects of hospital mergers on bilateral bargaining, accounting for composition, is Craig et al. [7], which uses detailed data on hospital supply purchase orders issued by a sample of U.S. hospitals from 2009 to 2015. The authors find that, for a fixed basket of top hospital supply categories, the average merger target saved 1.9%, while the average acquirer achieved no savings. Heterogeneity in effect estimates was consistent with mergers inducing a small increase in hospital buyer power that is (1) driven by local returns to scale, and (2) more influential for merger targets than for acquirers. There was little evidence that savings, where they exist, are mediated by supplier market structure.

Several studies have examined the effects of strong purchasers on drug prices. A key finding in this literature is that buyers' ability to credibly exclude suppliers can be as important, or even more important, than buyer size. Duggan and Scott Morton [18] estimate that drug "formularies," which give insurance plans a mechanism to exclude suppliers, were crucial in restraining drug costs during the early rollout of Medicare Part D, the federal prescription drug benefit for the elderly in the U.S. They find that Part D led to a substantial relative decline in branded pharmaceutical prices, but only in drug classes where exclusion was statutorily allowed *and* where multiple substitutes were available on the market.

The importance of upstream competition for leveraging buyer power is echoed by other studies of drug pricing. Ellison and Snyder [19] find that large purchasers (chain drugstores) extract lower antibiotic prices from manufacturers than small purchasers (independents), but only for drugs with multiple competitors. Lakdawalla and Yin [42] find that exogenous increases in enrollment enable insurers to negotiate lower drug prices with pharmacies, but these buyer size discounts were smaller in drug classes where manufacturers extracted monopoly rents and left little surplus for insurers and pharmacies to divide. Looking across low- and middle-income countries, Dubois et al. [16] find that centralized procurement is associated with large discounts relative to decentralized procurement, and the discounts vanish when the drug is supplied by a monopolist.

The interaction between buyer size and supplier competition has also been emphasized in the literature on insurer-hospital bargaining. Staten et al. [64] argue that insurer size alone does not confer the power to extract price concessions from hospitals. In order to extract discounts, an insurer must also be able to credibly threaten to send its enrollees elsewhere, and such threats are undermined by patient loyalty to hospitals. Ho and Lee [37] provide a framework for exploring these forces. In their model, managed care organizations (MCOs) with market power compete for enrollees *and* negotiate with hospitals over the prices of hospital services. MCOs can threaten to exclude hospitals from their network. Household premiums are set via bargaining between employers and MCOs. Subsequent to these negotiations, households enroll with MCOs as a function of their premiums and provider networks, experience healthcare needs, and choose hospitals for treatment. The authors estimate this upstream-downstream bargaining model using detailed data on prices, premiums, enrollment, and hospital admissions for public employees in California.

In this model, equilibrium prices in a given MCO-hospital negotiation are a function of several forces that map the above notions of "hospital and insurer loyalty." For example, if dropping the hospital from the MCO's network leads to a large drop in enrollment, then the hospital can command a higher price. Similarly, prices will be increasing in a recapture effect, which represents the profits that a hospital will obtain if loyal enrollees re-sort into other MCOs when the hospital is excluded from the current MCO's network.

The Ho and Lee [37] results present nuanced evidence on buyer power in healthcare markets. First, in an option demand setting where employers negotiate premiums, removing an MCO can lead to positive *or* negative effects on remaining MCOs' premiums. Second, these premium effects can counteract or reinforce the remaining MCOs' increased market power with respect to hospitals, with ambiguous implications for hospital prices on net. Finally, premium and price effects are quite heterogeneous across markets, though consumer welfare always decreases when an MCO is removed, due to reduced product variety.

12.1.2 Applications to Supplier Market Power: Mergers and Hospital-Insurer Bargaining

Bargaining has been especially influential in the realm of antitrust, particularly in the analysis of horizontal mergers and market power. For example, the Federal Trade Commission's standard model for evaluating hospital mergers is a bargaining model [20]. In recent cases, court opinions have relied heavily on bargaining theory [50].

Gowrisankaran et al. [25] estimate a bargaining model of competition between hospitals and MCOs and use the estimates to evaluate the effects of hospital mergers. They find that MCO bargaining restrains hospital prices significantly. In a counterfactual analysis, they find that a proposed hospital acquisition in Northern Virginia would have significantly raised hospital prices, and remedies based on separate bargaining would not alleviate the price increases.

Gowrisankaran et al. [25] hold bargaining parameters fixed in their merger simulations, so price effects are driven by the impact of the merger on gains from trade (and internalization of cross-elasticities). In a model that estimates bargaining ability parameters, Lewis and Pflum [44] find that more of the observed price gap between system and non-system hospitals can be attributed to bargaining parameter differences than to differences in gains from trade driven by local market concentration.

The result that bargaining power parameters explain a substantial portion of the variation in prices is a recurring phenomenon in this literature. As these parameters are in part residuals, they could in principle capture many unmodeled phenomena internal (including firm organizational structure, information, incentives, management, and leadership) or external to the firm (including exclusionary contracting, quantity-based contracting, or other unmodeled features of the full vertical supply chain or contract space). Much of the subsequent literature has sought to increase the scope of the models and data in order to capture these elements of various bargaining scenarios in healthcare. A large part of the rest of the chapter discusses these extensions and related work.

12.2 Modeling Network Formation

Real world trading networks in business-to-business markets are rarely exogenously determined or costless to form (and reform). As in other contexts, these factors can lead to selection in who contracts with whom, potentially affecting demand and supply estimation. They can also change the outside options in negotiations relative to the "frictionless" NiN models we have discussed thus far. These are potentially important issues in considering how insurers construct their provider networks and how hospitals construct their supplier networks. New research is making strides toward quantifying the magnitudes of these issues.

12.2.1 Strategic Exclusion

The discussion in the previous sections focused on how buyers and sellers split their gains from trade, holding all other agreements fixed. The model assumes that all agreements involving positive gains from trade will be made in equilibrium. Exclusion is an off-equilibrium threat.

Contrary to this notion, exclusion is an increasingly pervasive phenomenon in healthcare markets. For example, insurers form restrictive formularies, pharmacy networks, and provider networks [31, 49, 52, 62]. Several theories of bargaining provide useful intuition as to what might be happening. Gal-Or [21] presents a stylized bargaining model in which insurers can reduce hospital prices in "exclusionary" contracts in which each insurer forecloses all but one hospital. However, if horizontal differentiation between hospitals is sufficiently large, and when the likelihood of becoming sick is sufficiently high, the only equilibrium that can arise is non-exclusionary. In a similar vein, Dana [12] and Inderst and Shaffer [41] present models in which a merged buyer's bargaining advantage is mediated by buyers' demand commitments. The welfare implications of such demand commitments are complex. Some buyers will consume their less preferred product, but benefit on net from lower prices. In the healthcare context, similar tradeoffs precipitated the managed care backlash of the 1990s [32], as well as conflicts between physicians and hospitals regarding hospital attempts to sole-source medical devices [51].

A substantial body of reduced form empirical evidence supports the notion that exclusion can reduce insurer spending via price reductions. For example, many state Medicaid programs, which provide health insurance to low-income consumers, have been shown to successfully leverage restrictive formularies to lower retail drug expenditures [13, 26, 49]. In a similar vein, Sorensen [61] showed that the ability of Connecticut MCOs to channel enrollees to hospitals (i.e., their demand commitments) was a far more important determinant of negotiated hospital prices than MCO size.

Only very recently, a structural empirical literature has emerged that models equilibrium exclusion and demand commitments that provide buyers additional leverage to reduce negotiated prices. For example, Ho and Lee [38] propose the "Nash-in-Nash with Threat of Replacement" model (NiNTR), in which buyers can threaten to replace suppliers with viable alternative suppliers that are outside the network. The NiNTR solution looks similar to NiN, but with the additional requirement that insurer j will never pay hospital h more than its outside option of dropping h from the network and adding the best non-contracted alternative hospital k to the network (at k's reservation price). They also define a stability condition for NiNTR prices to be an equilibrium: a given network $\mathcal{G}$ is stable at NiNTR prices if, and only if, the network does not exclude any hospital that generates higher bilateral surplus with the insurer than any included hospital.

In order to make this intuition concrete, Ho and Lee [38] use the data and parameters from Ho and Lee [37] to simulate the counterfactual premium, price, and welfare effects of one insurer offering a restrictive hospital network. They estimate that, with a narrow network, the insurer would have been able to negotiate steep discounts. On average, consumers would benefit from the narrow network, as the resulting decrease in premiums would offset the consumer surplus loss of having access to fewer hospitals. However, consumer surplus varies widely: some consumers, such as those living close to excluded hospitals, would experience significant harm.

Ghili [24] and Liebman [45] propose alternative extensions of the Nash-in-Nash framework to accommodate equilibrium exclusion. Like Ho and Lee [38], Ghili [24] allows an insurer to threaten to replace any contracted hospital in its network with one outside its network. To rationalize observed variation across plans in network breadth, he assumes that different plans have different "economies of scale," captured by fixed costs of including additional hospitals in network. Liebman [45] proposes a different model, in which insurers commit to network size in an initial stage of the game. Prices are then determined as the result of an alternating offers bargaining game between all hospitals and insurers, where upon disagreement in bargaining for a given insurer-hospital pair, a replacement hospital may be randomly chosen.

12.2.1.1 Selection on networks

Shepard [58] focuses on how exclusion interacts with patient selection. A large theoretical and empirical literature suggests that more generous insurance plans will attract more costly enrollees. If insurers are not perfectly able to adjust premiums as a function of enrollees' risk, then costly enrollees will be less profitable to insurers.[5] This study focuses on a key aspect of plan generosity that interacts with insurer-hospital bargaining: whether plans cover the best-regarded academic (or "star") hospitals. Using rich data on claims and plan choices from Massachusetts' health insurance marketplace for low-income individuals, CommCare, Shepard [58] shows that consumers with a pre-existing attachment to star hospitals in Massachusetts are both very costly to insure and also far more likely to choose a plan covering star hospitals.

[5] "Risk adjustment" is a tool regulators use to limit insurers' incentive to seek low-risk enrollees. Risk adjustment works by measuring medical risk factors (e.g., age and diagnoses) and compensating plans that attract observably sicker people.

This form of selection provides a strong inducement for plans to drop star hospitals from their networks.

12.2.1.2 Quality regulation

A natural concern is that welfare is harmed when intermediary firms exclude suppliers. This might be particularly problematic in the healthcare setting, where excluding a high-quality provider or product may be a life-or-death matter and consumers may be insufficiently informed about tradeoffs. For example, Gruber and McKnight [31] find that the marginal enrollee in limited provider network plans does not simply avoid high-cost providers: she consumes less healthcare services overall.

The health economics literature has pursued this issue in a few different ways. Some papers have used structural model estimates to evaluate the effects of policy interventions that regulate network size. E.g., Ghili [24] and Liebman [45] study the effects of "network adequacy" rules that require minimum levels of coverage of local providers, finding that such standards would increase hospital prices and, perhaps, insurer premiums. Shepard [58] uses his structural estimates to evaluate the welfare effects of a targeted subsidy for plans that cover star hospitals. He finds that these policies would decrease welfare, as they would entail healthcare cost increases exceeding the increase in consumers' value for the hospitals.

In some instances, whether due to binding regulations or due to more informal pressures from healthcare suppliers or consumers, buyer firms opt not to fully exclude suppliers and instead rely on *partial* exclusion for leverage in bargaining. Starc and Swanson [62] consider the Medicare Part D context, in which plans are prohibited from excluding many retail pharmacies. Recently, many Part D plans have established restrictive "preferred pharmacy networks," where preferred status means reduced out-of-pocket costs to enrollees. In order for partial exclusion to result in a demand commitment, enrollees must respond to reduced out-of-pocket costs by frequenting preferred pharmacies. Starc and Swanson [62] show that: adoption of preferred networks is associated with selection of low-cost enrollees, consistent with Shepard

[58]; enrollees respond significantly to pharmacy "preferred status"; and preferred-network plans negotiate lower prices for drugs, with no effect on consumer access.[6] Unsurprisingly, the effects of preferred pharmacy networks disappear in plans that cover primarily subsidized beneficiaries who face low out-of-pocket prices no matter the pharmacy.

12.2.2 Frictions in network formation

The Ghili [24] study mentioned above rationalizes exclusion via fixed costs of adding and maintaining a buyer-supplier relationship. These costs can make it optimal to form a trading network that is smaller than the full network, and thus provide insurers a credible threat to replace an in-network hospital with an out-of-network one. To address the potential computational challenges involved in estimating a model with a large number of potential network configurations by, the paper uses a moment inequalities estimator derived from stability conditions on the observed networks in order to estimate the fixed costs of contracting. Applied to a health insurance market in Massachusetts, Ghili's estimated model finds that fixed costs of network formation add up to approximately one-third of insurer profits.

12.3 New Directions: Contracts, Organizations, and Information

Many of the models and applications discussed thus far have explicitly or implicitly assumed that the contracting parties have full information about all model parameters, for themselves and all parties who could potentially be included in the trading network. The contracting space is typically limited to linear prices, exchanged bilaterally, that only impact each other via their impact on equilibrium quantities. The players themselves are abstract entities, reducing complex and heterogeneously

[6] Similar "steering" effects are examined in the case of tiered hospital networks in Prager [53] and vertically integrated insurer-hospitals in Cuesta et al. [9].

skilled and motivated people and organizations down to a few parameters. Though these simplifying assumptions may be good approximations to reality in some contexts, in other cases they may miss important features of the market. Recent research has made progress toward better understanding and/or loosening these restrictions, but there are many opportunities for important contributions.

12.3.1 Enhancing the Contracting Space

Contracts in healthcare can be complex, and sometimes that complexity is critical for understanding equilibrium outcomes. An important example in drug procurement has been most-favored-nation (MFN) clauses or other types of "reference pricing" where the outcomes of prices negotiated in other agreements enter the negotiation directly through the contract stipulations, not only via their effects on demand. Scott Morton [57] and Duggan and Scott Morton [17] demonstrate these effects in studies of the U.S. Federal Government's introduction of an MFN clause on pharmaceutical prices supplied to Medicaid in the 1990s. Firms had to provide drugs to Medicaid at their lowest price. However, the rule resulted in higher prices to some non-Medicaid drug consumers.

More recently, a few papers have structurally modeled and estimated the impact of reference pricing on equilibrium prices, quantities, and entry patterns. Dubois et al. [15] consider the effects of a hypothetical U.S. reference pricing policy that would cap prices in U.S. markets by those offered in Canada. Counterfactuals based on their estimated model predict modest consumer welfare gains in the U.S., substantial consumer welfare losses in Canada, and an increase in overall pharmaceutical profits. Maini and Pammolli [47] also study the issue of reference pricing for pharmaceuticals, focusing on how reference pricing policies affect drug entry timing across countries within the EU. While they abstract from modeling the bargaining process underlying their pricing policy function, they consider both the direct externality imposed by reference pricing, and also the indirect externalities imposed on choice sets due to strategic entry delays (which are an optimal response to the reference pricing).

Another important feature of insurer-provider contracting is the desire to induce multiple providers to jointly balance the overall health benefits and financial costs of the care they provide. This desire has motivated both public and private payers in the U.S. to establish provider contracts with financial rewards/penalties based on *all* costs and consequences for a defined set of patients or episode of care (e.g., "Accountable Care Organizations" and "Comprehensive Care for Joint Replacement"). These efforts may be important in contexts where narrowly focused contracts have unintended consequences. For example, the literature on drug formularies in state Medicaid programs [13, 26, 49] finds that restrictive formularies may result in offsetting increases in other healthcare expenditures because drugs and other healthcare products and services are substitutes in the production of health. This may impose an externality on health insurance programs [63]. Further, Cooper et al. [6] show that many hospitals are staffed by specialists like emergency physicians, radiologists, and anesthesiologists that cannot be easily avoided by patients admitted at the hospitals where they practice. The result is that such specialists, even those staffed at in-network hospitals, can opt out of insurers' *physician* networks and charge inflated prices without sacrificing demand, and this lucrative outside option enables them to command high in network prices.

12.3.2 Asymmetric Information Bargaining

There is currently no standard approach for introducing asymmetric information explicitly to the Nash-in-Nash framework. This is unfortunate as much of the debate regarding transparency in healthcare hypothesizes about how such information may directly affect the bargaining problems between hospitals and insurers [34] or hospitals and device manufacturers [46].

Grennan and Swanson [29] study the latter context by examining what happens when hospitals obtain access to "benchmarking" data on the prices other hospitals pay for the same medical devices. They find that savings from access to this information are largest for physician preference devices, where high-price, high-quantity hospital-brand combinations average 3.9% savings, versus 1.6% for commodities.

The paper offers two theoretical models that could explain these savings: an asymmetric information bargaining model where hospitals are uncertain about manufacturers' bargaining parameters [55], and a model where bargaining parameters represent the outcome of an agency problem between hospital owners and the administrators who negotiate prices, so that benchmarking data allows owners to better monitor administrator effort [39]. They find evidence for both, but stronger evidence for the model of asymmetric information about bargaining parameters. They also model a role for externalities: transparency might discourage suppliers from agreeing to low prices with any buyer because that price can then become information that other buyers will use against the supplier, but they don't find empirical evidence of this effect.

12.4 Discussion: Progress and Opportunities for Bargaining in Healthcare and Beyond

The healthcare sector is one where most prices are set via business-to-business negotiations, and thus many important policy questions depend on bargaining outcomes across buyer-supplier networks. Because the healthcare setting has recently provided researchers with relatively rich data to model and estimate the surplus creation and division process, it has been at the forefront of much of the recent literature on empirical studies of bargaining. In many regards this literature has experienced a great deal of success in that the tools and approaches have quickly become influential, in particular with regard to antitrust in hospital and insurer markets.

However, the empirical bargaining literature (in healthcare and more broadly) is still young, and there are many challenges to tackle before researchers will have a toolkit that allows them to model the many interesting and important research questions that remain. There are currently very few structural papers that go beyond Nash-in-Nash to incorporate the phenomena documented in Sects. 12.1.1 and 12.2. Work that improves tractability (e.g., allowing endogenous network formation for counterfactuals with a high-dimensional player space, or incorporating externalities in structural models of bargaining under asymmetric information) or sheds further light on the importance and validity of modeling assumptions (e.g., fixed costs of adding a trading partner) would be a strong contribution.

Even less well-understood are the formal and informal contracts that exist between and within healthcare suppliers, or how those contracts may be disrupted in counterfactual scenarios. First, hospital surplus is to a great extent governed by physicians who recommend hospitals for inpatient and outpatient care and choose medical device brands (which are paid for by hospitals) to use in procedures.[7] Historically, physicians and hospitals were financially and organizationally distinct co-producers of care with strong informal ties and explicit prohibition of "kick-back" arrangements, but recent decades have seen growth in hospital ownership of physician practices and gainsharing. The literature (and policymakers) have not yet grappled with the contracting relationships between physicians and hospitals as co-producers of care.

Second, the bargaining parameters estimated in the Nash-in-Nash framework are often an empirically important but not well understood "residual" in the sense that they will tend to absorb any modeling or measurement error in the relationship between gains from trade and prices. Empirically, bargaining parameters capture the relative weight put on buyer and supplier surplus necessary to explain price variation as a function of added value variation. Theoretically, they are often modeled as discount factors in a multi-stage bargaining game. In the real world, they may proxy for a host of factors—impatience, opportunity costs of time, laziness, fear of negotiation breakdown—that will depend on leadership, management, and incentives within firms. Work that advances our understanding of what real-world factors bargaining

[7] Relatedly, physician relationships with medical device and pharmaceutical manufacturers may impact both hospital/insurer ability to credibly exclude those manufacturers' products and researchers' ability to use choice patterns to infer consumer welfare [30].

parameters capture, perhaps involving new ways of incorporating those factors into surplus calculations, would be tremendously beneficial.

We anticipate that the ubiquity of bargaining, the welfare at stake, and the large amounts of detailed data available to researchers will continue to make healthcare applications important for empirical bargaining research in the future.

References

1. Nick Bloom, Raffaella Sadun, and John VanReenen. Healthy business? Managerial education and management in healthcare. *Review of Economics and Statistics*, 102 (3): 506–517, July 2020.
2. Zach Y. Brown. An empirical model of price transparency and markups in health care. working paper, 2019.
3. Cory Capps, David Dranove, and Mark Satterthwaite. Competition and market power in option demand markets. *RAND Journal of Economics*, 34 (4): 737–763, 2003.
4. Dennis W. Carlton and Mark Israel. Proper treatment of buyer power in merger review. *Review of Industrial Organization*, 39 (1/2): 127–136, 2011.
5. Tasneem Chipty and Christopher M. Snyder. The role of firm size in bilateral bargaining: A study of the cable television industry. *Review of Economics and Statistics*, 81 (2): 326–340, May 1999.
6. Zack Cooper, Fiona Scott Morton, and Nathan Shekita. Surprise! Out-of-network billing for emergency care in the United States. *Journal of Political Economy*, 128: 3626–3677, 2020.
7. Stuart V. Craig, Matthew Grennan, and Ashley Swanson. Mergers and marginal costs: New evidence on hospital buyer power. *RAND Journal of Economics*, 52(1): 151–178, 2021.
8. Greg Crawford and Ali Yurukoglu. The welfare effects of bundling in multichannel television. *American Economic Review*, 102 (2), April 2012.
9. Jose Ignacio Cuesta, Carlos Noton, and Benjamin Vatter. Vertical integration between hospitals and insurers. working paper, 2019.
10. Janet Currie, Mehdi Farsi, and W. Bentley Macleod. Cut to the bone? Hospital takeovers and nurse employment contracts. *ILR Review*, 58 (3): 471–493, 2005.

11. David M. Cutler and Fiona Scott Morton. Hospitals, market share, and consolidation. *JAMA*, 310 (18): 1964–70, November 2013.
12. James Dana. Buyer groups as strategic commitments. *Games and Economic Behavior*, 74 (2): 470–485, 2012.
13. David Dranove. Medicaid drug formulary restrictions. *The Journal of Law and Economics*, 32 (1): 143–162, 1989.
14. David Dranove and Richard Lindrooth. Hospital consolidation and costs: Another look at the evidence. *Journal of Health Economics*, November 2003.
15. Pierre Dubois, Ashvin Gandhi, and Shoshana Vasserman. Bargaining and international reference pricing in the pharmaceutical industry. working paper, 2019a.
16. Pierre Dubois, Yassine Lefouili, and Stephane Straub. Pooled procurement of drugs in low and middle income countries. Working paper, March 2019b.
17. Mark Duggan and Fiona Scott Morton. The distortionary effects of government procurement: Evidence from Medicaid prescription drug purchasing. *Quarterly Journal of Economics*, 121: 1–31, February 2006.
18. Mark Duggan and Fiona Scott Morton. The impact of Medicare Part D on pharmaceutical prices and utilization. *American Economic Review*, 100 (1): 590–607, March 2010.
19. Sara F. Ellison and Christopher M. Snyder. Countervailing power in wholesale pharmaceuticals. *Journal of Industrial Economics*, 58 (1): 32–53, March 2010.
20. Joseph Farrell. Economics at the FTC: Hospital mergers, authorized generic drugs, and consumer credit markets. *Review of Industrial Organization*, 39: 272–282, 2011.
21. Esther Gal-Or. Exclusionary equilibria in health-care markets. *Journal of Economics and Management Strategy*, 6 (1): 5–43, 1997.
22. Joshua S. Gans and Stephen P. King. Exclusionary contracts and competition for large buyers. *International Journal of Industrial Organization*, 20 (9): 1363–1381, 2002.
23. Martin Gaynor and Robert J. Town. Competition in health care markets. In Thomas G. McGuire, Mark V. Pauly, and Pedro Barros, editors, *Handbook of Health Economics*, volume 2, pages 499–637. Elsevier B. V., 2012.
24. Soheil Ghili. Network formation and bargaining in vertical markets: The case of narrow networks in health insurance. Working paper, February 2018.

25. Gautam Gowrisankaran, Aviv Nevo, and Robert Town. Mergers when prices are negotiated: Evidence from the hospital industry. *The American Economic Review*, 105 (1): 172–203, 2015.
26. Henry Grabowski. Medicaid patients' access to new drugs. *Health Affairs*, 7 (5): 102–114, 1988.
27. Matthew Grennan. Price discrimination and bargaining: Empirical evidence from medical devices. *American Economic Review*, 103 (1): 145–177, February 2013.
28. Matthew Grennan. Bargaining ability and competitive advantage: Empirical evidence from medical devices. *Management Science*, 60 (12): 3011–3025, 2014.
29. Matt Grennan and Ashley Swanson. Transparency and negotiated prices: The value of information in hospital-supplier bargaining. *Journal of Political Economy*, 128 (4): 1234–1268, 2020.
30. Matthew Grennan, Kyle Myers, Ashley Swanson, and Aaron Chatterji. No free lunch? Welfare analysis of firms selling through expert intermediaries. Available at SSRN: https://ssrn.com/abstract=3216172, March 2021.
31. Jonathan Gruber and Robin McKnight. Controlling health care costs through limited network insurance plans: Evidence from Massachusetts state employees. *American Economic Journal: Economic Policy*, 8 (2): 219–50, May 2016.
32. Jay Hancock. 'Narrow networks' trigger push-back from state officials. *Kaiser Health News*, November 2013.
33. C. Scott Hemphill and Nancy L. Rose. Mergers that harm sellers. *The Yale Law Journal*, 127 (1), 2018.
34. HHS Press Office. Trump administration announces historic price transparency requirements to increase competition and lower healthcare costs for all americans. *HHS.gov*, November 2019.
35. Katherine Ho. The welfare effects of restricted hospital choice in the US medical care market. *Journal of Applied Econometrics*, 21 (7): 1039–1079, 2006.
36. Katherine Ho. Insurer-provider networks in the medical care market. *American Economic Review*, 99(1): 393–430, 2009.
37. Katherine Ho and Robin S. Lee. Insurer competition in health care markets. *Econometrica*, 85 (2): 379–417, 2017.
38. Katherine Ho and Robin S. Lee. Equilibrium provider networks: Bargaining and exclusion in health care markets. *American Economic Review*, 109 (2): 473–522, February 2019.

39. Bengt Holmstrom. Moral hazard in teams. *The Bell Journal of Economics*, 13 (2): 324–340, Autumn 1982.
40. Henrick Horn and Asher Wolinsky. Bilateral monopolies and incentives for merger. *RAND Journal of Economics*, 19: 408–419, 1988.
41. Roman Inderst and Greg Shaffer. Retail mergers, buyer power and product variety. *Economic Journal*, 117 (1): 45–67, 2007.
42. Darius Lakdawalla and Wesley Yin. Insurers' negotiating leverage and the external effects of Medicare Part D. *Review of Economics and Statistics*, 97 (2): 314–331, 2015.
43. Angelica LaVito. Trump administration opens up more drugs covered by Medicare to price negotiations. *CNBC.com*, August 2018.
44. Matthew Lewis and Kevin Pflum. Diagnosing hospital system bargaining power in managed care networks. *American Economic Journal: Economic Policy*, 7 (1): 243–74, 2015.
45. Eli Liebman. Bargaining in markets with exclusion: An analysis of health insurance networks. Working paper, January 2018.
46. Keith D. Lind. Understanding the market for implantable medical devices. *AARP Public Policy Institute*, 2017.
47. Luca Maini and Fabio Pammolli. Reference pricing as a deterrent to entry: Evidence from the European pharmaceutical market. working paper, 2019.
48. Howard P. Marvel and Huanxing Yang. Group purchasing, nonlinear tariffs, and oligopoly. *International Journal of Industrial Organization*, 26 (5): 1090–1105, 2008.
49. William J. Moore and Robert J. Newman. Drug formulary restrictions as a cost-containment policy in Medicaid programs. *The Journal of Law and Economics*, 36 (1): 71–97, 1993.
50. Aviv Nevo. Mergers that increase bargaining leverage. Remarks as Prepared for the Stanford Institute for Economic Policy Research and Cornerstone Research Conference on Antitrust in Highly Innovative Industries, January 2014.
51. W. C. Nugent, C. M. Kilo, C. S. Ross, A. S. Marrin, D. M. Berwick, and J. Roessner. *Improving Outcomes and Reducing Costs in Adult Cardiac Surgery*. Institute for Healthcare Improvement, Boston, MA, 1999.
52. Daniel Polsky, Zuleyha Cidav, and Ashley Swanson. Marketplace plans with narrow physician networks feature lower monthly premiums than plans with larger networks. *Health Affairs*, October 2016.
53. Elena Prager. Health care demand under simple prices: Evidence from tiered hospital networks. *American Economic Journal: Economic Policy*, 12 (4): 196–223, 2020.

54. Elena Prager and Matt Schmitt. Employer consolidation and wages: Evidence from hospitals. *American Economic Review*, 111(2): 397–427, 2021.
55. Ariel Rubinstein. A bargaining model with incomplete information about time preferences. *Econometrica*, 53 (5): 1151–1172, 1985.
56. Matt Schmitt. Do hospital mergers reduce costs? *Journal of Health Economics*, 52: 74–94, 2017.
57. Fiona Scott Morton. The strategic response by pharmaceutical firms to the Medicaid most-favored-customer rules. *The RAND Journal of Economics*, 28 (2), 1997.
58. Mark Shepard. Hospital network competition and adverse selection: Evidence from the Massachusetts health insurance exchange. Working paper, October 2016.
59. Christopher M. Snyder. A dynamic theory of countervailing power. *Rand Journal of Economics*, 27: 747–769, 1996.
60. Christopher M. Snyder. Why do larger buyers pay lower prices? Intense supplier competition. *Economics Letters*, 58: 205–209, 1998.
61. Alan Sorensen. Insurer-hospital bargaining: Negotiated discounts in post-deregulation Connecticut. *Journal of Industrial Economics*, December 2003.
62. Amanda Starc and Ashley Swanson. Preferred pharmacy networks and drug costs. *American Economic Journal: Economic Policy*, 13(3): 406–446, 2021.
63. Amanda Starc and Robert J. Town. Externalities and benefit design in health insurance. *Review of Economic Studies*, September 2019.
64. Michael Staten, William Dunkelberg, and John Umbeck. Market share and the illusion of power: Can Blue Cross force hospitals to discount? *Journal of Health Economics*, 6 (1): 43–58, 1987.
65. Robert J. Town and Gregory Vistnes. Hospital competition in HMO networks. *Journal of Health Economics*, 20 (5): 733–752, 2001.

13

Bargaining and Climate Change Negotiations

Alejandro Caparrós

13.1 Introduction

Climate change is one of the main challenges faced by humankind and over the last decades countries have tried to find a global response to this challenge through intense negotiations. Unfortunately, results have been, at best, mixed. Game theoretic analysis of International Environmental Agreements (IEA) has been a very active research area over the past three decades (Finus and Caparrós 2015). Although this literature does not apply exclusively to the climate change problem, there is no denying that climate change has been the main motivation. Although most of this literature abstracts from the negotiating process, this chapter focuses on the papers that have indeed modeled climate change negotiations, or parts of it.

A. Caparrós (✉)
Department of Economics and Finance, Business School,
University of Durham, Durham, UK
e-mail: alejandro.caparros@durham.ac.uk

E. Karagözoğlu and K. B. Hyndman (eds.), *Bargaining*,
https://doi.org/10.1007/978-3-030-76666-5_13

To model negotiations, the most obvious approach is to base the analysis on the Nash Bargaining Solution (NBS) or the Rubinstein Bargaining Solution (RBS), and this has been the path followed by most of the papers discussed below. However, recent developments have diminished the relevance of many of these papers for the analysis of current climate change negotiations. The reason is that climate change negotiations have moved away from what was basically a burden-sharing agreement, the Kyoto Protocol, to a pledge and review process, the Paris Agreement. Yet, at least without modifications, the NBS and the RBS are appropriate for analyzing burden-sharing agreements but not necessarily for the process launched by the Paris Agreement. This could be seen as diminishing the relevance of bargaining theory in this context but I will argue that, on the contrary, this opens up opportunities for future research, as recent advances are showing that properly modified bargaining models continue to be relevant. Furthermore, the flexibility of bargaining models makes them better candidates to analyze current negotiations than alternative modeling frameworks (see Finus and Caparrós [2015] for other frameworks used to analyze IEA).

Before moving on, I briefly describe the history of climate change negotiations. This will allow us to compare the theoretical analyses with this benchmark. In 1992 virtually all the countries in the world signed and ratified the United Nations Framework Convention on climate change (UNFCCC). The UNFCCC's objective is to achieve the "stabilization of greenhouse gas concentration in the atmosphere at a level that would prevent dangerous anthropogenic inference with the climate system" (UNFCCC 1992). In 1997 the Kyoto Protocol was signed, engaging the countries included in Annex I (OECD and economies in transition) to reduce their overall emission by five percent in 2012 compared to 1990. The main feature of the Kyoto Protocol is that it was negotiated as a burden-sharing agreement. That is, countries bargained over the contribution that each party should do, and once signed and ratified, the agreement became 'binding' under international law.[1] As efforts to extend the Kyoto approach beyond the first commitment period (2008–2012) failed, negotiators agreed in 2015 on the Paris Agreement. This agreement specifies the goal of the UNFCCC, stating that countries aim at "holding the increase in the global average temperature to well below 2°C above pre-industrial levels and [...] pursue efforts to limit the temperature increase to 1.5°C above pre-industrial levels" (UNFCCC 2015). The main feature of the Paris Agreement is that it does not have short-term commitments, but rather it urges countries to periodically submit their voluntary commitments, their Nationally Determined Contributions (NDCs). These NDCs (pledges) are not legally binding, not even under international law.[2] This approach is less ambitious than a binding burden-sharing agreement, but the advantage is that the Paris Agreement covers 96% of current emissions, while the potential successor to the Kyoto Protocol, negotiated in parallel, only covered 14%. The reason for this is that under the Paris Agreement developing countries also agreed to submit NDCs. It is also relevant to note that there are two types of NDCs: unconditional ones, where the country states the abatement that it pledges to do irrespectively of the behavior or other countries; and conditional ones, where the country pledges additional abatement efforts that it is willing to do in return for (technology or monetary) transfers. The latter have been used mainly by developing countries (Rogelj et al. [2016] show that about 80% of the NDCs have a conditional component).

There are other parts of the Paris Agreement which are also relevant and imply negotiations. Article 6 states that countries may cooperate, bilaterally or regionally, to increase the reach of their abatement targets, as this can significantly reduce costs and allow for more ambitious goals (Mehling et al. 2018). Article 9 considers monetary transfers from developed countries to assist developing countries in their efforts to mitigate and adapt to climate change. Developed countries have agreed to mobilize a substantial amount of money, although this commitment is carefully worded to minimize any binding interpretation and, as for

[1] Even an agreement that is 'binding' under international law is weak, as countries can abandon it at any time (as Canada did just before the end of the first commitment period of the Kyoto Protocol).

[2] Only procedural obligations are binding in the Paris Agreement.

targets, this global financial goal is not broken down into individual contributions. The approved text is as follows: "prior to 2025 the Conference of the Parties [...] shall set a new collective quantified goal from a floor of USD 100 billion a year" (UNFCCC 2015).

To focus more on the detailed negotiations, as some papers have done, I will now briefly describe how climate change negotiations unfold. Every year negotiators sent by the countries meet for two weeks. Delegates meet and discuss the different proposals and, if all delegates agree on a particular text, a general assembly is called and all participating countries confirm the agreement, if they so wish. If the agreement is signed, it then needs to be ratified to come into force, usually by a given percentage of all countries involved. In most democratic states, this implies that the parliament and/or the senate need to accept the agreement. If all these steps are successful and the agreement was meant to be binding under the international law, countries are bound to the terms of the agreement.

'Coalitions' have played a significant role in these negotiations since the early nineties (Hampson and Hart 1995). During each round of negotiations countries have organized themselves into 'coalitions,' such as the Group of 77 and China or the Coalition of Rainforest Nations. This concept of 'coalition' differs from the one used in most of the literature on game theory and IEA (Finus and Caparrós 2015), where a coalition is a group of countries that have decided to determine their abatement efforts jointly. In international negotiations, however, a 'coalition' is a group of countries that have decided to join forces during the negotiations, generally meeting in private to agree on common positions. In other words, the Coalition of Rainforest Nations is not a coalition according to most of the literature on IEA. To avoid confusion, I follow Caparrós and Péreau (2013) and use the term 'negotiation-coalition' to refer to the coalitions set-up for negotiation purposes. These negotiation-coalitions (NC) have been relatively stable and always formed between developed or between developing countries.

No model has thus far been able to capture all the details of the negotiation process just described, but there have been several attempts to capture key characteristics of this process. I first discuss models that were developed having the Kyoto Protocol in mind, in Sect. 13.2, before describing recent efforts to model the Paris Agreement, in Sect. 13.3.

13.2 Modeling the Kyoto world

13.2.1 The Basic Model

As the reader of this book is well aware, the basic bargaining model introduced by Rubinstein (1982) describes the process through which negotiating agents try to reach an agreement. The player opening the negotiations makes an offer, a proposed sharing of a resource of known size (e.g., a cake). The other player can accept the offer, in which case the negotiation ends, or reject it and make a counter-offer. This counter-offer may be accepted or rejected with a new counter-offer, and so on (this process can potentially go on forever and only ends if an agreement is reached). Rubinstein proves that every bargaining game that satisfies a set of reasonable assumptions has a unique subgame perfect equilibrium (SPE), which is reached immediately. A direct application of Rubinstein's model to a negotiation between the geopolitical North and the geopolitical South over climate change would be as follows. I use this simplified scenario as a benchmark to compare other models below.

The gross payoff before transfers, V_i, of both players ($i = N, S$, where N represents the North and S the South) depends on abatement made by the North, q_N, and the South, q_S. More precisely, benefits, B_i, depend on the abatement efforts made by both players but costs, C_i, are only supported by the player i involved in the abatement effort (the benefit function is supposed to be concave and the cost function convex). The functions B_i and C_i are supposed to capture the discounted stream of future constant benefits and costs, respectively, associated with a level of abatement. Thus, we have (for $i, j = N, S$ and $i \neq j$): $V_i(q_i, q_j) = B_i(q_i, q_j) - C_i(q_i)$.

The game starts at the non-cooperative equilibrium, where both players follow the Nash equilibrium. I denote the corresponding abatement by q_N^{nc} and q_S^{nc}. To focus on the simplest case, assume that there is a negotiation about the transfer, τ, that the North should grant to the South to move from the non-cooperative to the cooperative solution. Abatement efforts in the cooperative solution are determined using the standard procedure and noted q_N^c and q_S^c. The transfer τ can be seen as a simple form of issue linkage, as side payments are not necessarily monetary. The net payoff functions, after transfers, for both players of an agreement reached at period t over a transfer τ from the North to the South are: $U_N(\tau, t) = V_N^{nc} + \delta_N^t(V_N^c - V_N^{nc} - \tau)$ and $U_S(\tau, t) = V_S^{nc} + \delta_S^t(V_S^c - V_S^{nc} + \tau)$, where δ_N^t and δ_S^t are the discount factors of the North and the South, respectively, $t = \{0, 1, ...\}$ the periods in which the offers or counter-offers are made, $V_i^{nc} = V_i(q_i^{nc}, q_j^{nc})$ and $V_i^c = V_i(q_i^c, q_j^c)$. The RBS is the unique SPE given by the two following conditions (Rubinstein 1982; Muthoo 1999): $U_N(\tau^S, 0) = U_N(\tau^N, 1)$ and $U_S(\tau^N, 0) = U_S(\tau^S, 1)$, where τ^i denotes offers proposed by player i. The first equation states that the North is indifferent, in terms of expected payoffs, in regards to accepting the Southern offer, τ^S, in the current period, or rejecting it and making in the following period the counter-offer τ^N, which will be accepted by the South. The second equation reflects the same indifference for the South. Assuming that the North makes the first offer, the equilibrium transfer is: $\tau^* = \varphi(V_N^c - V_N^{nc}) - (1 - \varphi)(V_S^c - V_S^{nc})$, with $\varphi = \delta_S(1-\delta_N)(1 - \delta_N\delta_S)^{-1}$. Hence, the transfer depends positively on the marginal gain of the North and negatively on the marginal gain of the South. As this is at the basis of several of the results discussed below, note that if the disagreement points, V_N^{nc} and V_S^{nc}, could be modified in a pre-negotiations stage the distribution of the surplus would be modified.

As shown by Rubinstein (1982), under perfect information the equilibrium offer is proposed by the North in the first round and is immediately accepted by the South, i.e., $\tau^N = \tau^*$. Hence, the transfer τ^* implies that each player gets its perpetual disagreement payoff V_i^{nc} and a share of the additional surplus created. As it is well known, when the time between offers becomes infinitely small, or the discount factors tend to one, the SPE of Rubinstein's model converges to the asymmetric Nash Bargaining Solution (Muthoo 1999). More precisely, the RBS converges to the asymmetric NBS if the discount rates of the agents are not identical, while it converges to the NBS if both agents share the same discount rate (in other words, the discount rates are at the origin of the asymmetry). This provides a strategic justification of the NBS and also shows that this concept should be used when the time between offers is arbitrarily small, which may be interpreted as bargaining situations in which the absolute magnitudes of the frictions in the bargaining process are small (Muthoo 1999).

Rotillon and Tazdaït (1996), Rotillon et al. (1996) and Chen (1997) present early applications of bargaining theory to the analysis of global IEA. As Rubinstein's model abstracts from enforcement issues, which are key in most analyses of IEA, Hovi (2001) presents a model that incorporates enforcement issues into a two-stage bargaining model. The first stage is a direct application of Rubinstein's model, as the one described above. However, after an agreement is reached in the first stage, the players move on to a second stage where they play a prisoners' dilemma over the implementation of the agreement with an infinite time horizon. Nevertheless, as the equilibrium in the first stage needs to be subgame perfect and there are only two players, most of the results obtained with a direct application of Rubinstein's model continue to hold.

In the bilateral bargaining process described above uniqueness is ensured by Rubinstein's alternative-offers procedure (Schelling 1956). However, requiring unanimity in the multilateral bargaining case may yield multiple equilibria, as shown by Shaked (reported by Sutton [1986]) in the 3-player case and by Herrero (1985) in the *n*-player case. Given the limited predictive power of models with multiple equilibria, there are different proposals aimed at restoring uniqueness by modifying the structure of the game. One alternative is to focus solely on the case where the history of the negotiations has no impact, as the notion of Stationary SPE may be used to restore uniqueness. As the restriction on the strategy space in this case is rather strong, the second alternative considered is the one introduced by Suh and Wen (2006), who propose a series of bilateral negotiations. This is the approach followed in several of the applications to IEA so far. Once uniqueness is restored the results obtained for multilateral negotiations are rather similar to those obtained for bilateral negotiations, although the richer framework allows discussion of issues that are irrelevant in the two-player case.

In their analysis of climate change negotiations, Rotillon et al. (1996) consider a single North and *n* Southern players. The aim is to study the formation of NC in complete information according to their degree of complementarity and substitutability. Southern players are called complementary when all have to sign the agreement to be effective and substitutable otherwise. The bargaining process follows the alternating-offers procedure and uniqueness is ensured because it is modeled as a set of bilateral agreements. The results show that when all players are perfectly complementary, they act separately, and that when they are perfectly substitutable, they act jointly. As Southern countries were most likely substitutable in the Kyoto world analyzed in this section (as only developing countries had commitments and North–South negotiations were mostly done in the context of the Clean Development Mechanism), the Southern countries had a strong incentive to talk with a single voice in these negotiations. This was actually the case, as G77 and China acted united.

In Caparrós and Péreau (2013) incentives to form NC were analyzed in a world with two Northern and two Southern countries. Negotiations take place à la Rubinstein and uniqueness is maintained because the model assumes a set of bilateral agreements. As in Rotillon et al. (1996), the central question is whether or not there is a natural tendency for this type of negotiation to be carried out between NC, but now the focus is on whether the incentives to form this NC come from efficiency gains or from the potential to gain bargaining power. Efficiency gains refer to the direct gains that countries can expect when they negotiate together, minus what they can expect negotiating separately (due to fixed-costs savings, or because players expect different commitments while acting together instead of separately). Even if efficiency gains do not exist, the authors show that countries are not indifferent about negotiating together or separately. Furthermore, these additional motivations, based purely on bargaining power, go in the opposite direction for the North and the South. This implies that bargaining power never favors a negotiation between a single Northern NC and a single Southern NC. In their framework, this implies that in equilibrium there are two bilateral agreements, instead of a single global agreement. This also implies that the first-best is not attained.

Another variation of the basic game can be found in Okada (2007), who discusses a truly multilateral bargaining process, showing that there is a unique Stationary SPE and that this equilibrium converges to the asymmetric NBS as the probability of stopping negotiations becomes close to zero, which is similar to assuming that the discount factor tends to one. The article then moves on to a numerical illustration of the bargaining outcome without fully analyzing the details of the multilateral bargaining process.

13.2.2 Variations on a Theme

In this section, I discuss several issues that have been analyzed based on developments of the basic model discussed above.

13.2.2.1 The Role of a Leader

The difference in ambition between the EU climate policy and that of the rest of the world is so stark that the question of the role of unilateral action has been repeatedly addressed. Brandt (2004) argued that unilateral action may have a role to play if it can be used as a signal to show that costs are relatively low. Benedick (1998, 2007) has argued that the almost unilateral action taken in the late 1970s by Australia, Canada, Norway, Sweden and the US to individually and separately ban the use of CFCs in aerosol spray cans, demonstrated to skeptics that reducing emissions was feasible at a reasonable cost. This enabled the subsequent signature of the Montreal Protocol, a protocol that is frequently depicted as the paramount example that international cooperation can indeed work. Whether this would also work for climate change is unclear. Although climate policy has been relatively successful in Europe, it is true that costs related to climate policy have in fact been rather modest, especially for the sectors included in the EU emission trading system. However, the analysis in Brandt (2004) also requires costs to be clearly correlated and it is unclear whether the US or developing countries see the costs in Europe as relevant to them.

In any case, the pioneer analysis of the role of unilateral actions was proposed in Hoel (1991) and was more pessimistic, showing that unilateral actions by one country may trigger lower reductions in the other countries. In Hoel (1991) unilateral action can take two forms, as countries can commit to (i) a unilateral reduction of emissions even if an agreement is not reached or (ii) an over fulfillment of the negotiated agreement. In the first case the commitment alters the disagreement point used to determine the NBS and the consequence is that when one country commits to a unilateral action, its bargaining power is reduced. In the game outlined in the previous sub-section, a unilateral commitment by the North implies that it abates $q_N^{nc} + x$ instead of q_N^{nc} if no agreement is reached. This implies that the North has weakened its bargaining position. As Hoel (1991) shows, it also implies that total emissions may increase and global welfare may be reduced as a consequence of the unilateral action. If the second derivative of the cost function in Country 1 is relatively high, at the equilibrium, compared to that in Country 2 total emission will increase (i.e., Country 2 increases emissions more than Country 1 reduces emissions), while they will both decrease their emissions if the opposite relation holds.

In the second type of commitment considered in Hoel (1991), both countries bargain over a uniform reduction and one country commits to a given additional effort. In the model outlined in the previous sub-section, this implies that the North commits to abate $q + x$ if an agreement is reached. This type of commitment will in general reduce total emissions, as long as the second derivative of the cost function of the committing country is not too large, at the equilibrium.

Ward et al. (2001) discussed the role of potential leaders in climate change negotiations, focusing on the competition between leaders who can each offer package deals to attract support of veto players. However, given that the US has had a modest role in leading climate change negotiations, studies focusing on a single leader are probably more relevant in the current context. In this line, Caparrós and Péreau (2017) consider a gradual agreement formation game where a single leader, e.g., the EU, gradually extends a binding agreement in a sequential bargaining setting, following a similar pattern to that observed for trade agreements. Formally, the leading country endogenously decides whether to negotiate multilaterally or sequentially over climate change (the choice is determined by the convexity of the transferable utility game and the free-rider payoffs of the followers). Except in a few clearly defined cases, the outcome of the negotiation process is always the grand coalition, although the process may take some time as the leader may choose a sequential path.[3] The authors also analyze the role of a facilitating agency, which has the power to shape the negotiation process but not the power to impose a precise outcome. They show that, under certain conditions, it is able to favor a multilateral negotiation, which implies that the globally efficient outcome is attained earlier.

13.2.2.2 Features of International Negotiations

I now discuss papers that have focused on some of the key features of international negotiations, such as the role of delegation and ratification (see Sect. 13.1). Schelling (1956, 1960) initiated the discussion on delegation and Jones (1989) formalized it. More related to IEAs, Segendorff (1998) analyzes strategic delegation in a model where two countries bargain over the provision of a transboundary public good. In each country a principal has the option to delegate the negotiation to an agent. The game has two stages: first, both principals simultaneously choose agents, second, agents bargain over the provision of the public good. Segendorff (1998) considers a weak and a strong delegation model, the difference being that in the former the breakdown allocation is carried out by the principal, while in the latter the agent also decides on the breakdown allocation. Principals choose agents that have lower preferences for the public good than their own because this lowers the reservation utility and increases their bargaining power. That is, as in Beccherle and Tirole (2011) and Urpelainen (2012), the players use the pre-negotiation stage to modify their disagreement point to gain bargaining power. However, as both adopt this strategy, delegation makes at least one of the principals worse off compared to the case where the principal negotiates. When delegation is strong this effect can more than offset the gains from reaching an agreement. The analyses of strategic delegation just described are developed further in Buchholz et al. (2005),

[3] The authors show that this holds even if one assumes, as it is standard in IEA coalition formation games, that the remaining countries continue to cooperate if one player leaves the agreement. They also show that, even in this framework, a sequential path may lead to a stable grand coalition, even if negotiating directly a stable grand coalition is not possible. Note that in this framework each agreement has to grant all signatories its free-rider payoff, and not only its disagreement payoff as in a standard bargaining game.

confirming Segendorff's (1998) results. Buchholz et al. (2005) extend the analysis to different types of transboundary pollution, showing that the incentive to elect delegates who pay lower attention to the environmental problem becomes stronger when negotiating global public goods. The authors show that when voters anticipate a bargaining process their incentives to misrepresent their preferences increases. Thus, the median voter can be better off in a situation where elected countries determine their policy independently.

The analysis of delegation was extended to *n* players by Harstad (2008), including the analysis of the role of side payments. Harstad confirms that with side payments each principal appoints a delegate that values the project less in order to increase bargaining power. Side payments turn out to have a negative effect if the heterogeneity is small and at the same time the uncertainty and the value of the project are large.

As discussed in Sect. 13.1, agreements signed by negotiators need to be ratified by different parliaments before entering into force. Schelling (1960) highlighted, informally, this feature and Putnam (1988) analyzed this issue using a two-level game. This issue was subsequently analyzed in Iida (1993), Haller and Holden (1997) and Tarar (2001). These analyses find that Schelling's conjecture, that a tough ratification constraint can be a bargaining advantage, holds. Courtois and Tazdaït (2008) apply Putnam's structure to a climate negotiation between the South and two separated Northern players, showing that a parliament that is reluctant to ratify an agreement increases the bargaining power of the players. Tarar (2005) focuses on the exact nature of the constituency defining the ratification constraint (although not applied to climate change negotiations, the paper is still relevant for these negotiations). In the first option considered, the executive (negotiators) has a national constituency while the legislators who have to ratify the agreement have local ones (as in the US). As predicted by Schelling's conjecture, in this case the negotiators benefit from being constrained, unless the constraint is so tough that no agreement is possible.

13.2.2.3 Future Binding Negotiations

Buchholz and Konrad (1994), Beccherle and Tirole (2011) and Urpelainen (2012) all analyze the impact that expecting a bargaining process over abatement in the future may have on technology investments (see also Harstad 2012, 2016). These analyses were particularly relevant before the Kyoto Protocol was signed, and again on the road to Paris, as the world had abandoned the Kyoto Protocol and a future (potentially binding) agreement was expected. Buchholz and Konrad (1994) analyze a two-stage game where countries decide first their technology and then move on to a second stage where abatement efforts are negotiated according to the NBS. Countries choose their technology and hence modify the utility frontier and the disagreement point. Given the influence of the disagreement point on bargaining power, both countries have an incentive to adopt a technology with high costs per unit of abatement. In a related but more general model, Beccherle and Tirole (2011) focus on the consequences of delaying a binding agreement (see also Tirole 2012). Both countries have an incentive to set high levels of pollution in the first stage, as this credibly commits to a high level of pollution in the second stage. This increases the bargaining power in the second stage, which is analyzed using the NBS. Harstad (2012, 2016) further investigates the role of incomplete contracts. His results confirm that countries invest less if future negotiations are expected.

13.2.2.4 Asymmetry of Information

Asymmetry of information is a key ingredient of any international negotiation, and several analyses of climate change negotiations have focused on this feature. In most of the analyses discussed below information is shared via signaling, as discussed by Spence (1974), where an informed agent takes costly actions that reveal its information, or its type. In this context, information about relative costs of abatement is shared, or not, to gain bargaining power. Rotillon and Tazdaït (1996) analyze a bargaining process that is based exclusively on the North's initiatives, while the South merely accepts or rejects the different offers. Caparrós et al. (2004) present a more direct application of Rubinstein's framework to climate change negotiations under asymmetric information. The payoffs are a simplified version of those shown in the previous subsection, where costs functions are not explicitly modeled and, instead, the South has a minimum requirement for the transfer. All the elements of the negotiation are known, except the minimum amount of transfers that is acceptable to the Southern countries (they can have 'weak' or 'strong' requirements). As is standard in this type of models, the authors find pooling and separating equilibria. The results show that the asymmetry of information favors the weak South in both cases, but especially in the pooling equilibrium. As there is a monotone relation between the probability attached by the North of facing a strong South and the emergence of the pooling equilibrium, if the South were able to send a signal showing that it has high abatement costs (strong transfer requirements) in a pre-negotiation phase, it would be interested in doing so. In Buchholz and Konrad (1994) and Beccherle and Tirole (2011) pre-negotiation actions are used to commit to low abatement efforts, here pre-negotiation signals are used to show that the country has high abatement costs, even if this is not the case. Caparrós et al. (2004) extended their analysis to one North and two Southern players, which can both be strong or weak, while Bayer and Urpelainen (2013) essentially analyze the opposite scenario, proposing a game with one recipient and two donors. Jakob and Lessman (2012) also analyze one-sided asymmetric information, which can refer to the North or to the South. They also consider the possibility that countries 'cheat' by entering an IEA without fulfilling their commitments. They assume that after an agreement is struck, players play a one-shot game in pure strategies, where they decide to fulfill, or not, their commitments. Their analysis highlights a situation that may be relevant in actual climate change negotiations: the North is interested in engaging in early abatement to credibly signal its type, even though the involved costs exceed the benefits enjoyed in the first period, while the South prefers to delay action.

13.3 The Paris Agreement Arrives, New Models Are Needed

The world has moved away from binding burden-sharing agreements and has embraced instead a system based on voluntary contributions announced through pledges (NDCs). Theoretical analyses have not yet incorporated this tendency, although there are several ongoing efforts in this direction. As discussed in Sect. 13.1, the main feature of the Paris Agreement is that countries no longer negotiate burden-sharing agreements. Instead, each country submits, independently, its conditional and/or unconditional NDCs.

Harstad (2020a) and Caparrós (2020) are two contemporaneous[4] papers that attempt to model the Paris Agreement in a bargaining framework. To some extent these models can be seen as complementary, as the former considers only unconditional NDCs while the latter considers both, but focuses more on conditional NDCs.

In Harstad (2020a) each country quantifies its own contribution, the unconditional NDCs described in Sect. 13.1.[5] Then, the author assumes that the set of pledges must be unanimously accepted. If at least one country does not accept the NDCs submitted by all the other countries, all countries have to submit new NDCs. This yields a novel bargaining game, with potential application to other areas. The author further introduces uncertainty over which pledges will be accepted, captured through uncertainty over the discount factors. This allows him to show that there exist equilibria which improve over the situation that would prevail in the absence of any agreement. More precisely, assuming uncertain tolerance for delay, the author shows that equilibrium pledges (NDCs) coincide with an asymmetric Nash bargaining solution. That is, each equilibrium pledge maximizes an asymmetric Nash product where the weights reflect differences in the discount rates, but also the extent of uncertainty in

[4] Early versions of both papers were presented at the WCERE 2018.

[5] The author complements the analysis with a discussion of the differences between the Kyoto Protocol and the Paris Agreement in Harstad (2020b). In this paper, the bargaining protocol proposed in Harstad (2020a) is embedded in a dynamic game with several relevant features, such as endogenous technology and participation.

shocks and the correlation in shocks across the parties. Since the equilibrium weights vary from one party's pledge to another's, the bargaining outcome is not Pareto optimal. As noted above, the bargaining game combines a focus on unconditional pledges with a need for unanimous approval. The focus on unconditional pledges can be justified by the fact that developed countries have sent unconditional pledges, so that the analysis covers a significant share of total emissions. The need for unanimous approval is more problematic. Pledges are, in principle, excluded[6] from the unanimity rule, as countries merely "communicate" their pledges (NDCs), which are recorded in a public registry by the secretariat (Article 4.2).

Caparrós (2020) is another paper that attempts to model the Paris Agreement. To do so, the paper introduces a model where a long-term non-binding agreement is followed by a series of short-term interactions, in a stochastic environment. Short-term interactions are modeled as a bargaining game in which countries submit conditional and unconditional pledges (NDCs), which are not binding and not subject to the approval by other countries. Then, eventually, countries bargain over the conditions set out in the conditional pledges (as noted in Sect. 13.1, about 80% of the pledges submitted have a conditional component). This negotiation happens in an implementation phase, intended to capture negotiations under articles 6 and 9 of the Paris Agreement (see Sect. 13.1). However, backing-off from the initial terms proposed in the conditional pledges has reputational costs. The bargaining part of the model extends to a multilateral framework the bilateral bargaining game with partial commitment analyzed by Muthoo (1996) using the NBS and by Leventoglu and Tarar (2005) using the RBS (as the paper uses the RBS, it is closer to the latter). The paper also analyzes long-term

[6] New agreements by the Conference of the Parties (COP) are usually subject to the unanimity rule (or at least to an absence of an objection). In fact, this was the reason why the Copenhagen Accord, a predecessor to the Paris Agreement that included pledges, was not adopted as a decision of the COP in 2009. However, the Paris Agreement has followed a different route. The Paris Agreement itself was adopted unanimously as a decision of the COP in 2015. Countries were then invited to communicate their first pledges before or at the time of ratification, and to communicate new pledges every five years. That said, the fact that pledges are public, and that countries may decide not to take any emission abatement action if they do not like the pledge made by one particular country, could be seen as a weak form of unanimity.

provisions that are non-comprehensive, because countries do not agree on investments, and non-contingent, as agreements cannot depend on the state of nature finally observed. This long-term provision (a part of the Paris Agreement itself) is modeled as an agreement that can be abandoned if it is not profitable to all parts (see footnote 1). The results show that the pledge mechanism, followed by an implementation phase, can implement the first-best in the short term, and that the surplus is shared according to the relative importance of the cost-of-revoking the pledges. It is also shown that without a long-term provision there is underinvestment. However, even if the agreement does not cover investments, a long-term contingent provision can implement the long-term first-best, and a long-term non-contingent provision can bring the world closer.

Before concluding, let me briefly discuss which ones of the results discussed in Sect. 13.2 are more likely to be still relevant in the new framework. Analyses of unilateral actions and the role of a leader remain relevant for a post-Paris world, because countries can decide to submit NDCs that are comparatively more ambitious, as the EU has done. Delegation and ratification is probably less relevant, as the Paris Agreement has a very long time horizon and it has already been negotiated (although some details are still being negotiated, in particular referring to articles 6 and 9) and the pledges (NDC) are not subject to any negotiation. The role of future binding contracts is still relevant, but shifting the focus to agreements signed developing articles 6 and 9 of the Paris Agreement. Finally, asymmetry of information is certainly still relevant, but the analysis would need to be adapted, to focus either on information regarding future NDCs or on information that is relevant for articles 6 and 9.

13.4 Conclusion

This chapter has discussed papers that have used bargaining theory to analyze climate change negotiations. The basic bargaining model is optimistic, although developments of this model tend to temper this optimism. In any case, this literature offers insights that are relevant to analyze international negotiations on climate change. However, most available papers have been written having in mind a burden-sharing agreement, such as the Kyoto Protocol, while climate negotiations have moved on and the Paris Agreement is the new kid in town. There are several ongoing attempts to model this agreement, showing that a properly modified bargaining game can be used to model this new framework. Analyzing the robustness of the different results discussed above in this new framework opens up exciting avenues for future research.

Acknowledgements Financial support from the Spanish National Research Plan, through project TrEnGood (ECO2017-84461-R), is acknowledged.

References

Bayer, P. and Urpelainen, J., 2013. Funding Global Public Goods: The Dark Side of Multilateralism. *Review of Policy Research* 30(2): 160–189.

Beccherle, J. and Tirole, J., 2011. Regional Initiatives and the Cost of Delaying Binding Climate Change Agreements. *Journal of Public Economics* 95(11–12): 1339–1348.

Benedick, R.E., 1998. *Ozone Diplomacy: New Directions in Safeguarding the Planet*. Enlarged Edition. Harvard University Press, Cambridge.

Benedick, R.E., 2007. Avoiding Gridlock on Climate Change. *Issues in Science and Technology* 23: 2.

Brandt, U.S., 2004. Unilateral Actions, the Case of International Environmental Problems. *Resource and Energy Economics* 26: 373–391.

Buchholz, W., Haupt, A. and Peters, W., 2005. International Environmental Agreements and Strategic Voting. *Scandinavian Journal of Economics* 107(1): 175–195.

Buchholz, W. and Konrad, K.A., 1994. Global Environmental Problems and the Strategic Choice of Technology. *Journal of Economics* 60(3): 299–321.

Caparrós, A., 2020. Pledge and Implement Bargaining in the Paris Agreement on Climate Change. IPP-CSIC Working Paper 2020-3. Madrid.

Caparrós, A. and Péreau, J.-C., 2013. Forming Coalitions to Negotiate North-South Climate Agreements. *Environment and Development Economics* 18: 69–92.

Caparrós, A. and Péreau, J.-C., 2017. Multilateral Versus Sequential Negotiations over Climate Change. *Oxford Economic Papers* 69(2): 365–387.

Caparrós, A., Péreau, J.-C. and Tazdaït, T., 2004. North-South Climate Change Negotiations: A Sequential Game with Asymmetric Information. *Public Choice* 121 (3–4): 455–480.

Chen, Z., 1997. Negotiating an Agreement on Global Warming: A Theoretical Analysis. *Journal of Environmental Economics and Management* 32: 170–188.

Courtois, P. and Tazdaït, T., 2008. Accord climatique: Concessions et ratifications. *Revue Économique* 59: 719–735.

Finus, M. and Caparrós, A., 2015. *Game Theory and International Environmental Cooperation: Essential Readings*. Edward Elgar, Cheltenham.

Haller, H. and Holden, S., 1997. Ratification Requirement and Bargaining Power. *International Economic Review* 38(4): 825–846.

Hampson, O. and Hart, M., 1995. *Multilateral Negotiations: Lessons from Arms Control, Trade, and the Environment*. The Johns Hopkins University Press, Baltimore and London.

Harstad, B., 2008. Do Side Payments Help? Collective Decisions and Strategic Delegation. *Journal of the European Economic Association* 6(2–3): 468–477.

Harstad, B., 2012. Climate Contracts: A Game of Emissions, Investments, Negotiations, and Renegotiations. *Review of Economic Studies* 79(4): 1527–1557.

Harstad, B., 2016. The Dynamics of Climate Agreements. *Journal of the European Economic Association* 14(3): 719–752.

Harstad, B., 2020a. Pledge-and-Review Bargaining: A Theory. Mimeo (version March, 1).

Harstad, B., 2020b. Pledge-and-Review Bargaining: From Kyoto to Paris. Mimeo (version March, 1).

Herrero, M.J., 1985. N-player Bargaining and Involuntary Unemployment. Ph.D dissertation, LSE, London.

Hoel, M., 1991. Global Environmental Problems: The Effects of Unilateral Actions Taken by One Country. *Journal of Environmental Economics and Management* 20: 55–70.

Hovi, J., 2001. Decentralized Enforcement, Sequential Bargaining, and the Clean Development Mechanism. *Nordic Journal of Political Economy* (27): 135–152.

Iida, K., 1993. When and How Do Domestic Constraints Matter? Two-Level Games with Uncertainty. *Journal of Conflict Resolution* 37: 403–426.

Jakob, M. and Lessmann, K., 2012. Signaling in International Environmental Agreements: The Case of Early and Delayed Action. *International Environmental Agreements: Politics, Law and Economics* 12(4): 309–325.

Jones, S. R., 1989. Have Your Lawyer Call My Lawyer. *Journal of Economic Behavior and Organization* 11: 159–174.
Leventoglu, B. and Tarar, A., 2005. Prenegotiation Public Commitment in Domestic and International Bargaining. *American Political Science Review* 99(3): 419–433.
Mehling, M.A., Metcalf, G.E. and Stavins, R.N., 2018. Linking Climate Policies to Advance Global Mitigation. *Science* 359(6379): 997–998.
Muthoo, A., 1996. A Bargaining Model Based on the Commitment Tactic. *Journal of Economic Theory* 69: 134–152.
Muthoo, A., 1999. *Bargaining Theory with Applications.* Cambridge University Press, Cambridge.
Okada, A., 2007. International Negotiations Con Climate Change: A Noncooperative Game Analysis of the Kyoto Protocol. In: R. Avenhaus and I.W. Zartman. *Diplomacy Games.* Springer, Berlin.
Putnam, R.D., 1988. Diplomacy and Domestic Policies: The Logic of Two-Level Games. *International Organization* 52: 427–460.
Rogelj, J., Elzen, M., Höhne, N., Fransen, T., Fekete, H., Winkler, H., Schaeffer, R., Sha, F., Riahi, K. and Meinshausen, M., 2016. Paris Agreement Climate Proposals Need a Boost to Keep Warming Well Below 2 °C. *Nature* 534: 631–639.
Rotillon, G. and Tazdaït, T., 1996. International Bargaining in the Presence of Global Environmental Change. *Environmental and Resource Economics* 8: 293–314.
Rotillon, G., Tazdaït, T. and Zeghni S., 1996. Bilateral or Multilateral Bargaining in the Face of Global Environmental Change? *Ecological Economics* 18: 177–187.
Rubinstein, A., 1982. Perfect Equilibrium in a Bargaining Model. *Econometrica* 50: 97–109.
Segendorff, B., 1998. Delegation and Threat in Bargaining. *Games and Economic Behavior* 23: 266–283.
Schelling, T.C., 1956. An Essay on Bargaining. *American Economic Review* 46(3): 281–306.
Schelling, T.C., 1960. *The Strategy of Conflict.* Harvard University Press, Cambridge.
Spence, A.M., 1974. *Market Signaling—Informational Transfer in Hiring and Related Processes.* Harvard University Press, Cambridge.
Suh, S.-C and Wen, Q., 2006. Multi-agent Bilateral Bargaining and the Nash Bargaining Solution. *Journal of Mathematical Economics* 42(1): 61–73.

Sutton, J., 1986. Non-cooperative Bargaining Theory: An Introduction. *Review of Economic Studies* 53: 709–724.

Tarar, A., 2001. International Bargaining with Two-Sided Domestic Constraints. *Journal of Conflict Resolution* 45(3): 320–340.

Tarar, A., 2005. Constituencies and Preferences in International Bargaining. *Journal of Conflict Resolution* 49(3): 383–407.

Tirole, J., 2012. Some Political Economy of Global Warming. *Economics of Energy and Environmental Policy* 1(1): 121–132.

UNFCCC, 1992. United Nations Framework Convention on Climate Change. Available at unfcc.int.

UNFCCC, 2015. Adoption of the Paris Agreement (FCCC/CP/2015/L.9/Rev. 1). Available at unfcc.int.

Urpelainen, J., 2012. Technology Investment, Bargaining, and International Environmental Agreements. *International Environmental Agreements* 12: 145–163.

Ward, H., Grundig, F. and Zorick, E.R., 2001. Marching at the Pace of the Slowest: A Model of International Climate-Change Negotiations. *Political Studies* 49: 438–461.

14

Bargaining and War

Bahar Leventoğlu

14.1 Crisis Bargaining

War destroys the resources of all engaged parties. Therefore, the surplus parties can divide after war is always smaller than the surplus they could divide before war. Then why do rational actors not agree to a negotiated settlement they would all prefer to the war outcome? This question constitutes the central puzzle in the rationalist paradigm on war. This puzzle manifests itself in bargaining models of war as in Fearon's (1995) pioneering work "Rationalist Explanations for War".

The formal approach to war as a bargaining process can be traced back to Schelling (1960) (see Powell 2002). In this survey, my point of departure will be Fearon (1995). I will focus on models with dyads and conclude by arguing that multilateral models of bargaining and war remain as one of the most promising areas of research. Space limitations

B. Leventoğlu (✉)
Duke University, Durham, NC, USA
e-mail: bl38@duke.edu

E. Karagözoğlu and K. B. Hyndman (eds.), *Bargaining*,
https://doi.org/10.1007/978-3-030-76666-5_14

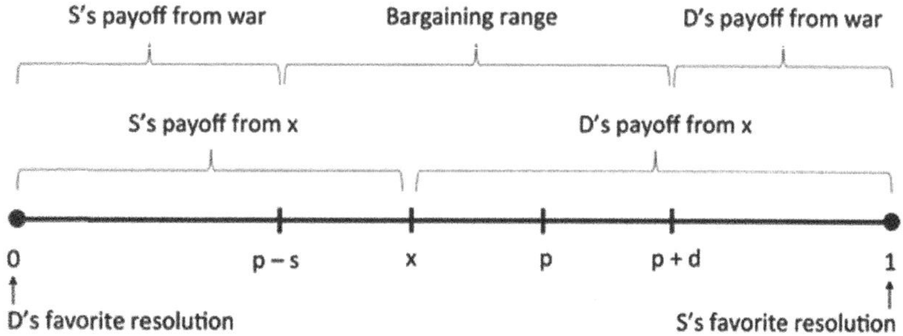

Fig. 14.1 Bargaining range in the conflict

do not allow for a more comprehensive review.[1] I will also not be able to cover the Economics literature on bargaining breakdowns.[2]

14.2 The Basic Framework and Fearon's Rationalist Accounts of War

Bargaining models of war build on the assumption of anarchy. There is no supranational authority to make and enforce law in the international arena and stop war from happening (Waltz 1959). War remains as an option for all parties in the conflict and provides a lower bound for payoffs for rational agents.

Consider a conflict between two rational states S and D over a pie of size 1. Let $x \in [0, 1]$ denote a resolution. S and D derive payoffs of x and $1 - x$ from the resolution, respectively. War is a costly lottery. If the states fight, S prevails with probability p, D prevails with probability $1 - p$, and the winner gets the entire pie. The cost of fighting to S and D is s and d, respectively. Therefore, S's payoff from fighting is $p - s$, and D's payoff from fighting is $1 - p - d$.

---

[1] See Powell (2002), Fey and Ramsay (2007), Kydd (2010), Jackson and Massimo (2011) and Baliga and Sjöström (2013) for surveys of literature with different perspectives.

[2] E.g., see Brito and Intriligator (1985) for a model war with bargaining and Fernandez and Glazer (1991) for a theory of union strikes in wage bargaining.

A rational agent prefers a peaceful resolution to fighting if and only if the payoff from the resolution is at least as high as the payoff from fighting. S would accept a resolution $x \in [0, 1]$ if $x \geq p - s$ and D would accept it if $1 - x \geq 1 - p - d$, equivalently $x \leq p + d$. Therefore, there always exists a bargaining range of negotiated settlements $x \in [p - s, p + d]$ that both sides would prefer to war. Figure 14.1, replicated from Fearon (1995), illustrates this range.

Assume that either state can initiate a war. Then any negotiated settlement must be in the bargaining range for both parties to agree. Let $q \in [0, 1]$ denote the status quo. If $q \in [p - s, p + d]$, each state prefers status quo to war and status quo prevails. Suppose $1 - q < 1 - p - d$, equivalently $q > p + d$. Then, D is dissatisfied with the status quo and would go to war unless the status quo is revised in his favor. To model the bargaining process, assume that S makes a take-it-or-leave-it offer of x. If D accepts S's offer, x becomes the negotiated settlement, otherwise war breaks out. The best S can do is to offer the least that D would accept, which is D's war payoff. So, S offers $1 - x = 1 - p - d$ for D and she collects $x = p + d > p - s$, which she prefers to war. The dispute is settled peacefully under complete information.

The literature has long argued that informational asymmetry among parties is one of the causes of costly fighting (Powell 1987).[3] Two prominent examples are uncertainty on the resolve of countries (Morrow 1985) and uncertainty on relative strength of states in war (Blainey 1988). Fearon argues that "the cause of war cannot be simply lack of information, but whatever it is that prevents its disclosure." Therefore, his first explanation focuses on rational incentives that explain why states cannot remedy informational problems.

Suppose that a resolved D's cost of fighting is $d = d_l$ and an unresolved D's cost is $d = d_h > d_l$. D knows his own type, S only knows that D is unresolved with probability α. Rationality implies that both types of D accept any offer greater than or equal to $1 - p - d_l$ and the unresolved type accepts any offer greater than or equal to $1 - p - d_h$. So, only these two offers matter for S. $1 - p - d_l$ settles the dispute

[3] Myerson and Satterthwaite (1983) show a general impossibility of ex post efficient mechanisms without outside subsidies under private information.

peacefully, $1 - p - d_h$ yields resolved type fighting. S faces a tradeoff between the non-risky peaceful resolution and the risky offer that may lead to war. S's expected payoff from the peaceful resolution is $p+d_l$ and her expected payoff from the risky offer is $\alpha\ (p+d_h)+(1-\alpha)(p-s)$. If the latter is greater, this "risk-return" trade-off resolves in favor of the risky offer and war breaks out between S and a resolved D. A similar risk-return trade-off emerges when uncertainty concerns relative strength of the states.

Fearon's second explanation relates to commitment problems. Modify the complete information model as follows: S wins the war with probability p_f if S attacks first, with probability p_s if D attacks first, and with probability p if both states attack simultaneously, where $p_s < p < p_f$. Under the assumption of anarchy, there is no mechanism to make states commit to not attacking. If states agree to a resolution x, then x would be peaceful only if it provides each state with at least its war payoff when it attacks first. This implies $x > p_f - s$ and $1-x > 1-p_s-d$, that is, $p_f-s < x < p_s+d$. If $p_f-s > p_s+d$, incentives for preemptive war preclude the existence of a bargaining window for peaceful resolution.

A second and empirically more relevant commitment problem relates to preventive motivations against large and rapid changes in distribution of power (Taylor 1954; Organski 1958). Modify the model as follows: States play the game twice and consume the flow of benefits in both periods. Relative strength of power evolves in favor of D in the second period. S wins the war with probability p_1 and $p_2 < p_1$ in the first and second periods, respectively. There is no discounting. If war breaks out in the first period, the winner collects benefits in both periods. Let x_1 and x_2 be S's share from peaceful resolutions in the first and second period. Rationality and no commitment imply $1 - x_2 \geq 1 - p_2 - d$, or $x_2 \leq p_2 + d$. The maximum S can get in the first period is $x_1 = 1$, so S's payoff from peaceful settlements in both periods is bounded from above by $1+p_2+d$. If S fights in the first period, she wins the war with probability p_1 and collects the benefits in both periods, so her payoff from war is $2p_1-s$. If $2p_1-s > 1+p_2+d$, or $0 < p_2 < 2p_1-s-d-1$, then a declining S prefers fighting in the first period in order to avoid bigger concessions in the second period.

Fearon's third explanation relates to issue indivisibilities such as territorial disputes. Which are also a form of commitment problem (Powell 2006). I will focus on informational and commitment problems below.

14.3 Informational Problems

14.3.1 Dynamic Bargaining

Only one actor can make an offer in Fearon's take-it-or-leave-it model. Powell (1996a, 1999) shows that the risk-return trade-off emerges in presumably more natural bargaining environments, in which both states can offer and counteroffer. Powell generalizes the alternating offers model of Rubinstein (1982) by adding the option of going to war and private information about cost of war. D is said to be dissatisfied if he prefers war to accepting what he would be offered in the underlying Rubinstein bargaining game. Powell shows that in any perfect Bayesian equilibrium of the game, no dissatisfied D ever rejects an offer in order to make a counteroffer. So, a dissatisfied D either accepts the offer or goes to war in any equilibrium. Then S's optimal strategy becomes a take-it-or-leave-it offer as in Fearon. The duration of bargaining depends on which state makes the initial offer, but the probability of war is independent of which state makes the initial offer. Powell (1996b) applies this model to address whether war is less likely when there is an even distribution of power, as argued by the balance-of-power school (Claude 1962; Morgenthau 1966; Mearsheimer 1990; Wright 1965; Wolfers 1962) or when there is a preponderance of power, as argued by the preponderance-of-power school (Blainey 1988; Organski 1958; Organski and Kugler 1980).

14.3.2 Bargaining Power

Leventoğlu and Tarar (2008) argue that the risk-return trade-off is the unique perfect Bayesian equilibrium outcome in Powell's model because it gives all the bargaining power to the satisfied state and this rules out any incentive for the dissatisfied state to make a counteroffer. This is achieved in Powell's model by the assumption that a state goes to war only in periods in which the other side makes an offer. Leventoğlu and Tarar modify Powell's model by allowing states to go to war after the rejection of an offer in any period, rather than just in periods in which the other side makes an offer. Unlike Powell, they show that when the dissatisfied state is not too impatient, equilibria exist in which a peaceful agreement is reached through the offer-counteroffer process. This finding implies that, unlike in Fearon's original argument, private information leads to war only in conjunction with other factors that impact or explain impatience of states in negotiations, such as domestic political vulnerability, exogenous obstacles that hinder ability to make counteroffers quickly, bargaining tactics that create incentives to strike quickly, or actions that lock states into war.

14.3.3 Robust Predictions: Mechanism Design Approach

As shown by Leventoğlu and Tarar (2008), model predictions may not be robust to model specifications. In an earlier work, Banks (1990) formulates a two-state crisis bargaining with one-sided private information as a mechanism design problem. He derives results that hold in equilibrium of any bargaining game that the states may play. Such generalization cannot provide precise predictions for states' behavior, but it offers comparative statics results that hold in every equilibrium of every possible game the states may play. Since this approach is relatively rare in the literature, I will discuss it in more detail below.

The building block of Banks' approach is a Bayesian-Nash revelation principle (d'Aspremont and Louis-Andre 1979), which yields a set of incentive compatibility constraints that must be satisfied in every equilibrium of every game that may be played. Assume D's cost can take value $t \in T = [t_l, t_h]$, where t is D's type and it is private information. The probability distribution of t is common knowledge. A game form consists of actions A_S for S and A_D for D and an outcome function with two components: $g_p(a_S, a_D) \in [0, 1]$ is the expected value of

D's share from a peaceful resolution and $g_w(a_S, a_D) \in [0, 1]$ is probability of war when S and D's actions are a_S and a_D, respectively. S and D choose actions simultaneously. Let σ_S and $\sigma_{D(t)}$ be perfect Bayesian equilibrium strategies of S and D of type-t in the game induced by S and D's payoff functions. The outcome of this equilibrium can be written as D's expected share from the peaceful settlement

$$y(t) = g_p(\sigma_S, \sigma_D(t))$$

and the probability of war

$$\pi(t) = g_w(\sigma_S, \sigma_D(t))$$

If type=t D plays $\sigma_{D(t)}$, his expected payoff is

$$U(t; y, \pi) = \pi(t)(1 - p - t) + (1 - \pi(t))y(t)$$

and if he plays $\sigma_{D(t')}$, his expected payoff is

$$U(t', t; y, \pi) = \pi(t')(1 - p - t) + (1 - \pi(t'))y(t')$$

$(y(\cdot), \pi(\cdot))$ is a function of D's type only and it is called a direct mechanism. $(y(\cdot), \pi(\cdot))$ is incentive compatible if $U(t; y, \pi) \geq U(t', t; y, \pi)$ for all $t, t' \in T$, namely a type-t D derives at least as much from reporting his true type to the direct mechanism as he would by reporting another type. The revelation principle states that any outcome that can be obtained as perfect Bayesian equilibrium of a game can be obtained by an incentive compatible mechanism. So, the following inequalities must hold for any two $t, t' \in T$:

$$\pi(t)(1 - p - t) + (1 - \pi(t)) \cdot y(t) \geq \pi(t')(1 - p - t) + (1 - \pi(t')) \cdot y(t')$$

$$\pi(t')(1 - p - t') + (1 - \pi(t')) \cdot y(t') \geq \pi(t)(1 - p - t') + (1 - \pi(t)) \cdot y(t)$$

Summing up these inequalities and canceling out yields $\pi(t) \geq \pi(t')$ for all $t, t' \in T$ such that $t' \geq t$. A smaller t means more resolved D. Then this result means the more resolved D is the more likely a war is in any perfect Bayesian equilibrium of any game between S and D.

Given the anarchic nature of the game, D's share of a peaceful settlement must also be at least as large as his war payoff. This implies an individual rationality constraint:

$$y(t) \geq 1 - p - t$$

for all $t \in T$. Since also $\pi(t) \geq \pi(t')$ for $t' \geq t$,

$$\pi(t)(1 - p - t) + (1 - \pi(t)) \cdot y(t) \leq \pi(t')(1 - p - t) + (1 - \pi(t')) \cdot y(t)$$

Combining this with the first incentive compatibility constraint,

$$\begin{aligned} \pi(t')(1 - p - t) + (1 - \pi(t')) \cdot y(t') &\leq \pi(t)(1 - p - t) + (1 - \pi(t)) \cdot y(t) \\ &\leq \pi(t')(1 - p - t) + (1 - \pi(t')) \cdot y(t) \end{aligned}$$

we obtain

$$\pi(t')(1 - p - t) + (1 - \pi(t')) \cdot y(t') \leq \pi(t')(1 - p - t) + (1 - \pi(t')) \cdot y(t)$$

which implies $y(t) \geq y(t')$ for $t' \geq t$, i.e., D's expected share from a peaceful settlement increases with his resolve.

These strikingly general monotonicity results are derived by easy manipulations of the incentive compatibility and individual rationality constraints. They robustly predict that a more resolved D runs a higher risk of war but also expects a higher share in a peaceful resolution.

Fey and Ramsay (2011) generalize this when both S and D have private information about their types but the joint distribution of types is common knowledge. Unlike Banks, this generalization also captures uncertainty about countries' relative strength and allows for evaluation of consequences of different types of uncertainties mentioned above.

Like Banks, Fey and Ramsay impose an individual rationality constraint to model the anarchic nature of the international system. They also account for the potential of the bargaining process to reveal information about types, so their individual rationality constraint is satisfied with updated belief after such information revelation. They model uncertainty about resolve as independent private values for cost of war. Bank's monotonicity results generalize to this setting.

In this independent private values model, they also obtain a unique peaceful equilibrium with voluntary agreements, in which each state gets a share proportional to its relative strength, i.e., S gets p and D gets $1-p$. Comparing this finding with Powell (1996b) is worthwhile. Powell calculates probability of war as a function of the disparity between the status quo disparity of distribution of benefits and the distribution of the expected benefits from war. He shows that this disparity must be small for a peaceful agreement to emerge in the unique equilibrium of his model. These two results are not contradictory. Powell's result holds true for an institutional setting that can be modeled precisely through a Rubinstein bargaining model under the shadow of war. On the other hand, Fey and Ramsay show that there exist other institutional settings in which a peaceful agreement would be achieved even when the disparity is large enough to guarantee war in Powell's setup.

Uncertainty over relative strength is a case of interdependent values, since a state's relative strengths necessarily define the other state's relative strength. Fey and Ramsay show that, when each state receives a private signal about their relative strength, there does not exist any game with an always peaceful equilibrium when the sum of costs of war is not too large.

14.3.4 Resolution of Informational Problems

If informational problems cause war, are there other institutions that may mitigate the problem? Ramsay (2011) studies a crisis bargaining game with two-sided incomplete information. Unlike in the previous models, he assumes that states can engage in diplomatic communication through a cheap talk game before the bargaining starts. Ramsay shows that, although the messages in the cheap talk game do not change the fundamentals of the game, players credibly communicate with each other about their values for the outcome in equilibrium. Such communication may change the continuation payoffs. In Ramsay's model, this happens especially when the bargaining game has multiple equilibria. The cheap talk diplomacy reveals information and helps players coordinate their actions and decreases ex ante probability of war.

If diplomatic channels are closed, can fighting resolve the very problem of informational asymmetry that causes inefficient fighting at the first place? After all, the assumption of war as a game-ending costly lottery contrasts with the perception of war as part of the bargaining process (von Clausewitz 1976; Schelling 1960). Slantchev (2003a) argues that warfare communicates information about players, and it ceases to be useful when it loses its informational content and ends with negotiated settlement if it has not ended before by a military decisive victory. To formalize this argument, Slantchev embeds war as a stochastic process between two players in an alternating offers bargaining game. Victor of a battle is determined randomly, and a country must win a certain number of battles to win the war decisively. When *D* has private information on relative strength, *D*'s decision to accept or reject an offer and his offer to *S* reveal information. *D* may manipulate that information. But, fighting necessarily reveals information about the distribution of power, so fighting has a valuable information content. Learning during fighting happens through strategic information revelation on the negotiation table and involuntary information revelation on the battlefield. When players' expectations converge sufficiently and battles no longer reveal information, the dispute settles peacefully.

Powell (2004a) models war as a simpler stochastic process: War may end with decisive victory by one of the states or the game proceeds to the next period, in which *S* makes all the offers. Unlike in Slantchev (2003a), in Powell's model, *S* can be uninformed about either *D*'s resolve or his relative strength. In the generically unique Bayesian equilibrium under either scenario, *S* screens *D* by making new and increasing offers as long as D keeps rejecting the offers. More resolved and more powerful types of D accept higher offers and informational asymmetry is resolved in equilibrium.

In contrast to the models above, Leventoglu and Metternich (2018) build a model of civil wars with imperfect information but no informational asymmetry. In their model, the government faces a rebel group. The success of a rebel attack depends on the size of those who participate in violent and non-violent anti-government activities and the strength of the rebels. The society has common beliefs about rebels' strength, but nobody knows it. Like in (2003a), fighting reveals information about the rebels' strength, which influences middle-class' support for rebels. They show that fighting ends with concessions from the government when the society's belief about rebels' strength becomes favorable enough to induce middle-class participation in non-violent anti-government activities.

14.4 Commitment Problems

14.4.1 Lack of Commitment to Future Redistribution

Fearon (2004) identifies several empirical regularities related to civil war duration. Civil wars emerging from coups and revolutions, civil wars in Eastern Europe and former Soviet Union and anti-colonial civil wars tend to be short; civil wars that involve land conflict between an ethnic minority and a dominant ethnic group and civil wars in which rebels derive major funding from contrabands tend to be longer. Fearon explains these patterns by the inability to commit to future redistribution after shift of power. Since this theme appears repeatedly in the literature, it is worth to summarize Fearon's model here.

Fearon sets up a complete information dynamic game with a government and a rebel group. They interact successively in an infinitely repeated game which starts with peace. The government controls the flow of resources. Each period, nature determines whether the government is weak or strong, then the government decides how to distribute resources. All parties observe the government's strength. Rebels cannot fight during strong times, so a strong government does not redistribute.

When the government is weak, rebels decide whether to fight or not, which may end the game with rebels' victory, or the game proceeds to the next period. This is the commitment problem rebels face during weak times. They choose between accepting the government's current offer and risk future redistribution, or fight now and possibly win autonomy when they can. If weak times are not likely, the government would not redistribute most of the time and the rebels would prefer to fight whenever they get a chance to do so.

This is the same mechanism Acemoğlu and Robinson (2001) use to explain political transitions. In their model, the elite controls the government and decides on redistribution and whether to extend the franchise to the poor. The poor can attempt a game-ending revolution when the elite is in control. Extending franchise eliminates the possibility of revolution and brings democracy. The elite may attempt a coup under democracy. The state of the economy is determined by nature every period. Both revolt and coup attempt are very costly when the economy is booming, incentives to revolt and for coup attempt emerge only during economically bad times. Since revolution and coup are not possible during good times, elite under autocracy and poor under democracy cannot commit to redistribution during economically good times, the elite does not redistribute, and the poor impose a high tax rate under democracy during good times. Lack of commitment during good times creates incentives for the poor to revolt under autocracy and for the elite to attempt a coup under democracy during bad times. The commitment mechanism can explain transition to and consolidation of democracy, and unconsolidated democratic transitions. Leventoğlu (2005, 2014) uses the same mechanism to study the impact of social mobility on political transitions and on middle-class behavior.

14.4.2 Shift of Power and Persistent Fighting

Powell (2012) links three regularities of interstate and civil wars to shifts in the distribution of power: periods of persistent fighting exist, fighting ends in negotiated settlements as well as in military decisive outcomes, fighting may reoccur. Powell explains these regularities through the role of fighting to forestall adverse shifts in an infinite horizon stochastic game with a government in control of resources and a rival faction. Each period, the government makes a take-it-or-leave-it-offer, the rival decides whether to accept or fight the government. The state consolidates and the distribution of power shifts in favor of the government unless the government and the rivals fight. Fighting may end the game decisively in favor of one of the parties, or the game may proceed to the next period stochastically. The rival faces a tradeoff between accepting and benefiting from an offer today at the expense of facing a stronger government tomorrow. Since the government cannot commit to future redistribution, this means smaller offers in future. This tradeoff may resolve in favor of persistent fighting in equilibrium.

14.4.3 Robust Predictions: A Unifying Approach

Powell (2004b) offers a unifying perspective on commitment problems. He shows that a common mechanism is at work in a diverse set of inefficient bargaining breakdowns. Powell formulates the mechanism through an inefficiency condition in dynamic stochastic games as follows: Two players, S and D, are trying to divide a flow of a pie of size one every period. They discount future payoffs by δ. Normalize payoffs so that the lifetime surplus from the flow of pies is 1. Let k denotes the state of the world. For example, k may represent state of economy in Acemoğlu and Robinson (2001), government strength in Fearon (2004), a consolidated state or an unconsolidated one in Powell (2012). Transition of k may be stochastic as in Acemoğlu and Robinson (2001) and Fearon (2004), or deterministic as in Powell (2012). Let $M_j(t, k)$ be j's minmax payoff in the continuation game starting in state k in period t, $j \in \{S, D\}$. Then S must offer D at least $M_D(t, k)$ to avoid a costly fight. Suppose that distribution of power shifts in favor of S in state k'. Assume that the state transitions from k to k' in period $t+1$ so that S becomes more powerful in $t + 1$. The most S can offer to D in period t is 1. She can credibly commit to offering a lifetime payoff of $1 - M_S(t + 1, k')$ in period $t + 1$, since S would not settle down for anything less than her minmax payoff. Then the maximum possible payoff that D can expect in period

t, whether in or out of equilibrium, is $(1-\delta)+\delta(1-M_S(t+1,k'))$. If this is less than D's minmax payoff of $M_D(t,k)$ in period t,

$$M_D(t,k) > (1-\delta)+\delta(1-M_S(t+1,k')),$$

then there exists no credible sequence of negotiated resolutions that will avoid costly fighting. Let us employ this in Powell (2012). Suppose that fighting ends decisively with probability α. In that case, probability of S's victory is p if the state is not consolidated and $p+\Delta$ if the state is consolidated. Players' minmax payoffs are obtained when they fight until one faction is eliminated. For simplicity, assume that the pie is destroyed when the players fight and each pays a cost of c. Let F_S be S's minmax payoff when the state is not consolidated. This can be computed recursively as

$$F_S = -(1-\delta)c + \alpha(p\cdot 1 + (1-p)\cdot 0) + (1-\alpha)\delta F_S$$

which yields

$$F_S = \frac{\alpha p - (1-\delta)c}{1-\delta(1-\alpha)}$$

Let F'_S be S's minmax payoff when the state is consolidated, similarly let F_D and F'_D be D's minmax payoffs in the corresponding states of the world. These can be computed in the same way as

$$F'_S = \frac{\alpha(p+\Delta)-(1-\delta)c}{1-\delta(1-\alpha)}, \quad F_D = \frac{\alpha(1-p)-(1-\delta)c}{1-\delta(1-\alpha)}$$
$$\text{and } F'_D = \frac{\alpha(1-p-\Delta)-(1-\delta)c}{1-\delta(1-\alpha)}$$

The inefficiency inequality can be written as

$$F_D > (1-\delta)+\delta(1-F'_S)$$

Again, for simplicity, take δ to 1, this inequality becomes $\Delta > 0$. In other words, when players are patient enough, even a small shift in distribution of power causes persistent fighting. Powell's condition $F_D - \delta F'_D > 0$ also becomes $\Delta > 0$. That is the same inefficiency inequality.

14.4.4 Resolution of Commitment Problems

When war ends in a negotiated settlement, the termination of war must be a consequence of the resolution of its causes (Blainey 1988), so a rationalist theory must explain how war breaks out and how fighting resolves its causes so that it terminates. When informational problems cause war, fighting may resolve the very reason of the war by revealing information credibly (Slantchev 2003a). In the absence of a similar account with commitment problems, any war that terminates with a negotiated settlement can only be explained by incomplete information (Gartzke 1999). Leventoğlu and Slantchev (2007) provide a theoretical explanation to this question in a complete information model.

In their model, actors can fight repeatedly and keep negotiating. Resources are fixed, they are destroyed by war and an agreement on the division of benefits does not necessarily end the war automatically. Parties may renege on the agreement and attempt to use newly acquired resources to extract further concessions. These assumptions allow for peace to happen endogenously only after fighting resolves the commitment problem by destroying enough resources.

By appealing to Powell's (2004b) inefficiency condition, they derive a sufficient condition for most deterrent threats in the future, which creates incentives for peace today. Their theoretical argument illustrates how "implementing an agreement cannot be expected to enable one of the parties to overturn it and enforce a still more favorable agreement" (Wagner 2000). The first-strike advantage in military victory remains constant in their model, but the continuation benefits from first-strike change as the resources shrink with the duration of fighting. Hence, the solution to the commitment problem involves eliminating incentives for first strikes and renegotiations by fighting certain number of battles, which opens a window of opportunity for a peaceful settlement that can be supported by fully credible threats in the future.

In Leventoğlu and Slantchev's model, redistribution of resources impacts how long states survive in continued war. Fearon (1996) analyzes a complete information model in which redistribution of resources leads to redistribution of power. In Fearon's model, p is an increasing function of x. Agreement on x does not end the game, it changes the status quo and shifts the distribution of power. Although actors cannot commit themselves to not increase their demand after power shift, no war breaks out in the unique subgame perfect equilibrium of the game. One of the states may keep acquiring additional chunks of the pie sufficiently small for the other to agree to it rather than fighting. Such salami tactics may eventually lead the other state to lose sovereignty. Fearon predicts that periods of offense dominance in military technology will see a long-term trend of increasing concentration and elimination of smaller states and consolidation of larger federations while periods of defense dominance in military technology will see a counter-trend toward deconcentration via successful secessionist movements.

Efficient bargaining in Fearon's model depends crucially on p being a continuous function of x. Contrast this to Acemoğlu and Robinson's (2001) costly political transitions predictions from this perspective. In their model, shift of power is also endogenous but it is discontinuous and may lead to inefficient political transitions.

If shifts in distribution of power lead to inefficient war, then why does the rising state not offer today concessions of capabilities that will reduce his expected power tomorrow? Chadefaux (2011) develops a model with endogenous power sharing. Unlike in Fearon, p is a continuous monotone function of military resources. He shows that all subgame perfect equilibria are peaceful when states can negotiate over military resources in addition to the issue in dispute.

Slantchev (2003b) asks a different but equally interesting question: Can war break out under complete information and without commitment problems even when peace can be supported in equilibrium? Since war is costly and risky, it is not obvious why and how states would ever play such an inefficient equilibrium while it is possible to avoid costs of war in another equilibrium? Slantchev provides an affirmative answer to this question by constructing an equilibrium with fighting. Given that both rationalist explanations of war are ruled out, what explains war in Slantchev's model? The Folk Theorem states that, as long as players are patient enough, any feasible outcome can be obtained in a subgame equilibrium of a repeated game (Friedman 1971; Fudenberg and Maskin 1986). Since inefficient fighting is a feasible outcome, the theorem implies that it can be supported in equilibrium if parties are sufficiently patient, which Slantchev also assumes.

14.5 Discussion and Future Directions

Bargaining models have become an integral part of rationalist school of war. Much has been argued with the help of such models, and much remains to be said. This survey aims to give a short but coherent picture of how bargaining models have shaped major rationalist explanations of war and offer some future research directions. The survey begs for more. For example, on the technical front, I could have spent more space on models that allow the bargaining process to continue after fighting (in addition to the ones discussed above, e.g., Filson and Werner 2002; Smith and Stam 2004; Wagner 2000; Wittman 1979). Models discussed above embed commitment to some degree, such as committing to agreements, committing to fighting after ending negotiations. Relaxing these assumptions may affect predictions to some degree (Fey et al. 2013; Fearon 2013). Having both informational and commitment problems may impact the resolution of the conflict (Wolford et al. 2011). Endogenizing the distribution of power through pre-bargaining military investment influences not only the level of deterrence but also how the dispute is resolved and may lead to bluffing (Leventoğlu and Tarar 2005; Fearon 2018). Domestic politics such as leadership turnover (Wolford 2012) or audience costs (Leventoğlu and Tarar 2005; Tarar and Leventoğlu 2009, 2012) may change the nature of bargaining significantly. Mediation by a third party changes information and beliefs in equilibrium and its impact may depend on mediator's information, preferences and bias (Kydd 2003, 2006; Beardsley 2008; Favretto 2009; Fey and Ramsay 2010). There is also a growing interest in explanations of war through mutual optimism (Fey and Ramsay 2007) and how to reinterpret them in the rationalist framework (Slantchev and Tarar 2011).

Also, there is a large body of work that builds on game theoretic models without embedding a bargaining process.

The models I covered in this survey and majority of other work build on the assumption of dyads. However, rarely a conflict involves only two actors. Multilateral nature of conflict manifests itself even in two-state conflicts as audience cost (Fearon 1994). This theory assumes that leaders suffer audience costs when they back down from an ongoing conflict or from their promises. Lack of micro foundations for audience costs is a significant drawback in a rationalist explanation. Also, recent experimental work shows that audiences can punish leaders both for being inconsistent as in the traditional audience cost literature and for threatening to use force in the first place (Kertzer and Brutger 2016). Explicitly modeling audiences as rational actors, how alternative forms of audiences costs emerge, and how and to what extent audience incentives to punish leaders aggravate or mitigate informational and commitment problems offer a promising avenue for future research.

Treating multilateral conflict as dyadic is problematic both empirically and theoretically. Poast (2010) shows that dividing actors in a multilateral event into a series of dyadic relations leads to model misspecification statistical bias in empirical work. Similarly, one may be tempted to interpret theoretical models with two actors as modeling dyadic alliances in multilateral conflict. This approach would assume existence of a representative actor for each alliance, which requires further restrictive assumptions on actors' preferences. Embedding alliance formation (Smith 1995) as a coalition formation game in crisis bargaining remains mostly unexplored.

Third party intervention in the form of threatening with punishment to promote cooperation and intervention in the form of mediation and monitoring to mitigate informational problems remain an active area of debate. Although this area is relatively more developed, there is still more to be done to model all three players as rational actors in a crisis bargaining framework. I refer the reader to Kydd (2010) for an extensive discussion of the literature and avenues for future research.

The literature on bargaining and war has culminated in a coherent set of theoretical predictions on mechanisms that cause bargaining breakdowns and war. Testing these predictions in data and experiments remains to be one of the urgent and promising areas.

References

Acemoğlu, Daron and James A. Robinson. 2001. "A Theory of Political Transitions." *American Economic Review* 91(4): 938–963

Baliga, Sandeep and Tomas Sjöström. 2013. "Bargaining and War: A Review of Some Formal Models," *Korean Economic Review*, Winter 29(2): 235–266.

Banks, Jeffrey. 1990. "Equilibrium Behavior in Crisis Bargaining Games." *American Journal of Political Science* 34: 599–614.

Beardsley, Kyle. 2008. "Agreement without Peace? International Mediation and Time Inconsistency Problems." *American Journal of Political Science* 52(4): 723–740.

Blainey, Geoffrey. 1988. *The Causes of War*, 3rd Edition. New York: Free Press.

Brito, D. and M. Intriligator. 1985. "Conflict, War and Redistribution," *American Political Science Review*, vol. 79, 943–957.

Chadefaux, Thomas. 2011. "Bargaining over Power: When do shift in power lead to war?" *International Theory* 3(2): 228–253.

Clausewitz, Carl von. 1976. *On War*. Princeton: Princeton University Press.

Claude, Inis L. 1962. *Power and International Relations*. New York: Random House.

d'Aspremont Claude and Louis-Andre Gerard-Varet. 1979. "Incentives and Incomplete Information." *Journal of Public Economics* 11: 25–45.

Favretto, Katja. 2009. "Should Peacemakers Take Sides? Major Power Mediation, Coercion and Bias." *American Political Science Review* 103(2): 248–263.

Fearon, James D. 1994. "Domestic Political Audiences and the Escalation of International Disputes." *American Political Science Review* 88(3), 577–592

Fearon, James D. 1995. "Rationalist Explanations for War." *International Organization* 49(3): 379–414.

Fearon, James D. 1996. "Bargaining over Objects that Influence Future Bargaining Power." Unpublished Manuscript.

Fearon, James D. 2004. "Why Do Some Civil Wars Last So Much Longer Than Others?" *Journal of Peace Research* 41(3): 275–301.

Fearon, James D. 2013. "Fighting rather than Bargaining." Paper presented at the 2007 Annual Meetings of the American Political Science Association, Chicago, August 30-September 2, 2007.

Fearon, James D. 2018. "Cooperation, Conflict and the Costs of Anarchy." *International Organization* 72(3): 523–559. Cambridge.

Fey, Mark and Kristopher W. Ramsay. 2007. "Mutual Optimism and War." *American Journal of Political Science* 51(4): 738–754.

Fey, Mark and Kristopher W. Ramsay. 2010. "When is Shuttle Diplomacy Worth the Commute? Information Sharing Through Mediation." *World Politics* 62(4): 529–560.

Fey, Mark and Kristopher W. Ramsay. 2011. "Uncertainty and Incentives in Crisis Bargaining: Game-Free Analysis of International Conflict." *American Journal of Political Science* 55(1): 149–169.

Fey, Mark, Adam Meirowitz and Kristopher W. Ramsay. 2013. "Credibility and Commitment in Crisis Bargaining." *Political Science Research and Methods* 1(1): 27–52.

Fernandez, R. and J. Glazer. 1991. "Striking for a Bargain Between Two Completely Informed Agents." *American Economic Review* 81(1): 240–252.

Filson, Darren and Suzanne Werner. 2002. "A Bargaining Model of War and Peace: Anticipating the Onset, Duration, and Outcome of War." *American Journal of Political Science* 46(4): 819–837.

Fudenberg, Drew and Eric Maskin. 1986. "The Folk Theorem in Repeated Games with Discounting or with Incomplete Information." Econometrica 54(3): 533–554.

Friedman, James W. 1971. "A Noncooperative Equilibrium For Supergames." *Review of Economic Studies* 38: 1–12.

Gartzke, Erik. 1999. "War is in the Error Term." *International Organization* 53(3): 567–587.

Jackson, Matthew O. and Massimo Morelli. 2011."The Reasons for Wars," in The Handbook on the Political Economy of War by Christopher J. Coyne and Rachel L. Mathers (Editors).

Kertzer, Joshua D. and Ryan Brutger. 2016. "Decomposing Audience Costs: Bringing the Audience Back into Audience Cost Theory." *American Journal of Political Science* 60(1): 234–249

Kydd, Andrew. 2003. "Which Side Are You On? Bias, Credibility, and Mediation." *American Journal of Political Science* 47(4): 597–611.

Kydd, Andrew H. 2006. "When Can Mediators Build Trust?" *American Political Science Review* 100(3): 449–462.

Kydd, Andrew H. 2010. "Rationalist Approaches to Conflict Prevention and Resolution." *Annual Review of Political Science* 13: 101–121

Leventoğlu, Bahar. 2005. "Social Mobility and Political Transitions." *Journal of Theoretical Politics* 17(4): 465–496.

Leventoğlu, Bahar and Ahmer Tarar. 2005. "Prenegotiation Public Commitment in Domestic and International Bargaining." *American Political Science Review* 99(3): 419–433.

Leventoğlu and Slantchev. 2007. "The Armed Peace: A Punctuated Equilibrium Theory of War." American Journal of Political Science 51(4): 755-771.

Leventoğlu, Bahar and Ahmer Tarar. 2008. "Does Private Information Lead to Delay or War in Crisis Bargaining?" *International Studies Quarterly* 52(3): 533–553

Leventoğlu, Bahar. 2014. "Social Mobility, Middle Class and Political Transitions." *Journal of Conflict Resolution* 58(5): 825–864.

Leventoğlu, Bahar and Nils Metternich. 2018. "Born Weak, Growing Strong: Anti-Government Protests as a Signal of Rebel Strength in the Context of Civil Wars." *American Journal of Political Science* 62(3): 581–596.

Mearsheimer, John J. 1990. "Back to the Future: Instability in Europe after the Cold War." *International Security* 15(1): 5–56.

Morgenthau, Hans J. 1966. *Politics Among Nations*, 4th Edition. New York: Alfred Knopf.

Morrow, James D. 1985. "A Continuous-Outcome Expected Utility Theory of War." *Journal of Conflict Resolution* 29: 473–502.

Myerson, Roger B. 1979. "Incentive Compatibility and the Bargaining Problem." *Econometrica* 47(1): 61–73.

Myerson, R.B., and M.A. Satterthwaite. 1983. "Efficient Mechanisms for Bilateral Trading." *Journal of Economic Theory* 29(2).

Organski, A. F. K. 1958. *World Politics*. New York: Alfred Knopf.

Organski, A. F. K. and Jacek Kugler. 1980. *The War Ledger*. Chicago, IL: University of Chicago Press.

Poast, Paul. 2010. "(Mis)Using Dyadic Data to Analyze Multilateral Events." *Political Analysis* 18: 403–425

Powell, Robert. 1987. "Crisis Bargaining, Escalation, and MAD." *American Political Science Review* 81(3): 717–735.

Powell, Robert. 1996a. "Bargaining in the Shadow of Power." *Games and Economic Behavior* 15(August): 255–289.

Powell, Robert. 1996b. "Stability and the Distribution of Power." *World Politics* 48 (January): 239–267.
Powell, Robert. 1999. *In the Shadow of Power: States and Strategies in International Conflict*. Princeton, NJ: Princeton University Press.
Powell, Robert. 2002. "Bargaining Theory and International Conflict." *Annual Review of Political Science* 5(1): 1–30.
Powell, Robert. 2004a. "Bargaining and Learning While Fighting." *American Journal of Political Science* 48(2): 344–361.
Powell, Robert. 2004b. "The Inefficient Use of Power: Costly Conflict with Complete Information." *American Political Science Review* 98(2): 231–241.
Powell, Robert. 2006. "War as a Commitment Problem." *International Organization* 60(1): 169–203.
Powell, Robert. 2012. "Persistent Fighting and Shifting Power." *American Journal of Political Science* 56(3): 620–637.
Ramsay, Kristopher W. 2017. "Information, Uncertainty, and War". *Annual Review of Political Science* 20.
Ramsay, Kristopher W. 2011. "Cheap Talk Diplomacy, Voluntary Negotiations, and Variable Bargaining Power." *International Studies Quarterly* 55(4): 1003–1023.
Rubinstein, Ariel. 1982. "Perfect Equilibrium in a Bargaining Model." *Econometrica* 50(January): 79–109.
Schelling, Thomas. 1960. *The Strategy of Conflict*. Cambridge, MA: Harvard University Press.
Skyler J. Cranmer, Bruce A. Desmarais & Justin H. Kirkland. 2012. "Toward a Network Theory of Alliance Formation." *International Interactions* 38:3, 295–324
Slantchev, Branislav L. 2003a. "The Principle of Convergence in Wartime Negotiation." *American Journal of Political Science* 97(4): 621–632.
Slantchev, Branislav L. 2003b. "The Power to Hurt: Costly Conflict with Completely Informed States." *American Political Science Review* 97: 123–133.
Slantchev, Branislav L. and Ahmer Tarar. 2011. "Mutual Optimism as a Rationalist Explanation of War." *American Journal of Political Science* 55(1): 135–148.
Smith, Alastair. 1995. "Alliance Formation and War." *International Studies Quarterly* 39(4): 405–425
Smith, Alastair and Allan C. Stam. 2004. "Bargaining and the Nature of War." *Journal of Conflict Resolution* 48(6): 783–813.

Tarar, Ahmer and Bahar Leventoğlu. 2009. "Public Commitment in Crisis Bargaining." *International Studies Quarterly* 53: 817–839.
Tarar, Ahmer and Bahar Leventoğlu. 2012. "Limited Audience Costs in International Crises." *Journal of Conflict Resolution* 57(6): 1065–1089.
Taylor, A. J. P. 1954. *The Struggle for Mastery in Europe, 1848–1918*. London: Oxford University Press.
Taylor, R. Harrison. 1994. "Peace, War and the Balance of Power." *American Political Science Review* 88(3): 593–607.
Wagner, R. Harrison. 2000. "Bargaining and War." *American Journal of Political Science* 44(3): 469–484.
Waltz, Kenneth. 1959. *Man, The State and War*. New York, NY: Columbia University Press.
Wittman, Donald. 1979. "How a War Ends: A Rational Model Approach." *Journal of Conflict Resolution* 23(4): 743–763
Wolfers, Arnold. 1962. *Discord and Collaboration: Essays on International Politics*. Baltimore, MD: Johns Hopkins University Press.
Wolford, Scott, Dani Reiter and Clifford J. Carrubba. 2011. "Information, Commitment and War." *Journal of Conflict Resolution* 55(4): 556–579.
Wolford, Scott. 2012. "Incumbents, Successors, and Crisis Bargaining: Leadership Turnover as a Commitment Problem." *Journal of Peace Research* 49(4): 517–530.
Wright, Quincy. 1965. "The Escalation of International Conflicts." *Journal of Conflict Resolution* 9(4): 434–449.

15

Bargaining in Operations Management Research

Andrew M. Davis

15.1 Introduction

Operations management investigates how companies can take inputs, convert them into end products and services, and deliver them to customers in a way that maximizes profits. As globalization increases it is becoming increasingly difficult for a company to accomplish such a task by itself. Instead, companies must rely on working with others in complex supply chains to take raw materials and generate a final product for customers. As one might imagine, an innumerable number of these business-to-business interactions occur every day and involve bargaining, which is where operations management research has recently turned its attention.

Some of the research areas that fall within operations management (OM) include, but are not limited to: forecasting, production, queuing,

A. M. Davis (✉)
SC Johnson College of Business, Cornell University, Ithaca, NY, USA
e-mail: adavis@cornell.edu

E. Karagözoğlu and K. B. Hyndman (eds.), *Bargaining*,
https://doi.org/10.1007/978-3-030-76666-5_15

inventory management, quality, project management, and supply chain management. Many of these areas entail direct interactions among companies. For example, companies may bargain over forecasts, payment terms, inventory levels, quality requirements, and deadlines. When establishing such terms, it is not uncommon for two companies to come to an agreement that generates an efficiency loss. In particular, an alternative set of contract terms may exist that leads to higher combined profits. A significant portion of bargaining research in OM focuses on investigating ways for companies to more readily identify and agree on such first-best terms. These often include the incentive structure of the contract, the type of relationship between the parties, the information available, and the bargaining institution utilized while negotiating.

In this chapter I summarize the OM research related to bargaining. I focus almost exclusively on behavioral research, which typically includes controlled human-subjects experiments. This is for two reasons. First, bargaining in practice almost always involves human managers. Second, the theoretical bargaining models used in OM stem from the economics literature, such as Stackelberg games, Nash bargaining [18], and Rubinstein bargaining [21]. Admittedly, there are some exceptions to this, which I highlight in Sect. 15.4, but otherwise, theoretical bargaining papers are relatively rare in the OM literature.

In the next section I highlight some of the features that distinguish OM bargaining research from other domains. These features generally aim to add a certain level of realism while maintaining the structure of the problem. In Sect. 15.3 I summarize some of the behavioral papers that examine bargaining through ultimatum offers. While bargaining is not necessarily the focal point of these papers, it is an important aspect that cannot be overlooked. In Sect. 15.4 I highlight the behavioral work that investigates unstructured bargaining processes, which includes settings where one or both parties can make unlimited offers, send feedback, or communicate through chat boxes. I then conclude in Sect. 15.5 by detailing some of the well-established bargaining results in the OM literature and some opportunities for future work. Lastly, I provide a list of behavioral OM papers related to bargaining at the end of the chapter in Table 15.1.

15.2 Features of Bargaining Research in OM

The methods of behavioral OM research are firmly rooted in experimental economics. For instance, most behavioral bargaining papers investigate settings where each party aims to maximize profit. Like economics, when examining such settings it is common practice to use cash incentives that are directly tied to the participants' earnings. Another example of the correspondence between behavioral OM and experimental economics is that both fields prohibit the use of deception. However, aside from these methodological similarities, behavioral OM research typically incorporates a set of features that distinguishes it from the economics literature. These features collectively attempt to add a layer of realism to the bargaining setting without overly detracting from the main structure of the problem.

Before turning to some of these features, it is useful to briefly outline the baseline bargaining setting in OM, depicted in Fig. 15.1. Consider a two-stage supply chain consisting of a single buyer and single supplier. The buyer wishes to procure a quantity of a single product from the supplier and sell it to end demand. The buyer receives a price for each unit sold and the supplier incurs a cost for each unit produced, where the buyer's selling price and supplier's production cost are common knowledge. The buyer and seller engage in a bargaining process over the wholesale price, in which the buyer will pay the supplier for each unit

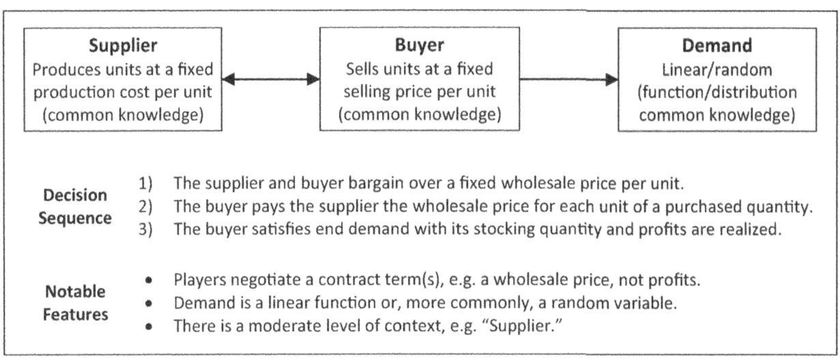

Fig. 15.1 Baseline bargaining experiment setting in OM

purchased. After this the buyer orders a stocking quantity at the fixed wholesale price, faces end demand, and profits are realized.

One might recognize, in Fig. 15.1, that in the baseline setting the two parties do not bargain over the split of a fixed pie or joint surplus. Rather, they bargain over contract parameters, such as a wholesale price, which is then tied to profits. This feature provides two benefits. First, it allows for a relatively accurate representation of a negotiation in practice between two companies. Second, given the existing work in experimental economics, this aspect allows researchers to determine if it leads to different outcomes compared to bargaining over direct payoffs. For example, past economics research has shown considerable evidence of fairness concerns when negotiating a split of a pie. To complement this, recent OM research has found that when buyers and suppliers negotiate over contract terms, rather than profits, they agree on a "superficially fair" set of contract terms that are roughly in the middle of the contracting space, even though they do not necessarily equalize expected profits [7].

Another feature of OM bargaining experiments pertains to the structure of end customer demand. There are typically two approaches employed in the literature: a linear downward sloping demand function or a random variable (usually uniform or normal). Early OM research, which was closely tied to experimental economics, explored a linear demand function. However, a majority of the recent bargaining papers consider the latter option, which is motivated by the fact that demand is usually random in practice. Aside from realism, random demand also allows researchers to investigate other unique aspects of bargaining. For instance, in such a setting there is inherent inventory risk in that, if demand is lower than the stocking quantity (which is set prior to observing demand), there may be unsold units leftover with minimal or no value. Recent behavioral OM research has shown that the party incurring the inventory risk earns a significantly lower share of the overall supply chain profit, despite the theory predicting a 50/50 split [3].

While bargaining experiments within OM tend to avoid background stories and hypothetical vignettes, they often incorporate a certain amount of context. This is admittedly a challenge: researchers wish to make their work more applied, but, at the same time, do not want any context to drive results. Therefore, while the degree of context may vary in OM, it almost always involves two aspects. The first is referring to the two parties as a buyer/retailer or supplier/wholesaler/manufacturer, as opposed to generic labels such as Player A and B. The second involves describing the problem as if two companies in a supply chain are interacting and trying to maximize their profits, as opposed to a more abstract environment. This minimal amount of context provides a certain level of practicality for business environments while also maintaining the primary structure of the problem.

These three features lend themselves to a variety of interesting problems within bargaining. For example, by negotiating over contract terms as opposed to payoffs, different contract structures (e.g., wholesale price, buyback, revenue share, etc), which are equivalent in theory, may lead to different outcomes with human decision-makers. Further, different demand functions, demand distributions, and bargaining institutions may impact behavior in unexpected ways as well. Much of the recent bargaining research in OM is exploring these types of topics and more.

15.3 Ultimatum Offers

Initial bargaining research in behavioral OM employed a highly structured form of bargaining: take-it-or-leave-it ultimatum offers. In this section I summarize some of the behavioral papers using ultimatum offers in human-to-human experiments, separated between full and asymmetric information (note that I drop the "OM" qualifier hereafter, as all referenced papers are from the OM literature, unless otherwise noted).

Before proceeding it is worthwhile to note that the primary focus of the following papers is not necessarily the bargaining dynamics. Rather, these papers investigate broader problems where bargaining is an integral component. One example of this is the problem of double marginalization in supply chains, where there is an efficiency loss due to two companies making independent decisions and seeking to maximize their own profits, as opposed to working cooperatively [22]. As mentioned previously, because the two companies interact directly with one another, bargaining cannot be overlooked. While more recent studies investigate how alternative bargaining institutions can alleviate this problem, traditional behavioral research attempts to identify solutions that include contracts, relationships, and/or incentives. Hence, while bargaining details are included in each of the following papers, it is not always the main objective of interest.

15.3.1 Full Information

One of the earliest papers to study the double marginalization problem within the literature, between two human participants, is Ho and Zhang [10]. They consider a full information setting where a manufacturer, with a fixed production cost, makes an ultimatum wholesale price offer to a retailer. The retailer then has the ability to reject the wholesale price, which leads to an outside option profit of zero, or, to accept it and set a selling price. Because demand is linear in price, the retailer's selling price determines the final quantity and demand. Following both decisions profits are earned, where double marginalization leads to an efficiency loss. Given that it is one of the first papers on contracting and bargaining in the field, Ho and Zhang [10] neglect to incorporate some of the features mentioned previously in this chapter, and instead opt for a more abstract context, such as referring to each role as Player A and Player B.

Ho and Zhang [10] compare three alternative contracts to one another in their setting, with the goal of alleviating the double marginalization problem: a regular wholesale price contract, a two-part tariff (TPT), and a quantity discount (QD) contract. While the latter two contracts are theoretically equivalent in their ability to generate full efficiency, (i.e., the fixed fee in the TPT can be divided by the quantity to obtain an average wholesale price under QD), Ho and Zhang observe that in a human-subjects experiment, the QD contract achieves the highest efficiency. However, neither the TPT nor QD contract achieves 100% efficiency. Instead, the observed channel efficiency is 69.51% in the TPT and 76.37% in the QD contract. Pertaining to bargaining, this difference is largely driven by rejection rates. When conditioning on acceptances, channel efficiencies become 93.62% and 92.87%. Ho and Zhang then demonstrate that a model of reference dependence, where the fixed fee is perceived as a loss and the retailer's selling price is perceived as a gain, can largely account for the decisions in their data.

Loch and Wu [16] examine a setting similar to the one in Ho and Zhang [10] where one party proposes its own margin of a product (similar to a wholesale price) and the responder sets its own margin for selling the product (similar to a retail selling price). Demand is linear in the sum of the margins. Whereas Ho and Zhang [10] evaluate how the TPT and QD contract fare at increasing efficiency in a single anonymous interaction between parties, Loch and Wu [16] experimentally manipulate how existing positive relationships and profit status influence efficiency in a repeated environment. In particular, they conduct three experimental treatments. The first is a baseline control where the two parties are initially matched without any communication. The second treatment represents a scenario where the two parties have an existing positive relationship. For instance, before beginning the game, the two parties meet each other, exchange names, and shake hands. The third treatment again includes initial matching without pre-play interaction, but after each round of decisions, the results screen includes an additional column depicting which of the two parties earned the higher profit and is declared the "winner."

Loch and Wu [16] observe that the second treatment, which is meant to reflect a positive relationship, leads to higher cooperation and reciprocity. As a consequence, both players set lower margins and achieve a higher overall efficiency (although still less than 100%). On the other hand, the third treatment, which makes profit comparisons salient by declaring a winner each round, leads to more competition and reduces overall efficiency.[1]

Davis et al. [6] extend the previous works by incorporating random demand and by focusing on how the location of the inventory risk (i.e., who incurs the cost of unsold inventory) impacts outcomes. Specifically, they evaluate a wholesale price contract where a supplier with a fixed

[1] A recent study by Lee et al. [14] attempted to replicate the results of three behavioral papers. While two of the studies were successfully replicated, the authors were unable to replicate the results of the third, which was Loch and Wu [16]. Therefore, the results of Loch and Wu [16] may not be robust to different subject pools.

production cost proposes an ultimatum wholesale price to a retailer. The retailer either rejects the offer or accepts it and sets a stocking quantity. After both decisions are made random demand occurs. The retailer earns its fixed selling price for each unit sold minus the wholesale price for each unit of the stocking quantity, and the supplier earns the wholesale price (less its production cost) for each unit of the stocking quantity. Davis et al. [6] consider two scenarios. The first is identical to the one just described, where the retailer incurs the inventory risk, referred to as a "push" setting. The second flips decisions such that the retailer proposes a wholesale price per unit it is willing to pay to the supplier, and the supplier then responds by either rejecting it or setting a stocking quantity. Thus, the supplier incurs the inventory risk. As demand is realized, the retailer fulfills it by pulling the product from the supplier's quantity, referred to as a "pull" setting.

Davis et al. [6] find wholesale prices are set too generously by proposers in both the push and pull settings, compared to the normative theory, and that the pull setting leads to higher efficiency. They find that a behavioral model which combines loss aversion with random errors (for the accept/reject decision), captures the data well. They then test this model in an out-of-sample advance-purchase discount (APD) contract experiment, which differs in allowing both parties to share the inventory risk. Davis et al. [6] observe that their behavioral model predicts decisions better than the normative theory in the APD contract and that the APD contract weakly Pareto dominates the push contract.

15.3.2 Asymmetric information

The papers in the previous subsection assume full information of cost, price, and demand information. In practice, however, companies bargaining with one another may have private information. This might include a retailer having more accurate information about demand or a supplier having better information about its production cost. Ozer et al. [19] consider the former setting with ultimatum offers, where a buyer (which they refer to as a manufacturer) has private forecast information about demand. Their problem includes the following five steps: (1) the buyer observes a private demand signal and sends forecast information to the supplier, (2) the supplier invests in capacity, (3) random demand occurs and the buyer places an order to the supplier, (4) the supplier fulfills as much of the buyer's order as possible, (5) the buyer sells to end demand. Ozer et al. explore this game in a variety of experimental conditions, such as single versus repeated interactions, low versus high capacity costs for the supplier, and low versus high demand uncertainty.

In all of the cases described above, the normative theory predicts that a buyer should inflate its forecast when sending information to the supplier and that the supplier should never trust the information sent from the buyer. However, experimentally, Ozer et al. [19] find that the two parties exhibit trust and trustworthiness, increasing efficiency relative to the normative predictions in all treatments. They develop a behavioral model where buyers exhibit trustworthiness (i.e., buyers incur disutility from sending erroneous information), and suppliers trust this information more than the normative theory predicts, and show that it captures the data well.[2]

Beer et al. [1] examine whether trustworthiness can be signaled in supply chains in a slightly different environment than Ozer et al. [19]. In particular, they study a setting where a supplier chooses between a general investment or a buyer-specific investment. The general investment provides the supplier with a higher outside option, in the case where no subsequent deal is agreed upon, and the buyer-specific investment provides a higher profit for the buyer for a given supplier effort level. Therefore, the buyer-specific investment can jointly benefit both parties (but only if the buyer chooses to offer a higher price).

After the supplier makes its investment choice, the buyer then makes an ultimatum price offer to the supplier. Finally, the supplier then chooses to reject the buyer's price, or, to accept it and choose a costly effort level. Beer et al. [1] study this problem in multiple experimental conditions, such as when the investment decision is endogenous versus exogenous and the two parties engage in a single versus repeated interaction. Overall, they find that buyer-specific investments can signal

[2] Ozer et al. [20] extend this work by investigating how levels of trust and trustworthiness differ between the United States and China.

trustworthiness of suppliers and increase overall efficiency. They also show that these benefits are stronger under repeated interactions.

Kalkanci et al. [11] consider a setting where a buyer has better demand information than a supplier. As opposed to focusing on issues of trust, they examine how the level of contract complexity affects outcomes under ultimatum offers. In each round of the game, a supplier first proposes a wholesale price to the buyer. The buyer then rejects the offer or sets a stocking quantity. After this, random demand is realized and profits are earned.

Kalkanci et al. [11] evaluate three different contracts in this setting. The first is the standard wholesale price contract. The second and third increase in complexity by offering quantity discounts through multiple wholesale prices. In the second contract, the supplier proposes two wholesale prices and a quantity breakpoint, where the lower wholesale price applies if the buyer orders more than the quantity breakpoint. The last contract is similar but increases complexity further by allowing the supplier to propose three wholesale prices and two quantity breakpoints. Given this experimental setup, the normative theory predicts that going from one to two to three wholesale prices should increasingly benefit the supplier. However, Kalkanci et al.'s [11] experimental results suggest that the one-price contract performs just as well as, or better than, the more complex variants when including rejections.

Davis and Hyndman [2] study a principal-agent type setting where a retailer attempts to induce a high-quality product from a supplier. The supplier can exert high effort, which is costly but assures a high-quality product, or low effort, where there is a 50/50 chance the product is high quality. The retailer can make an ultimatum offer to the supplier through a monetary incentive, such as a bonus for high quality, a relational incentive, such as a long-term relationship where there is the prospect of punishment, or a combination of both.

Davis and Hyndman [2] observe that relational incentives (i.e., long-term relationships) increase both efficiency and the likelihood of a high-quality product, compared to a short-term relationship. They also find that the interaction between monetary and relational incentives is non-monotonic. Specifically, less efficient monetary incentives (i.e., highly discounted bonuses) crowd out the benefits of relational incentives and yield a lower efficiency compared to when there is no monetary incentive, but highly efficient monetary incentives complement relational incentives and lead to significant efficiency gains.

15.4 Unstructured Bargaining

More recent behavioral work extends the ultimatum offers setting and allows for more natural bargaining processes. Because these bargaining processes take a variety of forms (e.g., one-sided repeated offers, unlimited back-and-forth offers, chat box communication, etc) I will collectively refer to these papers as using "unstructured" bargaining protocols. Unlike those papers employing ultimatum offers, these works provide more details relating to bargaining dynamics, as opposed to accept/reject decisions and efficiency results. As in Sect. 15.3, I will separate these papers between full information and asymmetric information environments.

Before turning to the behavioral papers with unstructured bargaining under full information, a brief comment on the theoretical bargaining literature is in order. In particular, the ultimatum papers summarized in Sect. 15.3 rely almost exclusively on a Stackelberg leadership model. Therefore, there is not much room for a new theoretical contribution. This is not necessarily true for unstructured bargaining settings. One notable example is Lovejoy [17], who introduces the "balanced-principal" bargaining model. In it, he considers a multi-tier supply chain which includes a buyer bargaining with several tier 1 suppliers, who bargain with several tier 2 suppliers, etc. Another example is Feng et al. [8], who theoretically investigate an alternating offer bargaining process with asymmetric demand information. I refer the interested reader to their works for more details.

15.4.1 Full Information

In the behavioral unstructured bargaining literature, Haruvy et al. [9] consider a classic game where a manufacturer, with a fixed production cost, proposes contract terms to a retailer under full information. If the retailer accepts the offer it then sets a selling price, where demand is linear in price. They conduct an experiment which manipulates the contract type, wholesale price versus TPT, and the bargaining process, ultimatum versus sequential offers with concessions. Haruvy et al. [9] design this alternative sequential bargaining protocol in a way that only slightly deviates from the ultimatum setting. Specifically, the manufacturer first makes an offer to the retailer. If the retailer chooses to reject it, then the manufacturer can make another offer which must be an improvement for the retailer (i.e., a concession by the manufacturer). This process continues for up to five minutes. If time ends without an acceptance, then the manufacturer makes a final ultimatum offer.

Aside from observing that the TPT generates higher efficiency than the wholesale price contract, Haruvy et al. [9] find that their sequential bargaining process achieves higher efficiency across both contract types. Turning to bargaining dynamics, initial offers by manufacturers in the sequential process are nearly the same as offers under the ultimatum protocol. When one combines this with concessions in the sequential bargaining protocol and similar rejection rates between the two bargaining institutions, then the sequential bargaining protocol achieves higher efficiency and benefits the retailer. They develop a behavioral model based on reciprocal concessions and loss aversion, and demonstrate that it fits the data well.

Davis and Leider [7] investigate a slightly different supply chain setting. In their study each round begins with a supplier and retailer dynamically bargaining over contract terms under full information. Unlike past behavioral bargaining research, both parties can make unlimited offers and provide limited feedback over a fixed timeframe. If the two parties come to an agreement, then the supplier, which already has a minimal level of capacity, chooses to incur a cost and invest in additional capacity or not. Following this, random demand and profits are realized: the retailer sells products at a fixed selling price per unit and the supplier manufacturers products instantly at zero cost to satisfy retailer demand.

Davis and Leider [7] show that, theoretically, there are a number of contracts which can induce the supplier to invest in first-best capacity levels. The contracts they explore include the quantity premium (QP) contract, quantity commitment (QC) contract, option (OP) contract, and service-level agreement (SLA). While all are theoretically equivalent at achieving first-best outcomes, Davis and Leider observe that, experimentally, the OP contract and SLA perform considerably better than the other alternatives. After analyzing their bargaining data, Davis and Leider find that this result is driven by "superficial fairness." In particular, in all of the contracts retailers and suppliers place more emphasis on negotiating the wholesale price component of the contract, while overlooking any additional coordinating parameters. As a consequence, wholesale prices end up roughly halfway between the retailer's selling price and the supplier's production cost, even though this does not necessarily lead to equitable payoffs.

Davis and Hyndman [3] investigate multidimensional bargaining under wholesale price contracts with full information. Each round of their game begins with a retailer, who has a fixed selling price, and a supplier, who has a fixed production cost, dynamically bargaining over contract terms. The bargaining protocol they employ is similar to Davis and Leider [7] in that both parties can make unlimited offers and provide limited feedback over a fixed timeframe.[3] Davis and Hyndman [3] develop a set of normative theoretical benchmarks for this setting and then administer a human-subjects experiment that manipulates two factors. The first factor is which party incurs the inventory risk: the retailer, the supplier, or the location is endogenously determined in the bargaining process. The second factor varies in which contract terms are included in the bargaining process. In the first variant, both parties only negotiate the wholesale price. After coming to an agreement, the party incurring the inventory risk unilaterally sets the stocking quantity. In the second variant, both the wholesale price and stocking quantity are bargained over simultaneously. Overall, this experimental design means that one (wholesale price), two (wholesale price and quantity), or three (wholesale price, quantity, and risk location), contract terms may be included in the bargaining process.

The main result from Davis and Hyndman [3] is that both parties earn higher expected profits when the two parties negotiate the wholesale

[3] They also consider an ultimatum setting.

price and stocking quantity simultaneously, compared to just the wholesale price. They also find that the inventory risk holder is always the disadvantaged party, which contradicts the standard theoretical prediction. They then show that an anchoring bias, especially on mean demand and the superficially fair wholesale price, can account for decisions in their data.

Leider and Lovejoy [15] examine a three-tier supply chain with horizontal competition and sequential bargaining between tiers. Specifically, each game begins with two suppliers (tier 2) who simultaneously negotiate transfer prices with two manufacturers (tier 1). The suppliers and manufacturers may have different costs, which are full information. In this bargaining stage, each manufacturer negotiates separately with each supplier for a fixed time frame, and attempts to come to an agreement with only one of the suppliers. This means that each manufacturer only comes to an agreement with one supplier, but a supplier can have agreements with both manufacturers (and indeed supply both). After this, the transfer prices and updated costs are revealed to all five participants in the chain, and the single retailer then bargains with the manufacturers. Once an agreement is made between a manufacturer and the retailer, the round ends and profits are earned.

Aside from the three-tier setting with horizonal competition, another unique aspect of Leider and Lovejoy [15] is the bargaining protocol they utilize. In each negotiation, between both the suppliers/manufacturers and the manufacturers/retailers, they allow for unlimited offers over a fixed timeframe with chat box messages. Among other results, Leider and Lovejoy [15] observe that differences in costs can lead to significantly different profit distributions. For instance, they find that profits increase within a tier as competition decreases within a tier, but that profits decrease with less competition in other tiers. They then demonstrate that the balanced-principal model [17] does well at capturing the data, as opposed to more classic bargaining models. In terms of bargaining dynamics, they observe an anchoring bias on initial offers where agreed upon terms are roughly in the middle of these opening offers.

15.4.2 Asymmetric information

One of the newer topics in bargaining involves unstructured bargaining with asymmetric information . Davis and Hyndman [4] consider such a setting where a retailer, with a fixed selling price per unit, and a supplier, with a fixed production cost per unit, dynamically negotiate a wholesale price and stocking quantity simultaneously over a fixed timeframe. During this time, both parties can make unlimited offers and send limited feedback. If they come to an agreement, random demand and profits are realized. Importantly, they assume that the retailer's selling price is common knowledge, but the supplier's production cost information may be full or private information. Specifically, in one treatment, the supplier's cost is known by the retailer, but in the other treatment, the retailer only knows that the supplier's cost is one of three values.

Davis and Hyndman [4] develop a set of normative benchmarks and behavioral hypotheses and then test them in a controlled laboratory environment. Whereas the theory predicts that suppliers should benefit from private cost information, they observe that high-cost suppliers (i.e., less favorable suppliers) are disproportionately disadvantaged. In particular, their bargaining data show that retailers, when negotiating with a supplier who has private cost information, make opening offers that are equivalent to the lowest cost supplier under full information. In other words retailers, under private information, act as if they are always negotiating with the lowest cost supplier and make low opening wholesale price offers. Because final agreements are anchored on these low opening offers, high-cost suppliers earn significantly low splits of overall supply chain expected profits under private information. Davis and Hyndman [4] then proceed to administer an experiment where suppliers have the ability to disclose their private cost information, and find that this action significantly increases the profits of high-cost suppliers, which contradicts the standard theory.

Davis et al. [5] also consider an unstructured bargaining protocol with asymmetric information. However, they extend the previous work by considering a game where a single assembling original equipment manufacturer (OEM) must procure two components from two different suppliers, both of whom have private cost information. Davis et al.

explore a TPT where the OEM has the ability to bargain with the two suppliers either simultaneously or sequentially. They also consider two bargaining institutions, ultimatum offers versus unstructured bargaining. Under simultaneous ultimatum bargaining, the OEM makes an ultimatum offer to supplier 1 and to supplier 2 at the same time (the offers may be different). Profits are earned only if there is an agreement with both suppliers. Under sequential ultimatum bargaining, the OEM first makes an ultimatum offer to supplier 1 and then the OEM makes an ultimatum offer to supplier 2. Again, there must be an agreement with both suppliers to earn positive profits. The unstructured bargaining setting is similar except that the OEM simultaneously makes back-and-forth offers with both suppliers under the simultaneous setting, versus bargaining with supplier 1 and then supplier 2 under the sequential environment.

Davis et al. [5] derive a number of theoretical predictions for their setting. After testing these predictions in a human-subjects experiment they find that when the OEM can make ultimatum offers they earn significantly more profits by contracting sequentially with suppliers, which runs counter to theory. They also administer a set of experiments between an OEM and a single supplier, which effectively serve as a baseline and are designed in a way such that the potential outcomes are equivalent to their assembly setting with two suppliers. Comparing the two to each other, they find that their assembly treatments achieve lower overall supply chain profits versus the dyadic environment between an OEM and a single supplier.

15.5 Established Results and Future Directions

Despite being somewhat young, the bargaining literature has identified a number of interesting results. At the same time, there are also considerable opportunities for future research. Below I attempt to summarize some of the more well-established results along with opportunities for future work.

15.5.1 Established Results

Within ultimatum offers, one robust result pertains to the effectiveness of coordinating contracts at improving overall supply chain profits. In particular, theory predicts that a number of alternative coordinating contracts (e.g., buyback, revenue sharing, service-level agreement) should be able to increase total supply chain profits over traditional wholesale price contracts and achieve first-best outcomes. However, multiple human-subject bargaining studies have reported that (a) while coordinating contracts do indeed provide a modest benefit over wholesale price contracts, they almost never achieve first-best outcomes, and (b) wholesale price contracts perform relatively well compared to the normative predictions (e.g., Kalkanci et al. [11]).

A second common result that has appeared in ultimatum offer bargaining experiments is that models which incorporate certain behavioral biases are better at explaining decisions than the normative theory. Specifically, while there is a myriad of behavioral biases that may exist in practice, three notable ones have emerged in the behavioral literature: (a) social preferences, (b) loss aversion and reference dependence, and (c) trust and trustworthiness, particularly in settings with asymmetric information.[4]

While the number of papers on unstructured bargaining is limited, one preliminary result suggests that relaxing the rigid structure of a negotiation can be beneficial for the supply chain. For instance, Haruvy et al. [9] show that simply allowing one side to make repeated offers, versus a one-shot ultimatum offer, can increase supply chain profits. Further, Davis and Hyndman [3] find that allowing both parties to bargain over two contract terms simultaneously (a wholesale price and quantity, versus only a wholesale price) leads to a Pareto improvement. Overall, these insights indicate that simply altering the bargaining institution can lead to supply chain gains and even win–win outcomes.

[4] Random errors and bounded rationality are often used in bargaining studies as well, usually in conjunction with one of the biases mentioned above, to provide a further improvement of the behavioral model's fit.

A second established result in unstructured bargaining research suggests that there are two common bargaining biases: (a) "superficial fairness," where pairs tend to agree on contract terms that are in the middle of the contracting space, even though they may not translate into equal expected profits, and (b) anchoring, where initial offers significantly influence agreed upon terms (which is consistent with the bargaining literature in economics and psychology). In addition, while more work needs to be done on unstructured bargaining with asymmetric information, early work indicates that uninformed parties may take advantage of "strategic ignorance" and achieve more favorable outcomes than theory predicts.

15.5.2 Future Directions

Turning to opportunities for future work, early research on bargaining focused on the simplest setting, such as one-shot interactions and ultimatum offers. Yet, in practice, companies often interact with the same supply chain partners over long-time horizons and through unstructured bargaining environments. With the exception of Leider and Lovejoy [15], the field has yet to investigate an unstructured bargaining environment with repeated interactions between parties. This will undoubtedly yield insights into how factors such as reputation and reciprocity, among others, influence bargaining dynamics and outcomes.

Another opportunity for future work on bargaining relates to renegotiation. As mentioned previously, OM research aims to be slightly more applied by incorporating features such as random demand. When there is randomness, either from demand or elsewhere (e.g., a supply disruption), initial contracts may need to be renegotiated. However, this topic has not been closely examined in the literature. Now that there is a reasonable body of work on bargaining over initial contract terms it would be interesting to see how renegotiation in alternative bargaining environments affects outcomes.

Most bargaining studies consider a simple supply chain structure: one buyer and one supplier. They also tend to exogenously match individual buyer/supplier pairs prior to negotiating. In reality however, supply chains might (a) be multi-tiered, (b) have multiple firms at each tier, and (c) endogenously form such that companies choose who to contract with. Therefore, future bargaining research that investigates multi-tier supply chains, chains with multiple firms, and/or endogenous supply chain formation could be interesting.

Another opportunity for future work relates to more relaxed bargaining protocols. As the field evolves from ultimatum offers , to one-sided repeated offers, to unlimited back-and-forth offers by both parties, it is natural to extend this further and attempt to mimic an even more realistic bargaining environment. This might include chat box communication or even face-to-face negotiations. Although the downside of this is that, as negotiations become more realistic, they also become more difficult to control. Therefore, researchers must continue to be careful to balance realism with the ability to obtain clear cause-and-effect results.

Lastly, one might note that almost all of the papers discussed in this chapter focus on bargaining over contract terms. Yet, bargaining is an integral aspect of other environments as well. For instance, managing supply chain disruptions, forecasting, and project management, are but a few examples where bargaining is important but has not been thoroughly studied in the literature. In sum, there is no doubt that it is an exciting time to be conducting research on bargaining. With the past ten plus years of research to build off of, I look forward to seeing how future research extends this work and generates further insights for practice.

Table 15.1 Behavioral OM papers related to bargaining

Reference	Bargaining	Information	Demand	Contracts	Interaction	Biases
Ho and Zhang [10]	Ultimatum	Full	Linear	WP, TPT, QD	Single	Reference dependence, QRE
Loch and Wu [16]	Ultimatum	Full	Linear	WP	Repeated	Status, reciprocity
Davis et al. [6]	Ultimatum	Full	Random	WP, APD	Single	Loss aversion, random errors
Ozer et al. [19]	Ultimatum	Asymmetric	Random	WP	Single/repeated	Trust
Katok and Pavlov [13]	Ultimatum	Asymmetric	Linear	MOQ	Single	Fairness, random errors
Katok et al. [12]	Ultimatum	Asymmetric	Linear	WP	Single	Fairness
Kalkanci et al. [11]	Ultimatum	Asymmetric	Random	WP, QD	Single	Fairness, random errors
Ozer et al. [20]	Ultimatum	Asymmetric	Random	WP	Single/repeated	Cultural differences, trust
Beer et al. [1]	Ultimatum	Asymmetric	NA	WP	Single/repeated	Trust, reciprocity
Davis and Hyndman [2]	Ultimatum	Asymmetric	NA	Deferred Pmt	Single/repeated	Fairness
Leider and Lovejoy [15]	Unstructured	Full	NA	WP	Repeated	Anchoring, risk aversion, altruism
Haruvy et al. [9]	Unstructured	Full	Linear	WP, TPT	Single	Concessions

Reference	Bargaining	Information	Demand	Contracts	Interaction	Biases
Davis and Leider [7]	Unstructured	Full	Random	WP,QP,QC,OP,SLA	Single	Superficial fairness
Davis and Hyndman [3]	Unstructured	Full	Random	WP	Single	Superficial fairness, anchoring
Davis et al. [5]	Unstructured	Asymmetric	Linear	TPT	Single	Fairness
Davis and Hyndman [4	Unstructured	Asymmetric	Random	WP	Single	Anchoring, concessions

Note WP=Wholesale price, TPT=two-part tariff, QD=quantity discount, QRE=quantal response equilibrium, APD=advance-purchase discount, MOQ=minimum-order quantity, QP=quantity premium, QC=quantity commitment, OP=option, and SLA=service-level agreement. Not all of these papers are explicitly covered in this chapter.

References

1. Ruth Beer, Hyun-Soo Ahn, and Stephen Leider. Can trustworthiness in a supply chain be signaled? *Management Science*, 64 (9): 3974–3994, 2018.
2. Andrew Davis and Kyle Hyndman. An experimental investigation of managing quality through monetary and relational incentives. *Management Science*, 64 (5): 2345–2365, 2018.
3. Andrew Davis and Kyle Hyndman. Multidimensional bargaining and inventory risk in supply chains: An experimental study. *Management Science*, 65 (3): 1286–1304, 2019.
4. Andrew Davis and Kyle Hyndman. Private information and dynamic bargaining in supply chains: An experimental investigation. *Forthcoming, Manufacturing & Service Operations Management*, 23 (6): 1449–1467, 2021. https://doi.org/10.1287/msom.2020.0896.
5. Andrew Davis, Kyle Hyndman, Anyan Qi, and Bin Hu. Procurement for assembly under asymmetric information: Theory and evidence. *Forthcoming, Management Science*, https://doi.org/10.1287/mnsc.2021.4000, 2021.
6. Andrew Davis, Elena Katok, and Natalia Santamaría. Push, pull, or both? a behavioral study of how the allocation of inventory risk affects channel efficiency. *Management Science*, 60 (11): 2666–2683, 2014.
7. Andrew M. Davis and Stephen Leider. Contracts and capacity investment in supply chains. *Manufacturing & Service Operations Management*, 20 (3): 403–421, 2018.
8. Qi Feng, Guoming Lai, and Lauren Xiaoyuan Lu. Dynamic bargaining in a supply chain with asymmetric demand infinitely. *Management Science*, 61 (2): 301–315, 2015.
9. Ernan Haruvy, Elena Katok, and Valery Pavlov. Bargaining process and channel efficiency. *Management Science*, 66 (7): 2845–2860, 2020.
10. Teck-Hua Ho and Juanjuan Zhang. Designing pricing contracts for boundedly rational customers: Does the framing of the fixed fee matter? *Management Science*, 54 (4): 686–700, 2008.
11. Basak Kalkanci, Kay-Yut Chen, and Feryal Erhun. Complexity as a contract design factor: A human-to-human experimental study. *Production and Operations Management*, 23 (2): 269–284, 2014.

12. Elena Katok, Tava Olsen, and Valery Pavlov. Wholesale pricing under mild and privately known concerns for fairness. *Production and Operations Management*, 23 (2): 285–302, 2014.
13. Elena Katok and Valery Pavlov. Fairness in supply chain contracts: A laboratory study. *Journal of Operations Management*, 31: 129–137, 2013.
14. Yun Shin Lee, Yong Won Seo, and Enno Siemsen. Running behavioral operations experiments using amazon's mechanical turk. *Production and Operations Management*, 27 (5): 973–989, 2018.
15. Stephen Leider and William S. Lovejoy. Bargaining in supply chains. *Management Science*, 62 (10): 3039–3058, 2016.
16. Christoph Loch and Yaozhong Wu. Social preferences and supply chain performance: An experimental study. *Management Science*, 54 (11): 1835–1849, 2008.
17. William S. Lovejoy. Bargaining chains. *Management Science*, 56 (12): 2282–2301, 2010.
18. John F. Nash. The bargaining problem. *Econometrica*, 2 (18): 155–162, 1950.
19. Ozalp Ozer, Yanchong Zheng, and Kay-Yut Chen. Trust in forecast information sharing. *Management Science*, 57 (6): 1111–1137, 2011.
20. Ozalp Ozer, Yanchong Zheng, and Yufei Ren. Trust, trustworthiness, and information sharing in supply chains bridging china and the u.s. *Management Science*, 60 (10): 2435–2460, 2014.
21. Ariel Rubinstein. Perfect equilibrium in a bargaining model. *Econometrica*, 50 (1): 97–109, 1982.
22. Joseph J. Spengler. Vertical integration and antitrust policy. *Journal of Political Economy*, 58 (4): 347–352, 1950.

Part III

Advances in Bargaining Research: New Platforms, Challenges and Techniques

16

Field Experiments in Bargaining

Burak Dindaroğlu and Seda Ertac

16.1 Introduction

Bargaining remains ubiquitous despite the prevalence of anonymous, decentralized markets for most goods and services. Understanding price formation and surplus division in bargaining contexts has therefore been of significant interest to economists.

There is a large literature that studies bargaining behavior in the laboratory. Laboratory experiments provide numerous advantages in the context of bargaining. Bargaining behavior is contingent on valuations and costs, which are not directly observable. Laboratory experiments that

B. Dindaroğlu
İzmir Institute of Technology, Urla, Turkey
e-mail: burakdindaroglu@iyte.edu.tr

S. Ertac (✉)
Koç University, Istanbul, Turkey
e-mail: sertac@ku.edu.tr

E. Karagözoğlu and K. B. Hyndman (eds.), *Bargaining*,
https://doi.org/10.1007/978-3-030-76666-5_16

induce valuations (Smith 1982) create settings in which all key parameters can be controlled by the experimenter. This allows direct tests of economic theory. While the laboratory provides strict control, the question of whether behavior in the lab is externally valid in natural contexts is a major empirical question. Field experiments offer a middle ground between naturally occurring data (which is often plagued by issues such as selection) and context-free laboratory experiments, and have proven useful for studying numerous topics in economics (DellaVigna 2009; Banerjee and Duflo 2017). In this chapter, we provide an overview of field experiments that study bargaining behavior and the determinants of bargaining outcomes.

Comparisons of laboratory and field experiments in economics have been the topic of a methodological discussion, with different studies highlighting the relative merits of field experiments (Harrison and List 2004) and lab experiments (Falk and Heckman 2009). This discussion points to the complementarity of lab and field methods and highlights that there are specific questions that will be better suited for each. The key advantage of field experiments lies in their realism. In many of the studies we consider, the field context offers an opportunity to use a setting that is very difficult, if not impossible, to create in the lab. On the other hand, a key problem with field experiments is the difficulty of inducing valuations, especially if researchers work within a naturally existing context of transactions. Some solutions to this problem have been attempted. For example, List (2004a, 2004b) studies negotiations over a collectible sports card that is rendered useless outside of the experiment by painting a moustache on it. This allows capturing the field context and knowledge through the use of a familiar item, while inducing valuations at the same time. Another approach is to obtain the distribution of "homegrown" valuations by means of a truthful revelation mechanism (e.g., second-price auctions or Becker-DeGroot-Marschak-type mechanisms) within the natural field context.[1]

Field experimentation usually operates under a trade-off between control and realism. However, the field can also help researchers exert

[1] As an example, Dindaroğlu and Ertac (2020) elicit livestock sellers' valuations through an incentive compatible mechanism, by actually purchasing sheep from them during the Feast of Sacrifice in Turkey.

control through the natural properties of the setting, without sacrificing realism. One example is Castillo et al. (2013), who use a unique feature of the taxicab market: the ability to send a signal to the next seller in line that the buyer has low valuation for the service. This feature makes it possible for the researcher to manipulate the seller's beliefs about the buyer's value naturally. Andersen et al. (2018) exploit differences in existing forms of social organization by conducting experiments in matrilineal and patriarchal societies. This gives the authors the ability to identify the effects of social organization, which would not be possible to create in the laboratory. Iyer and Schoar (2015) illustrate brilliant uses of the field context by creating random variation in unobservable characteristics of the bargaining setting and the contracting environment, namely the relationship-specificity of the transaction and the presence of reputation effects. In these respects, field experiments can provide ways of collecting data that can better capture individuals' behavior in natural settings.

Methodologically, field experiments in our review either (i) use naturally existing properties of the field to obtain treatment and control groups, (ii) intervene within a naturally occurring market context through explicit treatments and randomization, or (iii) use a field-specific subject pool to bring some realism from the field context. To follow the Harrison and List (2004) classification, we include natural, framed as well as artefactual ("lab-in-the-field") field experiments in our review.

Existing field experiments on bargaining exhibit great variety in the topics and questions that have been addressed, as well as in the field contexts in which these questions are investigated. Several themes emerge that are taken up by multiple studies, and we organize our review around these topics of interest. A relatively large number of studies use a bargaining mechanism to detect the presence of discrimination in the marketplace. Researchers have also focused on bargaining within the household , both regarding fertility and resource allocation decisions. Here, gender differences in the willingness to negotiate and bargaining outcomes have also been a major focus. Another common theme is the study of culture and ethnicity in relation to bargaining, for which the field context and the use of non-student subject pools have provided ample opportunities to conduct informative experiments.[2] We confine our attention to field experiments that specifically use a bargaining mechanism, and hence provide insights into the way bargaining procedures and outcomes relate to the treatments considered in each line of inquiry.

An important and sizeable set of field experiments use experimental bargaining protocols to test key propositions of economic theory, both in general and specialized contexts. Notably, bargaining experiments have been used for testing whether markets based on sequential bilateral bargaining interactions converge to Walrasian equilibrium, a fundamental question in economics. Researchers have also used specific field contexts to design experiments to infer the causes of inefficiencies in bargaining. These highlight important and significant interactions of experiments with economic theory, an area where field experiments will keep providing opportunities to enhance our understanding.

16.2 Discrimination in the Marketplace

Since the outcome of bargaining is an allocation of the total trading surplus, settings in which bargaining transactions naturally occur provide direct opportunities to detect and study discrimination. Discrimination is a topic that benefits greatly from the realism offered by the field, as the precise context in which discrimination occurs can be studied in detail, and laboratory studies of discrimination may be plagued by potential experimenter demand effects that manifest in subjects' unwillingness to look biased.

Field experiments on discrimination usually rely on an audit-based or a correspondence method. The former involves the use of recruited auditors acting either as buyers or sellers, and performing bargaining transactions with actual trading partners. This method allows randomization of buyer (seller) characteristics or behavior, at the cost of observing natural bargaining responses from the seller (buyer) side alone. This

[2] The use of non-student subject pools also provides clues as to whether negotiation behavior of different groups (e.g., entrepreneurs vs. the general public in Artinger et al. 2015) differ, due to self-selection into occupations or differences in life experiences.

problem does not hinder studies of discrimination, for which experimental observation of one side of the market at a time suffices. Auditors usually perform a scripted bargaining routine and may be paid a fixed fee per bargaining transaction and/or be the residual claimants of any surplus obtained if exchange takes place. Correspondence studies rely on communication (usually an inquiry or application) through mail. This method has been particularly popular for studying discrimination in the labor market (Bertrand and Duflo 2017).

Audit studies have been criticized on the grounds that the group attribute is not truly randomized (Heckman and Siegelman 1992; Ayres and Siegelman 1995). Indeed, identification may not be as sharp as in true randomization since the success of the experiment rests on the quality of the matching between auditors. Another criticism is that auditors may not be acting naturally, especially if they are told the purpose of the study before the experiment takes place. An obvious rule of thumb is to keep this information hidden from them unless the experimental design and the external environment dictate otherwise. Correspondence studies do not suffer from these criticisms and are easier to conduct since they do not require recruiting, training, and monitoring auditors. The downside, however, is that the data collected tend to be coarse, as interaction with subjects is quite limited. This makes it difficult to obtain multiple rounds of sequential offers, and studies usually observe a single initial offer by the seller, akin to observations from an ultimatum game.

A common problem in the bargaining literature studying discrimination is the identification of the source of observed differences in bargaining outcomes among groups of interest. Animus or taste-based discrimination refers to discrimination due to a distaste for a particular group of market participants (Becker 1957). Statistical discrimination refers to discrimination based on perceived statistical properties that may vary across groups (Phelps 1972; Arrow 1973).

Ayres (1991) and Ayres and Siegelman (1995) perform the flagship study of this literature, which involves audit-based field experiments at new-car dealerships in the Chicago area. The experiment uses trained pairs of buyers to bargain with dealers following a scripted protocol. One individual in each pair is always a white male and matched in order to isolate the effect of gender and race. The negotiations begin by the auditor soliciting a price for a particular car. The bargaining protocol consists of an initial counteroffer that equals the authors' estimate of the marginal cost of the car to the seller. After this first round, testers either respond with a "split-the-difference" strategy or one of "fixed concession". Negotiations end when the salesperson accepts an offer or refuses to bargain further.

The study finds evidence for discrimination against non-whites and females. Specifically, initial and final offers by the seller are strongly associated with both gender and race, with white males being quoted lower prices than females or African-Americans. While the study does not clearly distinguish between statistical or taste-based discrimination, the authors use the field context to obtain clues to suggest a distinction, such as information on the ethnicity of the salesperson, owner, employees, and customers, as well as neighborhood characteristics. Minority ownership or neighborhood effects are never significant, and no significant effects of employee characteristics are found. These findings point to the presence of statistical rather than taste-based discrimination.

An influential study by List (2004a) offers innovative uses of the field context to identify the sources of discrimination in the marketplace. The study involves field experiments conducted in the market for collectible sports cards. Subjects are recruited among buyers or sellers in the market. Buyers' task is to enter the marketplace and purchase a particular card for as little as possible, subject to a maximum reservation value. Earnings are the difference between the reservation value and the purchase price. Seller subjects are either dealers or nondealers who are naturally there to sell the card in question.

List observes that women and non-whites are given inferior deals in initial prices and final offers. This is true in both buyer and seller positions, but consumer-side discrimination is stronger. Interestingly, experience in the market helps avoid the discriminatory outcome in prices, but at additional cost: final offers do not exhibit discrimination among experienced nondealer buyers, but these buyers need to commit more time to obtain the final offer. Three more experiments are conducted to identify the sources of discrimination, which collectively point to the conclusion that the nature of discrimination is statistical. A dictator game rules out animus, and a market experiment singles out deliberate statistical discrimination as the only explanation. With a second-price auction and a survey of sellers, List confirms that sellers have reasonable knowledge of reservation value distributions for the different groups.

Castillo et al. (2013) conduct a field experiment in the taxi market in Lima, Peru, to study how gender affects bargaining outcomes. Auditors in the buyer role follow a scripted bargaining protocol whereby they always respond by offering a fixed and pre-determined maximum willingness to pay. The authors find that men face higher initial and final prices as well as higher rejection rates, indicating potential discrimination against men. To analyze discrimination patterns further, they use a unique feature of the field setting and introduce a treatment whereby the driver receives a signal about the valuation of the buyer before bargaining. In the taxi market in Lima, while a negotiation takes place, it is common for a second taxi to pull up and wait for a potential failure. Hence, it becomes possible for the buyer to visibly reject the offer of the first taxi and come to negotiate with the second, sending a signal to the second driver that the buyer has low valuation. They find that gender differences in initial and final offers, as well as rejection rates, disappear in this second negotiation. This again provides evidence for statistical, rather than taste-based discrimination.

Another study conducted in the taxi market is by Michelitch (2015), this time in Ghana. The study documents an interesting case of discrimination in bargaining, in which sellers discriminate based on partisanship during election times. Field experiments are conducted during three different time periods around Ghana's 2008 national elections. The study focuses on ethnic and partisan group identifications, which together create four possible treatments in bargaining encounters. Subjects from four ethnic groups are recruited as taxi passengers. Negotiations occur in free form, and the parties learn one another's ethnicity through language and accent and infer partisanship based on the typical nesting of ethnic groups in parties. Co-ethnic riders are always able to obtain a lower price from drivers than non-coethnic riders. They also find discrimination based on partisanship, in that prices for non-coethnic riders sharing the driver's political party are significantly lower, while they are significantly higher for non-coethnics affiliated with the opposing political party. Interestingly, this latter difference only occurs during election times.

Zussmann (2013) performs a correspondence study on an online advertising platform in Israel. He sends 8,000 pairs of emails from fictitious buyers, paired in a way in which one states a distinctly Arab, and the other a distinctly Jewish name. The responses reflect the presence of discrimination against Arab buyers. Specifically, the response rate to Jewish emails was found to be 22% higher than to those with Arab names. Importantly, discrimination responds to monetary incentives: when an Arab buyer offers the car's posted price he obtains the same response rate as a Jewish buyer who requests a 5–10% discount relative to the posted price. In a supporting experiment, many fictitious advertisements are posted on the same platform, again signaling ethnicity by name. The results show that Arabs are discriminated against in seller roles as well.

The study's argument for statistical rather than taste-based discrimination is based on two observations: First, Arab buyers discriminate against sellers from their own ethnic group as well, albeit to a lesser extent than Jewish buyers. Second, responses to an additional questionnaire indicate that the discrimination exhibited by Jewish buyers is not associated with those questions capturing prejudicial tastes, but only associated with the (payoff-relevant) belief that Arabs are more likely than Jews to cheat. While the questionnaire reveals notable animus-based discrimination in attitudes and in daily lives on the part of a large share of Jewish buyers, differences in market interaction remain consistent with statistical discrimination.

Hanson and Hawley (2011) use a correspondence experiment to test for discrimination in the market for rental housing. They send solicitation emails to landlords using names that are easily associated with being white or African-American. They also randomize a signal of social status. They find discrimination against African-Americans, which is more severe in neighborhoods that are near tipping points in racial composition. Interestingly, they find no evidence of discrimination when the email content insinuates high social status, again signaling the presence of statistical discrimination.

A general takeaway from this literature on bargaining and discrimination is that discrimination is ubiquitous, but it tends to be statistical, even in environments in which subjects exhibit clear animus against a particular group. When group identification does play a role, as in Michelitch (2015), it is observed to be short-lived and confined to particular time periods. Based on this, one is tempted to conclude that economic incentives tend to curb animus-based discrimination in the marketplace. Taste-based discrimination in many economic settings is costly to the discriminating party, and economic incentives do prevail in the end. Statistical discrimination, on the other hand, is very common and can help maximize profits—in fact, experienced sellers/buyers tend to perform better statistical discrimination (List 2004a).

16.3 Bargaining Within the Household

Not all bargaining contexts involve negotiation over a sales price. Many decisions made in a household are made by pairs that may have different preferences, and this pair decision-making usually involves significant negotiation. The household therefore offers a unique setup for studying bargaining behavior, particularly in terms of how the distribution of bargaining power affects outcomes. Indeed, a small number of field experiments study negotiations within the household, focusing mainly on resource allocation and bargaining power.

Ashraf et al. (2014) study household bargaining on fertility decisions by controlling the way couples gain access to concealable contraceptives. They conduct a field experiment in a large family clinic in Zambia, which provides women with vouchers that guarantee free access to contraceptives. The experiment creates variation in bargaining power by randomly assigning usage rights over the voucher. In one treatment, the woman can access the voucher alone, while in the other access requires the signature of both husband and wife, giving the husband veto power on the use of contraceptives.

The results show that women who were entitled to contraceptive use on their own were more likely to use them, and therefore less likely to give birth. Requiring the consent of the husband reduced contraceptive use by 19% (25% in the subsample of potential responders). A significant proportion of women either hid or misrepresented the aim of the voucher, thereby documenting the role of moral hazard in household fertility decisions. The results suggest inefficiencies in household bargaining around fertility, as women use contraceptives at higher rates in the individual treatment even if their preferences for children are aligned with those of their husbands in the short term.

Beblo and Beninger (2014) study bargaining for resource allocation within the household with an artefactual field experiment in Germany. Each couple was given four units of an experimental currency that allowed consumption from nearby department stores of cosmetics, fashion/sports, or electronics. The couples first made choices of consumption bundles individually, and then jointly. In each of the joint decisions, the distribution of the vouchers among husband and wife differed.

The results show that the allocation of consumption among the couple is influenced by the distribution of the vouchers between them. Couple choices are found to be always closer to the females' preferences, indicating higher female bargaining power in the household. The authors also find that female bargaining power increases with the number of children in the household and household income, and decreases in the woman's age and the man's education level.

Another study that deals with female bargaining power within the household is by Bulte et al. (2015). Here, the authors use exogenous spatial variation in male to female ratios in China due to the one-child policy, to study the effects of the sex ratio on the bargaining power of spouses in a field experiment. Their first measure of bargaining power is subjective, obtained by separately asking the wife and husband a standard question about power and decision-making in the household. Second, they record who oversees financial matters in the household. The third measure is obtained from public good contribution experiments in the vein of Carlsson et al. (2012).

Their main finding is that sex ratio and bargaining power are positively correlated. Specifically, a one standard deviation increase in the male to female ratio increases the probability that the woman's preferences dominate collective decision-making by 15%. Also, female bargaining power increases with the difference in women's and men's education levels, the wealth of the woman's parents, and is higher if the household moves in with the parents of the bride. On the other hand, female bargaining power falls with household income, and as the distance to the wife's parents increases.

16.4 Gender and Bargaining

While all of the household studies mentioned above allude to the role of gender, gender difference in bargaining has been a major topic of research (Babcock and Laschever 2003). In addition to laboratory experiments, field experiments have also been conducted to address gender differences in the willingness to bargain and in bargaining outcomes. This line of work is part of a large research agenda that aims to understand the sources of gender differences in economic behavior and outcomes, as well as the policy question of how to mitigate these differences, especially when they lead to inefficiency (Croson and Gneezy 2009).

Leibbrant and List (2015) use a natural field experiment to look for a particular factor that may contribute to the gender-wage gap, by testing whether there exist gender differences in initiating wage negotiations during the job application process. They place job advertisements with potentially high stakes and observe the behavior of applicants during application as well as in follow-up communication. They create random variation in job characteristics by creating ads that explicitly state whether the final salary is negotiable, or do not mention negotiability at all, as well as posting general or only sports-related ads, within a 2x2 factorial design. They show that if there is no explicit statement in the job offer that the wage is negotiable, men are more likely to negotiate for a higher wage, whereas women are more likely to signal that they would work for a lower wage. These differences disappear when the job postings explicitly state that the wage offer is negotiable. Men also prefer job environments with ambiguous rules for wage determination, leading to a larger gender gap for such jobs.

Most studies in western countries report women to be less successful in bargaining (Babcock and Laschever 2003), but it is difficult to identify whether this is due to discrimination, bargaining power, inherent gender-specific traits, or the cultural environment. Andersen et al. (2018) bring interesting evidence to the table by studying how bargaining behavior changes by gender in patriarchal and matrilineal societies. They conduct field experiments in an open-air market in Northeast India, using scripted bargaining by hired subjects who were residual claimants of bargaining gains for tomatoes.

In the same study, Andersen et al. (2018) also conduct an alternating-offer "lab-in-the-field" experiment with induced values, in order to identify gender differences in buyer and seller roles, which cannot be reliably identified in the field due to self-selection into market roles. Their main finding is that females obtain a larger share of the surplus in the matrilineal society than males. This is true in both field and lab experiments. The result is reversed within the patriarchal society, where males outperform females. This is in contrast to the evidence from the western world and suggests that observed differences have a cultural basis. Interestingly, being assigned to the buyer or seller role turns out to be an important factor in bargaining outcomes. This points to the possibility of subjects carrying over experiences from their daily transactions into the experiment.

16.5 Role of Culture and Ethnicity

An interesting feature of Andersen et al. (2018) is its use of differences in social organization among two cultures as treatments. The study exploits cultural differences in social organization between two Indian tribal societies, the matrilineal Khasi and the patriarchal Kharbi. The results indicate that gender differences in bargaining outcomes are likely to be products of culture and the social organization in place, rather than of inherent gender-specific traits.

Studies have also focused on aspects of culture or social organization other than in relation to gender. Roth et al. (1991) conduct experiments of two-person ultimatum bargaining and multi-person market environments in the US, Japan, Israel, and Yugoslavia in order to study a potential role for cultural differences in bargaining outcomes. While these experiments are direct implementations of the ultimatum game, we consider them to be artefactual field experiments due to the diversity of the (non-student) subject pool used. The results show that bargaining outcomes differ from theoretical predictions (as usual in the ultimatum game), as well as from one another across different countries. The highest offers are made in the US and Yugoslavia, and the lowest ones in Israel, with Japan in the middle. The probability of rejection is inversely related to offers within countries, but not between countries. This supports the hypothesis that the differences are cultural. Similarly, Henrich et al. (2001) report results from ultimatum bargaining experiments conducted in 15 small-scale societies with different cultures and social organization. The results reveal significant differences across cultures, as well as from previous results obtained in developed countries. Importantly, group-level differences in outcomes are mostly explained by differences in economic and social organization and the degree of market integration. The Machiguenga of the Peruvian Amazon have a very non-cooperative culture and end up making (and accepting) the lowest offers. In contrast, the Lamalera of Indonesia and Aché of Paraguay have cooperative cultures in which collaborative hunting and meat sharing are common practices. These societies make the highest offers among all cultures. Au and Gnau of Papua New Guinea are communities in which circulation of goods takes place through gift exchange, and their behavior reflects this: They are inclined toward hyper-fair offers that leave more than 50% to the responder, which are frequently rejected. In gift cultures, accepting a gift creates an obligation of debt, which must be reciprocated (Mauss 2016). This is consistent with observations from these two cultures. Taken together, evidence from this set of cross-country field experiments indicates that cultural organization and practices affect bargaining behavior and outcomes significantly. This contrasts with market environments in which bargaining serves as a micro-foundation, as in Roth et al. (1991) and the related studies we review in the next section.

16.6 Efficiency and Welfare

Lab experiments of market mechanisms in the vein of Roth et al. (1991) discussed above are important for economics, as they allow testing fundamental propositions of economic theory, such as the efficiency of markets. The first market experiment was conducted by Chamberlin (1948), who used student subjects and fictitious commodities. The experiment and its variants have been repeated in various contexts with monetary incentives and reservation value inducement. Bilateral bargaining is a popular mechanism, even though competing mechanisms have been used. In what follows, we review this line of field experiments that use bargaining protocols (see Al-Ubaydli and List (2017) for a more general review of the literature on market experiments).

List (2004b) uses data from field experiments in sports cards and collector pin markets to test the classic theory of competitive Walrasian equilibrium. List creates variation in the underlying multilateral bargaining mechanism to see the convergence behavior of various micro-foundations for market equilibria. Subjects are recruited so that natural dealer and nondealer roles are mapped into seller and buyer roles in the experiment. As in List (2004a), valuations are induced by using a commodity that is familiar to all market participants but valueless outside the experiment. The market experiment lasts for five rounds with reassignment of valuations. After each agreement, the sale price is announced to the whole group. There are three treatments: one in which both supply and demand curves have finite slopes and are symmetric, one that induces a perfectly elastic demand curve, and another a perfectly elastic supply curve.

The results show that exchange prices converge to the Walrasian equilibrium after a few market periods. This is also true for severely asymmetric settings with infinitely elastic demand or supply curves, provided that participants have sufficient experience. Market experience has a lasting role, as more experienced participants extract higher surplus and execute more trades. List claims that few of the usual assumptions of Walrasian equilibrium are really necessary for convergence to occur in mature markets. Additional experiments are conducted with men-only and women-only groups, as well as an only-children group to isolate the role of experience. These experiments reveal that men execute more trades, but men and women obtain similar surplus conditional on making one. Again, convergence to Walrasian equilibrium is obtained if participants have enough experience.

Waichman and Ness (2012) study decentralized bargaining markets similar to those of List (2004b) by using students and farmers as (separate) subject pools. The latter group is chosen for their real market experience, as well as to test potential subject-pool effects. They find that markets with the two subject pools do not differ in terms of prices and quantities, while both are statistically different from the Walrasian equilibrium. Hence, market performance is not as efficient as predicted by the theory of competitive markets, though it achieves more than 80% of potential welfare. While efficiency levels are not statistically different between the two subject pools, farmers yield higher surplus to buyers compared to the student pool. The authors attribute this to the identification of farmers with sellers in their professional life. As in Michelitch (2015), this study points to an effect of subjective identification on bargaining outcomes, albeit without significant effects on market efficiency.

List and Price (2005) test and explore the theory of collusion, with multilateral bargaining experiments in the market for sports cards. In one treatment, sellers are explicitly told that they are not allowed to collude. In this case, multilateral bargaining converges to the Walrasian market equilibrium. In the other treatment, sellers are informed that they can engage in collusive practices. This leads to an outcome in which prices (quantities) are considerably above (below) equilibrium levels. The addition of imperfect price signals to the experiment reduces prices to intermediate levels. Experienced buyers could thwart off attempts to collude among sellers.

Innovative uses of the audit methodology have been employed by a sequence of field experiments by Iyer and Schoar (2015). In a first study, they perform an audit-based experiment with tailoring stores in India, to examine if reputational concerns lead sellers to refrain from renegotiation , causing a breakdown of efficient ex-post trade. The experimental design creates a situation in which the renegotiation of an initially agreed-upon contract may be called for and observes the seller's behavior in response to three treatments. The first treatment creates variation in the cost and bargaining power of the seller. The auditor declares that his situation is urgent and asks to obtain the garment in one day. This increases the tailor's cost but increases their bargaining power. They find that tailors did not initiate a renegotiation and instead either agreed to fill the urgent order with no price increase or told the auditor that they could not complete the order and returned the cloth. In the second treatment, the auditor re-initiates renegotiation by offering twice the original price to the seller. In this case, many sellers accept. This shows that sellers forgo mutually beneficial trade for reputational concerns. In the third treatment, auditors state that they were in town for a one-time event, or that they just moved into the neighborhood. Tailors were more likely to initiate a renegotiation and to renege on the delivery of the urgent order for out-of-state auditors compared to local auditors with whom reputational concerns are stronger. A final treatment tests the effects of repeated interactions to see whether sellers will initiate renegotiation under the possibility of higher continuation value. As expected, tailors were significantly less likely to initiate renegotiation , and more likely to fill urgent requests in this second visit. The study also recruited auditor tailors to call a random group of customers with urgent requests and offer to do the task immediately for a 10% increase in the agreed price. They find that 36 out of 41 accepted the renewed offer.

Overall, the evidence indicates that reputational concerns can create contract rigidity, preventing profitable trades and causing inefficiency in bargaining, as well as potentially leading to price stickiness.

In a second study, the authors conduct a field experiment in the wholesale market for pens, in which auditors place orders that vary in their relation-specificity, by buying generic or custom-made lots. This context is suitable for studying incomplete contracts and hold-up. They find that sellers require larger upfront payments for orders that necessitate relation-specific investments and use upfront payments as a screening mechanism to protect themselves against contract breach but remain vulnerable against ex-post opportunistic renegotiation . In the latter case, sellers are much more willing to renegotiate the order in case of custom pens, and orders for printed pens can be renegotiated for price cuts up to 30%.

However, sellers terminate bargaining in about 40% of the cases, essentially opting out for the zero salvage value of the order and accepting the resulting loss. This is similar to "irrational" rejections in the ultimatum game. Most sellers return the upfront payment when renegotiation fails, pointing to the role of reputational concerns.

It is of interest to economics to study the welfare and distributional implications of bargaining compared to a fixed-price equilibrium outcome. Such an examination requires either obtaining or estimating value distributions in the market. Keniston (2011) addresses this question using field data collected in the context of bargaining for autorickshaw transportation in Jaipur, India. He observes free-form bargaining transactions by hired surveyors, and those in which auditors make randomized (but pre-determined) counteroffers to drivers. The focus of the study is on developing a dynamic structural estimation procedure to recover key unobservables, such as valuations and the costs of bargaining in a game-theoretic setting. He finds that a switch to a fixed-price mechanism would raise overall welfare by 28%. In terms of the distributional effect, this would benefit high-valuation buyers since they would avoid bargaining costs. However, the bargaining mechanism carries substantial value for low-valuation buyers; 63% of buyers would prefer bargaining if a fixed-price market were available as a choice.

Welfare and distributional implications of bargaining are also studied by Bengtsson (2015), who offers an interesting policy argument for regulation. He argues that market regulations can be welfare-enhancing even if they are side-stepped regularly. As a result, informal bargaining can achieve the first-best outcome under simple regulation schemes. He constructs a model with these characteristics, which requires that regulations determine only the fallback outcome of market participants. He tests the predictions of the model using a field experiment in the taxi market in Cape Town, South Africa. Taxi drivers are required to use a meter for pricing, but compliance is not complete as drivers and passengers bargain to agree on a fixed fee instead of using the meter. A key ingredient is moral hazard, whereby drivers tend to take detours when the meter is running.

Bengtsson assigns half of the trips (undertaken by a research assistant acting as a tourist) to a fixed, unregulated fare with counteroffers, and half to a choice to use the regulated fare. Results reveal significant welfare gains from sidestepping the meter. Average distance travelled reduces by 10%, which also reduces carbon emissions by 8% compared to strict obedience to the meter. On the other hand, the average price is found to be the same across treatments. The findings suggest that regulations frame the informal bargaining procedure efficiently. Interestingly, while regulations—at the outset—seem to increase costs and emissions, it does not follow that deregulation will raise welfare in the market.

These findings offer potential lessons for regulation. Regulation usually exhibits a trade-off between ex-ante and ex-post efficiency. The study suggests that there is a mix of simple regulation and informal trade that is capable of implementing the first-best. If regulation provides an option but is not strictly enforced, the market may attain both ex-post and ex-ante efficiency.

16.7 Discussion and Possible Directions for Future Research

In addition to directly testing key assertions of economic theory, field experiments in bargaining have contributed to our understanding in various domains of economics, including discrimination, decision-making within the household, and the role of gender and culture. While the strict control provided by induced valuations in the laboratory is an asset, field experiments provide high external validity, particularly when bargaining behavior draws on context-specific characteristics and experiences that would be stripped in "sterile" bargaining settings created in the lab, or involves biases that would not surface in the lab under observability. We believe that there are important research questions in the context of bargaining where the field experimental literature can expand into and provide unique insights.

The relationship between field experimentation and theory is growing in various directions. However, a general lack of model-based testing or experimental tests of theoretical predictions needs to be noted. The contribution of field experiments in bargaining to the theory of bargaining itself has remained relatively limited. The canonical

Rubinstein-Stahl bargaining game produces a simple prediction under complete information, an assumption that does not match empirical reality. Naturally, there are various ways of incorporating incomplete and asymmetric information into bargaining settings, which produce a variety of theoretical models and predictions. The resulting difficulties in matching theoretical models to data are highlighted by the efforts of Kennan and Wilson (1989), who examine the ability of various bargaining models to explain data on labor negotiations. Price formation and resource allocation thus emerge as empirical questions in many bargaining settings, providing a challenge for empirical and experimental work to produce "good data". Using more detailed data on sequential offers from the field may offer some further possibilities in studying the role of different sources of uncertainty and information asymmetry, as well as testing predictions of corresponding theoretical models.

The literature has had great success in studying bilateral or multilateral bargaining environments as micro-foundations for generating a variety of market structures. Important results from the literature include convergence of the market to the Walrasian equilibrium prediction under very general conditions (List 2004b; Waichman and Ness 2012). Studies have already begun to move beyond competitive markets to study other market structures (List and Price 2005). Pushing the envelope in this line of inquiry to study various market structures in the field, perhaps in deeper dialogue with industrial organization, is an area with great potential and is likely to produce more field experiments in the future.

Studying inefficiencies and policies to mitigate these inefficiencies is also an area that is likely to grow significantly. An important example is studying various remedies or market interventions for externalities. We note that no field experiment has yet provided direct tests of Coasean predictions, just to name an important possible application.

Field experiments also offer opportunities to randomize on various attributes of the bargaining environment, such as dyads and groups in bargaining. As a result, field experiments can be used to manipulate group formation and study its effects. Finally, we note that coupling field experiments with naturally occurring data may provide important insights. Studying natural bargaining transactions in the market may help identify the role of duration and provide insights into the process of learning in asymmetric information settings. Insights from such observations can then be used to create randomized field experiments within the market or be taken to the laboratory for more controlled tests of theory.

References

Al-Ubaydli O, List JA (2017) Field experiments in markets. In: Banerjee AV, and Duflo E (eds) *Handbook of Field Experiments* Volume 1. North-Holland, Amsterdam and Oxford, pp. 271–307.

Andersen S, Ertac S, Gneezy U, List JA, Maximiano S (2018) On the cultural basis of gender differences in negotiation. *Experimental Economics* 21(4): 757–778.

Arrow KJ (1973) The theory of discrimination. In: Ashenfelter O, Rees A (eds) *Discrimination in Labor Markets*. Princeton University Press, Princeton, pp. 3–33.

Artinger S, Vulkan N, Shem-Tov Y (2015) Entrepreneurs' negotiation behavior. *Small Business Economics* 44(4): 737–757.

Ashraf N, Field E, Lee, Y (2014) Household bargaining and excess fertility: An experimental study in Zambia. *American Economic Review* 104(7): 2210–2237.

Ayres I (1991) Fair driving: Gender and race discriminations in retail car negotiations. *Harvard Law Review* 104: 817–872.

Ayres I, Siegelman P (1995) Race and gender discrimination in bargaining for a new car. *American Economic Review* 85(3): 304–321.

Babcock L, Laschever S (2003) *Women Don't Ask: Negotiation and the Gender Divide*. Princeton University Press, Princeton and Oxford.

Banerjee AV, Duflo E (2017) *Handbook of Field Experiments*, Vol. 1 and Vol. 2. Amsterdam and Oxford, North-Holland.

Beblo M, Beninger D (2014) Experimental Evidence on Bargaining Power Within Couples. Beiträge zur Jahrestagung des Vereins für Socialpolitik 2014: Evidenzbasierte Wirtschaftspolitik, Session: Family Economics, No. F03-V2.

Becker GS (1957) *The Economics of Discrimination*. The University of Chicago Press, Chicago.

Bengtsson N (2015) Efficient informal trade: Theory and experimental evidence from the Cape Town taxi market. *Journal of Development Economics* 115: 85–98.

Bertrand M, Duflo E (2017) Field experiments on discrimination. In: Banerje AV, and Duflo E (Eds.) *Handbook of Field Experiments* Volume 1. North-Holland, Amsterdam and Oxford, pp. 309–393.

Bulte E, Tu Q, List J (2015) Battle of the Sexes: How Sex Ratios Affect Female Bargaining Power. *Economic Development and Cultural Change* 64(1): 143–161.

Carlsson F, He H, Martinsson P, Qin P, Sutten M (2012) Household decision making in rural China: Using experiments to estimate the influences of spouses. *Journal of Economic Behavior & Organization* 84: 525–536.

Castillo M, Petrie R, Torrero M, Vesterlund L (2013) Gender differences in bargaining outcomes: A field experiment on discrimination. *Journal of Public Economics* 99: 35–48.

Chamberlin EH (1948) An experimental imperfect market. *The Journal of Political Economy* 56(2): 95–108.

Croson R, Gneezy U (2009) Gender differences in preferences. *The Journal of Economic Literature* 47(2): 448–474.

DellaVigna S (2009) Psychology and economics: Evidence from the field. *The Journal of Economic Literature* 47(2): 315–372.

Dindaroğlu B, Ertac S (2020) *Rubinstein Meets Abraham: An Empirical Study of Sequential Offer Bargaining during the Festival of Sacrifice*. Unpublished manuscript.

Falk A, Heckman JJ (2009) Lab experiments are a major source of knowledge in the social sciences. *Science* 326: 535–538.

Hanson A, Hawley Z (2011) Do landlords discriminate in the rental housing market? Evidence from an internet field experiment in US cities. *Journal of Urban Economics* 70: 99–114.

Harrison GW, List JA (2004) Field experiments. *Journal of Economic Literature* 42: 1009–1055.

Heckman J, Siegelman P (1992) The Urban Institute studies: Their methods and findings. In: Fix M, Struyk R (eds) *Clear and Convincing Evidence*. Washington, DC: Urban Institute Press.

Henrich J (2000) Does culture matter in economic behavior? Ultimatum game bargaining among the Machiguenga of the Peruvian Amazon. *The American Economic Review* 90(4): 973–979.

Henrich J, Boyd R, Bowles S, Camerer C, Fehr E, Gintis H, McElreath R (2001) In search of homo economicus: Behavioral experiments in 15 small-scale societies. *The American Economic Review* 91(2): 73–78.
Iyer R, Schoar A (2015) Ex post (in) efficient negotiation and breakdown of trade. *The American Economic Review* 105(5): 291–94.
Keniston DE (2011) Bargaining and welfare: A dynamic structural analysis. Unpublished manuscript.
Kennan J, Wilson R (1989) Strategic bargaining models and interpretation of strike data. *Journal of Econometrics* 4: S87–S130.
Leibbrandt A, List JA (2015) Do women avoid salary negotiations? Evidence from a large-scale natural field experiment. *Management Science* 61(9): 2016–2024.
List JA (2004a) The nature and extent of discrimination in the marketplace: Evidence from the field. *The Quarterly Journal of Economics* 119(1): 49–89.
List JA (2004b) Testing neoclassical competitive theory in multilateral decentralized markets. *Journal of Political Economy* 112(5): 1131–1156.
List JA, Price MK (2005) Conspiracies and secret price discounts in the marketplace: Evidence from field experiments. *The RAND Journal of Economics* 36(3): 700–717.
Mauss M (2016, org.1925) *The Gift: Expanded Edition.* Hau Books, Chicago.
Michelitch K (2015) Does electoral competition exacerbate interethnic or interpartisan economic discrimination? Evidence from a field experiment in market price bargaining. *American Political Science Review* 109(1): 43–61.
Phelps ES (1972) The statistical theory of racism and sexism. *American Economic Review* 62: 659–661.
Roth AE, Praskinar V, Okuno-Fujiwara M, Zamir S (1991) Bargaining and market behavior in Jerusalem, Ljubljana, Pittsburgh, and Tokyo: An experimental study. *The American Economic Review* 81(5): 1068–1095.
Smith V (1982) Experimental Economics: Induced value theory. *The American Economic Review* 66(2): 274–279.
Waichman I, Ness C (2012) Farmers' performance and subject pool effect in decentralized bargaining markets. *Economics Letters* 115: 366–368.
Zussmann A (2013) Ethnic discrimination: Lessons from the Israeli online market for used cars. *The Economic Journal* 123: F433–F468.

17

Bargaining in Online Markets

Matthew Backus, Thomas Blake, and Steven Tadelis

The significance of bargaining and negotiations in economic life has motivated a vast theoretical and experimental literature to the end of understanding how those who bargain find profitable deals, divide gains from trade, and avoid bargaining breakdown. The welfare and policy implications of a better understanding of bargaining are vast—from avoiding breakdown at the negotiating table as nations forge compromises to addressing climate change, to the entrepreneur designing

M. Backus (✉)
Columbia University, New York, NY, USA
e-mail: matthew.backus@columbia.edu

T. Blake
Amazon, San Jose, CA, USA
e-mail: tomblake@gmail.com

S. Tadelis
University of California, Berkeley, Berkeley, CA, USA
e-mail: stadelis@berkeley.edu

E. Karagözoğlu and K. B. Hyndman (eds.), *Bargaining*,
https://doi.org/10.1007/978-3-030-76666-5_17

markets in which parties bargain to realize gains from trade.[1] However, but for a few pioneering exceptions focusing on wage bargaining in labor negotiations Card [8], Card and Olson [9], Cramton and Tracy [11], that vast literature has forged ahead in the absence of guidance from the empirical analysis of bargaining in the field.

Much of the difficulty of studying bargaining in the field is inherent to the settings in which market participants elect to bargain instead of using other price-discovery mechanisms, e.g., fixed-price sales or auctions. Bargaining typically happens when both parties have some market power. If, alternatively, either side faces competition from a large and liquid set of substitutes, then there is little room for posturing, and so we would expect a fixed-price mechanism to dominate trade. This means that when two parties bargain over a deal, it is likely that the setting has some idiosyncrasies which are often difficult to quantify and compare across deals. These were the challenges of an early empirical literature that endeavored to study labor negotiations (see [7] for a summary). Negotiations between management and labor are particularly difficult to study because the terms are multidimensional, from wages to benefits and workplace conditions.[2]

Another challenge of studying bargaining in the field is that many negotiated contracts are set in the broader context of repeated interactions. A supplier may negotiate a rate with a downstream customer not merely with an eye to profits in that deal, but to the stream of profits they obtain by cultivating a long-term relationship. This continuation value is difficult to measure in the absence of a credible structural model of bargaining.

---

[1] Here we echo Crawford [12], who writes: "Bargaining, broadly construed, is a pervasive phenomenon in modern economies, ranging from labor negotiations to trade agreements to strategic arms limitation talks. One need only consider these examples in light of past experience to realize that the potential welfare gains from improving the efficiency of bargaining outcomes are enormous, perhaps even greater than those that would result from a better understanding of macroeconomic policy."

[2] Strikes in labor negotiations provided a unique opportunity to study delay as signaling . This idea found little empirical application outside of labor until Goetz [15], which introduced delay in a model of bargaining adapted to negotiations between Comcast and internet ISPs for local content provision.

Even when negotiated contracts are one-off events, empirical work is plagued by the lack of available data, particularly at the offer level. It is perhaps not surprising that U.S. Attorney's Offices do not want the patterns of their settlement offers to be public knowledge, and that executives would not want it to be known that they frequently budge from their opening offers when making acquisitions. Perhaps more perplexing is the general unavailability of offer-level data in real-estate negotiations. This hurdle, the fact that offer-level data is generally unavailable to researchers, is in our opinion the most severe. For posted-price markets, there are innumerable sources of data on market outcomes, e.g., Nielsen data in retail. Moreover, there is increasing availability of data on negotiated prices in markets with bilateral bargaining, e.g., content providers selling to cable companies, insurance reimbursement rates for hospitals, and medical device pricing to hospitals. However, there are still precious few sources of step-by-step *offer-level* data in bargaining markets. Exceptions of which we are aware include a dataset of 780 real-estate transactions in the UK from Merlo and Ortalo-Magné [19] and the post-auction negotiations of Larsen [17].

In this chapter, we summarize our work in exploring a new data source on bargaining and negotiations: the eBay Best Offer platform. We use this platform as an example of the many distributed peer-to-peer marketplaces that have proliferated in recent years. Agents in these marketplaces negotiate over physical goods (e.g., eBay, Craigslist, Etsy, Alibaba), short-term labor contracts (Upwork, Freelancer), vacation rentals (AirBnband VRBO), and home services (e.g., Thumbtack) to name a few. The rise of e-commerce in general has been a boon to researchers: transactions that might previously have generated little more by way of record than a paper receipt now generate a vast trove of data. These data include not only information about the culminated transaction, such as what was sold, when, and at which price, but also the pre-transaction behavioral data concerning clicks, queries, and marketing that lead up to transactions. Users exchange structured offers over common contract terms such as price, service dates, and unit volumes. They exchange messages over less common terms (e.g., a vacation rental's use of air conditioning or a coder's choice of software language).

We begin in Sect. 17.1 with a summary of the Best Offer bargaining environment on the eBay platform. We also highlight some basic descriptive facts: some of them evidence in favor of rational theoretical models of bargaining, and some seemingly inconsistent. Next we turn to our own findings from the setting, which focus on understanding bargaining as negotiation, i.e., involving some kind of communication . In Sect. 17.2, we consider the role of cheap-talk communication in negotiation on the platform, taking as an example something that had been previously attributed to behavioral biases: the use of round numbers. Then in Sect. 17.3 we consider the broader question of communication and bargaining efficiency in Best Offer negotiations. While the applications we discuss are the first to which we turned, they are by no means the only questions that could be asked in this environment. To that end, Backus et al. [2] made one year of Best Offer bargaining data publicly available. The interested reader can find it available at https://www.nber.org/data/bargaining/. We hope that these applications will inspire more research in bargaining and that the data made available will prove fruitful to future bargaining scholars.

17.1 eBay's Best Offer Platform

The eBay online marketplace is best known for its auctions, which offers a price-discovery mechanism for sellers who may not know the optimal price of the object they wish to sell, and was complemented by a reputation system, for buyers to make transactions with sellers they might not otherwise trust. However, the use of auctions has long been on the decline on eBay, as a fraction of sales volume, as documented by Einav et al. [13]. The vast majority of sales volume on the platform are for listings with a fixed "Buy-it-Now" (BIN) price. For a subset of these fixed-price listings, sellers enable the "Best Offer " (BO) feature, which allows buyers to make an offer to the seller, and potentially negotiate a price lower than the asking, or BIN price.[3]

[3] As documented by Backus et al. [2], sales that are bargained through the BO mechanism (that is, excluding BO listings that sold at the listed BIN price) have grown along with the

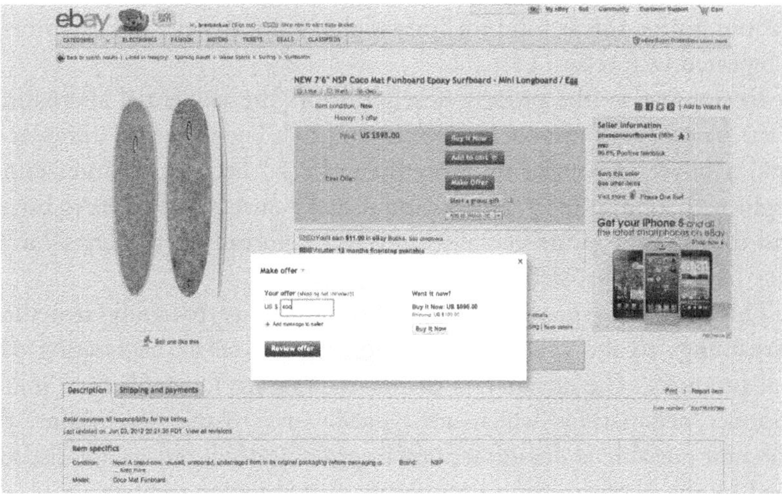

Fig. 17.1 Best offer on eBay (*Notes* This figure depicts a listing with the Best Offer feature enabled, which is why the "Make Offer" button appears underneath the "Buy It Now" and "Add to Cart" buttons. When a user clicks the Make Offer button, a panel appears, prompting an offer and, if desired, an accompanying message)

This process is depicted in Fig. 17.1, which depicts a fixed-price listing for a vintage box of cereal, on which the seller has enabled Best Offer as seen by the presence of the "Make Offer" button.[4] The buyer can click the "Buy it Now" button and purchase the product for $275, or they can click on the "Make Offer" button, which raises a pop-up screen with a numerical field for their offer. The buyer may also elect to add a brief text message to the seller, a feature to which we return in Sect. 17.3. Offers are valid for forty-eight hours, after which they expire and the buyer is no longer committed. The seller is notified of the offer and is given the option to accept—in which case the listing is closed and the buyer prompted for payment—reject, or counteroffer. If the seller makes

fixed-price portion of the marketplace , and by 2015 made up over 10% of sales volume on the U.S. website.

[4] Buyers can also observe that a listing is Best Offer enabled on the search results page, before they get to the View Item page depicted in Fig. 17.1. There, underneath the price, the text "or Best Offer " may appear.

a counteroffer, this is valid for forty-eight hours as well, and the process is repeated in reverse.

To summarize, the process closely mirrors the sequential alternating-offers bargaining protocol in Rubinstein [23]. There are two differences: first, a buyer can make at most three offers.[5] Second, all interactions begin with a buyer offer; sellers cannot make unsolicited offers to buyers and they cannot resurrect stalled or rejected threads, yet a buyer can (if they have not exhausted their three offers).

This marketplace offers a unique opportunity to study structured bargaining "in the wild," with real buyers and sellers negotiating over real products. The advantages of this dataset are fourfold: first, unlike contract negotiations which are typically over many dimensions, the outcome variable is one-dimensional: price. Indeed, buyers are discouraged by the platform from negotiating over shipping, preferring instead that they load it into the agreed-upon price. Second, there are almost no repeated interactions between buyers and sellers, and so we can treat them as anonymous, one-off bargaining games. This is in contrast with many business-to-business bargaining environments, which are typically characterized by persistent relationships, e.g., licensing and supplier contracts, or union contract negotiations. Third, bargainers who bargain more than once can be linked over time by the econometrician, allowing us to include buyer and seller fixed effects. Fourth, the dataset is very large. The publicly released version includes over 100 million BO listings.

Unsurprisingly, however, there is also a particular limitation of this dataset—there is substantial unobserved heterogeneity coming from the vast array of products that buyers and sellers negotiate over. There is little need to bargain over homogeneous products for which there is a thick market, in which case the market price would be known. Therefore the product inventory in the dataset is particularly idiosyncratic and unlikely to be well-described by observable characteristics. This makes it difficult to learn very much about a bargainer's reservation values or outside options.

[5] This was true during the period when we collected our data. The cap has since been increased.

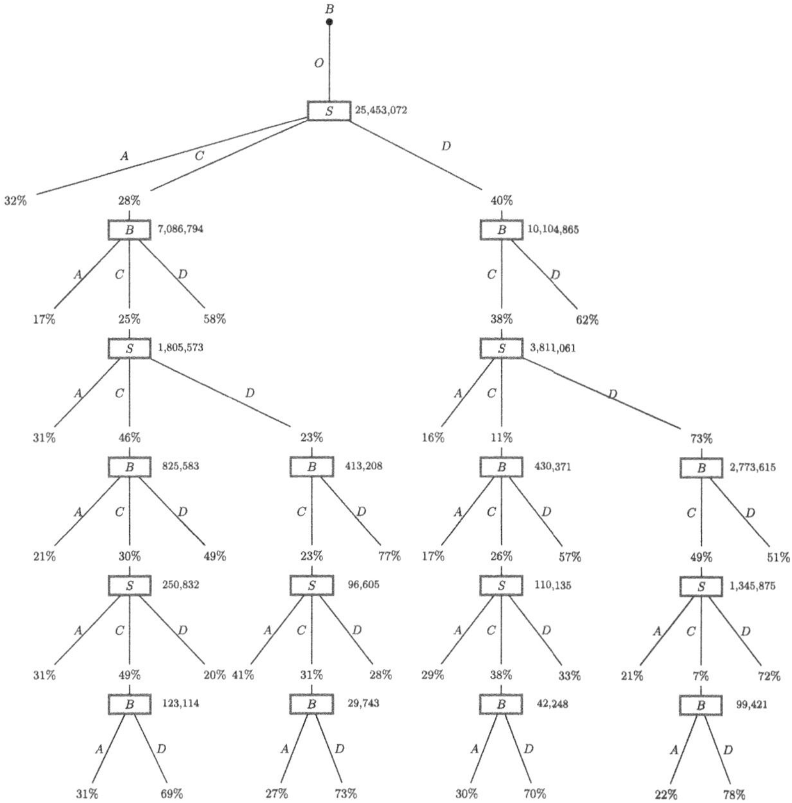

Fig. 17.2 Bargaining sequence patterns (*Notes* This figure summarizes the offer-level data in terms of the "game tree" of bargaining, and is borrowed from Backus et al. [2])

We begin with a few results that are immediate from the basic descriptives of the dataset. Figure 17.2, borrowed from Backus et al. [2], depicts an "empirical game tree"—the fraction of bargaining interactions that reach each node of the sequential bargaining game. Conceptually, we can think of the seller's BIN price as an initial offer to all potentially interested buyers, the first offer in a sequence is always made by a buyer, and so the first node is "B," after which buyers and sellers ("S") alternate. "A" means an offer is accepted; "C" means an offer is countered, and "D" means it was declined. We report both the number and fraction of offers that reach each node. For instance, just over 6 million cases (25%) fit the following path: an initial buyer offer is made, the seller declines (as in 40% of cases), and the buyer elects not to make another offer (as in 62% of such cases). From this figure we learn a few things. First, sellers are substantially more likely to accept an offer than buyers are. Second, we also see that frequently, if a seller declines a buyer offer (potentially allowing the offer to expire, as the dataset does not discriminate among methods of rejection), buyers re-approach the seller with a new offer (e.g., 38% of the time after a first offer is declined).

Many of the features of the dataset are broadly consistent with existing rational models of bargaining. For instance, buyers who select slower shipping methods, i.e., who may be more patient, also succeed in obtaining lower prices, consistent with the predictions of Rubinstein [23]. Of course, this is purely descriptive, and the correlation may be driven by other confounds such as a low reservation price.

Also, bargaining appears to be costly. In particular, for items that are listed at fixed prices under 50 dollars, buyers are relatively more likely to pay the seller's asking price rather than making an offer. And when the buyer does make an offer, the seller is much more likely to accept it than haggle. In particular, this supports the notion of fixed costs of bargaining. We observe that these fixed costs create qualitative differences above and below 50 dollars, which raises potential external validity concerns for the study of bargaining in laboratory settings, where stakes are low.[6]

Still other features of the data are more difficult to explain in standard theoretical models, even those that allow incomplete information and afford opportunities for bargaining breakdown. Two in particular stand out: reciprocal gradualism and split-the-difference behavior.

Backus et al. [2] document reciprocal gradualism in their dataset, which means that larger concessions by one party appear to be met with larger concessions by the other. This feature of real-life bargaining is notoriously difficult to explain in theoretical models. Compte and Jehiel [10] obtain it in the setting of baseball negotiations, but this exploits

[6] A similar observation, that bargaining entails fixed costs, motivates the study of negotiations in appliance sales by Jindal and Newberry [16].

the unique institutional environment of that setting, i.e., that disagreement payoffs depend on the sequence of offers. It may be possible to obtain a similar result if bargainers have reference-dependent preferences, however, this conjecture is unproven.[7]

A second robust and puzzling feature of the data is the predominance of so-called "splitting the difference." The puzzle has two features. The first, which is perhaps less surprising, is the fact of the behavior: that bargaining parties are discontinuously more likely to make an offer that is halfway between the two prior offers. The second, however, is that these offers appear to work, and introduce a non-monotonicity in the empirical relationship between the generosity of offers and the frequency with which they are accepted. That is, offers slightly higher than 50% (e.g., 55% of the other party's most recent ask) are less likely to be accepted even though they are more generous.[8] What is particularly puzzling about both of these phenomena is that the reference points according to which one splits the difference are endogenous; they are simply the prior two offers, one set by each bargainer. So, anticipating such behavior, it seems one would do well to engineer extreme reference points in your favor.

These descriptive results highlight both the strengths and weaknesses of bargaining theory, and offer paths for future empirical, experimental, and theoretical work. In particular, by highlighting features of real-world bargaining, the hope is to point to research avenues that can productively engage with bargaining practitioners. This is, of course, just a first step and there are myriad alternative settings in which we could learn even more about bargaining. Even within our setting, however, we have focused exclusively so far on the offers, counteroffers, and outcomes, and neglected communication between buyers and sellers. It is to this that we turn next.

[7] This suggestion is thanks to Philippe Jehiel.

[8] Substantially higher offers (e.g., 70%) are still more likely to be accepted as the non-monotonicity is a local phenomenon.

17.2 Cheap-Talk Signaling and Bargaining

Previously we documented a number of patterns in the data that are seemingly at odds with rational models of bargaining. Another such pattern is documented in Fig. 17.3. On the x-axis of that plot, we have the BIN price of the BO listing. On the y-axis, we have a scale from 0 to 1, and the object of interest is the ratio of the initial buyer offer in a bargaining interaction to the BIN price. To construct the scatter-plot, every point in the graph represents a group listings that all have the same BIN price *within* a unit interval according to the ceiling function. Concretely, consider an integer $z > 0$, we then take all listings with a BIN price of $x \in (z - 1, z]$ and group them together, and these listings correspond to the x-axis of the graph. Then, we calculate the ratio of

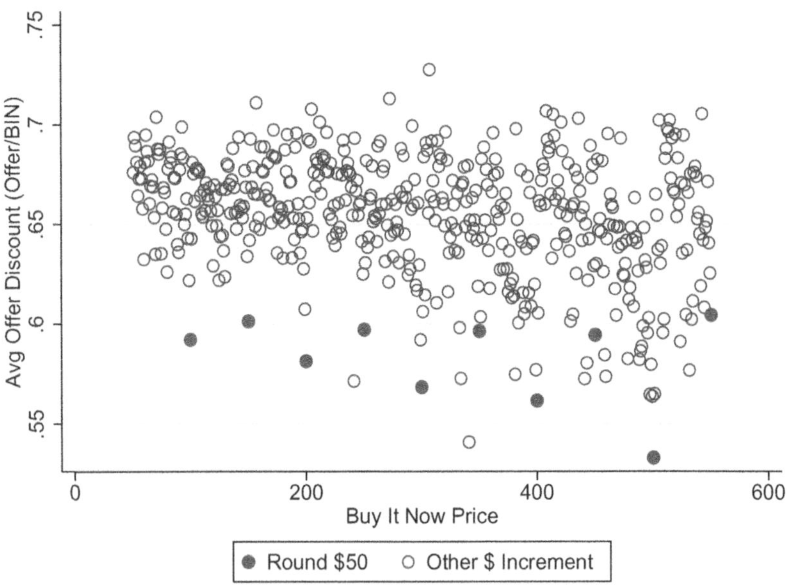

Fig. 17.3 Best offer on eBay (*Notes* This scatterplot presents average first offers, normalized by the BIN price to be between zero and one, grouped by unit intervals of the BIN price, defined by $(z - 1, z]$. When the BIN price is on an interval rounded to a number ending in "00" or "50," it is represented by a red circle. The figure is borrowed from Backus et al. [4])

the initial buyer offer for each of these listings and calculate the average of the ratios of all listings within such a group z, which corresponds to the y-axis of the graph. On average across all the points in the scatterplot, it appears that first offers arrive at somewhere near 65% of the BIN price. However, strikingly, if the BIN price is on a round "50" number, which we mark with a filled circle, we observe first offers between five and ten percentage points lower than other, precise number prices. A similar pattern persists for finally negotiated sale prices.

Why do round numbers fare so poorly? We were not the first to make this observation; indeed, a large literature in management and social psychology has documented it in lab experiments, see e.g., Mason et al. [18]. These papers attribute it to various perceptual biases around the use of round numbers, and conclude that bargainers should avoid the use of round numbers, favoring precise ones. However, this argument sits uneasily with economists—if the use of round numbers is a strictly dominated action then we should observe that rational bargainers avoid them. Instead, bargainers are discontinuously more likely to use round-number prices than precise number ones. Indeed, 5.3% of listings in the sample are priced at an exact multiple of $100. Why are they doing it wrong? In Backus et al. [4], we posit an alternative hypothesis, one that rationalizes the use of round numbers by sellers: round numbers are a cheap-talk signal of eagerness to transact, analogous to rug stores "going out of business," or forward compliments on a first date. In this light, the behavior may be entirely rational: impatient sellers (or, equivalently, sellers with worse outside options) will use round numbers to facilitate a transaction, albeit at a lower price, while patient sellers will use precise numbers and wait for higher-paying buyers.

To explore this idea in depth, we ask: what must be true in the equilibrium of a signaling game? If players are playing a separating equilibrium in which impatient sellers use round numbers and those who can hold out choose precise numbers, then (1) there must be *incentive compatibility*, a trade-off that makes some sellers prefer one outcome and others another; (2) sellers with different preferences must *sort*, i.e., if we split sellers by round- and precise-number usage, we should also see that these are fundamentally different kinds of sellers, and (3) buyers must *update* their beliefs, that is, see the signal and form beliefs about the seller's preferences that are consistent with the sorting. The extensive data generated by online transactions make the validation of this equilibrium uniquely feasible.

Incentive compatibility becomes transparent once we construct the analogue of Figure 17.3 for the likelihood of—and time to complete—a sale. In fact, round-number sellers are 15–20% more likely to sell and, conditional on sale, do so almost 30 days earlier. In other words, we can think of the use of round-numbers as akin to moving along a demand curve, trading lower prices for higher quantities. According to basic pricing theory, we expect sellers to do this as their costs change, and the intuition in a bargaining setting is no different. Patient sellers—equivalently, those with a high marginal or opportunity cost of transacting—will prefer a higher price and a lower quantity, and impatient sellers the opposite.

Do we observe sorting of patient and impatient sellers into round- and precise-number listing prices? We can test this by looking at cases where similar offers (as a fraction of the BIN) were made to both types of sellers. If precise-number sellers are the patient sellers of the marketplace , then they should be less likely to accept an offer, other things equal. Similarly, impatient sellers should jump to accept it. Indeed, this is borne out by the data. Taking the same offer (as a fraction of the asking price) to set "other things equal," precise number sellers are uniformly less likely to accept it, as depicted in Figure 17.4.[9]

The final diagnostic for a signaling equilibrium is that the signal is received—i.e., we need to show that buyers observe the signal and update their beliefs. This is particularly complicated because beliefs are unobservable. However, the behavioral data on buyers from the eBay platform affords an unusual opportunity. Buyers receive the "signal," i.e., see whether there is a round or a precise asking price, when they view listings on the search results page. As it turns out, round and precise listings are equally likely to appear on the search page, yet the data show that buyers are *systematically more likely* to click through to the next step, the

[9] Note that seller acceptance rates do not converge to one as the buyer's offer does—this may simply reflect the fact that many sellers are missing notifications that they have received an offer.

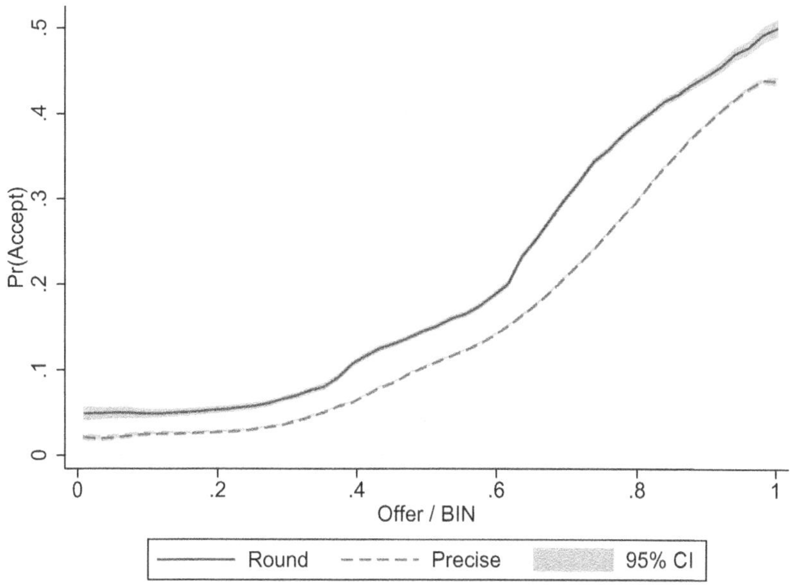

Fig. 17.4 Seller acceptance rates (*Notes* This figure depicts the polynomial fit of the probability of acceptance for a given offer (normalized by the BIN) on items with listing prices between $85 and $115, plotted separately for $100 "Round" listings and the remaining "Precise" listings. This figure is borrowed from Backus et al. [4])

detailed item page, for round-number listings than precise number ones. And conditional on clicking through and purchasing, they are *more likely to negotiate* (rather than take the BIN price) for round-number listings. This is consistent with the hypothesis that they (correctly) anticipate negotiating lower prices with round-number sellers.

At this point, the attentive reader may rightly object—are round-number listings similar to precise-number listings on other dimensions besides price? Maybe this constellation of results is all due to unobserved heterogeneity, which was highlighted as a limitation of the dataset in Sect. 17.1. To answer this concern, Backus et al. [4] identify a natural experiment—a garbling of the signal that exposes it to some buyers and obfuscates it to others.[10] In particular, sellers from the U.K. website of eBay (ebay.co.uk) have an option to pay for their listings to be cross-listed on the U.S. site. If they do so, these listings that are originally listed in British Pounds will also appear in U.S. search results, but prices will be converted automatically to U.S. Dollars using the current exchange rate. As a result, a listing that has a round BIN price in the U.K. will appear as a precise BIN price in the U.S., holding fixed all of the other characteristics of the item (including, importantly, those not observed to the econometrician). In this setting, we showed that the price effects of round-number signaling persist after controlling for unobserved heterogeneity.

Based on all of this evidence, we concluded that cheap-talk signaling offers the simplest, most coherent explanation for the behavior of buyers and sellers concerning round numbers. And yet, it seems implausible that buyers and sellers are all knowingly engaging in this behavior. The early papers documenting this phenomenon drew on the work of psychologists who document known perceptual biases around round numbers. How do we reconcile this with the heady assumptions on rationality required to rationalize a perfect Bayesian equilibrium? The work of Thomas et al. [25] offers a way out. They document perceptual biases around round numbers, but critically, they show that these biases are mediated by experience. In other words, while the mechanical truth of decision-making may be that we have heuristics that guide perception and influence behavior, these heuristics are consistent with observed experience and are in that sense functionally equivalent to rational expectations on the equilibrium path.

[10] The idea of using a garbling device to identify signaling appears also in Ambrus et al. [1]. There, the church, which serves as an intermediary in hostage negotiations between wealthy families and Tunisian pirates, must send couriers by foot to the town in which the family is located. Because the time required is unobservable to the pirates, they take this as a garbling device in the use of delay as a signaling device in negotiations and show that it predicts better bargaining outcomes, consistent with theory.

17.3 Protocol Design: Communication and Bargaining Breakdown

An important question for the bargaining literature, but also for the e-commerce platform regulating the bargaining itself, is: should buyers and sellers be allowed to communicate? From the perspective of the literature, this is an old question that relates to bargaining efficiency , and it does not help that theoretical models of communication in bargaining are divided on the efficiency implications of communication . While there may exist equilibria with credible communication in bargaining games, as in Farrell and Gibbons [14], it does not in general improve the efficiency of bargaining.

The experimental literature is rather more optimistic. In early work, Radner and Schotter [22] and Valley et al. [26] offer evidence that communication improves bargaining efficiency. Indeed, in the latter, it appears that subjects outperform the Myerson and Satterthwaite [20] upper bound on efficiency for incentive-compatible bargaining mechanisms in games with two-sided asymmetric information. The mechanism by which it does so, however, is unclear. It may be, e.g., that we over-communicate in cheap-talk games [6], we are averse to lying, or that we build amity and altruism through communication .

From the platform's perspective, however, there is an important caveat to the gains of bargaining efficiency. Platforms are particularly concerned about the risk of *disintermediation*; that is, when the buyer and the seller decide to cut out the middleman (and their fees) and instead transact independently, using the communication mechanism to foster off-platform contact. Indeed, the salience of this concern is highly predictive of the different platforms' choices regarding communication . Taobao, which does not tax transactions, allows free-form communication between bargainers with an on-site instant messenger service.[11] eBay, which charges fees between eight and twelve percent of the transaction price, allows brief text communication accompanying offers. And finally Amazon Marketplace, which charges fees between 15 and 25%,

[11] Taobao's instant messenger service was one factor in their success over the Chinese version of eBay, see Oberholzer-Gee and Wulf [21] for a discussion.

does not allow text communication on its bargaining mechanism (which is available only in a few narrow categories to begin with).

From a theoretical as well as a practical market design perspective then, it is important to understand how communication affects bargaining outcomes. To this end, Backus et al. [3] identify a natural experiment in the availability of communication in bargaining. Recall from Fig. 17.1 that there is an option to "add message to seller" when a buyer makes an offer. This requires an extra click, but it is available to both parties. Importantly, messages on the bargaining platform can only accompany a price offer.

Historically, this feature was unavailable on eBay.de, the German incarnation of eBay, while all other features of the Best Offer platform were equivalent to the U.S. (and other) sites. On May 23, 2016, the messaging feature was enabled on the German site, but it was only immediately available for buyers accessing the eBay.de marketplace from a computer browser, rather than a mobile app. Mobile app users, who made up approximately half of bargainers on the site, were not able to send messages.

The rollout of messaging in Germany offers a simple difference-in-differences design: before and after versus desktop and mobile. Backus et al. [3] use this natural experiment to identify the effect of the availability of communication on the likelihood that any particular bargaining interaction—inclusive of all offers between a buyer and a seller—ends in a transaction. They estimate the intent-to-treat effect to be approximately half a percentage point. This seems small, but it is important to remember that the magnitude is determined in part by the number of bargainers who actually take the feature up, i.e., "compliers," which in this case was only 6%. Adjusting for the compliance rate, the estimated effect of actually sending a message is 7 percentage points, against a baseline success probability of 44%. This implies that among compliers, the treatment effect of messaging was to increase the odds of a successful interaction by a staggering 15%.

The estimated effects in Backus et al. [3] were not realized immediately, however. Instead, they observe that although the take-up rate is almost instantaneous, the treatment effect takes a few weeks after introduction to stabilize. The paper argues that this is evidence of learning by bargainers who participate in multiple bargaining sequences. In an involved text analysis exercise, they document (1) that the text content of messages evolves over time, (2) that it becomes more similar, on a week-to-week basis, over time, and (3), that the changes are isolated among users who are repeat bargainers on the platform. In contrast, the text content of one-off buyers and sellers is stable over the ten weeks following the introduction of messaging.

The golden question for both academics and practitioners is, of course, what should we say when we bargain? The natural experiment in that paper does not offer an answer because it generates pseudo-experimental variation in the *availability* of communication , but not in the *content* of what is actually said. But as a second best, we might substitute an alternative question: what are more experienced sellers learning to say when they bargain? If sellers are learning from experience to bargain more effectively, then this offers some potential guidance for bargainers. At the very least, it reflects on existing work and has the potential to generate new hypotheses for what is to come.

Adopting the distributed multinomial regression framework of Taddy [24], they identify word pairs that are predictive of experience using the sample of observations in the ten weeks following the change. The exercise offers several reflections on messaging strategies. They find that inexperienced sellers are more likely to use effusive greetings, whereas more experienced sellers use polite, but restrained greetings. They also find that inexperienced sellers emphasize free shipping, which is salient in the listing, whereas experienced sellers are more likely to remind buyers of less-salient cost factors, e.g., the fact that PayPal and eBay charge them fees.

These findings are purely descriptive and may be context-specific, however, they offer a much-needed datapoint on communication in bargaining. Using natural language processing tools, exercises like this can describe what bargainers are actually doing in the field, and use that to motivate theoretical and experimental inquiry. Especially in light of the large positive effects of communication we found on eBay.de—a fourteen percent decrease in the rate of bargaining breakdown for interactions that involved a message after the change—we hope that this approach will foster a research agenda that helps us better understands the mechanisms by which communication affects bargaining.

17.4 New Tools and Directions

The Best Offer research agenda has offered an empirical setting in which to assess the performance of existing theoretical models and shows that on many elements, economic theory holds up surprisingly well. At the same time, however, it also raises new puzzles and opportunities for future research.

We observe evidence consistent with cheap-talk signaling in the strategic choices of bargainers, evidence that bargaining ability and patience matter for outcomes, and that bargaining itself is costly in a way that affects outcomes. Then again, we also observe puzzles. In the patterns of offers, we see reciprocal gradualism and splitting the difference, neither of which yet has a satisfying theoretical motivation. And in the messages that buyers and sellers send, we see what any practitioner surely already knows: that what we say when we bargain, and the opportunities we have to say it, matters greatly for determining outcomes.

In making the data public we hope to encourage new research on this question. Indeed, answers to these puzzles and others may lie in the Best Offer data. We believe, however, that growing this research agenda will also depend on finding new large-scale bargaining datasets. For example, Bagwell et al. [5] have constructed a novel large-scale dataset on the trade negotiations behind GATT. Moreover, we conjecture that with the emergence of online real-estate agent platforms (e.g., Redfin), there may one day be a large-scale dataset of offer-level bargaining for real-estate transactions.

While we pin much of our hopes on new data sources, we should also highlight the role of new tools. Especially insofar as we endeavor to think of bargaining as a communicative act, natural language processing tools for parsing text documents may prove critical to empirical attempts to understand bargaining. Best Offer bargaining has the advantage of being structured—every message is accompanied by a numerical offer in an alternating, sequential-offers setting. A similar advantage is shared by the GATT negotiations. While convenient, this is not generic to bargaining in the wild, and so we believe that new ML tools will have a central role in modeling unstructured bargaining.

References

1. A. Ambrus, E. Chaney, and I Salitsky. Pirates of the mediterranean: An empirical investigation of bargaining with transaction costs. *Quantitative Economics*, 9(1):217–46, 2018.
2. Matthew Backus, Thomas Blake, Bradley Larsen, and Steven Tadelis. Sequential bargaining in the field: Evidence from millions of online bargaining interactions. NBER Working Paper No. 24306, 2018.
3. Matthew Backus, Thomas Blake, Jett Pettus, and Steven Tadelis. Communication and bargaining breakdown: An empirical analysis. NBER Working Paper No. 27984, 2020.
4. Matthew Backus, Thomas Blake, and Steven Tadelis. Cheap talk, round numbers, and the economics of negotiation. NBER Working Paper No. 21285, 2015.
5. K. Bagwell, R. W. Staiger, and A. Yurukoglu. Multilateral trade bargaining: A first peek at the GATT bargaining records, 2017. Working paper, Stanford University.
6. Hongbin Cai and Joseph Tao-Yi Wang. Overcommunication in strategic information transmission games. *Games and Economic Behavior*, 56:7–36, 2006.
7. David Card. Strikes and bargaining: A survey of the recent empirical literature. *American Economic Review*, 80(2):410–415, 1990a.
8. David Card. Strikes and wages: A test of an asymmetric information model. *Quarterly Journal of Economics*, 105(3):625–659, 1990b.
9. David Card and Craig A. Olson. Bargaining power, strike durations, and wage outcomes: An analysis of strikes in the 1880s. *Journal of Labor Economics*, 13(1):32–61, 1995.
10. Olivier Compte and Philippe Jehiel. On the role of outside options in bargaining with obstinate parties. *Econometrica*, 70(4):1477–1517, 2002. ISSN 00129682.

11. P. Cramton and J.S. Tracy. Strikes and holdouts in wage bargaining: Theory and data. *American Economic Review*, 82(1):100–121, 1992.
12. Vincent P. Crawford. A theory of disagreemnt in bargaining. *Econometrica*, 50(3):607–637, 1982.
13. Liran Einav, Theresa Kuchler, Jonathan Levin, and Neel Sundaresan. Assessing sale strategies in online markets using matched listings. *American Economic Journal: Microeconomics*, 7(2):215–247, 2015.
14. Joseph Farrell and Robert Gibbons. Cheap talk can matter in bargaining. *Journal of Economic Theory*, 48(1):221–237, 1989.
15. Daniel Goetz. Dynamic bargaining and scale effects in the broadband industry. Working Paper, 2019.
16. Pranav Jindal and Peter Newberry. To bargain or not to bargain - the role of fixed costs in negotiations. *Journal of Marketing Research*, 55(6):832–851, 2018. Working Paper, Pennsylvania State University.
17. B. Larsen. The efficieny of real-world bargaining: Evidence from wholesale used-auto auctions. NBER Working paper 20431, 2018.
18. Malia Mason, Alice Lee, Elizabeth Wiley, and Daniel Ames. Precise offers are potent anchors: Conciliatory counteroffers and attributions of knowledge in negotiations. *Journal of Experimental Social Psychology*, 49:759–763, 2013.
19. Antonio Merlo and Francois Ortalo-Magné. Bargaining over residential real estate: Evidence from england. *Journal of Urban Economics*, 56(2):192–216, 2004.
20. R.B. Myerson and M.A. Satterthwaite. Efficient mechanisms for bilateral trading. *Journal of Economic Theory*, 29(2):265–281, 1983. ISSN 0022-0531.
21. Felix Oberholzer-Gee and Julie Wulf. Alibaba's taobao. Technical Report 9-709-456, Harvard Business School, 2009.
22. Roy Radner and Andrew Schotter. The sealed-bid mechanism: An experimental study. *Journal of Economic Theory*, 48(1):179–220, 1989.
23. A. Rubinstein. Perfect equilibrium in a bargaining model. *Econometrica*, pages 97–109, 1982. ISSN 0012-9682.
24. Matthew Taddy. Distributed multinomial regression. *The Annals of Applied Statistics*, 9(3):1394–1414, 2015.
25. Manoj Thomas, Daniel H. Simon, and Vrinda Kadiyali. The price precision effect: Evidence from laboratory and market data. *Marketing Science*, 29(1):175–190, 2010.

26. Kathleen Valley, Leigh Thompson, Robert Gibbons, and Max Bazerman. How communication improves efficiency in bargaining games. *Games and Economic Behavior*, 38(1):127–155, 2002.

18

Self-sufficient, Self-directed, and Interdependent Negotiation Systems: A Roadmap Toward Autonomous Negotiation Agents

Tim Baarslag, Michael Kaisers, Enrico H. Gerding, Catholijn M. Jonker, and Jonathan Gratch

18.1 Introduction

Negotiation, the process of joint decision-making, is pervasive in our society [23]. Whenever actors meet and influence each other to forge a mutually beneficial agreement, a form of negotiation is at work [44].

Negotiation arises in almost every social and organizational setting, yet many avoid it out of fear or lack of skill and this contributes to income inequality, political gridlock, and social injustice [18]. This has led to an increasing focus on the design of autonomous negotiators capable of

T. Baarslag (✉) · M. Kaisers
Centrum Wiskunde & Informatica, Amsterdam, The Netherlands
e-mail: T.Baarslag@cwi.nl

M. Kaisers
e-mail: Michael.Kaisers@cwi.nl

E. H. Gerding
University of Southampton, Southampton, UK
e-mail: eg@ecs.soton.ac.uk

E. Karagözoğlu and K. B. Hyndman (eds.), *Bargaining*,
https://doi.org/10.1007/978-3-030-76666-5_18

automatically and independently negotiating with others. This interest has been spurred since the beginning of the 1980s with the work of early flag bearers such as Smith [40] and Sycara [41].

Automated negotiation research is fueled by a number of benefits that computerized negotiation can offer, including better (win-win) deals, and reduction in time, costs, stress and cognitive effort on the part of the user. Moreover, autonomous negotiation will soon become not just desired but *required* in instances where the human scale is simply too slow and expensive. For instance, with the worldwide deployment of the smart electrical grid and the must for renewable energy sources, flexible devices in our household will soon (re-)negotiate complex energy contracts automatically. Another example is the rise of the Internet of Things (IoT), which will introduce countless smart, interconnected devices that autonomously negotiate the usage of sensitive data and make trade-offs between privacy concerns, price, and convenience.

To properly fulfill its representational role in an ever-dynamic environment, a negotiation agent has to balance and adhere to different aspects of autonomous behavior, including self-reliance and the capability and freedom to perform its actions, while at the same time remaining interdependent in its joint activity with the user. While many successes have been achieved in advancing various degrees of autonomy in negotiating agents, it is readily apparent that fully deployed and truly autonomous negotiators are still a thing of the future. Continued development will be required before agents will be able to forge even mundane agreements such as the personalized renewal of our energy or mobile phone contracts. This begs the obvious question: what is still lacking currently and what is needed for autonomous negotiators to be able to fulfill their promise?

C. M. Jonker
Delft University of Technology, Delft, The Netherlands
e-mail: C.M.Jonker@tudelft.nl

J. Gratch
University of Southern California, Los Angeles, CA, USA
e-mail: gratch@ict.usc.edu

This paper discusses the challenges and upcoming application domains for (almost) entirely autonomous negotiation on people's behalf. We describe the technological challenges associated with these future domains and provide a roadmap toward full autonomy, together with stops along the way, highlighting what we deem important solution concepts for enabling future autonomous negotiation systems. As a basis for our discussion, we provide a unifying view of autonomous negotiation based on three orthogonal dimensions of autonomy that research has focused on so far: being self-sufficient, self-directed, and interdependent. We argue that automated negotiation opportunities of tomorrow are calling for a combined effort in addressing these three pillars of a negotiator's autonomy.

This paper does not aim to survey all research or challenges in the field comprehensively, but rather presents pointers to what we consider important focal points for autonomous negotiation, now and in the future. We pinpoint and elaborate on the following major challenges for autonomous negotiation:

1. Domain knowledge and preference elicitation;
2. Long-term perspective; and
3. User trust and adoption.

Lastly, this paper also pays homage to the 2001 landmark publication by Jennings et al. [27] and asks what has happened, 16 years later, with the prospects and challenges of automated negotiation. We examine which main challenges have been addressed, and which stay relevant in a world that offers more opportunities for automated negotiation than ever before.

18.2 The Autonomy Diagonal of Negotiation

Autonomous negotiation is more than just *automated* negotiation; it is the freedom to negotiate independently. Rather than being unidimensional, autonomy incorporates at least two components [11]:

Table 18.1 Overview of major challenges in autonomous negotiation and the main dimensions of autonomy to which they relate. Each challenge is subdivided in building blocks along with example opportunities and a solution roadmap

Major challenge	Main autonomy dimensions	Building blocks	Example opportunities	Solutions roadmap
Domain knowledge and preference elicitation (Sect. 18.3.1)	Self-sufficiency & Interdependence	Preference elicitation on-the-fly	Privacy and IoT	Value of information indicators, robust performance estimates
		Domain modeling	Smart grids	Separate user/agent domain models, expert mappings
Long-term perspective (Sect. 18.3.2)	Self-sufficiency & Self-directedness	Repeated interactions	Communities, smart homes, autonomous driving	Temporally integrative negotiations, reputation metrics
		Non-stationary preferences	B2B, entertainment booking	Cost-efficient tracking, context-dependent models, preference dynamics
User trust and adoption (Sect. 18.3.3)	Self-directedness & Interdependence	Acceptability and participation	Conflict resolution, customer retainment	Co-creation, adjustable autonomy, transfer of control
		Transparent consequences	Sharing economy, decentralized marketplaces	Transparency and openness, worst-case bounds, risk measures

self-sufficiency (the capability of the actor to take care of itself) and *self-directedness* (the freedom to act within the environment and the means to reach goals). Following [28] we distinguish a third dimension called *support for interdependence*—being able to work with others and influence and be influenced by team members. Note that the notion of autonomy is notoriously difficult to capture (see [28] for an overview). We are concerned here with those aspects especially relevant for negotiation and for their autonomy in relation to their environment; an alternative, more self-contained definition, for example, is an agent's ability to generate its own goals [31].

We can distinguish three strands of research in automated negotiation that each cluster around one of the three dimensions of autonomy (Fig. 18.1):

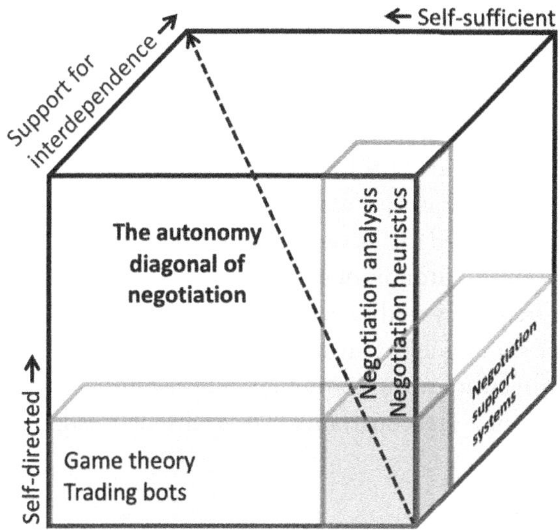

Fig. 18.1 By and large, negotiation research can be clustered around one of the three main orthogonal dimensions of autonomy: *self-sufficiency, self-directedness*, and *interdependence*. The efforts of the three need to be integrated to arrive at such truly autonomous negotiators that can progress along the *autonomy diagonal*

18.2.1 Negotiation Support Systems

These systems are designed to assist and train people in negotiation. Some of these systems, such as the Inspire system [29], have been widely employed in real-life. However, while negotiation support systems enable interdependence by design, humans predominately supervise and make decisions on the appropriate outcome, which results in low self-sufficiency and self-directedness.

18.2.2 Game Theoretical Approaches and Trading Bots

Game theory's dominant concern is with fully rational players and what each should optimally do. This approach is therefore called *symmetrically prescriptive* [37]. The focus is on either equilibrium strategies or protocols that can guarantee a good outcome for both players through mechanism design [44]. Agents have a reduced scope for self-directedness in such settings, as they are relatively simple and need to conform to certain strategies (e.g., to bid truthfully in an auction) [35]. Similarly, real-world trading bots mostly employ simple rule-based functions which have been hard-coded in advance. Examples of this type are among the most advanced autonomous negotiators in terms of self-sufficiency, such as high-frequency trading agents for financial exchanges, advertising exchanges, or sniping agents used in eBay [25]. While these approaches are able to function without human intervention and can be highly self-sufficient, they are constrained in terms of freedom to direct the process.

18.2.3 Negotiation Analytical Approaches

Negotiation analysis *prescribes* how players should act given a *description* of how others will act. That is, this field is concerned with an *asymmetrical prescriptive/descriptive* view of autonomous negotiation [37]. Much research on what are often dubbed simply 'negotiation agents' (or 'heuristics' in game theory literature) falls into this category; e.g., all negotiation agents from the annual automated negotiation competition [4]. A key feature of this approach is the agent's ability to make judgment calls without intervention (i.e., to construct beliefs based on partial information and act in best response to this belief, typically over opponent types or strategies), while the agent's preferences are often considered externally given. This locates the negotiation analytical approach around the self-directed axis.

As can be gleaned from the fields indicated above, autonomous negotiation has garnered attention from different research directions and has managed to advance in key aspects of autonomous behavior. As a result, we now have negotiators that exist independently in the real world, delegated with a gamut of available strategies to freely choose among, and that can engage in supportive interdependence; *just not all at the same time.*

This may explain why it has proven difficult to extend the progress made in this field to truly representative negotiating agents. Of course, we acknowledge that to a lesser degree, combined work on all dimensions has been performed (as depicted by the three-colored cube in the bottom right of Fig. 18.1); we simply argue that the main automated negotiation research lines have developed in parallel to one of the three autonomy directions. Research-wise, it is unquestionably a sound strategy to first explore the autonomy axes in separation. As Fig. 18.1 suggests, we can make substantive progress in autonomous negotiation by continuing to advance along *the autonomy diagonal*, which has inspired the focal points of the challenges we present in the next section.

18.3 Major Challenges

The various aspects of autonomy drive three major open challenges for autonomous negotiation, of which the overall theme can be summarized as *trusted and sustained representation.* We describe the challenges and their building blocks below, together with a number of explicit opportunities in each case (see Table 18.1 for an overview).

Just like autonomy itself, each challenge outlined here is *multi-dimensional*; i.e., each challenge pertains to at least two dimensions of autonomy, thereby providing the impetus to further advance along the autonomy diagonal. Note that many of these challenges intersect and cannot be entirely untangled; for example, adequate user preference extraction will not only increase the user model accuracy, but may also boost user trust .

18.3.1 Domain Knowledge and Preference Elicitation

Co-dependence between user and agent requires that they synchronize their world model. This requirement relates mainly to the agent's self-sufficiency and interdependence, which can be enhanced by imparting the agent with accurate and timely user preferences about the negotiation process and co-constructing the real-world intricacies of the domain.

18.3.1.1 Preference Elicitation on-the-Fly

In order to faithfully represent the user, an autonomous negotiator needs to engage with the user to make sure it constructs an accurate preference model. However, users are often unwilling or unable to engage with a negotiation system, and hence prudence needs to be exercised when interacting with the user to avoid elicitation fatigue. This is especially important in domains where people are notably reluctant to engage with the system at length, for instance in privacy negotiations.

As a consequence, automated negotiators of the future are required to not only strike deals with limited available user information, but also to assess which additional information should be elicited from the user, while minimizing user bother. This challenge is still as relevant (and for the most part still unaddressed) as when it was raised in [27]. However, as a way forward, we believe future research should particularly emphasize *preference elicitation on-the-fly*: that is, active preference extraction *during* negotiation(s). Potential benefits include a significantly reduced initial preference elicitation phase (as featured in many negotiation support systems) and the ability to select the most informative query to pose to the user at the most relevant time.

To facilitate this, new performance-based metrics are required that can assess how supplementary preference information influences negotiation performance. Adaptive utility elicitation models provide a good starting point for representing probabilistic utility-based preferences that allow for incremental updating over time (e.g., using Bayesian reasoning) in the vein of [12]. The viability of a negotiation query can for instance be measured in terms of the expected value of information [9] in order to assess the marginal utility of altering belief states.

Another challenge is for a negotiation strategy to determine its actions effectively in light of its imprecise information state. Techniques for decision-making under uncertainty could assist in this and could thereby give rise to novel negotiation strategy concepts, for instance by incorporating the notion of expected *expected* utility [10] to express the expected negotiation payoff over all possible instantiations of the user model.

The above discussion largely follows the standard assumptions of rational choice theory: i.e., that people's preferences can be accurately elicited. Unfortunately, several idiosyncrasies of human psychology complicate these assumptions. Not only do people often have difficulty explicitly expressing their preferences, a person's willingness to accept an agreement is also only partially determined by how they feel about the final agreement. For example, Curhan's Subjective Value Inventory [14] identifies four factors that predict which agreements people will accept. Besides feelings about the material outcome (e.g., 'the extent to which the terms of the agreement benefit you'), agreements are shaped by feelings about the self (e.g., 'did you lose face'), feelings about the process (e.g., 'did the counterpart listen to your concerns') and feelings about the relationship (e.g., 'did the negotiation build a good foundation for a future relationship').

Research also illustrates that elicited utility functions are highly sensitive to subtle contextual factors. For example, *framing effects* emphasize that preferences between outcomes can reverse depending on whether they are seen as losses or gains with respect to some reference point. In a negotiation, the reference point is often the perceived value that the other party receives, even though this knowledge doesn't change the individual's objective outcome. As a result, outcomes can be readily manipulated simply by changing the form and nature of information conveyed [22]. More broadly, valuations in a negotiation are shaped by emotion, including emotions that arise from the process, but also beliefs about what other parties feel (see, e.g. [8]). Given the highly context-sensitive nature of on-the-fly preference elicitation, such considerations will have to be taken into account in its design and implementation.

18.3.1.2 Domain Modeling

The quality of the negotiation outcome depends not only on the faithfulness of the preference model of an autonomous negotiator, but also on the accuracy of the domain model. The old 'garbage in, garbage out' truism applies here, as the quality of the offered solution depends so heavily on a correct domain description.

However, domain modeling, and certainly formal modeling, is an expertise that cannot be expected from an arbitrary user. Therefore, users require either expert guidance or explicit domain modeling support. Modeling in close cooperation with a domain expert runs the risk of perpetuating people's uncertainty about the model, thereby limiting their ability to make necessary adjustments. When modeling support is provided by the system, the knowledge representation language used will be inherently simple as it has to be understood by arbitrary negotiators. This is especially important in domains where users employ automated negotiation without any expertise, such as in the smart grid, which can result in the wrong evaluation of bids. Highly accurate models, on the other hand, also have their disadvantages: they can display complex non-linearities [26], in which case even assessing the utility of a proposal can prove NP-hard [15].

This inspires the following open research question: what is the impact of simplifying the domain and preference models to keep the layman user on board? An answer might come from using two models, as suggested in [24]: an accurate, but complex one that serves as a reference model for the agent, and a more comprehensive one for interaction with the user. Proper clarification and explanation could then be elicited from a process of co-creation [36] or participatory design [39] between modeling experts and domain experts. Ideally, a reflecting phase should be included during and after negotiations, in which the human (and perhaps eventually the agent) can provide feedback to allow for long-term co-evolution.

The above points also apply to the appropriateness and understandability of the protocol governing the negotiation. Typically, a pre-negotiation phase provides an opportunity for the negotiation parties to engage in a debate about what protocol to employ. A corresponding challenge is to construct a best practice repository for negotiation techniques, as mentioned in [27]. This has been tackled at least partially through recent efforts in creating a negotiation handbook for negotiation protocols [32].

Whatever approach is chosen, experts in formal modeling will be needed to instantiate a domain model that sufficiently captures all salient features. Those experts are pivotal to the negotiation agent business model and will be responsible for mapping user-understandable interests to the negotiation issues within complex domains. These are likely to become future jobs; i.e., real estate agents informing procurement agents of the future. Relevant research areas, and courses for training these experts, will be on collaborative and supportive modeling.

18.3.2 Long-Term Perspective

Given the effort involved in domain modeling and preference elicitation, the opportunities for automated negotiation are even clearer in domains where an agent frequently faces similar negotiation situations. Most research on negotiation agents, however, has focused on single encounters. The different challenges and opportunities for such long-term negotiations hinge on the volatility of both the opponent pool and the user's preferences.

18.3.2.1 Repeated Encounters

There are many propitious opportunities for applying negotiation in repeated encounters. For example, in community energy exchange [2], agents can trade energy from storage and local sources between neighboring homes and businesses. Another example is the smart home, where different occupants will have different needs and preferences and have to reach mutual agreements, e.g., about the temperature of the house and the use of devices. Other settings, in which the agent faces many different opponents, include self-driving vehicles, where vehicle-to-vehicle and vehicle-to-infrastructure negotiation can play an important role (e.g., negotiating priority at intersections).

Negotiation opportunities for isolated encounters can be very limited, since often a resource (e.g., electricity or giving way) is needed without necessarily offering anything immediately in return (except possibly money or virtual currencies). However, explicitly considering the *temporal dimension* allows agents to receive or concede something now in return for conceding or receiving the same resource later. In other words, single-issue, distributive negotiations can be turned into richer, multi-issue, integrative negotiations, with more scope to achieve win-win solutions [33].

A significant challenge for long-term reciprocal encounters is that future needs are often uncertain, and so it is difficult to commit to giving up or requesting specific future resources. Possible solutions involve money or virtual currencies which can be redeemed at a later stage and can undergo temporal discounting if necessary, but they do not address the distributive nature of multi-issue negotiation. They also introduce additional challenges: using actual money requires an exchange rate with the resources involved, while it may not be desirable to introduce money in certain settings; e.g., when they rely, to some degree, on unincentivized cooperation and altruistic behavior. Virtual currencies (including distributed ledger approaches) can be traded bilaterally in a 'like for like' manner, addressing the exchange problem, but then other issues arise, e.g., how much does each agent receive to begin with, what happens if an agent runs out, and to what extent do they provide a real incentive if agents can go into debt without any consequences?

Another possible solution is to rely on altruism and using trust ratings and reputation systems to provide the desired incentives (e.g., using favors and ledgers [33]). In such cases, 'altruism' can be a self-interested strategy if this is reciprocated at a later state, possibly involving a different opponent. While reputation mechanisms are well known to incentivize cooperation in the prisoner's dilemma, more research on this is needed in the context of (repeated) automated negotiation.

Unfortunately, negotiation methods that seek to identify efficient and fair (envy-free) agreements face, in addition to the above, a number of *psychological* challenges. People adopt a variety of interpretations as to what is fair and negotiations often involve disputes over which principle to apply [42]. For example, in the context of organ donation, the *equity principle* would allocate resources on the basis of ability, effort, or merit, the *equality rule* would treat individuals the same, whereas the *principle of need* is usually achieved by allocating according to individuals' medical condition, socio-economical status, or other relevant needs. Other complications involve moral constraints on certain exchanges. For example, it is considered morally repugnant to exchange money for bodily organs, so an agreement that combines material interests with sacred values may be seen as substantially worse than an independent evaluation of these elements would suggest [17].

Although these challenges might seem insurmountable, there are several ways to incorporate these biases into conventional computational methods. One approach is to incorporate psychological factors into the utility function. Indeed, Fehr and Schmidt have shown how this can be done without violating the basic tenets of utility theory [19]. Some of the challenges with fairness can be addressed by making the process more transparent (Sect. 18.3.3). Another approach is to incorporate modest psychological extensions to rational methods. For example, framing effects can be handled through the use of prospect theory (e.g. [43]).

18.3.2.2 Non-Stationary Preferences

While short-lived instantiations of representational agents may assume that there are some true and stationary preferences to be elicited from the user, in long-term negotiations, these very preferences may evolve over the course of weeks or months according to certain *preference dynamics*. If an autonomous negotiator acts on elicited information for an extended period of time without accounting for existing drift in preferences, it will erroneously fulfill outdated design objectives. Even if the drop in performance is noticed by the user, this leads to a plunge in user trust and adoption, or a de-facto shortened time of deployment. This is a typical example of opacity that can result from an excess of unchecked autonomy [34]. As a result, long-term negotiation requires an increase in co-dependence, at the cost of throttled-down self-directedness; e.g., by repeated assessment of the preference representation quality, with intermittent elicitation actions whenever their anticipated benefits exceed their costs.

This reframes the challenge posed in Sect. 18.3.1 of preference elicitation to *cost-efficient tracking of non-stationary preferences* in long-term negotiation, with possible applications ranging from leisure bookings to business-to-business (B2B) negotiations. Inspiration for tackling this challenge may come from the area of news recommender systems, which has embraced context-dependent models [1] and preference dynamics [30] in response to the inherent need to capture fast-paced preference evolution. Such models have promising merit for being transferred to negotiation strategies that balance the preciseness of preference representation with relevant and timely but costly elicitation, extending preliminary work in that area [5].

18.3.3 User Trust and Adoption

While the agent depends on the user for knowledge and guidance (as described in Sect. 18.3.1), the user relies on a self-directed agent for a good outcome. To alleviate unwillingness to relinquish control and to guarantee user satisfaction with and adherence to the final outcome, the user needs to trust the system through co-participation, transparency, and proper representation.

18.3.3.1 User Participation

Lessons learned from collaborative human-robot teams indicate that it is important to be able to escalate to the meta-level (i.e., have humans participate) when necessary [20]. The need for escalating to a higher authority applies whenever a negotiator represents a group or a company (e.g., a union, or stakeholder organizations in general). In such cases, the negotiator can only make deals that fall within certain margins. Take, for example, a helpdesk operator with a telecom provider, authorized to offer new deals on a contract renewal. She has only limited freedom in terms of the bounded range of possible deals she can sign off on; in fact, she does not even really possess the freedom to decide *whether* to negotiate. In case of doubt, the decision is escalated to a different authority level.

The idea of collaborative control, or mixed-initiative control (see e.g. [20, 21]) might become essential to obtain the most out of complex negotiations. In this envisioned line of research, each negotiation party consists of at least one human and one negotiation agent. The agent should do the brunt of the negotiation work to find possible agreements with the other negotiation parties and which can be presented to their human partners for feedback and new input. The research challenge is to determine when, how, and how often to switch the initiative from human to agent and vice versa.

18.3.3.2 Transparent Consequences

There is an inherent tension between increased self-directedness and trust , which dampens the adoption of increasingly autonomous negotiators: on the one hand, an autonomous negotiator's relevance is directly proportional to its ability to impact the user independently in meaningful ways (e.g., fiscal, well-being, reputation, and so on); but, in turn, the user's trust and willingness to relinquish control is conditional on understanding the agent's reasoning and consequences of its actions. The two can be reconciled by making the outcome space more *transparent* to the user, and by enabling the user to specify the permissible means in the form of *principles*. The challenge is that the negotiation agent's reasoning abilities may very well exceed the domain insights of a nonspecialist user, thus requiring a translation from stochastic performance models of self-directed expert reasoning into laymen terms that adequately convey expectations and risks.

Note that we suggest transparency as the key concept here, which subsumes Jennings' notion of predictability [27]. Predictability is essential toward the user to instill trust , but can be disastrous toward the opponent because of the potential for exploitability. We argue unpredictable behavior is in fact desirable as a negotiation tactic as a confusing and randomization device, as long as the consequences are transparently explained to the user.

The uncertainty inherent in negotiation can be captured in performance models and risk metrics, where the complexity should be scaled to the criticality of the consequences for the user. If the performance intervals are sub-critical, then simple guarantees on the range of possible outcomes may suffice (such as price bounds provided by Uber for individual rides), leaving it up to the user to build and judge the average performance model; otherwise, measures of risk are required, such as Conditional Value at Risk (CVar) [38].

In the end, the potency of autonomous negotiators is as much contingent on the acceptance by their users as by their counter-parties. Possible sources of resistance to adoption include established business models based on human inefficiencies (e.g., phone and media contracts) or anti-competitive practices (e.g., proprietary lock-in), which could become invalidated by autonomous (re-)negotiation. The most promising incubators of autonomous negotiators are ecosystems in which autonomous agents provide a unique source of societal value that is distributed over all stakeholders, as in the application of demand response for smart grids. Open platforms for value distribution have recently seen increased attention in flagship applications such as the cryptocurrency *bitcoin* and the decentralized World Wide Web *Blockstack* [3]. The digital API of these systems offers fertile grounds for a level playing field for competition and may soon provide a common interface for automated negotiators.

18.4 Concluding Observations

Autonomous systems that are capable of negotiating on our behalf are among society's key technological challenges for the near future, and their uptake is important for many critical economical application areas. In this paper, we present a roadmap to arrive at representative and trusted negotiators that are endowed with a long-term perspective. By continuing along this trajectory, negotiation research can address perhaps the biggest challenge of all: a coactive approach that simultaneously advances the autonomy of a negotiation agent in all its aspects.

Finally, looking even further forward, it is worth noting that people negotiate differently through intermediaries than they would face-to-face. The literature on *representation effects* suggests that people may show less regard for fairness and ethical behavior when negotiating through a third (human) party [13]. Indeed, human lawyers are ethically permitted and, to some extent, expected to lie on behalf of their clients [22]. This raises the question as to whether agents should similarly lie on behalf of a user. Analogous to recent research on ethical dilemmas in self-driving cars, people may claim that negotiation agents should be ethical, but sacrifice these ideals if it maximizes their profits. The natural dichotomy between recognizing the agent's autonomy and taking responsibility for its actions is best resolved by acknowledging user responsibility for the agent's design objectives (what should be achieved) and principles (how it should be achieved). This also illustrates an additional impetus for having humans understand the agent: feeling responsibility for the agent's actions implies an understanding what the agent is doing. Fortunately, some recent research on agent negotiators suggests that people may act more ethically when negotiating via computer agents [16], but far more research is needed to understand how *artificial representation effects* arise.

Acknowledgements This work was originally published in [6, 7]. This work is part of the Veni research program with project number 639.021.751, which is financed by The Dutch Research Council (NWO).

References

1. G Adomavicius and A Tuzhilin. Context-aware recommender systems. In *Recommender systems handbook*, pages 191–226. Springer, 2015.

2. M Alam, E H Gerding, et al. A scalable interdependent multi-issue negotiation protocol for energy exchange. In *IJCAI*, pages 1098–1104, 2015.
3. M Ali, J Nelson, et al. Blockstack: A global naming and storage system secured by blockchains. In *USENIX ATC*, pages 181–194, 2016.
4. T Baarslag, K Fujita, et al. Evaluating practical negotiating agents: Results and analysis of the 2011 international competition. *Artificial Intelligence*, 198:73–103, May 2013.
5. T Baarslag and M Kaisers. The value of information in automated negotiation: A decision model for eliciting user preferences. In *AAMAS 2017*, 2017.
6. T Baarslag, M Kaisers, E H Gerding, C M Jonker, and J Gratch. *Computers that negotiate on our behalf: Major challenges for self-sufficient, self-directed, and interdependent negotiating agents*, volume 10643 of *Lecture Notes in Computer Science*, pages 143–163. Springer International Publishing, Cham, 2017.
7. T Baarslag, M Kaisers, E H Gerding, C M Jonker, and J Gratch. When will negotiation agents be able to represent us? The challenges and opportunities for autonomous negotiators. In *Proceedings of the Twenty-sixth International Joint Conference on Artificial Intelligence*, IJCAI'17, pages 4684–4690, 2017.
8. B Barry, I S Fulmer, et al. I laughed, I cried, I settled: The role of emotion in negotiation. In *The handbook of negotiation and culture*, pages 71–94, 2004.
9. C Boutilier. A POMDP formulation of preference elicitation problems. In *AAAI*, pages 239–246, 2002.
10. C Boutilier. On the foundations of expected expected utility. In *IJCAI'03*, pages 285–290, 2003.
11. J M Bradshaw, P J Feltovich, et al. Dimensions of adjustable autonomy and mixed-initiative interaction. In *International workshop on computational autonomy*, pages 17–39. Springer, 2003.
12. U Chajewska, D Koller, et al. Making rational decisions using adaptive utility elicitation. In *AAAI*, pages 363–369, 2000.
13. D Chugh, M H Bazerman, et al. Bounded ethicality as a psychological barrier to recognizing conflicts of interest. *Conflicts of interest: Challenges and solutions in business, law, medicine, and public policy*, pages 74–95, 2005.

14. J R Curhan, H A Elfenbein, et al. What do people value when they negotiate? Mapping the domain of subjective value in negotiation. *Journal of Personality and Social Psychology*, 91(3):493, 2006.
15. D de Jonge, C Sierra, et al. *Negotiations over large agreement spaces*. PhD thesis, 2015.
16. C M de Melo, S Marsella, et al. Do as I say, not as I do: Challenges in delegating decisions to automated agents. In *AAMAS*, pages 949–956, 2016.
17. M Dehghani, S Atran, et al. Sacred values and conflict over Iran's nuclear program. *Judgment and Decision Making*, 5(7):540, 2010.
18. T Eisenberg and C Lanvers. What is the settlement rate and why should we care? *Journal of Empirical Legal Studies*, 6(1):111–146, 2009.
19. E Fehr and K M Schmidt. The economics of fairness, reciprocity and altruism–experimental evidence and new theories. *Handbook of the Economics of Giving, Altruism and Reciprocity*, 1:615–691, 2006.
20. P J Feltovich, B van Riemsdijk, et al. Autonomy and interdependence in human-agent-robot teams, 2012.
21. T Fong, C Thorpe, and C Baur. *Collaborative control: A robot-centric model for vehicle teleoperation*, volume 1. Carnegie Mellon University, The Robotics Institute, 2001.
22. J Gratch, Z Nazari, et al. The misrepresentation game: How to win at negotiation while seeming like a nice guy. In *AAMAS*, pages 728–737, 2016.
23. K L Harris. Content analysis in negotiation research: A review and guide. *Behavior Research Methods, Instruments, & Computers*, 28(3):458–467, 1996.
24. K Hindriks, C M Jonker, et al. Avoiding approximation errors in multi-issue negotiation with issue dependencies. In *ACAN*, 2008.
25. W Hu and A Bolivar. Online auctions efficiency: A survey of ebay auctions. In *WWW*, pages 925–934, 2008.
26. T Ito, M Klein, et al. A multi-issue negotiation protocol among agents with nonlinear utility functions. *Multiagent and Grid Systems*, 4(1):67–83, January 2008.
27. N R Jennings, P Faratin, et al. Automated negotiation: Prospects, methods and challenges. *GDN*, 10(2):199–215, 2001.
28. M Johnson, J M Bradshaw, et al. *The fundamental principle of coactive design: Interdependence must shape autonomy*, pages 172–191. Springer Berlin Heidelberg, 2011.

29. G E Kersten and G Lo. Negotiation support systems and software agents in e-business negotiations. In *ICEB*, pages 19–21, 2001.
30. L Li, L Zheng, et al. Modeling and broadening temporal user interest in personalized news recommendation. *Expert Systems with Applications*, 41(7):3168–3177, 2014.
31. M Luck, M D'Inverno, et al. *Autonomy: Variable and generative*, pages 11–28. Springer US, Boston, MA, 2003.
32. I Marsa-Maestre, M Klein, et al. From problems to protocols: Towards a negotiation handbook. In *Decision support systems*, 2013.
33. J Mell, G Lucas, et al. An effective conversation tactic for creating value over repeated negotiations. In *AAMAS '15*, pages 1567–1576, 2015.
34. D A Norman. The 'problem' with automation: inappropriate feedback and interaction, not 'over-automation'. *Philosophical Transactions of the Royal Society of London B: Biological Sciences*, 327(1241):585–593, 1990.
35. J Prause-Stamm. *Self-directedness and resoluteness. The two dimensions of autonomy*. PhD thesis, Humboldt-Universität zu Berlin, 2013.
36. E B-N Sanders and P J Stappers. Co-creation and the new landscapes of design. *Co-design*, 4(1):5–18, 2008.
37. J K Sebenius. Negotiation analysis: A characterization and review. *Management Science*, 38(1):18–38, 1992.
38. M Shafie-khah, D Z Fitiwi, et al. Simultaneous participation of demand response aggregators in ancillary services and demand response exchange markets. In *2016 IEEE/PES T&D*, pages 1–5, May 2016.
39. J Simonsen and T Robertson. *Routledge international handbook of participatory design*. Routledge, 2012.
40. R G Smith. The contract net protocol: High-level communication and control in a distributed problem solver. *IEEE Transactions on Computers*, 29(12):1104–1113, 1980.
41. K P Sycara. Arguments of persuasion in labour mediation. In *IJCAI*, volume 1, pages 294–296, 1985.
42. N A Welsh. Perceptions of fairness in negotiation. *Marquette Law Review*, 87:753, 2003.
43. R Yang, C Kiekintveld, et al. Improving resource allocation strategy against human adversaries in security games. In *IJCAI*, volume 22, page 458. Citeseer, 2011.
44. H P Young. *Negotiation analysis*. University of Michigan Press, 1991.

19

Using Machine Learning to Understand Bargaining Experiments

Colin F. Camerer, Hung-Ni Chen, Po-Hsuan Lin, Gideon Nave, Alec Smith, and Joseph Tao-yi Wang

19.1 Introduction

As all the chapters in this book discuss, bargaining is a fundamental economic activity. This chapter is about a general class of bargaining games in which there is private information about the amount that is being bargained over (often called the "pie size"). This class is most common in everyday bargaining. It is also interesting in both *theory* and *practice*.

C. F. Camerer · P.-H. Lin
California Institute of Technology, Pasadena, CA, USA
e-mail: camerer@hss.caltech.edu

P.-H. Lin
e-mail: plin@caltech.edu

H.-N. Chen
Ludwig Maximilians University of Munich, Munich, Germany
e-mail: hungni.chen@econ.lmu.de

E. Karagözoğlu and K. B. Hyndman (eds.), *Bargaining*,
https://doi.org/10.1007/978-3-030-76666-5_19

Theory is interesting because when there is private information and people are self-interested, theories based on individual rationality typically predict an inevitable loss of efficiency. That is, even when a bargain is mutually beneficial for both sides, they will not always come to agreement.

Private information bargaining is interesting in *practice* because, while inefficiencies are predicted by theory, it is also known that if there are observable statistical proxies for the hidden private information, then sets of rules (mechanisms) which use this information can improve efficiency [11, 12, 33]. Therefore, it is possible that methods for measuring private information can improve efficiency, even when bargainers voluntarily participate in systems using those measures.

There is a long history of using highly controlled laboratory experiments to study bargaining. We follow [8] to provide a brief description of this history to help explain why we are enthusiastic about modern applications of machine learning.

19.1.1 A brief history of bargaining experiments

Prior to breakthroughs on theories of structured bargaining, most experiments were conducted using unstructured communication. Research mainly focused on process-free solution concepts lead by the Nash bargaining solution [36], and their extensions (e.g., [28]). Numerous

G. Nave
University of Pennsylvania, Philadelphia, PA, USA
e-mail: gnave@wharton.upenn.edu

A. Smith (✉)
Virginia Tech, Blacksburg, VA, USA
e-mail: alecsmith@vt.edu

J. T. Wang
National Taiwan University, Taipei, Taiwan
e-mail: josephw@ntu.edu.tw

bargains [37, 40] led to an equal split of the amount of surplus available to share, which we refer to as "pie." When there are informational asymmetries, disagreements may occur because of coordination difficulties. Hence, Roth and colleagues have subsequent papers where players bargain over points which could be redeemed for different monetary values [39, 41, 42]. Theory predicts 100% agreement in these games, but experimental results show that a modest percentage of trials (10–20%) end in disagreement, likely due to differences regarding which "focal points" are acceptable.[1] Roth et al. [43] also drew attention to the "deadline effect," in which a large majority of agreements are made just before the (known) deadline.

Two pioneering papers, Ståhl [46] and Rubinstein [44] showed how noncooperative game theory might be used to improve the apparent precision of bargaining theories. Since then, almost all experimental studies have tested what happens in highly structured settings using variants of those early game structures [2]. In these theories and experiments, "structure" refers to theory clearly specifying the rules of how bargaining proceeds, which predictions of bargaining outcomes are sensitive to. That structural sensitivity proved to be enticing, because it created a cornucopia of interesting experiments testing whether bargaining was sensitive to structured features as theory predicted. This led to a burst of progress in experimental literature testing these theories [7].

Many other experiments have observed what happens in semi-structured bargaining in which there is *two-sided* private information [49]. The term "semi-structured" means that there is structure about bargainers' valuations and beliefs, but players may make offers at any time, and offers can be accompanied by natural language. These experiments typically find *fewer* disagreements than predicted by theory in face-to-face and unstructured communication via message-passing, comparable to findings in "cheap talk" games where senders willingly reveal "too much" [6, 10, 51].

---

[1] See the literature starting at Schelling [45] leading to Isoni et al. [25, 26], Hargreaves Heap et al. [22].

19.1.2 Returning to a Less Popular Route

Since the rise of structured bargaining theories, experimentation in economics on unstructured bargaining has all but disappeared. However, as shown by Karagözoğlu [29], there are many good reasons to investigate the process of unstructured bargaining, such as the need to satisfy procedural justice. Hence, Camerer et al. [8] return to this older venue, and explore unstructured bargaining with one-sided private information in laboratory experiment for the following reasons:

First, establishing more empirical regularities in naturally occurring settings is a prerequisite for theorizing. Since most natural two-player bargaining settings have little penalties for deviating from structured conventions, studying unstructured bargaining is of particular importance. In particular, strategic behavior under continuous-time interaction [16] should be documented, as well as deadline effects [18, 43] which are not predicted by most theories (though see [17]).

Second, theory can still be applied to make clear, interesting predictions even when bargaining is unstructured. For instance, clear predictions about unstructured bargaining can emerge, thanks to the wonderful "revelation principle" [34, 35]. This principle generates empirical predictions for noncooperative equilibria based purely on the information structure, regardless of the bargaining protocol.

Third, unstructured bargaining generates very rich data during the bargaining process. Players are allowed to make offers at any time, retract them, etc. Natural language can be analyzed, perhaps including vocal properties in verbal communication [9]. Self-reported and biological measures of emotion, cognitive effort, visual attention to display elements, and even neural activity can also be gathered.

Our view is that theoretical and experimental economists regarded these types of data as a nuisance—a "bug" in an experimental design rather than a "feature," especially if one does not have a theory to say anything about them. Nevertheless, when outcomes are systematically influenced by process variables, these empirical regularities would challenge existing equilibrium theories and invite new developments in theory.

To this end, we focus on predicting which bargaining trials will result in deals and strikes, using a penalized regression approach from machine learning to select predictive process features. Over-fitting is controlled by making out of sample, cross-validated predictions. We find that a machine learning predictive model based only on process features predicts strikes roughly as accurately as the pie sizes can while combining both process and pie size makes even better predictions.

Since practical negotiation advice often consists of simple heuristics, process data could also be very useful to carefully test them experimentally [38]. In particular, initial offers have long been postulated to serve as bargaining anchors, and perspective taking, as well as various other psychological manipulations could potentially bias bargaining outcomes [1, 20, 30, 32, 50]. However, Jeong et al. [27] show that making first offers in a "warm and friendly" communication style surprisingly leads to less favorable outcomes in buyer-seller bargaining, while Weir et al. [53] find a null result priming distributive and integrative language in the context of dam maintenance and wildlife preservation.

In this paper, we replicate Camerer et al. [8] whose design has its closest precursor in Forsythe, Kennan, and Sopher (henceforth FKS), as both studied unstructured bargaining with one-sided private information about the sizes of several possible pies [15]. With two possible pie sizes, FKS apply the revelation principle [34, 35] to identify a "strike condition" predicting when disagreements would be ex-ante efficient. They then experimentally verify (qualitatively) their theory with free-form communication. Camerer et al. [8] generalize the FKS model to allow for any finite number of pie sizes, resulting in equilibria which maximize efficiency or equality that create different predictions. Therefore, unlike FKS, their experimental design has 6 different pie sizes and record 10 seconds per trial of visible offers and counter-offers with little restrictions. This dynamic strategic environment with information asymmetry extends the recent literature on free form bargaining with full information [19, 23].

Our main finding, using National Taiwan University subjects and some small design changes, is a close replication of earlier results using US subjects in California. Agreements are often equal splits, even though the exact pie size is only known to one side. Deal rates do increase with pie size, but there is a lot of inefficiency—deal rates are too low—compared to revelation principle predictions. However, theory also predicts a break for uninformed offers for pies of \$4–6 compared to lower pie amounts, and this break is evident in the data. There are some experience effects (deal rates go up across trials in an experimental session). One session with twice-experienced subjects—repeating the entire experimental session—did not produce results much closer to equilibrium (to our surprise). There are also modest effects of gender. When females are informed, the deal rate is a bit higher and uninformed (males) get a little less, but the evidence is not statistically strong.

The reminder of this paper is organized as follows. In Sect. 19.2.1, we summarize qualitative properties of bargaining in equilibrium derived from mechanism design theory. The experimental design we replicate is presented in Sect. 19.2.2, and its general results summarized in Sect. 19.3.1. We replicate the machine learning results in Section 19.3.2. Finally, Sect. 19.4 points to possible new directions of future research.

19.2 Theory and Experiments

In this paper, we adopt the theoretical framework from Camerer et al. [8] to generate comparative statics predictions regarding the frequency of disagreements in each state with only the game structure, incentive compatibility (IC), and individual rationality (IR) constraints. Since the mechanism design approach only characterizes the class of possible equilibria rather than predicts specific outcomes, Camerer et al. [8] further take advantage of the focal points in this game to obtain testable predictions about both deal rates and payoffs in each state.

19.2.1 Theoretical Framework

In this unstructured bargaining game, two players bargain over an economic surplus or "pie," which is a random variable denoted by π. The finite set of true states indexed by $k \in \{1, 2, \ldots, K\}$, and the pie amount in state k is π_k. Without loss of generality, we assume $\pi_k > \pi_j$

when $k > j$. The informed player knows the true pie amount. The uninformed player does not know the pie amount, but knows the informed player knows it. The probability distribution over pie sizes $\Pr(\pi_k) = p_k$ is common knowledge. The payoff of the uninformed player is w, and is bargained over by the players continuously communicating their bids within a certain amount of time T—which is also common knowledge. If the players agree on w, then the informed player gets the rest of the pie $\pi - w$. If they do not agree on an allocation before the deadline, both players get nothing and we refer to this outcome as a disagreement, or in keeping with the motivation of Forsythe et al. [15], as a *strike*, while successful bargaining outcomes are *deals*.

From a mechanism design perspective, we can view this bargaining game as a process of transmitting private information regarding pie size from the informed player to the uninformed player. By the revelation principle [34, 35], we know that every Nash equilibrium in this bargaining game can be implemented in an incentive compatible direct mechanism where the informed player truthfully reports the actual state to a neutral mediator and the player's payoffs are equal to their payoffs in the original bargaining game.

Following Forsythe et al. [15] and Camerer et al. [8], in the direct mechanism the informed player announces that the state is $j \in \{1, \ldots, K\}$. Given the announcement, the neutral mediator determines the deal probability (γ_j) and the payoff to the uninformed player (x_j). The informed player gets the rest of the pie ($\gamma_j \pi_k - x_j$). Thus a mechanism involves $2K$ parameters, $\{\gamma_k, x_k\}_{k=1}^K$.

A mechanism is incentive compatible (IC) if it is optimal for players to reveal their private information. In our setting, this means that the informed player's expected payoff must be (weakly) maximized in the direct mechanism when she announces the true size of the pie. This requires

$$\gamma_k \pi_k - x_k \geq \gamma_j \pi_k - x_j, \quad \forall k \text{ and } \forall j \neq k. \tag{IC}$$

An IC-mechanism is individually rational (IR) when both players prefer to participate in it. Assuming the players' payoffs from not participating are zero, this means that for every state k the expected payoff to each player is positive, so that

$$\gamma_k \pi_k - x_k \geq 0, \qquad \text{(IR} - 1)$$
$$x_k \geq 0. \qquad \text{(IR} - 2)$$

A direct mechanism is interim-efficient if the payoff profile is Pareto-optimal for the informed player in each of the K possible states and the uninformed player (in expectation) [24].

Based on the IC, IR-1, and IR-2 conditions, Camerer et al. [8] prove the following two lemmas regarding bargaining outcomes and interim-efficient strikes.

Lemma 1 If the bargaining mechanism satisfies the IC, IR-1, and IR-2 conditions, then:

1. Deal rates are monotonically increasing in the pie size x_k.
2. The uninformed player's payoffs are monotonically increasing in the pie size.
3. The uninformed player's payoff is identical for all states in which the deal probability is 1.

Lemma 2 For any mechanism that satisfies the IR-1, IR-2, and IC conditions, strikes in state k are interim-efficient if

$$\frac{\pi_k}{\pi_{k+1}} < \frac{\left(1 - \sum_{j=1}^{k} p_j\right)}{\left(1 - \sum_{j=1}^{k-1} p_j\right)} = \frac{\Pr(\pi \geq \pi_{k+1})}{\Pr(\pi \geq \pi_k)}.$$

Note that $x_k = \gamma_k w_k$, where w_k is the uninformed player's payoff conditional on a deal being made in state k.

The IC, IR-1, IR-2, and strike conditions limit the scope of possible bargaining outcomes and predict when strikes are likely to occur. However, they are not sufficient to pin down the strike rates $1 - \gamma_k$ and the equilibrium payoffs w_k in each state. To make a more precise prediction, Camerer et al. [8] use an equilibrium selection approach which assumes that equal payoff splits are natural focal points. In the experiments, the possible states, π, take on values that are the integer dollar amounts between \$1 and \$6 with equal probability. Therefore, we can restrict the state space to $\{\$1, \ldots, 6\}$.

Absent other salient features of bargaining, the natural focal point is an equal split (i.e., $w_k = \frac{\pi_k}{2}$). Indeed, equal splits often emerge in bargaining experiments (e.g. [31]). Based on players' tendency to coordinate on the equal split allocation, Camerer et al. [8] propose that the equilibrium payoff of the uninformed player, conditional on a deal, will equal half of the pie size ($w_k = \frac{\pi_k}{2}$) as long as an equal split satisfies the IR and IC conditions (Lemma 1), and is subject to the efficiency conditions. By either prioritizing the former or the latter, Camerer et al. [8] derive two competing equilibrium predictions, which are **the efficient equilibrium**:

$$
\begin{aligned}
(w_1, w_2, w_3, w_4, w_5, w_6) &= \left(\tfrac{1}{2}, 1, \tfrac{3}{2}, 2, 2, 2\right), \\
(\gamma_1, \gamma_2, \gamma_3, \gamma_4, \gamma_5, \gamma_6) &= \left(\tfrac{2}{5}, \tfrac{3}{5}, \tfrac{4}{5}, 1, 1, 1\right).
\end{aligned}
$$

and **the equal split equilibrium**:

$$
\begin{aligned}
(w_1, w_2, w_3, w_4, w_5, w_6) &= \left(\tfrac{1}{2}, 1, \tfrac{3}{2}, 2, \tfrac{5}{2}, 3\right), \\
(\gamma_1, \gamma_2, \gamma_3, \gamma_4, \gamma_5, \gamma_6) &= \left(\tfrac{2}{7}, \tfrac{3}{7}, \tfrac{4}{7}, \tfrac{5}{7}, \tfrac{6}{7}, 1\right).
\end{aligned}
$$

See Online Appendix C for details of the derivation.[2]

19.2.2 Experiments

Camerer et al. [8] developed a novel experimental paradigm of dynamic bargaining that allows both parties to communicate offers whenever they please, while keeping their behavior tractable. This experiment was first conducted by Camerer et al. [8] (Experiment 1), which is the

[2] The experimental data and online appendix can be found on Open Science Framework https://osf.io/9j4cm/.

baseline treatment. We also report results from a follow-up experiment with the same design but with different treatments (Experiment 2). In this section, we first introduce the experimental design and then the treatments.

19.2.2.1 Design

Our experiment is a continuous-time bargaining game with one-sided private information. At the beginning of the experiment, subjects are assigned to one of the two roles: the informed player or the uninformed player. Players' roles are fixed for the session's 120 bargaining rounds.

In each round, each informed player is randomly matched with an uninformed player to bargain over a pie with a size unknown to the uninformed player. The pie size is an integer from 1 to 6, i.e., $\pi \in \{\$1, 2, 3, 4, 5, 6\}$ and drawn from a commonly known discrete uniform distribution. The informed player would know the pie size for that round after the draw is made.

Each pair bargained over the uninformed player's payoff w. Both players communicate their offers, in multiples of \$0.1,[3] using a mouse click on a graphic interface which was programmed with z-Tree software [13]. Both players start with two seconds to decide their initial bargaining position without seeing the opponent's position (Fig. 19.1A). The initial cursor location is randomized.

After initial locations are set, the players enter a 10-second bargaining round. They communicate the offers with mouse clicks (Fig. 19.1B). As both players' positions match, a green vertical stripe appears on the screen (Fig. 19.1C), and this position becomes the final deal if there is no change on the position in the following 1.5 seconds (or if the period ends, which ever came first).[4] If no deal is reached within 10 seconds,

[3] Camerer et al. [8] (Experiment 1) set the resolution to be in multiples of \$0.2, since they thought \$0.1 was too fine a resolution for coordinating in a short game. However, the result in Experiment 1 shows that players are able to coordinate in such a short period, so we increase the resolution to be in multiples of \$0.1 in Experiment 2.

[4] In Experiment 1, the offers have to match for 1.5 seconds in order to make a deal. In other words, the latest time where the players' bids can match is $t = 8.5$ seconds.

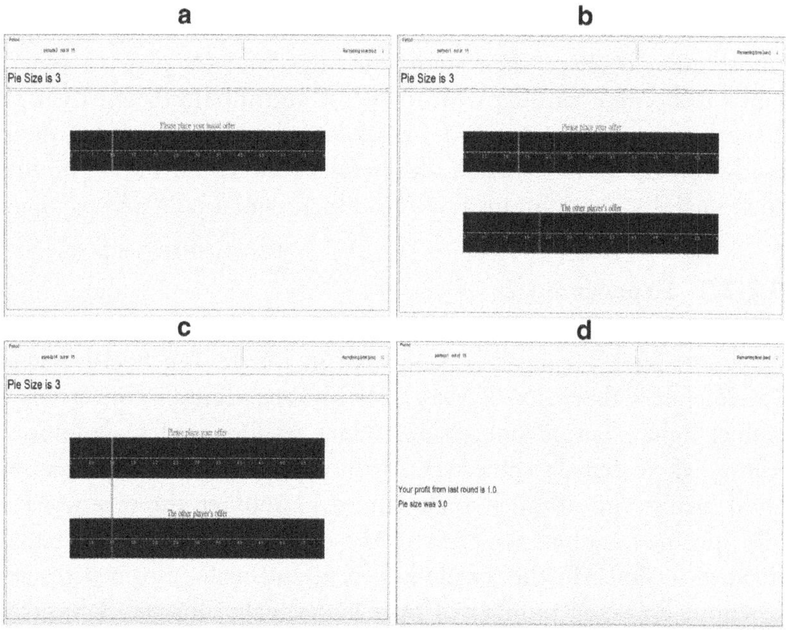

Fig. 19.1 (A) Initial offer screen: in the first two seconds of bargaining, both players can set their initial positions without revealing to the opponent. The pie size is on the top left corner and it only appears on informed player's screen. (B) Players communicate their offers using mouse click on the interface. (C) When two players' positions match, the green vertical stripe appears and this would be the deal if there is no change in the following 1.5 seconds. (D) After the bargaining round, both players would be notified about their payoffs and the pie size

both players earn nothing. After each round, the players are notified their payoffs and the actual pie size (Fig. 19.1D).

19.2.2.2 Experiment 1

Camerer et al. [8] conduct a total of eight experimental sessions in the Social Science Experimental Laboratory (SSEL) at Caltech and the California Social Science Experimental Laboratory (CASSEL) at UCLA. At the beginning of each session, subjects are randomly seated at isolated computer workstations and given printed versions of the instructions, which are also read aloud by the experimenter. All participants complete a short quiz to check their understanding. Subjects play 15 practice rounds to become familiar with the game and interface, and then play 120 real rounds. They are paid a randomly chosen 15% of the rounds, plus a show-up fee of $5. Each session lasts between 70 and 90 minutes, which includes check-in, instructions, experimental task, and payment.

19.2.2.3 Experiment 2

The follow-up experiment is conducted in the Taiwan Social Sciences Experimental Laboratory (TASSEL) at National Taiwan University. We conduct eight experimental sessions. Three sessions are female-informed sessions where female subjects take the role of informed players and played against uninformed male subjects. Another three sessions are male-informed sessions which have the opposite design to the female-informed sessions. In the female-informed and male-informed sessions, we require an equal number of male and female subjects. Subjects are only notified of this requirement when entering the experiment. In addition, we conduct one experienced session and one high-stake session in order to test whether our results are robust to experience and stakes. In the experienced session, we recruit subjects who have participated in one of the six previous sessions. In the high-stakes session, we multiply the stakes by 5. Notice that there is no gender constraint in the experienced and high-stake session.

The experimental procedures are the same in Experiment 1 and Experiment 2. In Experiment 2, participants' payoffs are based on their profits in a randomly chosen 10% of the rounds, plus a show-up fee of NT$ 100. Payoffs in the experiments are converted into NT$ according to a pre-set exchange rate (1 ECU = NT$15) specified in the instructions. In the high-stake session, the exchange rate is 1 ECU = NT$75 while the exchange rate is 1 ECU = NT$30 in the experienced session.

After 120 rounds of the bargaining game, we measure subjects' risk preferences and loss aversion by Dynamically Optimized Sequential Experimentation (DOSE) developed by Wang et al. [52]. In each round, subjects are asked to choose from 2 lotteries. Lottery 1 is a risky asset, while lottery 2 yields a fixed amount. There are 3 practice rounds and 40 paid rounds. At the end of the experiment, 12 rounds from the bargaining game and 1 round from DOSE would be drawn and realized. Before undergoing DOSE, all subjects evaluated their subjective willingness to take risk on a scale from 0 (not willing to take any risk at all) to 10 (willing to take any risk). The evaluation would not affect the payoff. Each session lasts around 2.5 hours.

19.3 Experimental Results

19.3.1 Basics

In this section, we focus on analyzing the deal rates across different treatments. See Camerer et al. [8] and Online Appendix A and B for further analysis on the payoffs and the bargaining dynamics.

Table 19.1 provides the summary statistics of average bargaining outcomes in different treatments. The average bargaining outcomes are similar across treatments. Differences in the average payoffs across treatments are less than \$0.1 and differences of average deal rates are within 5%. We highlight some of our findings in the following: The average surplus loss is the lowest in the experienced treatment and the highest in the male-informed treatment. Turning to the information value, which can be interpreted as the advantage of knowing the pie size, we observe that it is the largest in the experienced treatment and lowest in the baseline treatment. Bargaining outcomes are generally robust across different treatments and stakes on the aggregated level.

Next, we break down deal rates according to different pie sizes for different treatments. Figures 19.2 and 19.3 show that in all treatments, deal rates increase with the pie size. This confirms our theoretical prediction in Lemma 1. Moreover, deal rates in female-informed sessions and the experienced session are higher than the baseline sessions in all pies (except the largest pie). On the other hand, deal rates in male-informed sessions and the high-stake session are higher than the baseline in small pies ($\pi \leq 3$), but lower in large pies ($\pi \geq 4$).

Table 19.1 Summary statistics for different treatments

Treatment	Baseline	Female	Male	Experienced	High-Stake
Informed Payoff[a]	2.01	2.08	2.09	2.10	2.04
	(0.03)	(0.02)	(0.06)	–	–
Uninformed Payoff[a]	1.49	1.42	1.41	1.40	1.46
	(0.03)	(0.02)	(0.06)	–	–
Deal Rate	0.61	0.66	0.62	0.66	0.65
	(0.03)	(0.02)	(0.02)	–	–
Surplus Loss[b]	1.13	1.02	1.18	0.96	1.11
	(0.08)	(0.09)	(0.09)	–	–
Information Value[c]	0.40	0.51	0.49	0.54	0.42
	(0.03)	(0.05)	(0.06)	–	–

Means and standard errors (which are shown in parentheses) are calculated by treating each session's mean as a single observation. Since there is only one session for experienced and high-stake treatment, the standard errors for these two treatments are not computable.

[a] Averages are calculated for deal games only.

[b] Surplus loss = the mean expected loss of pie due to strikes.

[c] Information value = the mean difference between the informed and uninformed payoffs.

We defer further results from Experiment 2 to the Online Appendix. These results include analyses of the bargaining dynamics (see Online Appendix A) and testing predictions in Lemma 1 (see Online Appendix B). In general, the results in Camerer et al. [8] are replicated by Experiment 2. Besides the monotone increase of deal rates and payoffs, we also observe that the equal split allocation is the most salient focal point. Regarding the dynamics, we observe that the informed players' offers increase, and the uninformed players' demands decrease with time (within a trial). There is also a strong deadline effect—most of the deals are reached close to the deadline. Lastly, we analyze the differences in equilibrium selections using regression.

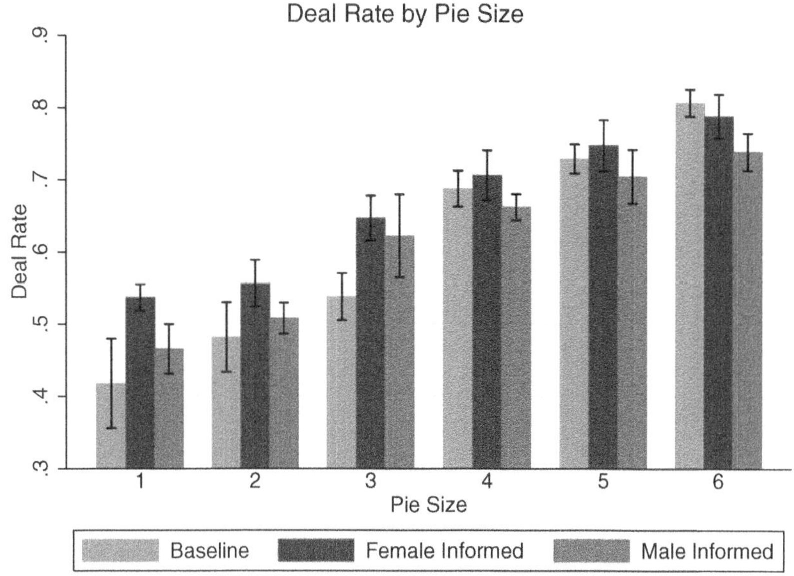

Fig. 19.2 The deal rates under different pie sizes and treatments. The green bars stand for the average deal rates of baseline sessions at different pie sizes. The blue and red bars are for female-informed sessions and male-informed sessions, respectively. The standard errors (overlaid on the bars) are calculated at the session level

19.3.2 Outcome Prediction via Machine Learning

The unstructured paradigm established by Camerer et al. [8] records a large amount of bargaining process data beyond initial demands and offers to predict disagreements before the deadline. Hence, we search for a small set of such features that is predictive, employing cross-validation [47] to control for over-fitting.

In this paper, we treat Experiment 2 as the lockbox test for the predictive model built in Camerer et al. [8]. Therefore, in this section we report the results from directly feeding the data from Experiment 2 into the model. First of all, we briefly introduce the algorithm here. We choose from the 35 behavioral features introduced by Camerer et al. [8]. Among them are the current difference between the offer and demand, the time since the last position change, and which player had changed his or

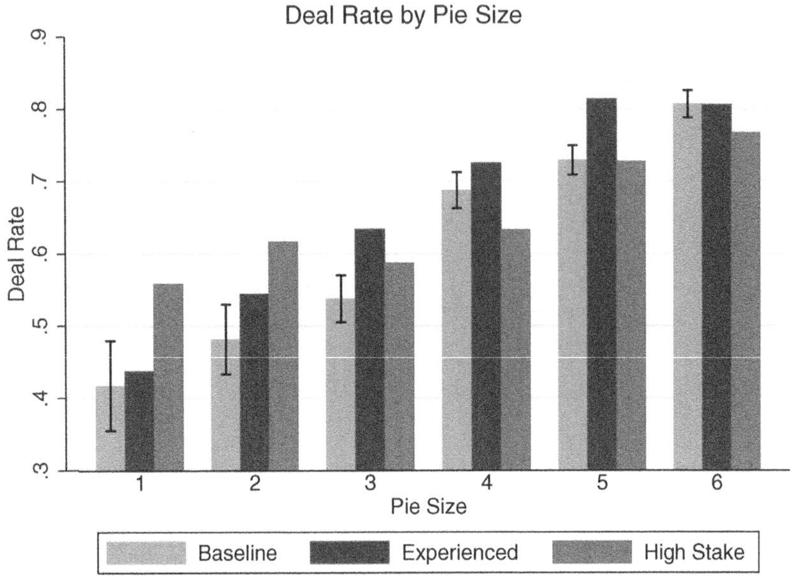

Fig. 19.3 The deal rates under different pie sizes and treatments. The green bars stand for the average deal rates of baseline sessions at different pie sizes. The blue and red bars are for the experienced sessions and high-stake sessions, respectively. The standard errors (overlaid on the bars) are calculated at the session level. Since there is only one session for experienced and high-stake treatment, the standard errors are not computable for these two treatments

her position in the game first. We compared three outcome prediction models at eight time points in the bargaining process (i.e., $1, 2, \ldots, 8$ seconds after bargaining starts). The first model relied only on the pie size, the second used only process features, and the third combined both. At each time point, we carried out the following nested cross-validation procedure: For each of the eight sessions in Experiment 2, we used the data of the remaining seven sessions to train our model. The model classifies trials into disagreements or deals by estimating a logistic regression with a least absolute shrinkage and selection operator (LASSO) penalty [48]. The tuning parameter, λ, is optimized via ten-fold cross-validation, performed within each training set. We then made out-of-sample outcome predictions (disagreement or deal) for the hold-out session.

To compare the three models, we use the "receiver operating characteristic" (ROC) curves [5, 21], standard in signal detection theory to quantify the performance of binary classifiers under various trade-offs between type I and type II errors. The 45-degree line in Fig. 19.4 indicates a random classifier whose true positive and false positive rates are identical. A better classifier has higher true positive rates (moving up on the y axis) and lower false positive rates (moving left on the x axis). The "area under the curve" (AUC), or difference between the ROC and the 45-degree line in the upper-left direction, is an index of how well the classifier does.

Figure 19.4 shows the ROC curve at $t = 2, 5, 7$ seconds for both Experiment 1 and 2. The ROC analysis indicates that process data do better than random at every time point in both experiments. Moreover, the fitness of models with process data increase with time, but the same is not true for the model with pie size only.

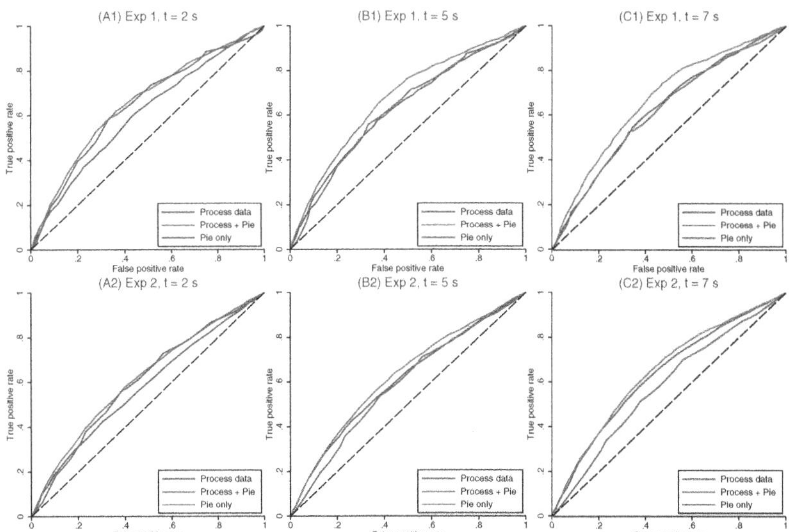

Fig. 19.4 Receiver operating characteristic (ROC) for predicting disagreements, two, five, and seven seconds into the bargaining game. The dashed lines represent the false and true positive rates of a random classifier. (A1-C1) show the data from Camerer et al. [8] (Experiment 1) and (A2-C2) plot the result from Experiment 2

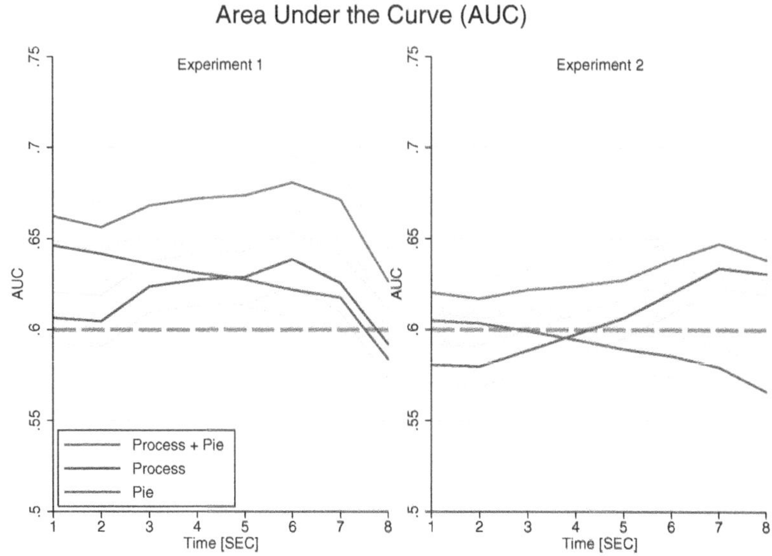

Fig. 19.5 Area under the curve (AUC) of disagreements classifiers using process data, pie size, and the two combined. Note that the classifier's input included only trials that were still in progress (when a deal has not yet been achieved), and excluded trials in which the offers and demand were equal at the relevant time stamp. The left figure is the original result from Camerer et al. [8] (Experiment 1) and the right one is the result from Experiment 2

While patterns of AUC are similar in Experiment 1 and 2, there are still some subtle differences. In Experiment 1, the model with pie and process features always has the best predictive power and the other two models are not so distinguishable in later seconds. On the other hand, even though the model with pie and process features is the best performing among the three, its predictive power is not significantly stronger than the model with process features only.

To further investigate which behavioral process features predict strikes, we follow Camerer et al. [8] and use a "post-LASSO" procedure proposed by Belloni et al. [3, 4]. Figure 19.6 summarizes the marginal effects of all process features (z-scored for every time point) in both experiments. The general feature patterns in Experiment 2 are consistent with those in Experiment 1. The current informed player's offer (positively correlated with a deal) and the current difference

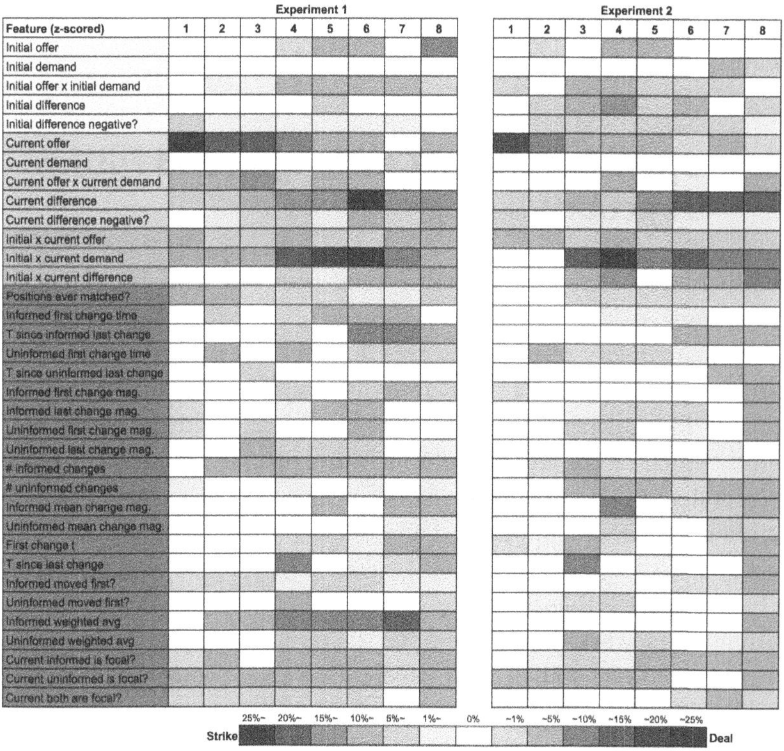

Fig. 19.6 Bargaining Process Features Selected by the Classifier for Outcome Prediction (Deal= 1) and Their Estimated Marginal Effects. The left panel is the result from Camerer et al. [8] (Experiment 1) and the right panel is the result from Experiment 2. The pie sizes are excluded

between the players' bargaining positions (positively correlated with a strike) are the most predictive process features. One surprising finding in Camerer et al. [8] is that initial bargaining positions contain predictive information regarding the possibility of reaching a deal, even as we approach the deadline, and even after controlling for current offers. In Experiment 2, such effect of initial positions is even stronger. We also find a negative interaction between initial offer and initial demand and a negative interaction between initial and current offer, which again confirms the arguments in Camerer et al. [8].[5]

19.4 Open Questions, Challenges, and Future Directions

Unstructured bargaining seems to hand over the reins of endogenous "treatments" to the experimental subjects. But if the goal is prediction rather than theory-testing, however, having a large amount of data is terrific. For machine learning applications, there is (almost) no such thing as too much data. Instead, the challenge lies in interpreting the results, which can be ad hoc and sometimes opaque. Besides, our replication results indicate that even a lot of process data in a highly controlled setting results in only modest AUC values, so there is still much room to improve.

Furthermore, theory-testing can still be done in a machine learning framework. In our example, the revelation principle, along with other restrictions, still delivers predictions about what will happen in equilibrium which are highly independent of the unstructured behavior. Everything depends on pie sizes. A lean predictive "machine" using only pie sizes therefore predicts comparably with one using many process features. One interesting question future studies should explore is whether alternative process models could predict significantly better, since our combined model improves only modestly beyond using only pie size.

Thirdly, Experiment 2 shows a modest effects of gender. While gender effects in bargaining are interesting, a lot more statistical power is probably needed. In fact, gender differences are likely to vary wildly across the globe, so a serious attempt to understand such differences must look at the influences of developmental life cycle, biological factors such as hormones, and cultural variation.

---

[5] However, not all effects are transparent; some even reverse across time (initial x current offer in Experiment 2).

We hope these data and methods inspire other experimenters from a range of social sciences to measure a lot more about what goes in the bargainers' bodies and brains, and results from their typing or talking, on during bargaining. For example, Forsythe et al. [14] allowed subjects to transmit verbal messages during bargaining. At the time, methods of analyzing natural language processing (NLP) were so primitive that they did not do any sophisticated analysis of those rich data. While they allowed messages and recorded them, they did not analyze them at all because they deemed the resulting game—treating messages as strategy choices—too complicated to solve. Using the messages as data in machine learning does not test a theory either, but it provides preliminary evidence of how features of messages influence agreement rates. Such evidence could provide inspiration for theory. For example, Jeong et al. [27] use NLP to analyze first offer messages to identify "warm and friendly" communications.

It is also notable that recording messages is very easy technically. NLP is one area of machine learning which is now hugely successful and improving by leaps and bounds every year. In general, machine learning methods are hungry for any such choice process data. And now we know what to do with them.

Appendix

The online appendix is available at https://osf.io/9j4cm/.

References

1. Daniel R Ames and Malia F Mason. Tandem anchoring: Informational and politeness effects of range offers in social exchange. *Journal of Personality and Social Psychology*, 108(2):254, 2015.
2. Lawrence M Ausubel, Peter Cramton, and Raymond J Deneckere. Bargaining with incomplete information. *Handbook of Game Theory with Economic Applications*, 3:1897–1945, 2002.

3. Alexandre Belloni, Daniel Chen, Victor Chernozhukov, and Christian Hansen. Sparse models and methods for optimal instruments with an application to eminent domain. *Econometrica*, 80(6):2369–2429, 2012.
4. Alexandre Belloni, Victor Chernozhukov, et al. Least squares after model selection in high-dimensional sparse models. *Bernoulli*, 19(2):521–547, 2013.
5. Andrew P Bradley. The use of the area under the roc curve in the evaluation of machine learning algorithms. *Pattern Recognition*, 30(7):1145–1159, 1997.
6. Hongbin Cai and Joseph Tao-Yi Wang. Overcommunication in strategic information transmission games. *Games and Economic Behavior*, 56(1):7–36, 2006.
7. Colin F Camerer. *Behavioral Game Theory: Experiments in Strategic Interaction*. The Roundtable Series in Behavioral Economics. Princeton University Press, 2003. ISBN 9780691090399.
8. Colin F Camerer, Gideon Nave, and Alec Smith. Dynamic unstructured bargaining with private information: theory, experiment, and outcome prediction via machine learning. *Management Science*, 65(4):1867–1890, 2019.
9. C Mónica Capra. Understanding decision processes in guessing games: A protocol analysis approach. *Journal of the Economic Science Association*, 5(1):123–135, Aug 2019. ISSN 2199-6784.
10. Vincent P Crawford. Lying for strategic advantage: Rational and boundedly rational misrepresentation of intentions. *American Economic Review*, 93(1):133–149, 2003.
11. Jacques Crémer and Richard P McLean. Optimal selling strategies under uncertainty for a discriminating monopolist when demands are interdependent. *Econometrica*, 53:345–361, 1985.
12. Jacques Crémer and Richard P McLean. Full extraction of the surplus in bayesian and dominant strategy auctions. *Econometrica*, 56(6):1247–1257, 1988.
13. Urs Fischbacher. z-tree: Zurich toolbox for ready-made economic experiments. *Experimental Economics*, 10(2):171–178, 2007.
14. Robert Forsythe, John Kennan, and Barry Sopher. Dividing a shrinking pie: an experimental study of strikes in bargaining games with complete information. *Research in Experimental Economics*, 4:223–268, 1991a.
15. Robert Forsythe, John Kennan, and Barry Sopher. An experimental analysis of strikes in bargaining games with one-sided private information. *American Economic Review*, 81(1):253–278, 1991b.

16. Daniel Friedman and Ryan Oprea. A continuous dilemma. *American Economic Review*, 102(1):337–363, 2012.
17. William Fuchs and Andrzej Skrzypacz. Bargaining with deadlines and private information. *American Economic Journal: Microeconomics*, 5(4):219–243, 2013.
18. Simon Gächter and Arno Riedl. Moral property rights in bargaining with infeasible claims. *Management Science*, 51(2):249–263, 2005.
19. Fabio Galeotti, Maria Montero, and Anders Poulsen. Efficiency versus equality in bargaining. *Journal of the European Economic Association*, 17(6):1941–1970, 2018.
20. Adam D Galinsky and Thomas Mussweiler. First offers as anchors: The role of perspective-taking and negotiator focus. *Journal of Personality and Social Psychology*, 81(4):657, 2001.
21. James A Hanley and Barbara J McNeil. The meaning and use of the area under a receiver operating characteristic (roc) curve. *Radiology*, 143(1):29–36, 1982.
22. Shaun Hargreaves Heap, David Rojo Arjona, and Robert Sugden. How portable is level-0 behavior? a test of level-k theory in games with non-neutral frames. *Econometrica*, 82(3):1133–1151, 2014.
23. Dorothea K Herreiner and Clemens Puppe. Equitable allocations in experimental bargaining games: Inequality a version versus efficiency. Technical report, Bonn econ discussion papers, 2004.
24. Bengt Holmström and Roger B Myerson. Efficient and durable decision rules with incomplete information. *Econometrica*, 51(6):1799–1819, 1983.
25. Andrea Isoni, Anders Poulsen, Robert Sugden, and Kei Tsutsui. Focal points in tacit bargaining problems: Experimental evidence. *European Economic Review*, 59:167–188, 2013.
26. Andrea Isoni, Anders Poulsen, Robert Sugden, and Kei Tsutsui. Efficiency, equality, and labeling: An experimental investigation of focal points in explicit bargaining. *American Economic Review*, 104(10):3256–3587, 2014.
27. Martha Jeong, Julia Minson, Michael Yeomans, and Francesca Gino. Communicating with warmth in distributive negotiations is surprisingly counterproductive. *Management Science*, 65(12):5813–5837, 2019.
28. Ehud Kalai, Meir Smorodinsky, et al. Other solutions to nash's bargaining problem. *Econometrica*, 43(3):513–518, 1975.
29. Emin Karagözoğlu. On "going unstructured" in bargaining experiments. In Jean-François Laslier, Hervé Moulin, M. Remzi Sanver, and William S.

Zwicker, editors, *The future of economic design: The continuing development of a field as envisioned by its researchers*, pages 295–304. Springer International Publishing, Cham, 2019. ISBN 978-3-030-18050-8.
30. Henrik Kristensen and Tommy Gärling. The effects of anchor points and reference points on negotiation process and outcome. *Organizational Behavior and Human Decision Processes*, 71(1):85–94, 1997.
31. Po-Hsuan Lin, Alexander L Brown, Taisuke Imai, Joseph Tao-yi Wang, Stephanie W Wang, and Colin F Camerer. Evidence of general economic principles of bargaining and trade from 2,000 classroom experiments. *Nature Human Behaviour*, 4(9):917–927, 2020.
32. Malia F Mason, Alice J Lee, Elizabeth A Wiley, and Daniel R Ames. Precise offers are potent anchors: Conciliatory counteroffers and attributions of knowledge in negotiations. *Journal of Experimental Social Psychology*, 49(4):759–763, 2013.
33. R Preston McAfee and Philip J Reny. Correlated information and mecanism design. *Econometrica*, 60(2):395–421, 1992.
34. Roger B Myerson. Incentive compatibility and the bargaining problem. *Econometrica*, 47(1):61–73, 1979.
35. Roger B Myerson. Two-person bargaining problems with incomplete information. *Econometrica*, 52(2):461–487, 1984.
36. John F Nash Jr. The bargaining problem. *Econometrica*, 18(2):155–162, 1950.
37. Rudy V Nydegger and Guillermo Owen. Two-person bargaining: An experimental test of the nash axioms. *International Journal of Game Theory*, 3(4):239–249, 1974.
38. Dean G Pruitt. *Negotiation behavior*. Academic Press, 2013.
39. Alvin E Roth. Toward a focal point theory of bargaining. *Game-Theoretic Models of Bargaining*, 259:265–267, 1985.
40. Alvin E Roth and Michael W Malouf. Game-theoretic models and the role of information in bargaining. *Psychological Review*, 86(6):574, 1979.
41. Alvin E Roth, Michael WK Malouf, and J Keith Murnighan. Sociological versus strategic factors in bargaining. *Journal of Economic Behavior & Organization*, 2(2):153–177, 1981.
42. Alvin E Roth and J Keith Murnighan. The role of information in bargaining: An experimental study. *Econometrica*, 50(5):1123–1142, 1982.
43. Alvin E Roth, J Keith Murnighan, and Françoise Schoumaker. The deadline effect in bargaining: Some experimental evidence. *American Economic Review*, 78(4):806–823, 1988.

44. Ariel Rubinstein. Perfect equilibrium in a bargaining model. *Econometrica*, 50(1):97–109, 1982.
45. Thomas Schelling. The strategy of conflict. Cambridge: Harvard University Press, 1960.
46. Ingolf Ståhl. Bargaining theory. PhD diss., Economic Research Institute at the Stockholm School of Economics (EFI), 1972.
47. Mervyn Stone. Cross-validatory choice and assessment of statistical predictions. *Journal of the Royal Statistical Society: Series B (Methodological)*, 36(2):111–133, 1974.
48. Robert Tibshirani. Regression shrinkage and selection via the lasso. *Journal of the Royal Statistical Society: Series B (Methodological)*, 58(1):267–288, 1996.
49. Kathleen Valley, Leigh Thompson, Robert Gibbons, and Max H Bazerman. How communication improves efficiency in bargaining games. *Games and Economic Behavior*, 38(1):127–155, 2002.
50. Dirk Van Poucke and Marc Buelens. Predicting the outcome of a two-party price negotiation: Contribution of reservation price, aspiration price and opening offer. *Journal of Economic Psychology*, 23(1):67–76, 2002.
51. Joseph Tao-yi Wang, Michael Spezio, and Colin F Camerer. Pinocchio's pupil: using eyetracking and pupil dilation to understand truth telling and deception in sender-receiver games. *American Economic Review*, 100(3):984–1007, 2010.
52. Stephanie W Wang, Jonathan Chapman, Erik Snowberg, and Colin F Camerer. Loss attitudes in the U.S. population: Evidence from dynamically optimized sequential experimentation (dose). *mimeo*, 2018.
53. Michael J Weir, Catherine M Ashcraft, Natallia Leuchanka Diessner, Bridie McGreavy, Emily Vogler, and Todd Guilfoos. Language effects on bargaining. *PLOS ONE*, 15(3):1–20, 03 2020.

20

Emotions in Bargaining

Gert-Jan Lelieveld and Eric van Dijk

Negotiations are often heated and highly emotional. This may be attributed to the fact that negotiations are mixed-motive situations, in which negotiators can be in competition with each other for certain resources, but at the same time need to cooperate to get to an agreement (Komorita & Parks, 1995). The tension between competition and cooperation elicits a wide variety of emotional experiences and emotional expressions. For example, when negotiating a new contract, employees may feel angry after being offered a poor deal, but also disappointed. Or, when negotiations are going well, they may feel happy or relieved. These emotions may affect their standing in the negotiation, but when communicated, also affect their negotiation partner. How emotions

G.-J. Lelieveld (✉) · E. van Dijk
Leiden University, Leiden, The Netherlands
e-mail: lelieveldgj@fsw.leidenuniv.nl

E. van Dijk
e-mail: dijk@fsw.leidenuniv.nl

E. Karagözoğlu and K. B. Hyndman (eds.), *Bargaining*,
https://doi.org/10.1007/978-3-030-76666-5_20

affect negotiations becomes even more complicated if one realizes that negotiators may try to regulate their emotions, or even misrepresent their emotions. Emotions that negotiators experience or express may lead negotiations to become more competitive or cooperative, depending on the interests that lie at the heart of the negotiation (Van Kleef & Côté, 2018). Insight into the dynamics of emotions is therefore critical to understand the trajectory of negotiations and to discover ways to make negotiations more successful.

In this chapter, we provide an overview of research on how emotions shape negotiations. Before doing so, however, it is important to discuss what we mean by emotions. Most theorists agree that emotions are the result of an evaluation of some event relevant to a particular concern or goal. Emotions differ from moods in that they are always about something, whereas moods "simply are" (Frijda, 1994). Emotions are directed toward a specific person, object, or event—people can feel happy after receiving a high offer, or angry at their opponent for withdrawing from the negotiation. Moods are less specific and not necessarily directed at anything. Furthermore, emotions are characterized by distinct subjective experiences, physiological reactions, and action tendencies (Ekman, 1993). Discrete emotions are therefore often more informative than diffuse moods, both to the individual experiencing them and to observers. Most of the empirical studies described in the current chapter discuss the effects of discrete emotions like anger, happiness, disappointment, and sadness, but some involve more diffuse positive and negative moods.

It is also useful to distinguish between integral emotions and incidental emotions (Loewenstein & Lerner, 2003). *Integral* emotions arise during the social interaction of interest and are relevant to the present judgments and/or decisions. For example, bargainers may experience increased levels of anger after receiving a low offer from their opponent. *Incidental* emotions can be considered spillovers from other situations which should be irrelevant to the present judgments and/or decisions. Bargainers may for example feel happy because someone else treated them nicely, which can make them act more cooperatively during the negotiation. In this review, we will discuss both types of emotions. We, for instance, describe studies on the effects of expressing (integral) anger over other's negotiation offers, but also the effects of (incidental) anxiety elicited by watching a movie prior.

Having defined the key concepts, we will now provide an overview of theory and research on the effects of emotions in bargaining. Section 20.1 focuses on how the experience of one's own emotions influences the bargaining process (i.e., intrapersonal effects). Section 20.2 reviews how emotional expressions influence the other party in negotiations (i.e., interpersonal effects). In Section 20.3 we focus on how emotions influence deceptive strategies in negotiations and how negotiators use their emotions to deceive their opponents. We conclude with suggestions for future research and a brief discussion of the practical implications.

20.1 The intrapersonal effects of emotions in bargaining

Intrapersonal effects of emotions describe how the experience of emotions affects one's own feelings, cognitions, and/or behavior. In negotiations, this involves how the experience of anger affects one's own concessions or how the experience of happiness influences one's own cooperativeness.

20.1.1 Relevant theories

One of the main theoretical models for intrapersonal effects of emotions is the mood-as-information model (also referred to as affect-as-information or feelings-as-information model; Schwarz & Clore, 1983). This model posits that people attend to their moods as a source of information, with different moods providing different types of information. For instance, an individual's liking for a person is partly based on the positive feelings when this person is around. The impact of feelings as a source of information increases when they are perceived to be relevant to the task at hand. Relevance is a broad concept, however, as misattribution may make even nonrelated information seem relevant. For example, applied to the negotiation context, the mood-as-information model would posit that incidental moods can influence the negotiation process, if people misattribute their mood to the negotiation process or negotiation partner.

The mood-as-information model focuses on general feelings and mood states and bases its predictions on the valence of affect (i.e., whether the mood or emotion is positive or negative). Such valence-based approaches cannot explain why different emotions with the same valence (e.g., anger and disappointment) may influence judgments and decisions differently. The appraisal-tendency framework (Lerner & Keltner, 2000) does allow for such effects. The framework distinguishes between a set of different appraisal dimensions like certainty, pleasantness, and control and posits that each emotion can be defined by a combination of these dimensions. Under this framework, any emotion, whether it is an incidental or integral emotion, can influence the negotiation, and each specific emotion has its own unique effect on the negotiation. The negative emotion anger may for instance affect the negotiation process differently than other negative emotions, like disappointment. This way, the framework can make more specific predictions about how emotions influence negotiations.

20.1.2 Empirical work

General affect. In line with the mood-as-information model, the early studies on intrapersonal emotion effects in negotiations focused mostly on general affect. Carnevale and Isen (1986) studied the influence of positive affect on negotiation strategies and outcomes. Prior to a negotiation (incidental) positive affect was induced in some participants by having them sort cartoons into a funny pile and a not as funny pile, and by giving them a gift. Results showed that positive affect increased the joint outcomes in the negotiation and reduced the use of contentious tactics. Anderson and Thompson (2004) also studied the intrapersonal effects of positive affect, by measuring negotiators' trait positive affect with the Positive And Negative Affect Schedule (PANAS; Watson, Clark, & Tellegen, 1988). Positive affect increased trust and facilitated joint gains, but more so for powerful negotiators than for less powerful negotiators. These studies thus demonstrate that positive affect increases cooperation in negotiations.

Baron et al. (1990) focused on the intrapersonal effects of negative affect. Participants first interacted with a confederate who expressed disagreement in a calm and non-provocative way or in an arrogant and provoking way. Subsequently, they engaged in a negotiation task with the confederate. Participants who were provoked made lower initial offers in the negotiation than those who had not been provoked. Interestingly, when participants were exposed to one of several treatments designed to induce positive affect (e.g., mild flattery or a small gift) this increased participants' preference for cooperation.

The findings above suggest that positive affect increases negotiators' willingness to cooperate while negative affect decreases cooperation. A later study that directly compared positive to negative affect supported this conclusion. Forgas (1998) manipulated affect using false feedback on a test of verbal abilities. Participants either learned that they performed well on the test or not. Participants in a positive mood (who received positive feedback) used more cooperative and integrative negotiation strategies than those in a neutral (who received no feedback) or negative mood (who received negative feedback).

Discrete emotions. In line with the appraisal-tendency framework, several studies have studied the effects of the experience of discrete emotions. Pillutla and Murnighan (1996) studied the effects of experienced anger in ultimatum bargaining. They showed that the reception of small and unfair offers evoked integral anger which, in turn, led participants to reject these unfair offers. Anger thus reduced cooperation. Follow-up research indicated that these detrimental effects are attenuated if bargainers can regulate their anger via reappraisal or distraction (Fabiansson & Denson, 2012), or by formulating an if-then plan about how to negotiate (Jäger, Loschelder, & Friese, 2017).

Allred et al. (1997) compared the intrapersonal effects of anger to the effects of compassion. In a job contract negotiation task, participants either learned that their opponent was responsible for behavior that affected them negatively (which induced anger) or that their opponent had no choice (which induced compassion). Angry participants (compared to compassionate ones) had less desire to work with their opponent in the future and achieved lower joint outcomes.

Other negative emotions have also been studied. Brooks and Schweitzer (2011) showed that incidental anxiety—induced by music and movie clips—harms negotiator behavior, such that it induces negotiators to expect lower outcomes, make lower first offers, exit the negotiation earlier, and as a result also obtain worse outcomes. They also found that these negative effects were less pronounced for individuals with high negotiator self-efficacy (i.e., those having the belief that they could succeed in the negotiation).

Ketelaar and Au (2003) investigated the effects of experienced guilt. They reasoned that the experience of guilt signals a blameworthy violation of a social norm, which may motivate people to increase their level of cooperation. Guilt was induced by asking participants to write about an experience where they felt guilty (i.e., inducing incidental guilt), or letting them rate their feelings of (integral) guilt after making an initial offer in an ultimatum bargaining context. The results showed that guilt led to more generous offers. These effects were later replicated in the context of divorce negotiations (Wietzker, Buysse, Loeys, & Brondeel, 2011).

In the domain of positive emotions, Shirako, Kilduff, and Kray (2015) studied the effects of sympathy in negotiations. Across five studies, negotiators responded to an opponent who was in a potentially vulnerable position (e.g., he/she had been working 18 hours per day for 5 years). The results showed that experiencing sympathy decreased value claiming and increased integrative bargaining.

Finally, Butt, Choi, and Jaeger (2005) compared the effects of four different types of emotion in a negotiation task that resembled the job contract negotiation used by Allred et al. (1997). Participants engaged in two negotiation sessions. After completing the first session, they received feedback about their performance. This feedback was designed to manipulate one of four emotions: pride (i.e., success due to self), gratitude (i.e., success due to counterpart), shame (i.e., failure due to self), or anger (i.e., failure due to counterpart). The results showed that whereas gratitude increased yielding behavior and joint gain, pride decreased yielding behavior and joint gain. Of the two negative emotions, anger, but not shame, led negotiators to take a more competitive and dominant stance.

20.2 The interpersonal effects of emotions in bargaining

Interpersonal effects of emotions refer to the influence of an individual's emotions on the feelings, cognitions, and/or behavior of others. In negotiations, one's anger may for instance inform observers how high one's subsequent offer will be or may elicit certain emotions in observers.

20.2.1 Relevant theory

Insights on the interpersonal effects of emotions highlight the social functions of emotional expressions. According to social-functional approaches of emotions (Keltner & Haidt, 1999; Van Kleef, De Dreu, & Manstead, 2010), emotions contain valuable information about the feelings and intentions of the sender. The Emotion as Social Information (EASI) model by Van Kleef et al. (2010) specifies two processes through which emotions may influence the behavior of others. Emotions affect others by providing relevant information about the intentions and/or feelings of the sender (the inferential path of the model), but also by affecting the emotions of others (the affective path of the model).

The inferential path rests on the notion that expressed emotions have informational value. Happiness, for instance, may signal that one is satisfied with the current situation, which may lead others to continue their current course of action. Sadness on the other hand signals a loss, which may lead others to offer help.

Emotional expressions may also elicit affective reactions in others, which can influence subsequent behavior. One way emotions can affect the emotions of others, is via emotional contagion (Hatfield, Cacioppo, & Rapson, 1994), where emotions spread from expresser to observer. A person's happiness, for instance, can be "caught", which leads others to become happy themselves. Emotions can also influence others by eliciting complementary emotions in them, which may influence subsequent behavior. Displays of anger, for instance, can elicit fear-related responses.

Whether inferential processes or affective reactions take precedence has been shown to depend on two factors (Van Kleef et al., 2010). One important factor is the observer's motivation and ability to process the information conveyed by the emotional expression. The more thorough the information processing, the stronger the predictive value of inferential processes; the shallower the information processing, the stronger the predictive value of affective processes.

The predictive strength of inferential versus affective reactions also depends on social-contextual factors that influence the perceived appropriateness of the emotional expression. When an emotional expression is perceived to be appropriate, the predictive value of inferential processes is stronger; when emotional expressions are perceived to be inappropriate, the predictive value of affective processes is stronger.

20.2.2 Empirical work

While the work on the interpersonal effects could be applied to general affect as well, most studies have concentrated on discrete emotions, which may be explained by the fact that others' discrete emotions have more informational value to negotiators.

Anger versus happiness. One of the first studies on the interpersonal effects of emotions in negotiations was conducted by Van Kleef, De Dreu, and Manstead (2004a), which focused on the emotional expressions of anger and happiness. Participants engaged with (simulated) opponents in a computer-mediated integrative negotiation task over a consignment of mobile phones. Over the course of six rounds, participants either received angry, happy, or neutral expressions. Negotiators with a happy opponent inferred that their opponent was lenient and easy to please. This led participants to make only minor concessions. Angry emotional expressions, however, signaled high limits, leading negotiators to conclude they were dealing with a tough opponent (see also Sinaceur & Tiedens, 2006). This led opponents to give in themselves, to not let the negotiation end in impasse. This study thus showed that it is better to express anger than to express happiness in a negotiation.

Research has, however, also documented detrimental effects of communicating anger in negotiations. The aforementioned study by Van Kleef et al. (2004a), showed that bargainers develop a more negative impression of an opponent who expresses anger in the negotiation. Also, negotiators dealing with angry opponents are less satisfied with the negotiation and are less willing to engage in future interaction (Van Kleef, De Dreu, & Manstead, 2004b). Moreover, negotiators with angry counterparts are more likely to exit the negotiation and choose an impasse because they consider their opponents to be selfish (Yip & Scheinsberg, 2017). In the context of coalition formation, negotiators form negative impressions of those who communicate anger, and are more likely to exclude them from coalitions and from obtaining a share of the payoff (Van Beest, Van Kleef, & Van Dijk, 2008).

These results suggest that expressions of anger may be dependent on specific moderators. In the following, we first discuss moderators that are related to the ability and motivation to process the information conveyed by the angry expression and then moderators related to the appropriateness of the angry expression.

Information processing as moderator of angry expressions. In line with the EASI model, Van Kleef et al. (2004b) identified the ability and/or motivation to process the information as a moderator. In a negotiation setting, they manipulated how much time participants had to reach an agreement and showed that participants with an angry opponent made more concessions than did those with a happy opponent, but only under low rather than high time pressure.

Several other personal and situational factors have been shown to moderate the effects of anger by influencing negotiators' information processing. Two of those factors are the competitiveness of the negotiation and relative power differences. Adam and Brett (2015) compared the effects of angry expressions in negotiations that balance cooperative and competitive elements to those in negotiations that are predominantly cooperative or predominantly competitive. They reasoned that balanced negotiations provide a more uncertain and ambiguous situation that induces negotiators to engage in systematic information processing and rely on diagnostic informational cues. In agreement with this, expressing anger elicited larger concessions than expressing no emotion, but only in balanced negotiations, and not in predominantly cooperative or competitive situations.

Relative power differences also influence information processing. Low-power negotiators may generally be more motivated to process the information conveyed by emotional expressions than high-power negotiators (Fiske, 1993). Using various operationalizations of power (e.g., the number of available alternatives), Van Kleef et al. (2006b) found that low-power negotiators were strongly affected by their opponent's emotions (i.e., they made more concessions to angry than to happy opponents), whereas those with high power were unaffected. Compatible effects were shown by other studies focusing on the moderating effects of power (Van Kleef et al., 2004b; Sinaceur & Tiedens, 2006; Van Kleef & Côté, 2007). Van Dijk et al. (2008) manipulated relative power in an ultimatum bargaining setting and showed that communicating anger may backfire for low-power bargainers. They explained this by showing that—similar to a process of emotion contagion—by communicating anger, low-power bargainers may fuel anger in their opponents (resulting in low offers).

Perceived appropriateness of the angry expression. Van Kleef and Côté (2007) directly manipulated the perceived appropriateness of the emotion. In a computer-mediated negotiation, participants either learned that an ethics committee had decided that it was not allowed to use pressure tactics or express negative emotions during the negotiation, or they did not receive this information. The results showed that negotiators who were confronted with angry opponents made fewer concessions when anger was considered inappropriate than when anger was considered appropriate, but only among those negotiators who were high in power.

Appropriateness of communicating anger is also dependent on the intensity with which anger is expressed. Adam and Brett (2018) manipulated high- versus moderate- versus low-intensity anger in one study by giving instructions to use aggressive sentences and raise their voice, and in another study by programming angry verbal reactions (high, moderate, or low in intensity) to negotiation offers. Results showed that high-intensity anger was considered more inappropriate and decreased concession making compared to moderate- and low-intensity anger.

How anger is communicated can also determine its perceived appropriateness and interpersonal effects. Steinel, Harinck, and Van Kleef (2008) distinguished between expressions of anger and happiness directed toward the person (e.g., "this person makes me really angry") and directed toward the negotiation offer (e.g., "this offer makes me really angry"). Their results showed that person-directed anger was considered less appropriate and elicited smaller concessions than offer-directed anger.

What is appropriate may also be culturally defined. Adam, Shirako, and Maddux (2010) studied the effects of angry expressions in negotiations across cultures. Focusing on the cultural background of the observer of the emotion, they showed that expressing anger elicited larger concessions from European American negotiators, but smaller concessions from Asian and Asian American negotiators, due to different cultural norms about the appropriateness of expressions of anger in negotiations. In later work, Adam and Shirako (2013) investigated the cultural background of the expresser of anger in negotiations. They showed that angry expressions elicited greater cooperative efforts when the expresser was East Asian than when the expresser was European American, because East Asian negotiators were perceived as tougher and more threatening. These findings indicate that emotional expressions of negotiators who are, based on stereotypes, considered less expressive (as is the case for East Asian negotiators), are more informative.

Moving beyond anger and happiness. While research on anger and happiness has received most attention, the field has also begun to explore the effects of other emotions. Van Kleef et al. (2006a) compared the interpersonal effects of the supplication emotions disappointment and worry (i.e., emotions communicating dependency and a need for support) to the appeasement emotions guilt and regret (i.e., emotions communicating that one has done something wrong). Their results showed that supplication emotions increased, and appeasement emotions decreased, concessions making in opponents, but only among those opponents high in dispositional trust.

Other studies compared the interpersonal effects of anger and disappointment. Both emotions can be used in negotiations to communicate dissatisfaction, but with markedly different effects on opponents. Lelieveld et al. (2012) showed that anger and disappointment evoke different affective reactions in others. In an ultimatum bargaining setting, anger either evoked reciprocal anger or complementary fear, depending on the relative power position of the expresser. Anger expressed by a high-power bargainer evoked complementary fear in opponents, which led opponents to make higher offers. In low-power positions, anger evoked reciprocal anger in opponents, which led opponents to make lower offers. In contrast, disappointment evoked complementary guilt in opponents, which elicited higher offers in opponents (see also Van Kleef & Van Lange, 2008), regardless of the expresser's power position. In later work, Lelieveld et al. (2013) demonstrated that anger and disappointment differ in the extent to which they communicate power or weakness. In four studies, they showed that whereas anger communicates power, toughness, and high limits in negotiations, disappointment communicates weakness, lenience, and low limits. This weakness can elicit cooperativeness and a social responsibility to help others, but only when it evokes guilt (see also Lelieveld et al., 2011). When participants negotiated as representatives or when they negotiated with an out-group member, they felt less guilty and therefore made lower offers to disappointed opponents, than in individual negotiations and when they negotiated with an in-group. Anger elicited high offers in opponents regardless of the type of negotiation or the group membership of the expresser.

Other discrete emotional expressions that have been studied are sadness and gratitude. Similar to the aforementioned effects of disappointment, Sinaceur et al. (2015) showed that expressions of sadness elicit concessions in opponents because it increases opponents' concern for the expresser. Participants made more concessions to sad opponents but only when they had a reason to experience concern for the expresser (e.g., when the expresser had low power). Similarly, expressions of gratitude in negotiations elicit cooperative behavior and increase benevolence perceived by counterparts, but only when the expression of gratitude is accompanied with cooperative behavior (Kong & Belkin, 2019).

Emotional inconsistency and ambivalence. So far, we discussed the interpersonal effects of single discrete emotions. It is, however, also possible to express more than one emotion during negotiations. Pietroni et al. (2008) studied the effects of anger and happy expressions in a two-issue negotiation, where participants had one high-priority issue and one low-priority issue. They received emotional expressions which were either angry or happy on the high-priority issue and angry or happy on the low-priority issue resulting in four different emotional response patterns. Results showed that happiness on the high-priority issue and anger on the low-priority issue reduced fixed-pie perceptions and increased integrative behavior. Anger on participant's high-priority issue and happiness on participant's low-priority issue, however, reduced integrative behavior.

Emotions may also differ over time. Sinaceur et al. (2013) studied the effects of emotional inconsistency, by manipulating emotions opponents expressed across several rounds of a negotiation. Across experimental conditions, opponents were either consistent in their expressions (e.g., always conveying anger) or inconsistent (e.g., sometimes communicating anger and sometimes happiness). Results showed that emotional inconsistency reduced feelings of control in counterparts and elicited greater concessions compared to a consistent communication of emotions. Filipowicz, Barsade, and Melwani (2011) studied the effects of emotional transitions, where bargainers either moved from anger to happiness or from happiness to anger during the negotiation. Three studies showed that expressing a transition from happiness to anger left a more positive impression on counterparts and, in turn, increased concessions in counterparts more than did express only anger during the negotiation.

Finally, Rothman (2011) studied the effects of expressing emotional ambivalence; the simultaneous experience of a positive and a negative emotion. She demonstrated that counterparts showed more dominant behavior toward ambivalent negotiators than toward happy, angry or non-emotional negotiators, because they perceived the ambivalent negotiator as more deliberative and submissive. In later work, Rothman and Northcraft (2015) showed that in negotiations that were more cooperative, this submissiveness led counterparts to come up with more integrative agreements, which increased value creation in the negotiation.

20.3 Emotion and deception in negotiation

20.3.1 Relevant theory

Negotiations offer many opportunities for deception. Emotions can play an important role here. Gaspar and Schweitzer (2013) proposed the Emotion Deception Model, which explains the willingness to deceive others on the basis of the emotions deceivers experience before making their decision as well as the emotions they anticipate to occur after having deceived their opponent. For example, the experience of anger can directly lead people to conceal information from their opponent (Yip & Schweitzer, 2016), and anticipated guilt or regret can lead people to refrain from using deception.

Methasani, Gaspar, and Barry (2017) extended the model by incorporating the influence of counterparts' emotional expressions on the decision to deceive in negotiations. In line with the EASI model, they proposed that emotional expressions of others may influence deception decisions via affective reactions (by evoking specific emotions in observers) or via inferential processes (by providing information that observers may use to guide their deception decision). Expressions of anger may for instance increase deceptive strategies in opponents, whereas expressions of happiness may decrease such strategies.

20.3.2 Empirical work

Intrapersonal effects. The research on the intrapersonal effects of emotions on deception has largely focused on three emotions: anger, anxiety, and envy. Olekalns and Smith (2009) used a negotiation task where participants negotiated about an employment contract. Using software that scanned text and categorized it in affective categories, they studied the relationship between anger and anxiety and the use of deception. They found that negotiators who expressed anger used more deception by misinforming their opponent (see also Yip & Schweitzer, 2016), whereas negotiators who expressed anxiety used more deception by concealing information.

Moran and Schweitzer (2008) found that the experience of envy also influences the use of deception. They manipulated envy by providing participants with upward social comparison information. Participants who experienced high levels of envy were more likely to lie to their opponent in the negotiation than participants who experienced low levels of envy.

Interpersonal effects. We are aware of only one study that investigated how bargainers' willingness to deceive may depend on the emotional expressions of their opponent. Van Dijk et al. (2008) studied the effects of anger expressions in an ultimatum bargaining setting where participants could misinform opponents about the value of the chips that were allocated. Results showed that participants were more deceptive toward angry bargainers than toward bargainers that expressed happiness . They reasoned that by deceiving the angry opponent, bargainers could make low offers without having to fear the consequences.

Emotion deception. The insights above all concentrate on the effects of own or other's emotions on the willingness to deceive others (e.g., by lying or concealing information). Note, however, that—given the interpersonal effects of emotions—it may also make sense to mislead others about one's own emotions. For example, one might deliberately exaggerate or downplay one's emotions. Emotional expressions can thus be used to deceive opponents in negotiations. This intriguing possibility was first addressed by Andrade and Ho (2009), who showed that bargainers may strategically modify the expression of anger to influence their opponent. Participants in their studies received an unfair offer from an opponent, after which participants were asked to indicate their level of anger. Subsequently, they learned that they would negotiate with the same person for another round. They were again asked to indicate their level of anger, but now learned that their reaction would be sent to the opponent. Results showed that participants then "gamed" their expression of anger by communicating higher levels of anger to their opponent than they had experienced.

Later work showed that when bargainers have more emotions to their disposal, this strategy changes. Van Dijk et al. (2018) demonstrated that when bargainers could also communicate disappointment (besides anger), participants chose to amplify their levels of disappointment, and were more diverse in their communications of anger. Some chose to exaggerate, whereas others chose to downplay their anger. They concluded that having an alternative means to signal disapproval in negotiations tempered the willingness to (strategically) communicate anger.

Negotiators should, however, make sure that when they choose to "game" their emotions, these expressions come across as authentic. Côté, Hideg, and Van Kleef (2013) studied the consequences of faking anger in negotiations. Results showed that faking anger decreases concession making in counterparts, and this effect was explained by reduced trust.

20.4 Conclusions and future directions

It is clear from this chapter that the experience and expression of emotions have a pervasive impact on how people negotiate. These effects are visible at the intrapersonal level and at the interpersonal level. Emotions affect the offers negotiators make, their willingness to give in, and the use of strategies like deception. The recent years have shown tremendous progress in the understanding of the various ways in which emotion shapes negotiations. Nevertheless, several important issues remain to be addressed.

One of these issues is that most of the research on the role of emotions in negotiations has used laboratory experiments. Although findings obtained with computer-mediated interactions are often similar to findings obtained with different paradigms, including surveys involving full-time workers (e.g., Van Kleef et al., 2006b), and face-to-face negotiations (e.g., Sinaceur & Tiedens, 2006), it may be important to study actual negotiators to see how the effects of emotions influence their decision-making and how they make use of emotional expressions. Such research may not only answer questions about the generalizability of the findings, but also can offer novel insights into the role of emotions in negotiation.

Our review reveals that most studies have focused on the effects of anger in negotiations. One positive aspect of this particular focus on anger is that the findings on the intrapersonal and interpersonal effects have been replicated across different studies, using different manipulations of anger (experience and expression). A downside of this focus on anger is that other negative emotions, like disappointment and anxiety, have received less attention. More research is needed to investigate whether findings on the effects of these emotions replicate across different negotiation settings. Studies on some emotions even seem absent (e.g., disgust and contempt). For a more complete picture, future research may benefit from investigating a broader range of discrete emotions. Moreover, it may be worthwhile to also include more positive emotions. It would, for example, be interesting to see whether emotions that increase perceived power, like pride, may have different effects on bargaining behavior than positive emotions that decrease perceived power, like gratitude.

In addition, it may be worthwhile to broaden the cultural perspective and study emotion effects in non-Western cultures. The few studies that have examined culture show that there are important differences between cultures in the intra- and interpersonal effects of emotions in negotiations (Adam & Shirako, 2013; Adam et al., 2010). Cultural norms may also determine which emotional expressions bargainers may (strategically) communicate in negotiations, which relates to the issue of appropriateness. For instance, bargainers in Eastern societies may prefer the less confrontational communication of disappointment over the expression (or exaggeration) of anger.

Taken together, this chapter clearly shows that emotional dynamics play a crucial role in negotiations, by influencing the cognitions and behavior of bargainers' own behavior and the behavior of counterparts. At the same time, the unanswered questions that remain stress the need for more research. Such research promises to enhance the understanding of the negotiation process, the factors that facilitate or hinder this process, and the (social) consequences of emotion in general.

References

Adam, H., & Brett, J. M. (2015). Context matters: the social effects of anger in cooperative, balanced, and competitive negotiation situations. Journal of Experimental Social Psychology, 61, 44–58.

Adam, H., & Brett, J. M. (2018). Everything in moderation: The social effects of anger depend on its perceived intensity. Journal of Experimental Social Psychology, 76, 12–18.

Adam, H., & Shirako, A. (2013). Not all anger is created equal: the impact of the expresser's culture on the social effects of anger in negotiations. Journal of Applied Psychology, 98, 785–798.

Adam, H., Shirako, A., & Maddux, W. W. (2010). Cultural variance in the interpersonal effects of anger in negotiations. Psychological Science, 21, 882–889.

Allred, K. G., Mallozzi, J. S., Matsui, F., & Raia, C. P. (1997). The influence of anger and compassion on negotiation performance. Organizational Behavior and Human Decision Processes, 70, 175–187.

Anderson, C., & Thompson, L. L. (2004). Affect from the top down: how powerful individuals' positive affect shapes negotiations. Organizational Behavior and Human Decision Processes, 95, 125–139.

Andrade, E. B., & Ho, T. H. (2009). Gaming emotions in social interactions. Journal of Consumer Research, 36, 529–552.

Baron, R. A., Fortin, S. P., Frei, R. L., Hauver, L. A., & Shack, M. L. (1990). Reducing organizational conflict: the role of socially-induced positive affect. International Journal of Conflict Management, 1, 133–152.

Brooks, A. W., & Schweitzer, M. E. (2011). Can Nervous Nelly negotiate? How anxiety causes negotiators to make low first offers, exit early, and earn less profit. Organizational Behavior and Human Decision Processes, 115, 43–54.

Butt, A. N., Choi, J. N., & Jaeger, A. M. (2005). The effects of self-emotion, counterpart emotion, and counterpart behavior on negotiator behavior: a comparison of individual-level and dyad-level dynamic. Journal of Organizational Behavior, 26, 681–704.

Carnevale, P. J., & Isen, A. M. (1986). The influence of positive affect and visual access on the discovery of integrative solutions in bilateral negotiation. Organizational Behavior and Human Decision Processes, 37, 1–13.

Côté, S., Hideg, I., & Van Kleef, G. A. (2013). The consequences of faking anger in negotiations. Journal of Experimental Social Psychology, 49, 453–463.

Ekman, P. (1993). Facial expression and emotion. American Psychologist, 48, 384–392.

Fabiansson, E. C., & Denson, T. F. (2012). The effects of intrapersonal anger and its regulation in economic bargaining. PLoS One, 7.

Filipowicz, A., Barsade, S., & Melwani, S. (2011). Understanding emotional transitions: the interpersonal consequences of changing emotions in negotiations. Journal of Personality and Social Psychology, 101, 541–556.

Fiske, S. T. (1993). Controlling other people: the impact of power on stereotyping. American Psychologist, 48, 621–628.

Forgas, J. P. (1998). On feeling good and getting your way: mood effects on negotiator cognition and behavior. Journal of Personality and Social Psychology, 74, 565–577.

Frijda, N. H. (1994). Varieties of affect: Emotions and episodes, moods, and sentiments. In P. Ekman & R. J. Davidson (Eds.), The nature of emotion: Fundamental questions (pp. 59–67). New York: Oxford University Press.

Gaspar, J. P., & Schweitzer, M. E. (2013). The Emotion Deception Model: A review of deception in negotiation and the role of emotion in deception. Negotiation and Conflict Management Research, 6, 160–179.

Hatfield, E., Cacioppo, J. T., & Rapson, R. L. (1994). Emotional contagion. New York: Cambridge University Press.

Jäger, A., Loschelder, D. D., & Friese, M. (2017). Using self-regulation to overcome the detrimental effects of anger in negotiations. Journal of Economic Psychology, 58, 31–43.

Keltner, D., & Haidt, J. (1999). Social functions of emotions at four levels of analysis. Cognition and Emotion, 13, 505–521.

Ketelaar, T., & Au, W. T. (2003). The effects of feelings of guilt on the behaviour of uncooperative individuals in repeated social bargaining games: an affect-as-information interpretation of the role of emotion in social interaction. Cognition and Emotion, 17, 429–453.

Komorita, S. S., & Parks, C. D. (1995). Interpersonal relations: Mixed-motive interaction. Annual Review of Psychology, 46, 183–207.

Kong, D. T., & Belkin, L. Y. (2019). Because I want to share, not because I should: Prosocial implications of gratitude expression in repeated zero-sum resource allocation exchanges. Motivation and Emotion, 43, 824–843.

Lazarus, R. S. (1991). Emotion and adaptation. New York: Oxford University Press.

Lelieveld, G. -J., Van Dijk, E., Van Beest, I., Steinel, W., & Van Kleef, G. A. (2011). Disappointed in you, angry about your offer: Distinct negative emotions induce concessions via different mechanisms. Journal of Experimental Social Psychology, 47, 635–641.
Lelieveld, G. -J., Van Dijk, E., Van Beest, I., & Van Kleef, G. A. (2012). Why anger and disappointment affect other's bargaining behavior differently: The moderating role of power and the mediating role of reciprocal and complementary emotions. Personality and Social Psychology Bulletin, 38, 1209–1221.
Lelieveld, G. -J., Van Dijk, E., Van Beest, I., & Van Kleef, G. A. (2013). Does communicating disappointment in negotiations help or hurt? Solving an apparent inconsistency in the social-functional approach to emotions. Journal of Personality and Social Psychology, 105, 605–620.
Lerner, J. S., & Keltner, D. (2000). Beyond valence: Toward a model of emotion-specific influences on judgment and choice. Cognition and Emotion, 14, 473–493.
Loewenstein, G., & Lerner, J. S. (2003). The role of affect in decision making. In R. Davidson, K. Scherer, & H. Goldsmith (Eds.), Handbook of affective science (pp. 619–642). New York: Oxford University Press.
Methasani, R., Gaspar, J. P, & Barry, B. (2017). Feeling and deceiving: A review and theoretical model of emotions and deception in negotiation. Negotiation and Conflict Management Research, 10, 158–178.
Moran, S., & Schweitzer, M. E. (2008). When better is worse: Envy and the use of deception. Negotiation and Conflict Management Research, 1, 3–29.
Olekalns, M., & Smith, P. L. (2009). Mutually dependent: Power, trust, affect and the use of deception in negotiation. Journal of Business Ethics, 85, 347–365.
Pietroni, D., Van Kleef, G. A., De Dreu, C. K. W., & Pagliaro, S. (2008). Emotions as strategic information: effects of other's emotions on fixed-pie perception, demands and integrative behavior in negotiation. Journal of Experimental Social Psychology, 44, 1444–1454.
Pillutla, M. M., & Murnighan, J. K. (1996). Unfairness, anger, and spite: emotional rejections of ultimatum offers. Organizational Behavior Human Decision Processes, 68, 208–224.
Rothman, N. B. (2011). Steering sheep: how expressed emotional ambivalence elicits dominance in interdependent decision making contexts. Organizational Behavior Human Decision Processes, 116, 66–82.

Rothman, N. B., & Northcraft, G. B. (2015). Unlocking integrative potential: Expressed emotional ambivalence and negotiation outcomes. Organizational Behavior Human Decision Processes, 126, 65–76.

Schwarz, N., & Clore, G. L. (1983). Mood, misattribution and judgments of well-being: Informative and directive functions of affective states. Journal of Personality and Social Psychology, 45, 513–523.

Shirako, A., Kilduff, G. J., & Kray, L. J. (2015). Is there a place for sympathy in negotiation? Finding strength in weakness. Organizational Behavior Human Decision Processes, 131, 95–109.

Sinaceur, M., Adam, H., Van Kleef, G. A., & Galinsky, A. D. (2013). The advantages of being unpredictable: how emotional inconsistency extracts concessions in negotiation. Journal Experimental Social Psychology, 49, 498–508.

Sinaceur, M., Kopelman, S., Vasiljevic, D., & Haag, C. (2015). Weep and get more: when and why sadness expression is effective in negotiations. Journal of Applied Psychology, 100, 1847–1871.

Sinaceur, M., & Tiedens, L. Z. (2006). Get mad and get more than even: When and why anger expression is effective in negotiations. Journal of Experimental Social Psychology, 42, 314–322.

Steinel, W., Van Kleef, G. A., & Harinck, F. (2008): Are you talking to me? Separating the people from the problem when expressing emotions in negotiation. Journal of Experimental Social Psychology, 44, 362–369.

Van Beest, I., Van Kleef, G. A., & Van Dijk, E. (2008). Get angry, get out: The interpersonal effects of anger communication in multiparty negotiation. Journal of Experimental Social Psychology, 44, 993–1002.

Van Dijk, E., Van Beest, I., Van Kleef, G. A., & Lelieveld, G. -J. (2018). Communication of anger versus disappointment in bargaining and the moderating role of power. Journal of Behavioral Decision Making, 31, 632–643.

Van Dijk, E., Van Kleef, G. A., Steinel, W., & Van Beest, I. (2008). A social functional approach to emotions in bargaining: When communicating anger pays and when it backfires. Journal of Personality and Social Psychology, 94, 600–614.

Van Kleef, G. A., & Côté, S. (2007). Expressing anger in social conflict: When it helps and when it hurts. Journal of Applied Psychology, 92, 1557–1569.

Van Kleef, G. A., & Côté, S. (2018). Emotional dynamics in conflict and negotiation: Individual, dyadic, and group processes. Annual Review of Organizational Psychology and Organizational Behavior, 5, 437–464.

Van Kleef, G. A., De Dreu, C. K. W., & Manstead, A. S. R. (2004a). The interpersonal effects of anger and happiness in negotiations. Journal of Personality and Social Psychology, 86, 57–76.

Van Kleef, G. A., De Dreu, C. K. W., & Manstead, A. S. R. (2004b). The interpersonal effects of emotions in negotiations: A motivated information processing approach. Journal of Personality and Social Psychology, 87, 510–528.

Van Kleef, G. A., De Dreu, C. K. W., & Manstead, A. S. R. (2006a). Supplication and appeasement in conflict and negotiation: The interpersonal effects of disappointment, worry, guilt, and regret. Journal of Personality and Social Psychology, 91, 124–142.

Van Kleef, G. A., De Dreu, C. K. W., Pietroni, D., & Manstead, A. S. R. (2006b). Power and emotion in negotiation: Power moderates the interpersonal effects of anger and happiness on concession making. European Journal of Social Psychology, 36, 557–581.

Van Kleef, G. A., De Dreu, C. K. W., & Manstead, A. S. R. (2010). An interpersonal approach to emotion in social decision making: The emotions as social information model. Advances in Experimental Social Psychology, 42, 45–96.

Van Kleef, G. A., & Van Lange, P. A. M. (2008). What other's disappointment may do to selfish people: Emotion and social value orientation in a negotiation context. Personality and Social Psychology Bulletin, 34, 1084–1095.

Watson, D., Clark, L. A., & Tellegen, A. (1988). Development and validation of brief measures of positive and negative affect: the PANAS scales. Journal of Personality and Social Psychology, 54, 1063–70.

Wietzker, A., Buysse, A., Loeys, T., & Brondeel, R. (2011). Easing the conscience: Feeling guilty makes people cooperate in divorce negotiations. Journal of Social and Personal Relationships, 29, 324–336.

Yip, J. A., & Schweinsberg, M. (2017). Infuriating impasses: Angry expressions increase exiting behavior in negotiations. Social Psychological and Personality Science, 8, 706–714.

Yip, J. A., & Schweitzer, M. E. (2016). Mad and misleading: Incidental anger promotes deception. Organizational Behavior Human Decision Processes, 137, 207–217.

21

Gender Differences in Negotiation and Policy for Equalizing Outcomes

María P. Recalde and Lise Vesterlund

21.1 Introduction

Gender differences in negotiation are frequently used to explain why men and women advance at different rates (e.g., Bertrand, 2018), why they select different occupations, and secure different compensation (e.g., Blau and Kahn, 2017). Indeed, field evidence is consistent with negotiation differences contributing to the persistent gender wage gap and to men and women holding different occupations and different ranks

Recalde acknowledges financial support from ARC grant DE190100585.

M. P. Recalde
University of Melbourne, Melbourne, Australia
e-mail: maria.recalde@unimelb.edu.au

L. Vesterlund (✉)
University of Pittsburgh, Pittsburgh, Pennsylvania, USA
e-mail: vester@pitt.edu

E. Karagözoğlu and K. B. Hyndman (eds.), *Bargaining*,
https://doi.org/10.1007/978-3-030-76666-5_21

within occupation (e.g., Greig, 2008; Card, Cardoso, and Kline, 2016; Säve-Söderbergh, 2019).

Considering the potential impact on labor-market outcomes, it is no surprise that substantive work has examined when and why men and women approach negotiation differently. The overarching conclusion is that there are gender differences in both willingness and ability to negotiate, and that these are sensitive to the characteristics of the negotiation (for reviews see Bowles et al. 2005; Bowles and McGinn 2008; Stuhlmacher and Walters 1999; Bertrand 2011; Azmat and Petrongolo 2014; Mazei et al. 2015; Kugler et al. 2018; and Hernandez-Arenaz and Iriberri, 2019a).

The striking finding by Babcock and Laschever (2003), that out of new MBA graduates 57% of men and only 7% of women negotiated the compensation for their first job, is one of many that point to the robust evidence that women less than men pursue negotiations. Although negotiation in the labor market is of key concern, the limited information on the value of the employee–employer match and the parties' outside options challenges inference on gender differences in negotiation.[1] Many studies instead rely on controlled experiments which similarly find that men negotiate more often than women (e.g., Bowles et al. 2005; Small et al 2007; Kray and Gelfand, 2009; Amanatullah and Morris, 2010; Kugler et al., 2018; Gihleb et al., 2020). The evidence is more mixed when examining the ability to negotiate. While some studies point to female employees securing worse outcomes than male employees (e.g., Dittrich et al., 2014; Barron, 2003), there is substantial evidence that the male advantage depends on the negotiation setting (Pradel et al. 2005).[2]

[1] See Andersen et al (2018b) for a field study where the value of the negotiated item is better assessed.

[2] A substantial literature examines if men and women receive differential treatment when bargaining. Ayres (1991, 1995) and Ayres and Siegelman (1995) report on an audit study for car sales, finding that single women are quoted higher prices than single men. Castillo et al. (2013) examine negotiations for taxi rides, finding that statistical discrimination drives gender differences in outcomes. Consistent with statistical discrimination, Busse et al. (2017) find, for buyers who appear uninformed, higher prices for women than men. However, audit studies instruct buyers on how to negotiate and do not capture differences in negotiation. List (2004) instead examines free-form negotiations over sports cards and finds that statistical discrimination gives rise to a male advantage. With transactions only occurring 3% of the time, it is however difficult to capture differences in negotiation.

Research points to a number of factors that affect gender differences in negotiation.[3] Differences are less pronounced when it is clear that something is negotiable and what the bargaining range is (Bowles et al., 2005; Rigdon, 2012; Kugler et al., 2018; Small et al., 2007; Leibbrandt and List, 2015). That is, ambiguity amplifies the difference. Differences also depend on whether the negotiation activates stereotypes (Kray et al., 2002), with differences increasing when female negotiation violates gender norms. The response to such stereotypes may result from stereotype threat, or from the correct expectation that backlash is greater toward women who violate gender norms (Bowles et al., 2007; Tinsley et al, 2009).[4] Gender differences are also found to be smaller when individuals negotiate on behalf of someone else rather than on behalf of themselves (Bowles et al., 2005; Amanatullah & Morris, 2010; Amanatullah & Tinsley, 2013) and when negotiation occurs in less competitive environments (Bowles et al., 2005).[5] Finally, the positional role matters with gender differences arising for the party with less power (Dittrich et al., 2014; Exley et al., 2020).[6]

Although gender differences in negotiation vary with the characteristics of the negotiation, there is consensus that the characteristics of labor-market negotiations are largely those that give rise to a gender gap in willingness and ability to negotiate. For example, labor negotiations

---

[3] While ultimatum games limit the negotiation interaction to a take-it-or-leave-it offer, the setting nonetheless provides insights on why women fare worse in negotiations (Eckel and Grossman 2001; Solnick 2001). Reviewing the literature, Eckel et al. (2008) conclude that women are more egalitarian, expect and ask for less, and are less likely to fail in reaching an agreement.

[4] For gender differences in negotiation expectation see also Eckel et al. (2008) and Andersen et al. (2018a).

[5] As for negotiation, the literature on competition reveals robust differences on the extensive margin (Niederle and Vesterlund 2007) and more context-dependent differences on the intensive margin (Gneezy et al. 2003). See Niederle and Vesterlund (2011) for a review, and Niederle and Vesterlund (2008) for the connection between negotiation and competition.

[6] Other factors may affect gender differences in negotiation including the sex of negotiating partners (Eckel and Grossman, 2001; Solnick, 2001; Bowles et al., 2007; Sutter et al., 2009; Hernandez-Arenaz and Iriberri, 2018), the framing as a negotiation or an ask (Small et al., 2007), communication mode (Bowles and Babcock 2013; Bowles 2013), and sharing norms (Hernandez-Arenaz and Iriberri 2019b). Differences in preferences, such as risk aversion and fairness concerns, may also play a role (see Croson and Gneezy 2009 and Niederle 2015 for a review). Finally, Bursztyn et al. (2017) find that single women opt out of negotiation because pursuing career enhancing actions may decrease their success in the marriage market.

are generally on behalf of oneself; tend to be competitive; and it is often ambiguous what may be negotiated.

Recognizing that men hold an advantage in labor-market negotiations has led to initiatives that aim to reduce differences in negotiation or in the effect such differences may have on outcomes. Some of these may be characterized as "fixing-the-women" initiatives, whether it be for women to negotiate more or improve their negotiation skills. Others instead center on "fixing-the-institution" and include a direct ban on negotiations, banning requests for salary history, and changing wage transparency. We will review the literature on each of these initiatives and the evidence on their effectiveness.

21.2 "Fixing the women"

The finding that men are more able and willing to negotiate in the labor market tempt recommendations that women should mirror their behavior by negotiating more and improving their negotiation skills. While there is substantial public support for such programs, there has until recently been little evidence on their effectiveness. This section reports on research studying these "fix-the-women" initiatives and their challenges.

21.2.1 Lean-In Recommendation

The finding that both men and women gain from negotiation and that women are less likely to pursue such opportunities suggests that women are leaving substantial lifetime earnings on the table (Babcock and Laschever, 2003). This has led to a push for women to negotiate more and to lean in (e.g., Sandberg 2013).

Exley, Niederle, and Vesterlund (2020, ENV henceforth) note that in making the recommendation for women to lean in and negotiate more, we are missing the counterfactual. Of course, the recommendation is harmless if the "worst that can happen is that they say no." However, there are many cases where instead negotiation is costly, and it is less clear that negotiating more improves outcomes.[7]

ENV design an experiment to examine the effect of increased negotiation. "Workers" and "firms" each perform a task, and then decide how to split the surplus of their joint efforts. They run two versions of their study: a "choice treatment," where workers are offered an initial wage and decide whether they want to accept it or instead negotiate; and an "always treatment," where workers still see an initial wage offer but have to negotiate. Negotiations may last up to 3 minutes and are done via anonymous chat messages. The joint firm-worker surplus is reduced in the event of a bargaining impasse, as the worker and the firm then each secure a payment that is lower than had the negotiation not been initiated.

The ENV choice treatment confirms that women don't enter all negotiations: 34% of the time they take the initial wage offer and opt out of the negotiation. This occurs although negotiations increase wages. In fact, there is very little downside to women negotiating: 74% secure final wages above the initially offered wage, and only 13% get a lower final wage. Confirming field evidence, women often avoid negotiations, although negotiations are beneficial.

To determine the counterfactual of increased negotiation, ENV compare the outcomes women achieve when they avoid some negotiations (choice treatment) to when they always negotiate (always treatment). The treatment where participants always negotiate backfires—there are no additional gains from negotiation and the share of negotiations that decrease earnings increase to 33%. Rather than improving women's earnings, the additional negotiations decrease earnings and make women worse off.

ENV show that selection is key to increased negotiations being costly. Women know when it is beneficial to negotiate and they use that knowledge to avoid costly negotiations in the choice treatment. Examination of the counterfactual makes clear that the finding that "women who enter

[7] Negotiations may be costly immediately (costs of time, disutility from asking); in the future (backlash, reputation, future negotiation); or there may be costs from bargaining impasse (affecting future collaboration, legal costs, or retraction of earlier offers).

negotiations gain from doing so" does not imply that all women should negotiate.

With the recommendation to lean in being directed at women, ENV also ask if men are better at deciding when to negotiate. Results confirm that men negotiate more often than women (74% vs 66% of the time) and that they too gain from negotiation. However, comparing the distributions of earnings between the "choice" and "always" treatments shows no evidence that their decisions are superior to women's. Nonetheless, ENV confirm a greater push for women to negotiate. Respondents of an online survey were more likely to recommend more frequent salary negotiations for women than for men (75 vs 54%). In fact, participants presented with information about the initial ENV experimental design were willing to pay to remove the worker's choice to opt out of the negotiation. This willingness to restrict the choice arises despite an asymmetry in information where the "paternalistic" participant only knows the distribution of initially offered wages, while the worker knows the initially offered wage and whether negotiation is likely to be beneficial. Importantly, this willingness to pay to remove the worker's negotiation choice is more prevalent when faced with a female than a male worker.

The ENV study demonstrates that people are willing to pay to remove women's choice to negotiate, even though women know whether negotiations benefit them, and increased negotiations decrease individual earnings. The study serves as a caution against the blanket recommendation that women should negotiate more.

21.2.2 Improving Negotiation Skills

Another approach to "fixing-women" is to improve their negotiation skills. Evidence that experience improves negotiated outcomes has fueled the expectation that negotiation training reduces the gender gap in compensation. For example, the American Association of University Women has initiated free nationwide negotiation workshops for 10 million women to "close the pay gap, one workshop at a time." Although substantial resources are used to improve negotiation skills, there is limited evidence of the impact such training has on salary negotiations, let alone on gender differences in outcomes.[8]

An exception is Stevens et al. (1993) which has 60 MBA students participate in two different negotiation programs. All participants first receive a basic 4-hour negotiation training and are then assessed through knowledge tests and salary negotiation simulations with confederates who provide raises based on the successful use of negotiation tactics. This first-stage assessment reveals a gender gap in negotiated salaries which is found to result from men and women setting different goals for the negotiation. Participants are then subjected to one of two negotiation training programs: one emphasizing goal setting, and the other augmenting training in goal setting with general self-management training.[9] A second-stage assessment reveals that although goal setting improves the skills of both men and women, it has no differential effect and does not eliminate gender differences in negotiation outcomes. The augmented training does, however, improve skills more for women than men, closing the gender gap. The authors find that augmented training works by increasing the perceived control women have over negotiation outcomes. Confidence is also shown to affect the effectiveness of training.

While Stevens et al. (1993) demonstrate that training can affect men and women differently, training effectiveness is assessed in an environment where the response to negotiation is gender neutral. There is ample evidence that the response to negotiation differs by gender, and that women more than men may experience backlash. For example, Bowles et al. (2007) report on experiments where participants evaluate hypothetical job candidates after seeing interview transcripts and videos. Treatments vary the candidate's gender and whether the candidate asks for higher compensation. Results show no gender difference in evaluation in the absence of pay requests, and lower evaluation scores for women who ask for higher compensation than men who do the same.

---

[8] Evidence on the effectiveness of negotiation training on outcomes is mixed (Movius 2008). For gender differences in negotiation performance, Mazei et al (2015) document that experience reduces gender differences.

[9] The augmented self-management training adds identifying performance obstacles, planning to overcome obstacles, self-monitoring progress, and self-administering rewards. There is no control group receiving no training in the study.

Further, requests for higher compensation decrease willingness to work with female candidates, while there is no effect for male candidates.

Importantly, Amanatullah and Morris (2010) show that backlash is anticipated by women. In an experiment that varies whether participants negotiate on behalf of themselves or on behalf of others, the authors ask participants to report the salary threshold above which they think they would be perceived as "pushy" and would cause the hiring manager to "punish them for being too demanding." Results show that women anticipate backlash when negotiating for themselves, but not for others. Further, the anticipated size of this backlash when negotiating for themselves is large with women asking for approximately 15% lower wages and making larger salary concessions than men.

This literature suggests that training programs may backfire if they encourage negotiations that subsequently result in backlash. Bowles and Babcock (2013) and Bear and Babcock (2017) explore negotiation tactics that account for gender norms and find that these can be effective in reducing the gender gap in negotiation outcomes. Bowles and Babcock (2013) show that relational accounts can improve negotiation outcomes for women by reducing social backlash. Relational accounts include techniques such as expressing concerns for organizational relationships and using a "supervisor-excuse" script that validates a negotiation initiation because someone else suggested it.

Bear and Babcock (2017) study priming techniques that reduce the gender incongruency women experience when they negotiate for themselves. They vary whether prior to negotiating participants: (1) think of situations where the use of assertive and forceful tactics helped them succeed in a negotiation, and (2) imagine that they are negotiating on behalf of a close friend. Participants were informed that these tactics improve performance when negotiating on behalf of self. Subjects participate in simulated face-to-face negotiations in a masculine buyer-seller environment. Results show that in the absence of primes, men outperform women. Gender differences, however, disappear with primes. An online study further investigates the effect of primes on negotiation aspirations and shows in the absence of a prime, women have lower negotiation-performance aspirations than men, while no gender differences arise under primes. Interestingly, the aspirations of men do not change across treatments while the aspirations of women do.

A recent study by Ashraf et al. (2020) explores the effect of negotiation training on education rather than labor-market outcomes. A field experiment with 2,366 grade 8 girls in Lusaka, Zambia randomizes girls into three treatments (within schools): negotiation training, safe space, and control. The negotiation treatment has participants attend six 2-hour training sessions with material similar to that of a modified MBA negotiation class. The safe space treatment consists of the same number of 2-hour sessions but instead has girls play games, work on homework, and spend time with each other.

Ashraf et al. (2020) find that negotiation training increases average school enrollment in grades 10 and 11 by 10% relative to the control treatment. The effect of the safe space treatment is smaller and not significantly different from the control or negotiation treatment when looking at overall school enrollment. However, analysis of enrollment in high-quality schools, which prepare girls for college entry exams, reveal no impact of the safe space treatment and a positive impact of the negotiation treatment. The impact on school enrollment grows over time, indicating that benefits accumulate and may spill over to the labor and marriage markets.

Together these studies suggest that negotiation training programs that are comprehensive enough to increase women's confidence and sense of control over the negotiation may reduce the gender gap in negotiation outcomes.[10] However, the evidence on the impact of pure negation training is more limited, and it is clear that such training needs to account for the potential for backlash. Additional work is needed to understand training effects on salary and promotion negotiations as well as impacts on the gender gap in labor-market outcomes.

[10] A recent study by McKelway (2019) examines self-efficacy/confidence training (rather than negotiation skills training) and finds it increased women's self-efficacy, employment, and income.

21.3 Fixing Institutions

It has been argued that the first step should not be to "fix the women", but rather the institutions in which they work. Several such initiatives seek to restrict negotiations by banning them, eliminating the possibility of inquiring about past salary history, and by making wages within organizations transparent. While the first two initiatives take as given gender differences in negotiation and attempt to remove the effects of such differences, the latter instead relies on the evidence that negotiation differences are more prevalent when the negotiation is ambiguous.

21.3.1 Banning Salary Negotiations

Evidence that gender differences in negotiation skill contribute to the gender wage gap along with concerns that negotiation skills rather than productivity differences lead to variation in compensation, has led some corporations to directly ban negotiations. For example, Reddit banned negotiations in 2015 with the aim of eliminating the disadvantage women have at the bargaining table. Other companies have followed, and the policy has been noted as an effective way of eliminating wage disparities (Kray, 2015). Negotiation bans, however, have their own challenges, as there is a risk associated with leaving it up to management to secure equal pay for men and women.

Gihleb, Landsman, and Vesterlund (2020, henceforth GLV) explore the effects of a negotiation ban. They argue that the extent to which a negotiation ban is effective in reducing the gender wage gap depends on the potential bias of the manager, and on why negotiation is effective in raising compensation. For example, they show in a simple theoretical model that if the decision to negotiate serves as a credible signal on productivity, and the productivity distribution of men dominates that of women, then men will negotiate more than women and secure higher earnings. A negotiation ban could backfire in such a setting as management will perceive men as more productive and pay them more than women. A negotiation ban may similarly backfire if management is biased against women and the negotiation serves to temper such biases.

GLV use a lab experiment to study the effect of a negotiation ban. They investigate manager-selected compensation in a between-subject design. In one treatment workers may negotiate with management and in another there is no negotiation option. Participants are matched in triads, with each triad consisting of one manager and two workers. The triad interacts for five rounds. Personal characteristics like age, gender, and area of study are revealed to the manager. The two workers must in each round perform a task, and their performance generates a profit for the manager and a surplus that the manager must distribute between the two workers. One worker is given a high-productivity task and the other a low-productivity task. Uncertainty over the relative productivity ensures variation in subjective assessment of worker effort and allows for negotiations to signal productivity.

GLV's negotiation treatment replicates the finding that men negotiate more than women. Further, negotiating only improves compensation for workers who are assigned the more productive task and it does so only for men. Hence, negotiations increase inequality both between and within the task and between men and women.

The negotiation ban is, however, shown to reduce inequality and the relative pay advantage of men on the high-productivity task. In contrast to the theoretical example and potentially biased management, GLV show, consistent with the recent push to ban negotiation, that the ban gives rise to equal compensation for men and women.

It may be questioned whether a negotiation ban is sustainable when other firms engage in negotiation; whether it is advisable in the long run, when high-quality employees may secure attractive outside offers and require retention packages; or whether a ban will only be adhered to by female workers. With these caveats in mind, the GLV evidence suggests that corporations who wish to compensate for ability rather than negotiation skill may benefit from eliminating negotiation with initial recruits of unknown ability.

21.3.2 Salary History Ban

A popular fix-the-institution initiative is to ban salary history requests, and thereby allow employees to break the path dependency of wages.[11] Such policies may, however, fail if employers statistically discriminate against women in the same way that they discriminate against Black and Hispanic men as a result of ban-the-box initiatives (see e.g., Agan and Starr 2018; Doleac and Hansen, 2018, 2020). Further, it may become a practice for workers to voluntarily disclose their salary histories, thus eliminating the impact of the policy.

Agan et al. (2020a) provides a theoretical examination of Salary History Ban (SHB) policies that incorporates workers' decision to voluntarily disclose salary information and examines the implications this has for different types of policy interventions. Using a survey they find that workers can be classified into three types: always disclosers (25%), never disclosers (17%), and policy compliers (58%); that men are more likely to always disclose and less likely to comply than women; and consistent with a contagion story, that willingness to disclose increases with the proportion of others who do.

Despite SHB concerns, empirical estimates point to the policy reducing the gender wage gap.[12] Exploiting variation in US states that have adopted SHB policies, McNichols (2019) and Sinha (2019) find a 3–4% point reduction in the gender pay gap and no impact on labor-force participation or turnover rates.

Experiments have also been used to study the impact of SHBs. Agan et al. (2020b) conduct a field experiment where recruiters evaluate job applications under randomly assigned salary-disclosure conditions. They find that recruiters offer candidates lower salaries when disclosure is banned. This is driven by lower beliefs about outside offers, lower candidate reservation wages, and lower candidate quality. Although the ban increases equality across candidates, gender results are mixed. Disclosure

[11] US estimates suggest that 25 to 50% of potential employees are asked to disclose past salary (Hall and Krueger 2012, Barach and Horton 2020, Agan et al. 2020a).

[12] By April 2019 some form of SHB was implemented in 12 states, 9 cities, and 3 counties in the US (Sinha 2019).

increases the salaries of men more than women, but it also improves the callback rates of women without affecting those of men.[13]

21.3.3 Transparency

Another class of interventions instead aims to increase pay transparency to reduce gender differences in negotiation. This includes permission to discuss salary information, disclosing pay ranges, reporting pay statistics by occupation and gender, and letting candidates know if and when compensation is negotiable. Transparency allows individuals to set similar negotiation expectations, and the hope that this reduces gender differences in negotiation has in part motivated public transparency policies.[14]

Indeed, Bowles et al. (2005) show that gender differences in negotiated outcomes increase with the negotiation's level of ambiguity. They find, in a survey of MBAs, that the gender gap in starting salaries is larger in industries with higher ambiguity in compensation. Similar results are seen in an experiment they conduct where participants negotiate the price of a good in a buyer-seller environment. Buyers are given the bargaining range in both a high- and a low-ambiguity treatment, with the latter adding a negotiation target. Results show gender differences in negotiation in the high- but not in the low-ambiguity environment.

Leibbrandt and List (2015) study the effect of ambiguity on job applications and salary negotiation decisions. In a field experiment with 2,422 job seekers, they compare the response to low- and high-ambiguity job postings. One treatment states that wages are negotiable and the other has no such statement. Results show higher application rates for men

[13] See also Barach and Horton (2020) which in an online labor market finds that removing salary history causes employers to search more and evaluate more candidates. As a result, candidates with lower past average wages are more frequently evaluated and hired.

[14] Laws requiring firms to disclose salary statistics by gender and occupation are now in place in numerous countries, including Australia, Austria, Denmark, Finland, Germany, and the UK. The US has also seen a push for increased transparency, e.g., executive orders were signed to prohibit federal contractors from retaliating against employees who discuss their compensation (2014), and to require firms with government contracts to report average salaries by gender (2016).

than women in both treatments. However, the reduction of ambiguity decreases applications from men, while it increases applications from women. Job applicants are classified into those that initiate negotiations for higher pay, signal willingness to work for lower pay, and those who do not initiate negotiations. When negation is ambiguous, men are more likely to initiate negotiations for higher pay and less likely to signal willingness to accept lower wages than women. However, these gender differences disappear when it is clear that wages are negotiable.

Further evidence on the effect of transparency is seen in work examining the impact of information on the compensation obtained by others. Major et al. (1984) conduct an experiment where participants choose their compensation after completing survey work for 20 minutes. Participants are given \$4 and decide how much to keep as pay. Participants record their pay and gender on a form which may or may not contain information on compensation of others. A baseline treatment keeps the form blank, while three social information treatments pre-fill the form making it seem as though the information reflects the compensation chosen by 8 previous participants. One treatment shows that 4 men and 4 women paid themselves \$2 on average, while the two others show the average pay as \$2.50 for one gender and \$1.50 for the other. Results reveal that men pay themselves nearly twice as much as women when no information is provided; however, the social information treatments cause men to decrease their pay, eliminating the gender gap.[15]

While Major et al. (1984) find a differential response to "transparency," they do not examine the effect on negotiation outcomes. Rigdon (2012) fills this gap in the literature by conducting an experiment where participants play a modified ultimatum game where roles as proposers and responders are earned at the beginning of the experiment. The game is as follows: responders first make a cheap-talk pay request, proposers then make a responder offer, and responders accept or reject the offer. Treatments vary whether participants receive information about the outcomes of previous sessions. A baseline treatment provides

[15] A second experiment pays participants \$4 and asks them to decide how much time they want to work. Consistent with women asking for lower pay, they find that women work longer than men and complete more and higher quality work.

no social information, another treatment shows participants the distribution of pay requests made by male responders in the baseline treatment, a third treatment additionally shows the average offer received per pay request. Participants do not know that they only see male-responder choices. The baseline treatment shows that women demand less, are given lower offers, and ultimately earn less than men. As in Major et al., these differences disappear when social information is provided.

The studies above suggest that transparency may help eliminate gender differences in negotiation initiation, salary requests, and negotiation outcomes. However, transparency policies may also affect the morale of workers, the productivity of firms, and the choices of employers.[16] Recent work uses legislation on transparency to estimate the effect on labor-market outcomes. Bennedsen et al. (2019) study the impact of a Danish law passed in 2006 requiring firms with 35 or more employees to report average salaries by occupation code and gender. They compare firms with 10 to 34 employees, which did not have to report salaries, to those with 35 to 50 employees who did. Results show that the transparency law reduced the gender pay gap by decreasing the wage growth for men relative to women. More women were hired and promoted as a result of the policy. Productivity, however, decreased as did costs, generating no overall impact on firm profits.

Baker et al. (2019) study the impact of public-sector salary-disclosure laws in Canada. The authors exploit variation in when and where the law took effect and find that the policy decreased the gender pay gap by 2% points (30%). Cullen and Pakzad-Hurson (2019) examine the effect of pay transparency using data from an online labor-market platform for low-skill work, TaskRabbit. Results show that employers are more likely to equalize pay when workers complete tasks that allow them to learn of the compensation of others, and this is further confirmed in an online experiment. Although the study is not centered around gender differences in negotiation, the authors provide insights for policies seeking to reduce the gender pay gap. They find that partial transparency policies which allow workers to endogenously choose whether to discuss

[16] See also Card et al. (2012), Breza et al. (2018), and Mas (2017).

salary information may backfire and cause the gender pay gap to increase because men and women have differential communication patterns.

21.4 Conclusion

Men more than women succeed when negotiating over labor-market outcomes, and gender differences in negotiation likely contribute to the gender wage gap and to horizontal and vertical segregation in the labor market. Numerous initiatives have been put in place to reduce the effect of gender differences in negotiation, and our chapter reviews recent advances in the literature to evaluate the potential impact of these policies.

Our review makes clear that the literature is still at its infancy and that many questions remain. The evidence points to serious challenges of "fix-the-women" policies. Encouraging women to negotiate more may backfire, because women correctly opt out of costly negotiations. Caution is also warranted when training women to negotiate, as such training, absent other interventions, may cause backlash or lower chances of employment. Women do not appear to be "broken" and policies to fix them may fail.

The evidence on the "fix-the-institution" initiatives suggests that these are more effective in reducing gender disparities in the labor market. Concerns of adverse effects of banning negotiations or salary history requests have not materialized, and the empirical evidence points to reductions in gender differences in negotiation outcomes. However, the evidence is limited. A full assessment requires an understanding of how these initiatives fare in the long run. The strongest and most consistent evidence to date is seen for increased transparency. Numerous studies confirm that gender differences in negotiation diminish when it is clear what to expect from the negotiation. While wage transparency should not be expected to eliminate all gender differences, the literature points to it as an effective first step organizations and governments can take if they wish to reduce gender differences in labor-market outcomes.

References

Agan, A., & Starr, S. (2018). Ban the box, criminal records, and racial discrimination: A field experiment. The Quarterly Journal of Economics, 133(1), 191–235.

Agan, A. Y., Cowgill, B., & Gee, L. (2020a). Do Workers Comply with Salary History Bans? A Survey on Voluntary Disclosure, Adverse Selection, and Unraveling. AEA Papers & Proceedings.

Agan, A. Y., Cowgill, B., & Gee, L. (2020b). Salary Disclosure and Hiring: Field Experimental Evidence from a Two-Sided Audit Study.

Amanatullah, E. T., & Morris, M. W. (2010). Negotiating gender roles: Gender differences in assertive negotiating are mediated by women's fear of backlash and attenuated when negotiating on behalf of others. Journal of Personality and Social Psychology, 98(2), 256.

Amanatullah, E. T., & Tinsley, C. H. (2013). Punishing female negotiators for asserting too much... or not enough: Exploring why advocacy moderates backlash against assertive female negotiators. Organizational Behavior and Human Decision Processes, 120(1), 110–122.

Andersen, S., Ertac, S., Gneezy, U., List, J. A., & Maximiano, S. (2018a). On the cultural basis of gender differences in negotiation. Experimental Economics, 21(4), 757–778.

Andersen, S., Marx, J., Nielsen, K. M., & Vesterlund, L. (2018b). Gender Differences in Negotiation: Evidence from Real Estate Transactions.

Ashraf, N., Bau, N., Low, C., & McGinn, K. (Forthcoming). Negotiating a better future: How interpersonal skills facilitate inter-generational investment. Quarterly Journal of Economics.

Ayres, I. (1991). Fair driving: Gender and race discrimination in retail car negotiations. Harvard Law Review, 817–872.

Ayres, I. (1995). Further evidence of discrimination in new car negotiations and estimates of its cause. Michigan Law Review, 94(1), 109–147.

Ayres, I., & Siegelman, P. (1995). Race and gender discrimination in bargaining for a new car. The American Economic Review, 304–321.

Azmat, G., & Petrongolo, B. (2014). Gender and the labor market: What have we learned from field and lab experiments? Labour Economics, 30, 32–40.

Babcock, L., & Laschever, S. (2003). Women Don't Ask: Negotiation and the Gender Divide. NJ Princeton University Press.

Baker, M., Halberstam, Y., Kroft, K., Mas, A., & Messacar, D. (2019). Pay Transparency and the Gender Gap. NBER.

Barach, M. A., & Horton, J. J. (2020). How do employers use compensation history?: Evidence from a field experiment. NBER.

Barron, L. A. (2003). Ask and you shall receive? Gender differences in negotiators' beliefs about requests for a higher salary. Human Relations, 56(6), 635–662.

Bear, J. B., & Babcock, L. (2017). Negotiating femininity: Gender-relevant primes improve women's economic performance in gender role incongruent negotiations. Psychology of Women Quarterly, 41(2), 163–174.

Bennedsen, M., Simintzi, E., Tsoutsoura, M., & Wolfenzon, D. (2019). Do firms respond to gender pay gap transparency? NBER.

Bertrand, M. (2011). New perspectives on gender. In Handbook of labor economics (Vol. 4, pp. 1543–1590). Elsevier.

Bertrand, M. (2018). Coase Lecture–The Glass Ceiling. Economica, 85(338), 205–231.

Blau, F. D., & Kahn, L. M. (2017). The gender wage gap: Extent, trends, and explanations. Journal of Economic Literature, 55(3), 789–865.

Bowles, H. R. (2013). Psychological perspectives on gender in negotiation. The Sage Handbook of Gender and Psychology, 465–483.

Bowles, H. R., & Babcock, L. (2013). How can women escape the compensation negotiation dilemma? Relational accounts are one answer. Psychology of Women Quarterly, 37(1), 80–96.

Bowles, H. R., Babcock, L., & Lai, L. (2007). Social incentives for gender differences in the propensity to initiate negotiations: Sometimes it does hurt to ask. Organizational Behavior and Human Decision Processes, 103(1), 84–103.

Bowles, H. R., Babcock, L., & McGinn, K. L. (2005). Constraints and triggers: Situational mechanics of gender in negotiation. Journal of Personality and Social Psychology, 89(6), 951.

Bowles, H. R., & McGinn, K. L. (2008). Gender in job negotiations: A two level game. Negotiation Journal, 24(4), 393–410.

Breza, E., Kaur, S., & Shamdasani, Y. (2018). The morale effects of pay inequality. The Quarterly Journal of Economics, 133(2), 611–663.

Bursztyn, L., Fujiwara, T., & Pallais, A. (2017). "Acting Wife": Marriage Market Incentives and Labor Market Investments. American Economic Review, 107(11), 3288–3319.

Busse, M. R., Israeli, A., & Zettelmeyer, F. (2017). Repairing the damage: The effect of price knowledge and gender on auto repair price quotes. Journal of Marketing Research, 54(1), 75–95.

Card, D., Cardoso, A. R., & Kline, P. (2016). Bargaining, sorting, and the gender wage gap: Quantifying the impact of firms on the relative pay of women. The Quarterly Journal of Economics, 131(2), 633–686.
Card, D., Mas, A., Moretti, E., & Saez, E. (2012). Inequality at work: The effect of peer salaries on job satisfaction. American Economic Review, 102(6), 2981–3003.
Castillo, M., Petrie, R., Torero, M., & Vesterlund, L. (2013). Gender differences in bargaining outcomes: A field experiment on discrimination. Journal of Public Economics, 99, 35–48.
Croson, R., & Gneezy, U. (2009). Gender differences in preferences. Journal of Economic Literature, 47(2), 448–474.
Cullen, Z. B., & Pakzad-Hurson, B. (2019). Equilibrium Effects of Pay Transparency in a Simple Labor Market.
Dittrich, M., Knabe, A., & Leipold, K. (2014). Gender differences in experimental wage negotiations. Economic Inquiry, 52(2), 862–873.
Doleac, J. L., & Hansen, B. (2018). The unintended consequences of "ban the box": Statistical discrimination and employment outcomes when criminal histories are hidden.
Doleac, J. L., & Hansen, B. (2020). The unintended consequences of "ban the box": Statistical discrimination and employment outcomes when criminal histories are hidden. *Journal of Labor Economics, 38*(2), 321–374.
Eckel, C. C., & Grossman, P. J. (2001). Chivalry and solidarity in ultimatum games. Economic Inquiry, 39(2), 171–188.
Eckel, C., De Oliveira, A. C., & Grossman, P. J. (2008). Gender and negotiation in the small: Are women (perceived to be) more cooperative than men? Negotiation Journal, 24(4), 429–445.
Exley, C. L., Niederle, M., & Vesterlund, L. (2020). Knowing when to ask: The cost of leaning-in. Journal of Political Economy, 128(3), 816-854.
Gihleb, R., Landsman, R., & Vesterlund, L. (2020). The Effect of Negotiation on Securing Equal Pay for Equal Work.
Gneezy, U., Niederle, M., & Rustichini, A. (2003). Performance in competitive environments: Gender differences. The Quarterly Journal of Economics, 118(3), 1049–1074.
Greig, F. (2008). Propensity to negotiate and career advancement: Evidence from an investment bank that women are on a "slow elevator." Negotiation Journal, 24(4), 495–508.
Hall, R. E., & Krueger, A. B. (2012). Evidence on the incidence of wage posting, wage bargaining, and on-the-job search. American Economic Journal: Macroeconomics, 4(4), 56–67.

Hernandez-Arenaz, I., & Iriberri, N. (2018). Women ask for less (only from men): Evidence from bargaining in the field. Journal of Economic Behavior & Organization, 152, 192–214.
Hernandez-Arenaz, I., & Iriberri, N. (2019a). A Review of Gender Differences in Negotiation. In Oxford Research Encyclopedia of Economics and Finance.
Hernandez-Arenaz, I., & Iriberri, N. (2019b). Gender Differences in Alternating-Offer Bargaining: An Experimental Study.
Kray, L. J. (2015, May 21). The best way to eliminate the gender pay gap? Ban salary negotiations. The Washington Post. https://www.washingtonpost.com/posteverything/wp/2015/05/21/the-best-way-to-way-to-eliminate-the-gender-pay-gap-ban-salary-negotiations/
Kray, L. J., Galinsky, A. D., & Thompson, L. (2002). Reversing the gender gap in negotiations: An exploration of stereotype regeneration. Organizational Behavior and Human Decision Processes, 87(2), 386–409.
Kray, L. J., & Gelfand, M. J. (2009). Relief versus regret: The effect of gender and negotiating norm ambiguity on reactions to having one's first offer accepted. Social Cognition, 27(3), 418–436.
Kugler, K. G., Reif, J. A., Kaschner, T., & Brodbeck, F. C. (2018). Gender differences in the initiation of negotiations: A meta-analysis. Psychological Bulletin, 144(2), 198.
Leibbrandt, A., & List, J. A. (2015). Do women avoid salary negotiations? Evidence from a large-scale natural field experiment. Management Science, 61(9), 2016–2024.
List, J. A. (2004). The nature and extent of discrimination in the marketplace: Evidence from the field. The Quarterly Journal of Economics, 119(1), 49–89.
Major, B., McFarlin, D. B., & Gagnon, D. (1984). Overworked and underpaid: On the nature of gender differences in personal entitlement. Journal of Personality and Social Psychology, 47(6), 1399.
Mas, A. (2017). Does transparency lead to pay compression? Journal of Political Economy, 125(5), 1683–1721.
Mazei, J., Hüffmeier, J., Freund, P. A., Stuhlmacher, A. F., Bilke, L., & Hertel, G. (2015). A meta-analysis on gender differences in negotiation outcomes and their moderators. Psychological Bulletin, 141(1), 85.
McKelway, M. (2019). Vicious and Virtuous Cycles: Self-Efficacy and Employment of Women in India.
McNichols, D. (2019). Information and the Persistence of the Gender Wage Gap; Early Evidence from California's Salary History Ban.

Movius, H. (2008). The effectiveness of negotiation training. Negotiation Journal, 24(4), 509–531.
Niederle, M. (2015). Gender. In The Handbook of Experimental Economics (Vol. 2). Princeton university press.
Niederle, M., & Vesterlund, L. (2007). Do women shy away from competition? Do men compete too much? The Quarterly Journal of Economics, 122(3), 1067–1101.
Niederle, M., & Vesterlund, L. (2008). Gender differences in competition. Negotiation Journal, 24(4), 447–463.
Niederle, M., & Vesterlund, L. (2011). Gender and competition. Annual Review of Economics, 3(1), 601–630.
Pradel, D. W., Bowles, H. R., & McGinn, K. L. (2005). When does gender matter in negotiations. Negotiation, 8(11).
Rigdon, M. L. (2012). An experimental investigation of gender differences in wage negotiations.
Sandberg, S. (2013). Lean In: Women, Work, and the Will to Lead. Random House.
Säve-Söderbergh, J. (2019). Gender gaps in salary negotiations: Salary requests and starting salaries in the field. Journal of Economic Behavior & Organization, 161, 35–51.
Sinha, S. (2019). Salary History Ban: Gender Pay Gap and Spillover Effects.
Small, D. A., Gelfand, M., Babcock, L., & Gettman, H. (2007). Who goes to the bargaining table? The influence of gender and framing on the initiation of negotiation. Journal of Personality and Social Psychology, 93(4), 600.
Solnick, S. J. (2001). Gender differences in the ultimatum game. Economic Inquiry, 39(2), 189–200.
Stevens, C. K., Bavetta, A. G., & Gist, M. E. (1993). Gender differences in the acquisition of salary negotiation skills: The role of goals, self-efficacy, and perceived control. Journal of Applied Psychology, 78(5), 723.
Stuhlmacher, A. F., & Walters, A. E. (1999). Gender differences in negotiation outcome: A meta analysis. Personnel Psychology, 52(3), 653–677.
Sutter, M., Bosman, R., Kocher, M. G., & van Winden, F. (2009). Gender pairing and bargaining—Beware the same sex! Experimental Economics, 12(3), 318–331.
Tinsley, C. H., Cheldelin, S. I., Schneider, A. K., & Amanatullah, E. T. (2009). Women at the bargaining table: Pitfalls and prospects. Negotiation Journal, 25(2), 233–248.

Index

A

Adverse Selection 63, 67
Affect-as-Information 435
Agenda 193, 195, 197
Alternating-offers Bargaining 14, 89, 96–101
Altruism 186, 379, 398
Ambiguity 457, 467, 468
Amendment Rule 183, 192
closed amendment rule 183, 192
open amendment rule 183
Anger 434–449
Appraisal-Tendency Framework 436, 437
Area Under the Curve 423, 424
Arrival of Information 62
Asymmetrically Prescriptive 392
Asymmetric Information 5, 14, 21, 26, 87, 263–265, 284, 321, 324, 327, 331, 333, 334, 361, 362
Auction 64, 204–208, 211, 212, 215–217, 219–223, 344, 349, 366–368
Audience Costs 309, 310
Autonomous Negotiation 5, 6, 388–390, 392, 393
Autonomous Negotiator 387, 388, 392, 394, 396, 399, 401, 402
Autonomy Diagonal 389, 391, 393, 394
Availability Heuristic 98

B

Ban-the-Box 466
Bargaining Impasse 17, 459
Bargaining Problem 11, 12, 88–96, 101, 102, 110, 111, 116, 122,

E. Karagözoğlu and K. B. Hyndman (eds.), *Bargaining*,
https://doi.org/10.1007/978-3-030-76666-5

131, 133, 134, 140, 147, 190, 228, 230, 231, 263
Baron-Ferejohn Model 19, 183, 184
Battle of the Sexes (BoS) 116–125
Becker-DeGroot-Marschak 344
Best Offer 6, 367–369, 380, 382
Bidding War 77
Bilateral Agreements 242, 278
Bilateral Oligopoly 227–229, 232, 233, 242
Bitcoin 402
Bounded Rationality 13
Bounds 137
Business-to-Business (B2B) 249, 253, 257, 264, 370, 390, 400
firm-to-firm 227, 228

C

Cheap Talk 25, 206, 222, 302, 368, 374, 375, 378, 379, 382, 409
Cheap Talk Diplomacy 302
Civil War 303, 304
Climate Change 4, 20, 23, 271–275, 277, 279, 280, 282–284, 287
Coalition 19, 153, 154, 157, 158, 160, 183–185, 187–191, 194–198, 231, 274, 280, 281, 441
Coase 56, 62–65, 69, 70, 72–74
Coasean 62, 69, 361
Coasean Forces 62, 69
Coase Conjecture 62–65, 70, 72, 73
Coase Theorem 23
Commitment 2, 3, 5, 12–25, 27, 28, 36–39, 41–56, 64, 74, 89, 95, 99, 100, 253, 258, 260, 273, 278, 280, 284, 286, 296, 297, 303–305, 307–310, 329, 337
Commitment Power 14, 17, 64, 74
Commitment Tactics 2, 12, 13, 19, 23, 27
Commitment Type 2, 36–39, 41–43, 45–56
Committees 124, 179–181, 183–188, 190, 191, 193, 195, 198
standing committee 180, 192, 198
Common Knowledge 65, 116, 118, 120, 123, 124, 211, 298, 301, 319, 331, 413
Communication 28, 110–112, 115, 116, 187, 188, 193, 194, 323, 327, 335, 347, 353, 368, 373, 379–382, 408–411, 427
Compactness 90, 133
Compensation 222, 460–462, 464, 465, 467–469
Complete Information 2, 14, 15, 20, 26, 101, 187, 277, 295, 296, 303, 307, 308
Complexity 262, 326, 402
Comprehensiveness 133
Compromise 56, 91, 111, 113, 126, 132, 142, 143, 160, 365
Concession 13, 19, 21, 22, 99, 296, 303, 307, 308, 328, 348, 372, 435, 440–445, 448
Concession Game 38, 39, 41–43, 45
Conditional Value at Risk 402
Continuous-time 3, 62, 67, 69, 73, 74, 76, 77, 82, 83
Continuous-Time Bargaining 416
Continuous-time Concession Game 43

First, as noted above, predicted efficiency depends only on the numbers of buyers and sellers (and hence the likelihood of frictions), not on the institution itself.

Hypothesis 1: For a given market (2×2 or 3×3), efficiency is the same across all three market institutions.

Second, there are usually unambiguous order relationships for the *transaction price*—the price at which the good is traded (which may differ from the posted price)—in both 2×2 and 3×3 markets.

Hypothesis 2: Transaction prices in the 2×2 market are the same under either haggling or flexible pricing, and lower under posting, while those in the 3×3 market are highest under haggling and lowest under posting.

Since expected profits for buyers and sellers depend only on profit per trade (determined by the transaction price) and the probability of trading (determined by efficiency, which does not vary across market institutions), the hypotheses for buyers' and sellers' profits follow immediately from Hypothesis 2.

Hypothesis 3: Sellers' profits in the 2×2 market are the same under either haggling or flexible pricing, and lower under posting. In the 3×3 market they are highest under haggling and lowest under posting.

Hypothesis 4: Buyers' profits in the 2×2 market are the same under either haggling or flexible pricing, and higher under posting. In the 3×3 market they are lowest under haggling and highest under posting.

10.2.3 Experimental Procedures

The experiment was conducted at Monash University; the 376 subjects were mainly undergraduates, recruited using ORSEE (Greiner 2015). There were at least ten markets in each of the six cells (see the online appendix for details). Some sessions with large numbers of subjects were

Summing up these inequalities and canceling out yields $\pi(t) \geq \pi(t')$ for all $t, t' \in T$ such that $t' \geq t$. A smaller t means more resolved D. Then this result means the more resolved D is the more likely a war is in any perfect Bayesian equilibrium of any game between S and D.

Given the anarchic nature of the game, D's share of a peaceful settlement must also be at least as large as his war payoff. This implies an individual rationality constraint:

$$y(t) \geq 1 - p - t$$

for all $t \in T$. Since also $\pi(t) \geq \pi(t')$ for $t' \geq t$,

$$\begin{aligned}\pi(t)(1-p-t) + (1-\pi(t)) \cdot y(t) \leq \pi(t')(1-p-t) \\ + (1-\pi(t')) \cdot y(t)\end{aligned}$$

Combining this with the first incentive compatibility constraint,

$$\begin{aligned}\pi(t')(1-p-t) + (1-\pi(t')) \cdot y(t') &\leq \pi(t)(1-p-t) \\ &\quad + (1-\pi(t)) \cdot y(t) \\ &\leq \pi(t')(1-p-t) \\ &\quad + (1-\pi(t')) \cdot y(t)\end{aligned}$$

we obtain

$$\begin{aligned}\pi(t')(1-p-t) + (1-\pi(t')) \cdot y(t') \leq \pi(t')(1-p-t) \\ + (1-\pi(t')) \cdot y(t)\end{aligned}$$

which implies $y(t) \geq y(t')$ for $t' \geq t$, i.e., D's expected share from a peaceful settlement increases with his resolve.

These strikingly general monotonicity results are derived by easy manipulations of the incentive compatibility and individual rationality constraints. They robustly predict that a more resolved D runs a higher risk of war but also expects a higher share in a peaceful resolution.

Fey and Ramsay (2011) generalize this when both S and D have private information about their types but the joint distribution of types

Continuous-time Limit 62, 67, 73, 74
Convexity 133, 280
Coordination 25, 110, 111, 114, 116–120, 122–124, 211, 409
Coordination Failure 25
Coup Attempt 304
Crisis Bargaining 52, 56, 293, 298, 301, 310
Cross-validated Predictions 411
Culture 345, 354, 355, 360, 443, 449

D

Deadline Effect 76, 77, 409, 410, 420
Decay of Commitment 18, 19
Delay/Delayed Agreement 13–16, 18, 19, 23, 25, 26, 63, 65, 69, 74, 78, 79, 81, 97–101, 104, 182, 183, 185–189, 193, 197, 263, 284, 285
  efficient delay 19
  inefficient delay 63, 65, 66
Delegation 20, 21, 24, 27, 281, 282, 287
Directed Search 204, 206, 222, 223
Direct Mechanism 299, 413, 414
Disagreement Point 90–93, 95, 102, 133, 135, 142, 239, 276, 280, 281, 283
Disagreement Value 188, 230, 231, 239
Discount Factor 22, 62, 82, 182, 186, 193, 194, 265, 276, 278, 285
Discrete Time 62
Discrimination 6, 238, 345–351, 354, 360
Distributive Negotiation 398
Distributive policy 157
Divide-and-Choose 142, 144
Domain Knowledge 389, 390, 394
Dynamically Optimized Sequential Experimentation 418
Dynamically Pareto Efficient 168, 169
Dynamic Bargaining 2, 25, 62, 63, 152, 167, 170, 192, 194, 196–198, 297, 415

E

EBay 6, 367–369, 374, 376, 378–381
Efficiency 4, 14, 16, 18, 19, 21, 56, 77, 82, 93, 97, 112, 114, 115, 122, 124, 125, 135–137, 153, 168, 169, 196, 203, 204, 208–210, 212–215, 242, 278, 318, 321–328, 356, 357, 360, 366, 368, 379, 408, 411, 415
Efficient 67, 82
Efficient Equilibrium 21, 22, 115, 415
Egalitarianism 132, 133, 137–141, 143, 144, 146, 147
Egalitarian Solution 134, 146
Egalitarian-Utilitarian Monotonicity 140, 141, 146
Elicitation Fatigue 394
Emotion Deception 446, 447
Emotions 5, 6, 20, 396, 433–440, 442–449
  discrete 434, 437, 440, 444, 445, 449

incidental 434–436, 438
integral 434, 436, 437
Emotions as Social Information (EASI) 439, 441, 446
Endogenous Status-quo 4, 151, 152, 164, 167, 169, 192, 194
Entitlements 112
Envy-freeness 143, 144, 399
Equal Sacrifice Solution 93
Equal Split 24, 111, 113, 114, 118, 125, 142, 193, 198, 215, 216, 221, 409, 411, 415
Equal Split Equilibrium 415
Exclusion 254, 257–261
Existence 14, 62, 153, 156, 162
Expected Utility Theory 88
Extended Kalai-Smorodinsky Solution 91

F

Fairness Norms 25
False Positive 423
Fertility 345, 351, 352
Field Experiment 344–349, 351–362, 463, 466, 467
Fixing-the-Institution 458
Fixing-the-Women 458
Flexible Pricing 204–210, 212, 213, 215, 220, 221
Focal Points 25, 28, 110–113, 116–118, 124–126, 389, 393, 409, 412, 415
Framing Effect 395, 399
Free Form Bargaining 411

G

Gamson's Law 184
Gender Difference 5–7, 345, 349, 353, 354, 426, 455–457, 461–464, 467–470
Gender Norms 457, 462
Gender Wage Gap 5, 7, 455, 464, 466, 470
Goal-Setting 461
Gupta-Livne Solution 92, 93, 95

H

Haggling 27, 46, 204–208, 210, 212, 213, 215, 220, 221
Happiness 434, 435, 439–441, 443, 445–447
Hazard Rate 25, 26
Healthcare 4, 5, 249–253, 255, 257, 258, 260, 262–266
Household 222, 255, 345, 351–353, 360, 388
Human-Robot Team 400

I

Ideal Payoff 134, 142
Ideal Point 90, 92, 93, 134
Immediate Agreement 19, 98, 100, 104, 185
Immediate Trade 63, 67, 74
Incentive Compatible 299, 344, 413
Incomplete Information 2, 15, 20, 25, 26, 28, 170, 302, 307, 372
Independence of Irrelevant Alternatives 90–92, 134, 141
Individually Rational 12, 413
Individual Monotonicity 90
Industrial Organization 227, 232, 234, 237, 241, 361

Inefficiency 14, 15, 18–21, 24, 27, 52, 169, 208, 305–307, 353, 358, 412
Inequality Aversion 100
Integrative Negotiation 390, 398, 437, 440
Interdependent Values 63, 64, 67, 69, 71, 73, 82, 301
Interim Efficient 414
International Environmental Agreements (IEA) 271, 272, 274, 277, 281, 284
Internet of Things 388
Interpersonal Utility Comparisons 135, 140

K

Kalai-Smorodinsky Solution 90, 91, 93, 95

L

Labor-market Negotiations 457, 458
Lean-In Recommendation 458
Least Absolute Shrinkage and Selection Operator (LASSO) 422
Legislative Bargaining 2, 4, 151, 152, 156, 160, 162, 168, 179
Legislator 153, 182, 190, 282
Limited Influence 98
Limited Sensitivity to Changes in the Conflict Point 92
Lockbox Test 421
Long-term perspective 389, 390, 397, 403
Loss Aversion 88, 94, 97–99, 324, 328, 333, 418

M

Machine Learning 5, 6, 408, 411, 412, 421, 426, 427
Majority Rule 19, 184, 186, 195
Managed Care Organization (MCO) 255, 256, 258
Market Design 380
Marketplace 6, 345, 346, 348, 351, 367–370, 376, 379, 380
Market Power 63, 228, 241, 244, 255, 256, 366
Markov Perfect 18, 27, 155, 193–195
Markov Perfect Equilibrium (MPE) 18, 155, 193, 194
Markov Stationary Equilibria 65
Matching Game 119, 122
Maxmin Share 144
Mechanism Design Approach 298, 412
Median Voter 162, 282
Mediation 3, 52, 53, 309, 310
Medicare 254, 260
Merger 5, 235, 238, 239, 252–254, 256
Midpoint Domination 141, 142
Midpoint Outcome on a Linear Frontier 141
Mimicking 25, 37, 42, 43, 54
Minimum Winning Coalitions 157, 183–185, 188, 189, 194, 196
Moderation 164–167
Mood 434–437
Moral Costs 25
Multi-issue Negotiation 398
Multilateral Bargaining Game 184

N

Nash Bargaining Solution 2, 3, 14, 16, 22, 83, 132, 146, 272, 276, 285
Nash Fiber 90
Nash-in-Nash (NiN) 4, 5, 228, 231, 232, 239, 240, 243, 251, 257, 258, 259, 263, 265
Nash Program 103
Natural Language 381, 382, 409, 410, 427
Negotiated Aspirations Solution 93, 94
Negotiation Skills 458, 460, 463, 464
Negotiation Support System 392, 394
Network 5, 239, 250, 251, 255, 257–261, 263–265
Non-stationary Equilibria 63, 65
(Non)stationary Types 3, 46, 47, 49, 50
NP-hard 396

O

One-sided Private Information 410, 411, 416
Operations Management 4, 5, 317
Outside Options 3, 24, 56, 62, 82, 83, 257, 370, 375, 456

P

Pareto Dominant 115
Pareto Efficient 11, 168, 169
Payoffs-as-you-go 46
Pay Transparency 467, 469
Peaceful Resolution 5, 295, 296, 299, 300
Penalized Regression 411
Perfect Bayesian Equilibrium 13, 297, 299, 300, 378
Poisson Intensity 71
Polarization 167
Pooling Equilibrium 284
Positive And Negative Affect Schedule (PANAS) 436
Post-Lasso Procedure 424
Posturing 81, 366
Preference Dynamics 390, 399, 400
Preference Elicitation On-the-fly 390, 394
Preponderance of Power 297
Price Posting 204, 216, 220, 221
  posted price 4, 204–208, 210–212, 216, 217, 219–222, 350
Privacy 77, 81, 388, 390, 394
Process Data 411, 421, 423, 424, 426, 427
Prospect Theory 88, 94, 102, 103, 399
Public Goods 189, 195, 282

Q

Quota Voting Rule 160

R

Random Proposer 18, 19, 154
Rational Type 2, 50, 54
Rawlsian Objective 134, 136, 137
Receiver Operating Characteristic Curve 423

Recognition Probability 165, 190, 192
Recognition Rule 182, 189
Reference Dependence 88–90, 94–96, 98, 99, 101–104, 323, 333, 373
Reference Function 91, 102
Reference Point 88, 89, 91–103, 186, 395
Regulation 236–240, 260, 359, 360
Renegotiation 232, 307, 334, 357–359
Reputational Bargaining 14, 15, 28, 36–38, 43, 48–51, 53–56
Reputational Coase Conjecture 37, 44
Restricted Monotonicity 92
Retrievability Bias 98
Revelation Principle 298, 299, 410–413, 426
Revoking Costs 21, 99
Revolt 304
Ricardian trade 242, 243
Riker's Size Principle 157
Rotating Dictator Equilibrium 159, 160, 169

S

Salary-Disclosure Laws 469
Salary History Ban 466
Salary History Requests 466, 470
Salary Negotiations 460, 461, 464
Scale Covariance 135, 139–142, 146, 147
Screening 65, 72, 78, 358
Self-directedness 390–392, 400, 401
Self-Management 461
Self-serving Bias 25
Self-sufficiency 390–392, 394
Self-supporting Reference Points 94
Semi-structured Bargaining 409
Separating Equilibrium 284
Signaling 283, 350, 366, 374–376, 378, 382
Simple Solution 161, 162
Single-issue Negotiation 398
Skimming Property 65
Smart Grid 396, 402
Smooth 62, 70, 79, 133–135, 138, 156
Spatial Policy 152, 153, 162
Statically Pareto Efficient 168, 169
Status-quo 15, 19, 151–154, 156, 158–161, 163–167, 169, 192–194, 295, 301, 308
Stereotype 457
Strategic Polarization 167
Strike 23, 77, 294, 298, 307, 366, 394, 411, 413, 414, 420, 424, 425
Strike Condition 411, 414
Strong Individual Rationality 135
Structured Bargaining 408, 410
Stubborn Type 14, 46
Subjective Value Inventory 395
Suppes-Sen Dominance 139
Supply Chain 244, 257, 317–321, 325, 327, 328, 330–335
Symmetrically Prescriptive 392
Symmetry 14, 90, 117, 134, 142, 209
Symmetry Based Compromise 142

T

Tacit Bargaining 115, 119

Take-it-or-leave-it Offer 74, 232, 236, 239, 241, 305
Tariffs 229, 241–244
Tempered Aspirations 92, 93
Terms-of-trade 242
Territorial Dispute 297
Training Program 462, 463
Transparency 77, 252, 263, 264, 390, 400, 402, 458, 467–470
True Positive 423
Trust 325, 326, 333, 368, 389, 390, 394, 398, 400–402, 436, 448
Trustworthiness 325, 326, 333
Tuning Parameter 422
Two-part Tariff (TPT) 322, 323, 328, 332, 337
Two-sided Private Information 63, 409

U

Ultimatum Game 24, 96, 101, 113, 159, 457, 468
Ultimatum Offers 318, 321, 324, 326, 327, 332–335
Unanimity Rule 19, 186, 188, 191, 195, 196, 286
Unobserved Heterogeneity 370, 377, 378
Unstructured Bargaining 25, 28, 318, 327, 331–334, 410–412, 426
User Trust and Adoption 389, 390, 400
Utilitarianism 132, 133, 137–141, 143, 146
Utilitarian Objective 134, 136, 137
Utilitarian Solution 134, 146

V

Verbal Communication 410
Veto Power 186–188, 194, 351

W

Wait-till-Deadline Strategy 74
Walrasian Equilibrium 346, 356, 357, 361
War of Attrition 37, 39, 47, 49, 55, 81
Weak Pareto Optimality 90, 134, 142
World Trade Organization (WTO) 229, 242, 243

The manufacturer's authorised representative in the EU is Springer Nature Customer Service Centre GmbH, Europaplatz 3, 69115 Heidelberg, Germany. If you have any concerns regarding our products, please contact ProductSafety@springernature.com

Printed and bound by CPI Group (UK) Ltd, Croydon, CR0 4YY
22/09/2026
02220984-0015